Argumentative
and Aggressive
Communication
Theory, Research, and Application

Andrew S. Rancer   *The University of Akron*

Theodore A. Avtgis   *West Virginia University*

SAGE Publications
Thousand Oaks ▪ London ▪ New Delhi

For information:

Sage Publications, Inc.
2455 Teller Road
Thousand Oaks, California 91320
E-mail: order@sagepub.com

Sage Publications Ltd.
1 Oliver's Yard
55 City Road
London EC1Y 1SP
United Kingdom

Sage Publications India Pvt. Ltd.
B-42, Panchsheel Enclave
Post Box 4109
New Delhi 110 017 India

Library of Congress Cataloging-in-Publication Data

Rancer, Andrew S.
Argumentative and aggressive communication: Theory, research, and application/Andrew S. Rancer, Theodore A. Avtgis.
    p. cm.
Includes bibliographical references and index.
ISBN 0–7619–3088–4 (cloth)—ISBN 0–7619–3089–2 (pbk.)
    1. Aggressiveness. 2. Communication. 3. Interpersonal communication.
I. Avtgis, Theodore A. II. Title.
HM1116.R36 2006
302.5′401—dc22   2005029362

06   07   08   09   10   9   8   7   6   5   4   3   2   1

Acquiring Editor:	Todd R. Armstrong
Editorial Assistant:	Deya Saoud
Project Editor:	Beth A. Bernstein
Copy Editor:	Toni Williams
Typesetter:	C&M Digitals (P) Ltd.
Indexer:	Rick Hurd
Graphic Designer:	Candice Harman

Contents

Preface

Communication traits have enjoyed a central position in the communication discipline for over 30 years. An examination of the content of the communication journals supports this assertion. Much research activity and theory building has focused on understanding how communication predispositions develop and how they influence one's behavior. Examination of the constructs of argumentativeness and verbal aggressiveness constitutes a large part of these research programs.

This book is designed to serve as a textbook for courses that deal with communication especially during disagreement, controversy, and conflict. While written for upper-level undergraduates, master's and doctoral students, researchers interested in the argumentativeness and verbal aggressiveness traits would also benefit from this material. Indeed, this text represents a thorough review of research and application efforts on argumentative and aggressive communication. This book is not intended to be a comprehensive review of human aggressiveness (which would fill dozens of volumes), but provides a robust treatment of primarily communication literature specific to the argumentativeness and verbal aggressiveness traits.

Our goal for this text was twofold. First, we wanted to produce a book that contained the most up-to-date information on argumentative and aggressive communication written in a way that is accessible to a wide variety of people (i.e., undergraduate students, graduate students, and researchers). Second, we wanted to produce a book that contains the most comprehensive review of argumentativeness and verbal aggressiveness written to date. As such, students, researchers, and even practitioners could use the text as a handbook from which to review the development of this line of inquiry and garner information and ideas for future research and training efforts.

One pedagogical feature of this text is the reflective discussion questions located at the end of each chapter. These questions serve to stimulate student self-reflection as well as classroom discussion. Students can also identify their own, and others', predispositions toward constructive and destructive communication by completing the numerous scales contained in the appendixes.

The research benefits of this text are that it reviews hundreds of studies and resources partitioned by communication context allowing the researcher to gain a comprehensive knowledge of argumentativeness and verbal aggressiveness simply by reading the specific chapters of interest. Finally, Chapter 12 provides those interested in argumentative and aggressive communication with suggestions from some of the leading scholars who have conducted research in this area.

Acknowledgments

The genesis of this project began with a need to bring together a massive body of research that was being conducted on argumentative and aggressive communication from several social science disciplines. Throughout the writing process we have been supported by many people without whom this project would have never come to fruition. First, we would like to thank our families through which everything is possible. Andrew would like to thank his wife Kathi and his daughter Aimee who provided the motivation, love, and food to see him through this process. Ted would like to thank his wife Mary for love and support throughout this project and his son Aiden for providing the reason and inspiration to complete it. He would also like to thank his parents Alex and Gloria for their generous support.

This project would not have been possible without the help and support of a number of other colleagues. First, we would like to acknowledge Dominic Infante. Dom is one of the rare breed of scholars who is not only world renowned for his research, but is also an excellent teacher and mentor. He encouraged us to go ahead with this project and provided a great deal of time and feedback to us. Joseph DeVito, whose own books have greatly influenced the discipline, provided numerous suggestions on how to enhance the content and appearance of the book.

We called on a number of distinguished and highly recognized communication scholars and asked them to contribute their thoughts about the future of research on argumentativeness and verbal aggressiveness. Despite their hectic schedules, none of them let us down. Their contributions have made Chapter 12 quite unique and extremely meaningful. In alphabetical order we thank Carolyn Anderson, Michael Beatty, Dominic Infante, Timothy Levine, Matthew Martin, James McCroskey, Scott Myers, Anne Maydan Nicotera, Jill Rudd, and Charles Wigley. We would also like to thank the numerous other scholars mentioned throughout this text, for their work is really the foundation of the content of this book.

We would like to thank SAGE Publications for assistance throughout this project. Our editor, Todd Armstrong, an early supporter of this project, provided much guidance especially in dealing with revisions. Deya Saoud, associate editor, always answered our questions and helped us meet our deadlines in a timely fashion. We would also like to thank Toni Williams, whose editing helped to improve the flow of the text.

Finally, we wish to thank the following reviewers:

Deborah J. Borisoff, New York University

Leda Cooks, University of Massachusetts at Amherst

Joseph A. DeVito, Hunter College of The City University of New York

Dominic Infante, Kent State University

Matthew M. Martin, West Virginia University

Anne Maydan Nicotera, Howard University

James C. McCroskey, West Virginia University

John G. Oetzel, University of New Mexico

R. Jeffrey Ringer, St. Cloud State University

Jill E. Rudd, Cleveland State University

Charles J. Wigley III, Canisius College

PART I

The Structure and Origin of Argumentative and Aggressive Communication

1

What Are Argumentative and Aggressive Communication?

To say that conflict exists everywhere would be to state the obvious. Conflict occurs between all people and in all contexts. If you were to review your interactions with people you encounter from day to day, you can probably recall numerous instances in which your communication with them was marked by disagreement. That is, you and others seem to see the world in very different ways, and the positions you hold on various issues seemed to be divergent.

For example, you may recall conversations you had with friends, such as, "What is the best comedy program on television?" "Which major in college creates the greatest chance for getting a job after graduation?" "Who makes the best pizza in the city?" "Which brand of jeans is the most attractive?" or "Which current musical performer or group is the best?" One of your authors can recall arguments he had with friends many years ago about who were the better musical groups: the Beatles or the Rolling Stones, the Temptations or the Four Tops. The excitement felt when arguments were presented on a variety of such subjects, and the feelings of satisfaction experienced when he was able to win them over to his side are still palpable decades later. Although the issues, topics, and characters have changed, these types of arguments and the positive feelings about arguing continue today.

You may even consider arguing with friends and colleagues fun or a type of recreational activity that is a satisfying alternative to watching television or listening to the radio (Rancer, Baukus, & Infante, 1985; Rancer, Kosberg, & Baukus, 1992). In this context, arguing with someone is seen as stimulating, exciting, and exhilarating, and the outcomes produced by a good argument are deemed constructive and beneficial. These feelings of excitement, interest, and enjoyment may have led you to believe that arguing is a constructive activity and an effective and satisfying way to communicate with people.

As you review your interactions with parents, relational partners, supervisors, spouses, colleagues, children, and even strangers, another, less favorable view of arguing may also emerge. You can no doubt recall instances in which an argument was anything but fun and constructive. That is, the argument you were in might have led to feelings of anger, hurt, embarrassment, or humiliation and may have even led to damaging or the termination of the interpersonal relationship. Perhaps you can recall an example of an argument that became so destructive that it quickly turned to name calling and may have culminated with the individuals engaged in some form of physical aggression (e.g., shoving, pushing, hitting) or other forms of violence. Although hopefully less common, these situations may have led you to believe that arguing is something to be avoided at all costs, even if it means having to suppress your true feelings and yield to another person's wishes. As such, you may have come to believe that arguing is a very destructive form of communication.

Examples of destructive communication behavior during conflict are often highlighted by stories in magazines, in newspapers, on radio, and on television. Political messages often contain these destructive forms of communication. For example, columnist George Will, writing about incivility, reported that during a congressional dispute, one member of Congress who was told to "shut up" retorted by calling his colleague a "wimp" and a "fruitcake" (Will, 2003). In the 1992 presidential campaign, President George H.W. Bush verbally attacked the competence of candidates Bill Clinton and Al Gore by stating, "My dog Millie knows more about foreign policy than these two Bozos" (Keen, 1996). Morning drive radio is peppered with attacks on people's character, competence, and physical appearance. Nationally syndicated radio programs such as *The Howard Stern Show* contain numerous instances of this type of communication. The use of profanity in communication is more ubiquitous than ever. Profanity is pervasive in movies and cable television programs and was becoming more commonplace even on broadcast television programs before the recent crackdown by the Federal Communications Commission (Peterson, 2000).

Constructive communication has taken a marked downturn, even in contexts in which officials and rules are supposed to prevail. According to reports in the media, if you watch children play organized sports you are likely to observe parents shouting at coaches, referees, and other players. Headlines such as "Father accused of biting son's coach" (2001) and "Hockey death no surprise to sports observers" (Bayles, 2000) have emerged in the past several years. This latter article describes the tragic outcome of a conflict between two parents attending their children's hockey scrimmage at an ice rink in Reading, Massachusetts, in July 2000. After exchanging hostile words over a physical altercation between their children, one of the parents became enraged and physically attacked the other and "beat him into a coma, witnesses said" (Bayles, p. 3A). The man who was attacked later died from those injuries.

Even the workplace is not immune from these forms of aggressive behavior. A new phenomenon is emerging and is being compared with road rage, the type of aggression experienced when driving: "a significant portion of the U.S. work force is suffering everything from uncomfortable and distracting incivilities to stress-induced attacks on trash cans, keyboards and even co-workers, all expressions of what one survey called 'desk rage'" (Girion, 2000, p. W1). The frequency of gossip, hostile e-mail messages, snide comments, and even physical aggression between managers and subordinates and between workplace colleagues has reportedly increased in recent years.

You may have even experienced some conflict today. Consider the following examples: As you got ready to prepare to go to class this morning, both you and your roommate may have wanted to use the bathroom at the same time. With only one bathroom in the apartment, this was impossible and an argument erupted about who should use it first. In a fit of frustration, your roommate says that it was probably a mistake for the two of you to live together and accuses you of being spoiled.

Later in the day, you call your mother and ask if you can borrow some money to repair your car. During the conversation, you and your mom get into it when she states that you lack control and spend your money recklessly. In your communication research class, the instructor hands back the results of the exam you took the other day. You receive a grade of C- and feel that you were graded unfairly. You follow the professor back to her office and argue that several of the questions were ambiguous and irrelevant to the chapters covered on the test. The professor decides not to yield to your challenge, and your grade of C- stands.

Later on, you open your cell phone bill and find roaming charges for calls that you understood to be unrestricted and part of the plan you signed up for. You call customer service and argue about exactly what is and what is not covered on your "unlimited" plan.

Looking forward to some evening relaxation, you and your significant other discuss where you will go out to eat for dinner. You want Chinese food; your partner wants Italian. An argument erupts when your partner calls you selfish and stubborn because you do not see the merits of Italian over Chinese food. These scenarios represent a few of the situations in which conflict may have emerged in your daily life. Of course, these are but a few of the many forms of conflict communication, but the latter examples typify verbal aggressiveness.

The Genesis of the Theory of Argumentative and Aggressive Communication

In 1978, one of the authors was a doctoral student in communication studies at Kent State University. He and his professor, Dominic Infante, were interested in developing a measure of interpersonal communication competence and were discussing what constitutes a competent interpersonal communicator. After a rather exhaustive review of literature, they identified a number of factors research had indicated might be associated with interpersonal communication competence. Among those factors identified were openness and self-disclosure, listening, feedback, supportive communication, empathy, trust, and perspective-taking ability. The list, however, seemed to contain only those factors that might come into play during interpersonal communication in which agreement and interpersonal bonding was the goal. In examining this list of interpersonal communication competence behaviors, they noted the absence of behaviors that deal with communication during interpersonal conflict, communication behaviors that are considered argumentative and aggressive in nature.

Much interpersonal communication takes place when individuals disagree with each other about important relationship issues or when individuals espouse significantly different positions on issues they feel are important to the relationship. After all, almost everyone has held a position contrary to their partner on an important (and sometimes unimportant) relationship issue. As a former intercollegiate debater and debate coach, as well as a student and scholar trained in argumentation, Infante suggested that it might be profitable to explore the influence of personality when people hold different positions on controversial issues. He observed that people seem to differ in their desire and motivation to engage in argumentative behavior. Some people may be seen as incessant arguers, who enjoy engaging in an argument with others no matter who they are arguing with or what the topic of the argument is. Some of these highly argumentative types even talk back to their radio when they disagree with what is being said on one of the many national and local talk radio programs.

It is also apparent that many other individuals rarely voice their position at all on controversial issues. Such people appear to avoid arguing with others, even when they are passionate about an issue and despite the fact that it would be in their best interests to do so. For still others, the tendency to argue seems to be influenced by factors in the situation; that is, they either increase or dampen their desire to argue depending upon who they are arguing with, what they are arguing about, and the situation or context in which the argument takes place. It was clear, however, that people seem to differ in their underlying motivation to engage in argumentative communication and thus a systematic program designed to study aggressive communication started. We began by defining aggressive communication and then developed a conceptualization and measure of one form of aggressive communication, argumentativeness. In so doing, we made sure to distinguish argumentativeness from another form of aggressive communication, verbal aggressiveness. A few years later, Infante and Wigley (1986) developed a more complete conceptualization and measure of verbal aggressiveness.

Purpose of This Book

It is the purpose of this book to review the journey that has been taken toward the development of what is called *the theory of argumentative and aggressive communication*. Hopefully by the end of this journey, you will better understand the differences between constructive and destructive communication exhibited when conflict exists or when people disagree with each other. As communication scientists, we believe that the most important "way of knowing" comes about as the result of "the activities of scholars committed to a scientific approach to generating answers to questions" (Beatty, 1996, p. 37). In this book we will identify a number of questions that have been raised about communication during disagreement, and through reviewing and synthesizing this body of research, we will attempt to provide some answers to those questions.

Several years ago, Infante and Rancer (1996) reached a number of conclusions about argumentative and aggressive communication based on the research available at that time. In this book, we will update many of those conclusions and attempt to articulate new ones as well. In summarizing that research over a decade ago, Infante and Rancer presented "the rather unequivocal conclusion that the effects of argumentativeness are constructive and those of verbal aggressiveness are destructive" (p. 345). We believe this conclusion is further strengthened by an examination of the studies reported here.

Part I will begin by defining the structure and origin of argumentative and aggressive communication. We will first present a conceptualization of argumentative and aggressive communication as they are situated within the cluster of other communication and personality traits. This section will also review the major approaches to studying argumentative and aggressive communication and present the issues related to the measurement of these predispositions. In Part II we will present a rather thorough review of how the argumentative and aggressive communication traits function in a variety of communication contexts. A plethora of research has been conducted over the past 25-plus years on the influence of argumentativeness and verbal aggressiveness in the relational and family context, in the organizational context, in the instructional context, in the intercultural context, in mediated contexts, and in persuasion and social influence situations. Much of that research will be discussed in this section of the book. Part III of the book will present suggestions based on this corpus of research regarding how one could modify these traits to enhance the chances of more effective and satisfying outcomes of communication encounters. This part of the book will also describe how knowledge and understanding of these traits has been, and can be, employed to try and overcome social and personal problems dealing with communication during conflict. The book will conclude with suggestions for future directions for research and theory-building efforts offered by some of the most noteworthy scholars in argumentative and aggressive communication.

The Importance of Communication Traits

If you were to search the literature in the communication discipline for the past 35 years, you would discover that communication traits and predispositions have occupied a central place. A large percentage of research and theory building activity has been directed at (a) identifying a cluster of communication traits, (b) understanding how these traits and predispositions emerge, and (c) determining how these traits influence our actual communication behavior in several communication contexts. Communication trait researchers believe that a better understanding of other people can be obtained by knowing the traits an individual possesses. By examining communication traits, scholars hope to identify ways in which individuals might be able to enjoy more favorable communicative outcomes in their lives. More specifically, these situations range from teaching argumentative skills to children and adults in an effort to de-escalate a volatile situation to helping employees interact with a difficult boss. The chapters throughout this book will highlight these and many other important communication goals.

Your exposure to traits probably goes back to your early experiences in school. You may recall that you, or someone you knew, was described as possessing a given personality trait. Shyness, friendliness, talkativeness, and assertiveness, for example, were potential traits ascribed to you or your friends by others. It is not difficult to conjure up images of individuals we know whose communication behavior is defined by those traits. One of the authors, in the second grade, was described as a troublemaker. You can probably imagine, without too much effort, the cluster of cross-situational behaviors that give the impression of a troublemaker.

The concept of a trait originated in personality theory. Psychologist Guilford (1959) defined a trait as "any distinguishable, relatively enduring way in which one individual differs from others" (p. 6). Another psychologist, Mischel (1968), suggested "a [personality] trait is a construction or abstraction to account for enduring behavioral consistencies and differences" (pp. 4–5).

Communication scholars Daly and Bippus (1998) suggest that communication and personality traits differ along several dimensions. For example, some traits are broad such as locus of control (i.e., the way in which people see their actions in relation to life's outcomes), whereas others are more narrowly focused such as communication apprehension (i.e., the fear associated with either real or anticipated communication with other people). Some traits highlight social characteristics such as shyness (i.e., the tendency to talk less than the typical person) while other traits are focused more on an individual's cognitive orientation such as dogmatism (i.e., closed-mindedness or the tendency to ignore the belief systems of other people that deviate from their own). Some traits are part of a larger conceptual framework or fit into a larger supertrait (e.g., Costa & McCrae's [1980] five factor model of personality; Eysenck & Eysenck's [1985] three dimensions of personality), whereas other traits stand alone (e.g., communicator style). Some traits are measured primarily as responses to questionnaires, whereas other traits are measured by observing a person's behavior (e.g., disclosiveness) (Daly & Bippus).

Regardless of how traits differ, the underlying assumption among communication trait theorists is that people differ from each other because of the different clusters of traits or predispositions that they possess. That is, trait theorists believe there is a great deal of variation in the way individuals interact with each other and respond to situational factors. The way a person responds, trait theorists believe, is primarily controlled by this cluster of traits. Scholars who adhere to the trait perspective of behavior suggest that individuals will most often respond to different situations with similar behavioral and interactional patterns (Nicotera, 1993, 1994; Rancer & Nicotera, in press).

That is not to say that situational influences do not have any impact on the way a person will respond communicatively in a given situation. The specific characteristics of each situation do impact somewhat the behavior of an individual. For example, consider Bob, who is absolutely terrified to speak at an interpersonal level. Let us also assume that in the past week Bob has experienced a great degree of loneliness. The loneliness (in this case a situational factor) will influence Bob's communication apprehension. Bob may want to be free from apprehension and appear interpersonally savvy. In this case, Bob's need to reduce the feelings of loneliness (a temporary state) serves to subdue his tendency for being apprehensive (an enduring trait). Some scholars believe that situational factors are more important in predicting an individual's behavior than are the cluster of traits belonging to that person. More specifically, they feel that factors in the given situation are more important than knowledge of a person's trait in predicting how people will interact and respond in that situation. Scholars who espouse this position are called *situationalists*. We will have more to say about this perspective in the next chapter. For now, we will again cite the work of Daly and Bippus (1998), who state, "Although situations clearly play a major role in affecting behavior, a situationalist perspective has not received either strong empirical or conceptual support" (p. 11). Indeed, the importance of traits has been underscored by numerous researchers (see especially Beatty, 1998; Daly & Bippus, 1998; Infante, 1987a; McCroskey, Daly, Martin, & Beatty, 1998). Perhaps most important, traits have been found to account for significant variability (i.e., the degree to which traits explain behavior and perception) in a person's actual communication and communication-based perceptions (Daly & Bippus; Rancer, 1998).

What Are Communication Traits?

Communication traits represent a subset of personality traits. More specifically, communication traits are personality-related traits that deal specifically with human symbolic behavior (i.e., communication). We can define a communication trait as "an abstraction constructed to account for enduring consistencies and differences in message-sending and message-receiving behaviors among individuals" (Infante, Rancer, & Womack, 2003, p. 77). An argument for this definition can be made because studying communication traits provides us with a degree of knowledge about what to expect from a person in a given situation. It can be very helpful to us if we have some idea of what to expect when we interact with a person whom we do not know or when we hear about someone we do know when in a novel situation or new context. Knowledge of people communication traits allows us to make relatively accurate predictions about how they will likely respond in different communication contexts (Infante et al., 2003).

Communication traits are considered part of the broader umbrella concept of personality traits, but are related more specifically to human symbolic behavior. As such, communication traits represent a subset of the larger set of personality traits. Employing an adaptation of Mischel's definition of a personality trait, a communication trait has been defined as "an abstraction constructed to account for enduring consistencies and differences in message-sending and message-receiving behaviors among individuals" (Infante et al., 2003, p. 77).

Before we present our conceptualization of aggressive communication traits, another general issue needs to be reviewed. Communication traits are considered *hypothetical constructs*. That is, they give meaning to certain communication behaviors and provide us with explanations about human communication that would not otherwise be available (Infante et al., 2003).

What is a hypothetical construct? Hypothetical constructs (such as attitudes) are invented by scholars and researchers in the social and behavioral sciences to represent something that might not be easily observed through the senses. Hypothetical constructs are invented in order that we may better or more completely explain behavior. For example, although we can measure your attitude toward an object (e.g., creamed corn), a person (e.g., Hillary Rodham Clinton), or an event (e.g., the war in Iraq), we cannot see your attitude. We can say, however, that you have a favorable or unfavorable attitude toward creamed corn. Thus, we can better explain your actual behavior regarding that object. Knowing your attitude toward creamed corn allows us to better explain and predict behaviors such as buying creamed corn at the supermarket, talking favorably about creamed corn with your friends and colleagues, asking for creamed corn at a restaurant, and the relative frequency of eating creamed corn as a side dish with dinner.

Like the hypothetical construct of attitude, communication traits are also considered hypothetical constructs. That is, we do not know that a particular trait is real (Infante et al., 2003). We continue to gather data to test our assumptions about the development, manifestation, and influence of communication traits. We continue to do this until another hypothetical construct is invented that might explain a set of behaviors or perceptions more completely and accurately.

Researchers have identified numerous communication traits and predispositions. Infante et al. (2003) developed a taxonomy (a classification system) in which to place these traits. Some traits can be classified as *apprehension traits*, such as the fear of communicating with others (e.g., communication apprehension), the tendency to initiate communication with others (e.g., willingness to communicate), or the fear of receiving information or communication from others (e.g., receiver apprehension). Some traits are classified as *presentation traits*, such as the overall impression people make when communicating (e.g., communicator style) and the amount and types of information people reveal when communicating with others (e.g., disclosiveness). Some traits are considered *adaptation traits*, such as the tendency to hold one's own opinions while respecting the opinions of others (e.g., rhetorical sensitivity), the tendency to consider the impression one makes on other people (e.g., self-monitoring), or the tendency to be fully engaged in conversations with others (e.g., interaction involvement). Finally, some traits fall under the classification schema as *aggressive traits*. It is this last class of traits that this book will focus on.

What Is Aggressive Communication?

Infante argues that while the study of aggression has a rich and productive history in psychology and other social science disciplines, the study of aggression in interpersonal communication was hampered by lack of a "comprehensive and unified conception of aggressiveness as a personality trait" (Infante, 1987a, p. 161). In an effort to provide a structure for the study of aggressive communication, Infante offered a definition of aggression in interpersonal communication:

> An interpersonal behavior may be considered aggressive if it applies force physically or symbolically in order, minimally, to dominate and perhaps damage or, maximally, to defeat and perhaps destroy the locus of attack. The locus of attack in interpersonal communication can be a person's body, material possessions, self-concept, position on topics of communication, or behavior. (Infante, 1987a, p. 158)

In an effort to better understand the definition of interpersonally aggressive behavior, we should break this definition down into its principle components. First, a distinction is made between physical and symbolic aggression. Physical aggression involves the use of the body to apply force, such as striking or hitting someone or something. Symbolic aggression involves the use of words or other nonverbal behaviors (e.g., gestures made with the face or body, tone of voice) toward someone or something. The large body of research on argumentative and aggressive communication has sought to understand more fully when, how, and why people use symbolic aggressive behavior.

Second, the definition of interpersonal aggression also suggests that physical or symbolic aggression is used to dominate and defeat something or someone (i.e., the locus, or the place where the attack is directed). Infante suggests that in interpersonal communication, the locus of attack could be another person's body, possessions, self-concept, or positions on controversial issues. For example, let us say Aimee wants to pressure Daniel into complying with a request to lend her his car when he is reluctant to do so. Aimee might use physical aggression (e.g., grabbing or shaking) or the threat of physical aggression in order to soften Daniel up and make him comply (e.g., "Give me the keys or I'll slap you!"). Aimee might attack Daniel's self-esteem by using profanity or by calling him names. This attempt at compliance gaining uses symbolic aggressive communication in the form of profanity or ridicule. Another person might attempt to induce compliance by presenting a threat to the relationship (e.g., "If you won't let me borrow your car, our relationship is over!"). Although these forms of physical and symbolic aggression (physical attacks, threats, and verbally attacking the self-concept of another) are not advocated by this book or the communication discipline, they are nevertheless used by some individuals to secure compliance from others (see research by Anderson & Rancer, 2003, for examples of such attacks).

Reading the above examples, one might conclude that all aggressive communication behaviors are bad. However, this is not the case. Some aggressive communication behaviors are inappropriate whereas others are considered appropriate. This is especially true if the behaviors involve two types of aggressive communication, assertiveness and argumentativeness. Consider the following example: Let us say you are required to participate in a group problem-solving activity in one of your courses. The other members of your group are having difficulty offering solutions, and the ideas of people who are offering solutions seem to you to be either impractical or foolish. Knowing that the group's grade will be based on the overall quality of the solution developed, you could take two different approaches. You could verbally attack the group's solutions, calling them ridiculous and impractical. In this case, your aggressive communication might be considered a bad thing and would do little to help the group. Or you could begin to present a series of arguments in favor of the solution you advocate. The other group members, having heard no better alternatives, like what you propose, accept the arguments you present in support of your position, and endorse your solution. In this example, your aggressive communication might be considered a good thing.

This duality of aggressive communication, the notion that aggressive communication can be considered good or bad, can be explained in a model of aggressive communication offered by Infante (1987a) in his personality approach to aggression. The Infante model provides the framework for the rest of the book and will be used as a way of classifying all forms of symbolic aggressive communication. Essentially, the model suggests that symbolic aggression can be divided into two categories, constructive and destructive. In addition, the model suggests that a cluster of four aggression-based personality traits influences and controls aggressive communication (Infante, 1987a; Rancer, 2004). Each of these traits interacts with factors in the environment to energize and produce message behavior (Infante, 1987a). Two of the traits are considered constructive, and two are destructive. According to this model, the decision to identify an act as constructive or destructive can be determined in one of the following ways: (a) when one person in a dyad feels that the act is constructive or destructive, (b) when both persons in the dyad agree on whether the act was constructive or destructive, (c) when an observer deems the act to be either constructive or destructive, and (d) whether the act is consistent with societal norms for classifying the act as constructive or destructive (Infante, 1987a, p. 163).

Constructive Aggressive Communication Traits

Assertiveness

According to the theory of aggressive communication, assertiveness and argumentativeness are considered constructive traits. Assertiveness is considered the more global of the two traits. If you possess the trait of assertiveness, you tend to be interpersonally dominant and forceful, and you use this trait to achieve personal goals while creating positive feelings in others (Infante, 1987a; Infante et al., 2003; Rancer, 2004). This conceptualization of assertiveness is derived from Costa and McCrae's (1980) trait model of personality. We will examine the relationship between Costa and McCrae's model and aggressive communication a bit later in this chapter. For now, we will just suggest that assertiveness is one of the six facets of the extraversion dimension in Costa and McCrae's model of personality.

Assertiveness is conceptualized as a constructive communication trait because it involves using verbal and nonverbal symbols to exert control, to obtain justified rewards, and to avoid violation of one's rights. Individuals who are assertive use symbols aggressively, but do so in a socially acceptable way. Assertive individuals stand up for their rights and express their thoughts, feelings, and beliefs in "direct, honest, and appropriate ways which do not violate another person's rights" (Lange & Jakubowski, 1976, p. 7). Other assertive behaviors include, but are not limited to, openness, refusal of unreasonable requests, absence of interpersonal anxiety, initiation of requests, spontaneous expression of one's feelings, refusal to be intimidated, outgoingness, willingness to take initiative, and active versus passive disagreement (Norton & Warnick, 1976, pp. 62–64).

Although assertiveness has been studied extensively in the discipline of psychology, communication researchers have not been as persistent in investigating this trait. As far back as 1985, Zakahi stated, "Very little assertiveness research has been conducted using communication variables" (p. 36). The status of assertiveness research in the communication discipline has not changed very much in the years since Zakahi's assessment. Of the few studies in the communication discipline that have investigated assertiveness, only a few have explored the trait-like aspect of assertiveness. In one such effort, Norton and Warnick (1976) examined the relationship between assertiveness and a presentation trait labeled communicator style. They identified the assertive individual as one who is predisposed to verbal behavior (as opposed to being anxious in communication situations) and as a person who tends to be precise, not easily persuadable, and contentious (i.e., overly quarrelsome). Assertive individuals are also talkative, leave an impression on others with whom they communicate, hold their own in interpersonal relationships, and are likely to be remembered by others (Norton & Warnick, p. 66).

It has been suggested that the characteristics of assertiveness could be clustered into four dimensions (Lorr & More, 1980). Directiveness involves taking charge of situations. Social assertiveness involves feeling comfortable around people and the ability to initiate conversations with a variety of people, including strangers. The defense of rights and interests involves standing up for one's rights, such as being able to confront others who are taking advantage of one. Independence involves the ability to maintain one's own personal convictions or position even when receiving pressure from others to conform (Infante et al., 2003, p. 93).

One instrument used to measure assertiveness is the Rathus Assertiveness Schedule, a 30-item, Likert-type scale with high reliability and validity (see especially, Beatty, Plax, & Kearney, 1984; Norton & Warnick, 1976; Rathus, 1973). Another scale used to measure assertiveness is Richmond and McCroskey's (1990) Assertiveness-Responsiveness Measure. Recent research on assertiveness in the communication discipline has examined assertiveness as a facet of assertiveness and responsiveness (Anderson, Martin, Zhong, & West, 1997; Bacon & Severson, 1986; Richmond & McCroskey; Rocca, Martin, & Toale, 1998). Assertiveness is the effort of a person to influence another person's thoughts or actions, whereas responsiveness refers to the individual's ability to express feelings and emotions (Bacon & Severson, p. 53). These two dimensions of assertiveness and responsiveness are considered important dimensions of communication competence (Richmond & McCroskey). Richmond and McCroskey, in developing a scale for the measurement of assertiveness and responsiveness, suggest that the following items tap the assertiveness dimension of personality: "defends own beliefs, independent, forceful, has strong personality, assertive, dominant, willing to take a stand, acts as a leader, and competitive" (p. 449). The other focus from the communication discipline on this trait usually explores the influence of assertiveness training (Ruben & Ruben, 1989). That is, the purpose of these efforts is to teach people low in (trait) assertiveness to communicate more assertively. For example, assertiveness training for women was particularly popular during the early days of the women's rights movement in the 1970s.

Argumentativeness

Like assertiveness, argumentativeness is also considered a constructive communication trait. Some conceptualizations or definitions of this trait place argumentativeness as a subset of assertiveness because all argument is considered assertive, but not all assertiveness involves argument (Infante, 1987a, p. 164). An example of this would be a request to a friend for help on studying for a communication theory exam. While this request is considered a compliance-gaining effort, it does not necessarily involve arguing. If your friend agrees with your initial request, "Can you help me study?" there is no need for you to say anything else. However, if you want to go to the movies and your friend wants to go swimming, you might need to present some arguments (e.g., "It is too cold to go swimming today!") to support your position. This latter example would be considered evidence of argumentative behavior.

In their conceptualization of the trait, Infante and Rancer (1982) defined argumentativeness as "a generally stable trait which predisposes the individual in communication situations to advocate positions on controversial issues, and to attack verbally the positions which other people take on these issues" (p. 72). Simply stated, a person's trait argumentativeness represents an underlying motivation to argue. Note here that the locus of the attack is on the position that the other person holds on the issue, not the person.

Here is an example of argumentativeness. Let us say that you and a friend are planning a spring break getaway vacation. You have a preference to go to Fort Lauderdale, Florida, while your friend prefers to go to South Padre Island, Texas. You are locked in a major disagreement with your friend because you want to travel together, you can only go to one location during the break, and you must make your travel plans very soon. The interaction might go something like this: You might say to your friend, "I understand that you want to go to South Padre Island, but I don't. South Padre Island may hold a great attraction for you because you've been there before, and you have some great memories of your times there. But I think it is too far to drive for only a week's vacation, and The Weather Channel reports that the weather in south Texas is too variable and often too cold in mid-March. Since we live in a cold weather climate and have felt frozen the entire winter, we want to be able to catch some decent rays and warmth, and I think Florida is a better bet."

Notice here some elements of the argumentativeness trait. You stated some understanding of your adversary's position on the controversial issue of where to go for spring break. You did not put your friend down for holding that position on the issue; rather, you provided some arguments, indeed some rudimentary evidence, to support your position on the issue. You attacked your friend's position (going to Texas for spring break); you did not attack your friend personally. You were constructive in asserting your position. And, you did not yield to the other person's position without defending your own position while attacking the other one. What you did in this example was to engage in argumentative behavior.

Categories of Trait Argumentativeness

Individuals can be categorized into five different types regarding predispositions to be argumentative. Although Chapter 3 will discuss in greater detail how we measure the argumentativeness trait, for now let us simply state that argumentativeness is composed of two dimensions: ARGap and ARGav. ARGap stands for your motivational tendency to approach arguments, and ARGav stands for your motivational tendency to avoid arguments. Thus, any individual can be placed into one of a set of categories of argumentativeness depending on his or her approach and avoidance scores. The categories represent the following:

1. Low argumentatives: these individuals have a low motivation to approach arguments and a high motivation to avoid arguments. Low argumentatives lack motivation and desire to argue across most situations and generally do not engage in much argumentative behavior (e.g., people who dislike talking about controversial issues because it makes them uncomfortable).

2. High argumentatives: these individuals have a high motivation to approach arguments and a low motivation to avoid arguments. High argumentatives experience little anxiety associated with argumentative communication and, indeed, often see arguing as an exciting intellectual challenge (e.g., people who love to discuss controversial issues and also find it enjoyable as well as exciting).

3. Conflicted-feelings moderate argumentatives: these individuals have a high motivation to approach arguments, but also have a high motivation to avoid arguments. These conflicted-feelings moderates are highly emotional when it comes to engaging in arguing. At the same time they both feel compelled to

argue due to their level of competitiveness, yet are also highly anxious about arguing due to the possible fear of failure. We suspect that moderate argumentatives who have conflicted feelings are more sensitive to factors in the argumentative situation, especially their perceptions of the importance and success of a particular argument. We suggest that these conflicted-feelings moderates argue mainly when the probability of success is high and the importance of failure is low. This is mainly due to their wish to avoid feeling anxious about the possibility of losing an important argument (e.g., these people often find themselves in arguments in an attempt to win, but do not necessarily enjoy the experience).

4. Apathetic moderate argumentatives: these individuals have a low motivation to approach arguments and concomitantly a low motivation to avoid arguments as well. These apathetic moderates are very low in emotion when it comes to engaging in argument. They feel very little motivation to argue and experience little to no anxiety over engaging in argument. We speculate that these apathetic moderate argumentatives generally tend to engage in argumentative behavior when the incentive of success is high and argue mainly for utilitarian (practical) reasons.

5. Neutral moderate argumentatives: a fifth category of moderate argumentatives has also been suggested. That is, individuals who are moderate in motivation to approach arguments and moderate in motivation to avoid arguments have also been identified (Hamilton & Mineo, 2002). These individuals will argue only when they see some good coming out of it and that they have a good chance of winning.

Because the argumentativeness trait, like many other traits, is normally distributed in the population (especially among individuals from Western cultures), we would expect that more people would fall into the moderate categories of argumentativeness, while fewer people would be high and low in argumentativeness. This issue remains somewhat unresolved empirically. For example, Hamilton and Mineo (2002), in arguing for the unidimensionality of the Argumentativeness Scale (a topic we will cover in Chapter 3) suggest "that the number of people who are apathetic moderates or conflicted moderates in the argumentativeness typology is relatively small" (p. 306).

Destructive Aggressive Communication Traits

Hostility

There are two destructive traits in Infante's model of aggressive communication, hostility and verbal aggressiveness. First, we will describe hostility, the more global of the two traits. Destructive symbolic aggression is classified as hostility. Hostility manifests itself in interpersonal communication when individuals use messages to express irritability, negativity, resentment, and suspicion (Buss & Durkee, 1957; Infante & Rancer, 1996). Infante et al. (2003) illuminate some of these characteristics of hostility: Irritability is exhibited by communicators who have a quick temper, show little patience, exhibit moodiness, and become exasperated when something goes wrong. Negativism is communicated by excessive pessimism about outcomes others are more favorable about, refusing to cooperate, and being antagonistic toward authority, rules, and social conventions. Resentment involves expressing jealousy and hatred and brooding about slights, either real or imagined, which causes anger to develop. Suspicion is communicated through distrust of others and by believing that others want to harm you (p. 95).

One of the leading researchers from the discipline of social psychology, Leonard Berkowitz, views hostility as "an attitude, a dislike of a particular person, object, or issue, accompanied by a desire to see this target injured or even destroyed" (Berkowitz, 1998, p. 264). This definition of aggressive and hostile behavior is consistent with the definition of verbal aggressiveness advanced by Infante (1987a).

Some individuals exhibit strong predispositions toward hostility, and as such, they are said to possess a hostile personality. Research by Zelli and Huesmann (1995) suggests that extremely hostile individuals tend to exhibit some common beliefs. For example, they see themselves as being persecuted by others (e.g., "People want to be mean to me"), see their world as a mean one (e.g., "People like doing things that bother me") and view themselves as more aggressive than others (e.g., "I'm a better fighter than most people"). In Costa and McCrae's (1980) trait model of personality, hostility is considered a facet of neuroticism. Each of these expressions of hostility is the result of the interaction between the trait dimension of hostility and factors in a given situation. That is, people who possess the hostility trait are likely to express hostility across many situations; however, certain situational factors may serve to either increase or dampen expressions of hostility. For example, a hostile person might be unlikely to exhibit this trait when communicating with superiors at work for fear of losing his or her job.

As with the trait of assertiveness, the hostile personality has been studied more extensively by psychologists and social psychologists than by communication scholars. In his early work, Berkowitz (1962) suggests that aggressive behavior is learned by individuals responding aggressively to aggressive cues. In particular, Berkowitz posits that frustrating and anger-inducing experiences produce hostile and aggressive behavior. Consequently, hostile behavior in response to anger-inducing stimuli is learned and can become habitual

(Infante, 1987a). Berkowitz suggests further that hostility can be influenced by the method in which an individual was punished in childhood. The influence of aggressive behavior emerges especially when attempting to influence others. If a child is subject to physical or corporal punishment (i.e., the child is hit), the child may reason that physical aggression is an effective compliance-gaining strategy. That is, the child may reason that "hitting someone must be a good method for getting your way; it sure worked on me" (Infante, 1987a, p. 179; Infante, 2005). Indeed, when compared with other students, children identified as school bullies report being hit more often by their parents and have parents who resort more often to corporal punishment as a method of solving problems with their children (Bosworth, Espelage, & Simon, 1999).

The hostile personality has not received a great deal of attention from scholars in the communication discipline, but comes out of the discipline of social psychology. Indeed, most of the measures of hostility were developed by psychologists and social psychologists. For example, one of the earliest hostility measures is the Buss and Durkee (1957) Hostility Inventory. This self-report instrument consists of 75 true–false items intended to measure one's propensity to engage in hostile behavior. The 75 items cluster into seven distinct traits: assault, indirect aggression, irritability, negativism, resentment, suspicion, and verbal aggression. Another self-report hostility instrument was developed by Siegel (1986). It consists of 38 items designed to measure aspects of angry feelings such as the frequency, duration, and magnitude of anger; the types of situations that provoke anger; and the individual's general way of expressing anger (Berkowitz, 1998, p. 272).

Research indicates that the predisposition toward hostility and aggressiveness can persist over many years and the trait is quite stable (Berkowitz, 1998). If individuals are hostile in their youth, then that knowledge is a good predictor of how hostile and aggressive they will be much later on in their life (Berkowitz, 1993).

Verbal Aggressiveness

The trait of verbal aggressiveness is considered to be a subset of hostility. Like hostility, verbal aggressiveness is considered part of the neuroticism dimension of personality (Costa & McCrae, 1980; Infante, 1987a). Argumentative behavior and verbally aggressive behavior are both considered attacking and aggressive forms of communication. However, presenting a definition of verbal aggressiveness will help you understand the difference between these two traits.

Verbal aggressiveness is defined as "the tendency to attack the self-concepts of individuals instead of, or in addition to, their positions on topics of communication" (Infante, 1987a, p. 164; Infante & Wigley, 1986, p. 61). When people direct their attack on the person's self-concept, ("You are such a liar!"), they are engaging in verbal aggression. A study by Kinney (1994) suggests there are three broad domains of self-concept attack: group membership (e.g., "Your family is a bunch of psychos!"), personal failings (e.g., "And how could we forget that business you ran into the ground five years ago!"), and relational failings (e.g., "Maybe your ex-husband wasn't so weird after all.").

Argumentativeness (the constructive trait) and verbal aggressiveness (the destructive trait) can be distinguished by the locus of the attack (i.e., the place where the attack is directed). When the attack is on the other person's position, it is considered an argumentative attack. When the attack is on the other person's self-concept, it is considered a verbally aggressive attack. As we will detail later in the book, many people confuse both communication traits, while others see any attack, even if it is directed at another person's position, as verbally aggressive communication.

The trait of verbal aggressiveness is measured by the Verbal Aggressiveness Scale developed by Infante and Wigley (1986). A copy of the scale and more details on its development will be presented in Chapter 3 and in Appendix A. For now, however, we will describe a taxonomy of verbally aggressive communication and describe what we believe causes the trait to be developed in individuals.

First, let us contrast an interpersonal interaction characterized by verbal aggression with one categorized as argumentative. In order to do so, let us return to the example presented earlier in this chapter. Recall the controversy you had with your roommate over the spring break getaway vacation (you wanted to go to Fort Lauderdale, Florida, while your friend preferred to go to South Padre Island, Texas). Unlike the argumentative encounter described earlier, the verbally aggressive interaction might go something like this: You might say to your friend, "I think you are so stupid for wanting to go to South Padre Island for spring break! The weather in south Texas in mid-March sucks. And, it is so far away. I'll probably have to drive most of the way because you are such a bad driver. Even worse, I'll get stuck with paying for all the gas, tolls, and food on the trip since you are such a cheap bastard." Although this interaction may seem closer to reality than the argumentative version, it is considered verbally aggressive and thus can be considered relationally destructive.

Several different types of verbally aggressive communication have been identified and several of them are evident in the preceding example. The first type is called competence attacks. Competence attacks are verbal attacks directed at another person's ability to do something. A general example of a competence attack would be a father saying to his son, "You can't do anything right!" or more specifically, "Give me that hammer, you can never put a nail in the wall correctly." Spouses can engage in competence attacks that instill hurt, pain, and embarrassment. One such competence attack that is exchanged in relationships marked by difficulty is "You are a lousy mother/father." In the dialogue example above, calling your friend a bad driver is an example of a competence attack. Recipients of competence attacks generally feel hurt, ashamed, and embarrassed. If the attacks persist in one area, those attacks may indeed cause a person to become less competent at the particular task and dampen that person's desire to perform that task or activity again.

Another type of verbally aggressive message is character attacks, attacks on another person's character. "You're a liar!" and "You're a cheater!" are two very typical forms of character attacks. Again, embarrassment, hurt, and psychological pain often result from character attacks. Profanity is a ubiquitous form of verbally aggressive message behavior. Some researchers define profanity in a very narrow way (e.g., "to treat [something sacred] with abuse, irreverence, or contempt" (Jay, 1992, p. 3). However, a more common interpretation suggests that profanity involves the use of obscene words, epithets, and vulgarities. Since most of us know profanity when we hear it, we will not provide a laundry list of profane or obscene words or phrases. Those wishing to review such a list can be directed to the work of Jay, whose book, Cursing in America, provides an extensive list of curses, profanity, blasphemy, obscenity, vulgarity, slang, epithets, and slurs. However, Jay makes it clear that anger is often expressed with profanity and taboo words and has developed a five-stage model designed to demonstrate that "taboo or obscene speech when used to express anger is coded speech" (Jay, p. 97). In the dialogue example above, calling your friend a cheap bastard would constitute a verbally aggressive attack using profanity.

Teasing and ridicule are also two forms of verbally aggressive message behavior. Although in conventional usage the terms teasing and ridicule are often used interchangeably, they are a bit different. In teasing, we make fun of, or playfully mock, another individual. The key element in teasing is the notion that it is a more playful form of verbal aggression. When we tease others and they become angry or annoyed at us, we tend to defend this verbal behavior by stating, "I was only kidding you, I was only teasing you." However, teasing can inflict psychological harm and damage on the target, thus fulfilling the objective of verbal aggression to inflict harm and pain on another. We are certain that you can recall an example of being teased sometime during your life, whether it was directed at your physical appearance (e.g., "You have a nose like a trumpet") or your level of skill at doing something (e.g., "You throw the ball like a baby"). We are also sure that, despite the number of years that may have passed, you remember the teasing episodes and the hurt and embarrassment they evoked. Closely related to teasing is another type of verbal aggression, ridicule. Ridicule is using words or deeds to evoke condescending laughter directed at another person. Children are particularly fond of using teasing and ridicule as forms of verbal aggression.

In order to understand and study teasing, DiCioccio (2001) developed the Teasing Communication Scale, which is used to assess differences in teasing messages. DiCioccio drew from the literature on verbal aggression and the use of personal idioms (expressions) to explore how and why teasing is used. Although the theory of aggressive communication suggests that teasing is a form of verbal aggression (Infante, 1987a; Infante, Riddle, Horvath, & Tumlin, 1992; Infante, Trebing, Shepard, & Seeds, 1984; Infante & Wigley, 1986), the research on personal idioms suggests that teasing is one type of personal idiom that could potentially have a beneficial dimension to interpersonal relationships (Baxter, 1992; DiCioccio).

Incorporating both theoretical frameworks, DiCioccio suggested that teasing has two dimensions, affectionate teasing and aggressive teasing. These two dimensions represent the constructive and destructive aspects of teasing. Affectionate teasing is considered a constructive form of communication and is used as a means to exhibit positive relational affect, to increase affinity between individuals, and to strengthen relationships. Affectionate teasing often acts like an inside joke between relationship partners that can bring them closer to each other. An example of affectionate teasing is when one person says to his or her partner during a trip, "Better hold onto these maps and directions because you know how good you are at finding places!" In this case, one partner is commenting on the other's geographic and directional challenges in an effort affectionately laugh at his or her shortcomings.

Aggressive teasing, however, is considered destructive communication and a form of verbal aggression. Hence, aggressive teasing has the goal of causing psychological pain and hurt. As a form of verbal aggression, aggressive teasing is often used as an expression of anger regarding a specific relational issue or as a way of expressing one's discontent with a partner or the relationship in general (DiCioccio, 2001). Using the above example, aggressive teasing would manifest itself when one partner says to the other, "It would be a good idea for you to finally use the map," and says it in a mocking way in which clearly the intention is to hurt by pointing out the other's shortcomings and poor sense of direction.

An 18-item Teasing Communication Scale (TCS) was developed (DiCioccio, 2001) that measures predispositions toward both affectionate and aggressive teasing. Some of the items in the scale include, "I use teasing as a way of expressing positive feelings about a relationship," "I make fun of other people when I know it will be amusing to both of us," "I purposely tease people to embarrass them in front of others," and "I poke fun at people to intentionally hurt their feelings." Among the many findings that emerged in her study, DiCioccio discovered that both the affectionate and the aggressive dimensions of teasing were correlated positively with trait verbal aggressiveness. This finding supports the relationship between aggressive teasing and verbal aggression, while contradicting the conceptualization of affectionate teasing. As DiCioccio suggests, perhaps all teasing is seen as aggressive in nature. As mentioned earlier, most people tend to remember the psychological pain and harm of being teased, even if those messages were delivered many years earlier.

Maledictions are verbally aggressive messages in which we wish someone harm. An example of one of the most ubiquitous maledictions in our culture is, "Drop dead!" Different cultures have idiosyncratic maledictions that do not appear to translate well into other languages and cultures. A malediction used among Eastern European immigrants to New York City was a phrase loosely translated into English as "You should swell up and die!" Another malediction heard in the workplace that is particularly cruel but humorous is "May you suffer from an injury not covered by Worker's Compensation!"

Threats are another form of verbally aggressive communication. When you threaten someone, you are expressly suggesting the intention to inflict pain (physical or psychological), injury, or another type of hurt on another person. If you grew up with a sibling, the following will probably ring true for you. A little brother or sister catches you doing something you should not be doing and proceeds to taunt you with the famous expression, "I'm telling Mom and Dad on you!" At that point, given that adolescents have relatively low skill in developing arguments, you reach into your verbal aggression arsenal and reply "You tell Mom or Dad on me and I will kill you!"

Another frequent form of verbal aggression is nonverbal verbal aggression. Nonverbal verbal aggression most frequently takes the form of speech-independent gestures, also called nonverbal emblems. Emblems are nonverbal behaviors that take the place of spoken words. The most common verbally aggressive emblem in our culture (and in many cultures around the world) is flipping the bird, or displaying the middle finger in the "up yours" gesture. Other forms of nonverbal verbal aggression include gritting one's teeth in anger, crinkling the nose, sticking out the tongue, making a fist and shaking it in front of someone, and using your index finger and thumb to form the letter "L" while holding it to your forehead to signify "loser."

Infante (1995b) expanded this original taxonomy of verbal aggressive messages by adding a few, including personality attacks (e.g., an attack on another person's personality such as saying "He's a timid fool"), negative comparison (e.g., "You are not as handsome/pretty as your brother/sister"), attacking the target's significant others (e.g., "Your children are so ugly"), blame (e.g., "You are the reason I am poor"), and disconfirmation (i.e., completely ignoring another person or making believe he or she does not exist).

Causes of Verbal Aggressiveness

Five causes have been offered to explain the development of verbal aggressiveness: psychopathology, disdain, social learning, the argumentative skill deficiency explanation (ASD), and genetics. We will describe each of them here.

Psychopathology occurs when an individual expresses previously repressed hostility. For example, some individuals may have been the victims of teasing, threats, or ridicule and they may have become deeply hurt by it. Because they may have been quite young, or lower in status and thus powerless to respond, they consequently had to hold these negative feelings inside and suppress the hostility they felt. Several years later, however, they may vent this repressed hostility by verbally attacking someone who reminds them of the individual or group who hurt them. Now, whenever they encounter an individual who reminds them of their previously held hurt, pain, and embarrassment, they employ verbal aggression as a primary message behavior. For example, suppose an individual had an unfortunate and negative encounter with a police officer early in life. A police officer may have yelled at, belittled, or physically mistreated him or her for an offense that may or may not have been committed. Years later, whenever this individual encounters a police officer, he or she is likely to use some form of verbal aggression (e.g., profanity or negative comparison) when communicating with or about the police. Treatment for this potential cause of verbal aggression goes beyond the scope of most communication specialists and a "psychopathological basis for aggression seems likely in some of the extreme cases, and its investigation is more appropriately reserved for trained psychologists" (Wigley, 1998, p. 194).

Disdain has been suggested as another potential cause of verbal aggressiveness (Infante et al., 1984). Disdain is considered severe dislike or even hatred for another person or object. Many of us might have been the victim of a verbal attack by someone who disliked us greatly. Thankfully, such experiences are infrequent for most people (except for those who work as customer service representatives!). When one expresses disdain for another person it is likely to be in the form of verbally aggressive communication. However, as Wigley (1998) suggests, disdain "helps us understand why some people are consistently verbally aggressive toward some individuals, but not toward others" (p. 194). Disdain, however, may not be a very powerful cause of verbally aggressive behavior because, for many of us, when we disdain someone or something, we seek to avoid that person or object as much as possible, and we normally avoid interacting with people we dislike greatly. It is during those instances in which we must interact with someone we disdain that the likelihood of using verbally aggressive communication increases. In addition, the verbally aggressive personality usually does not restrict verbal aggression to a particular group of individuals, but engages in it across a wide range of potential targets. Current thinking suggests that while psychopathology and disdain are potential causes of verbal aggressiveness, the next three potential causes are more likely the main contributors to an individual becoming verbally aggressive.

The social learning explanation suggests that we learn to become verbally aggressive from those around us whom we interact with or observe on a regular basis. Social learning theory suggests that our behavior is shaped by factors in the environment. As such, those individuals we frequently come into contact with can greatly influence our communication behavior and personality. However, social learning theory argues that people will only model behaviors if they themselves are reinforced for using those behaviors. If we are reared in a home in which verbal aggression was commonplace, then the social learning explanation suggests that we will either be predisposed to it, or not, depending upon how we observed the outcomes associated with this form of communication. For example, a child might learn to become verbally aggressive from his or her highly verbally aggressive father if the child observes that the father always gets his way when he uses it. Conversely, a child might learn not to be verbally aggressive if he or she observes that the father is continually punished for engaging in this type of communication behavior (e.g., is shunned by family and friends or loses a job as a result of it). If the environment we grew up in contained a great deal of verbally (and physically) aggressive messages and behaviors, then social learning theory argues we might engage in these forms of aggression if we observe benefits from using it. For example, the use of bullying behaviors by some students has been attributed to social learning (see Bosworth et al., 1999). Earlier it was suggested that verbal aggressiveness is a subset of hostility and as such can be considered an aspect of neuroticism (Infante, 1987a; McCrae & Costa, 1987). As Wigley (1998) suggests, "Because neuroticism appears to categorize a large number of negative characteristics, verbal aggressiveness might incubate and grow with this aspect of one's personality" (p. 195).

Another potential explanation for the development of verbal aggressiveness is called the inherited trait explanation. It has been argued by several communication scholars that verbal aggressiveness develops largely due to genetics (Beatty & McCroskey, 1997; Wigley). Beatty and McCroskey, working under the communibiological paradigm, conceptualize verbal aggressiveness as an expression of temperament. This perspective argues that people are born with a set of biologically determined temperaments that are relatively consistent throughout their lives.

Temperaments are behavioral tendencies that differentiate people. The communibiological perspective stands in direct opposition to the social-learning framework described earlier. While the social-learning framework suggests that verbal aggressiveness is a learned predisposition influenced by situational forces around us, the communibiological paradigm argues that a great deal of human behavior, and in this particular case verbal aggressiveness, is genetically determined. In other words, we inherit our verbal aggressiveness from our biological parents. Indeed, Beatty and McCroskey (1997) state, "From a communibiological perspective, situational or environmental explanations of verbal aggressiveness, or any other interpersonal process for that matter, should be proffered as a last resort, only after all neurobiological explanations have failed" (p. 450).

More specifically, Beatty and McCroskey (2001) suggest that three neurological circuits in the brain are the biological basis for verbal aggressiveness. One of those circuits is called the behavioral activation system, one is called the behavioral inhibition system, and one is the fight–flight system. While a complete discussion of these three systems is beyond the scope of this text, the identification of these systems as a part of the regions of the brain should help us understand if and when an individual's verbal aggressiveness becomes activated. For each of these three systems, Beatty and McCroskey (2001) identify which regions of the brain are involved and describe different types of brain and neurobiological chemical activity associated with each. In essence, they have identified a neurobiology of verbal aggressiveness. We will describe in more detail the relationship between the aggressive communication traits of argumentativeness and verbal aggressiveness and the measurement of temperament that has been linked to neurobiological activity later in this chapter (Valencic, Beatty, Rudd, Dobos, & Heisel, 1998).

Throughout the remainder of this text, you will encounter much discussion about another potential cause of verbal aggressiveness, the argumentative skill deficiency explanation for verbal aggressiveness. This explanation suggests that individuals become verbally aggressive due to a lack of motivation and skill in arguing. Individuals who lack motivation and skill in argumentative communication become easily frustrated when they are involved in a conflict situation. In addition, individuals with lower motivation and skill in argument have a great deal of difficulty in generating arguments to use. That is, people who have low motivation to argue, or who lack the skill to generate arguments, appear to quickly run out of things to say (i.e., arguments) during conflict episodes.

You may recall examples of this from your own life. Let us describe how this might play out. Do you ever recall, as a newly licensed driver, arguing with your parents about using their car? For example, you may have asked your dad to borrow the car to go on a date. In no uncertain terms he said, "No!" Frustrated, you attempted to argue in support of the request to borrow the car, by delivering one puny and weak argument (e.g., "All of my friends get to use their parents' cars"). Consequently, this argument was unsuccessful in getting your father to yield to your request. Because you dislike arguing, and have trouble generating any additional arguments, you could not think of any other arguments to present to him. Later, on the bus to your date's house, you can suddenly come up with much better arguments that you wish you could have generated earlier (e.g., "Traveling by car is much safer than taking the bus or subway"). Such is the case with individuals who are low in motivation and unskilled in arguing. They quickly exhaust their rather meager store of arguments during an argumentative encounter.

The argumentative skill deficiency explanation has been suggested as a cause for verbal aggression because during an argument we are in an attack-and-defend mode. If we cannot attack our adversary's position on the controversial issue by inventing and delivering arguments (i.e., engage in argumentativeness), we can either avoid the situation or more often resort to attacking their self-concept instead (i.e., engage in verbal aggression). The argumentative skill deficiency explanation for the development of verbal aggressiveness presents a rationale for the development of communication-based programs designed to enhance an individual's motivation and skill in argument. Indeed, some programs have already been designed and tested (see Chapter 10). Although the efficacy of the argumentative skill deficiency explanation for verbal aggression has been questioned (Hamilton & Mineo, 2002; Roberto, 1999), additional research will need to be conducted before its utility can be dismissed or retained. In review, Table 1.1 presents a summary of the four aggressive communication predispositions.

Infante, Riddle, et al. (1992) also discovered a few additional reasons individuals reported engaging in verbally aggressive communication. These include trying to appear tough, rational discussions that degenerate into verbal aggression, and wanting to be mean to others. Finally, verbally aggressive communication may be more common when the topic of disagreement is of greater importance to the interactants and the consequences of the conflict are very meaningful to those involved. Indeed, Martin, Anderson, and Horvath (1996) found that individuals high in verbal aggressiveness often perceive that their use of verbal aggression is justified.

Table 1.1   Argumentative and Aggressive Communication Predispositions

Trait	Definition	Orientation	Scales Used to Measure Trait
Assertiveness	Predisposition to be interpersonally dominant and forceful to achieve personal goals while creating positive feelings in others	Constructive	Rathus Assertiveness Schedule (1973); Richmond & McCroskey's Assertiveness-Responsiveness Measure (1990)
Argumentativeness	Predisposition to advocate positions on controversial issues and to verbally attack the positions of others	Constructive	Infante & Rancer's Argumentativeness Scale (1982); Roberto & Finucane's Adolescent ARG Scale (1977); Hinkle's ABCAS Instrument (1986)
Hostility	Predisposition to use messages to express irritability, negativity, resentment, or suspicion	Destructive	Buss & Durkee's Hostility Inventory (1957); Siegel's Multidimensional Anger Inventory (1986)
Verbal Aggressiveness	Predisposition to attack the self-concepts of individuals instead of, or in addition to, their positions on issues	Destructive	Infante & Wigley's Verbal Aggressiveness Scale (1986); Roberto & Finucane's Adolescent VA Scale (1997); Beatty, Valencic, Rudd, & Dobos's Indirect Interpersonal Aggressiveness Scale (1999)

Argumentative and Aggressive Communication Traits and Personality Theory

Throughout this chapter we have presented research that suggests the communication traits of argumentativeness and verbal aggressiveness (as well as assertiveness and hostility) are part of the larger theoretical framework of temperament and personality theory. To review, trait theorists believe there is a great deal of variation in the way individuals interact with each other and respond to situational factors. The way a person responds, trait theorists believe, is primarily controlled by this cluster of traits. Scholars who adhere to the trait perspective of behavior suggest that individuals will most often respond to different situations with similar behavioral and interactional patterns.

Although numerous theories and approaches to the study of temperament and personality exist, primarily from the discipline of psychology, two dominant theoretical approaches have emerged. In this section, we will briefly review these two trait and psychobiological theories of personality and describe how argumentative and aggressive communication traits are related to them.

Recently, communication scholars have employed trait and psychobiological theories of personality as frameworks to help explain the development of communication traits in general, and argumentative and verbally aggressive communication in particular (see Beatty & McCroskey, 2001). The frameworks developed by psychologists Eysenck and Eysenck (1985), as well as Costa and McCrae (1980), have been extremely helpful in this endeavor.

The Dimensions of Personality

The work of Eysenck and Eysenck (1985) resulted in the three-factor model of personality. This model argues that there are three superfactors (i.e., a trait that many other specific traits are part of) that underlie all personality: psychoticism, extraversion, and neuroticism (P-E-N). Eysenck and Eysenck's approach also suggests that personality is developed by genetic inheritance. Costa and McCrae (1980) extended the work of Eysenck and Eysenck by retaining the extraversion and neuroticism dimensions of Eysenck and adding three additional factors. Thus, they produced a five-factor model ("The Big 5") that consists of five personality traits: openness, conscientiousness, extraversion, agreeableness, and neuroticism (O-C-E-A-N). Before discussing the relationship between these personality traits and aggressive communication, let us define these traits. As there is considerable overlap between Eysenck and Eysenck's and Costa and McCrae's dimensions of personality, we will combine both sets of definitions when defining them.

Neuroticism refers to the dimension that ranges from a calm and relaxed nature to one that exhibits a great deal of nervousness. An individual's emotional stability and psychological adjustment is reflected by how neurotic the person is. Highly neurotic individuals are easily worried, are quick to anger, and have difficulty coping with stress. Individuals who score low in neuroticism are calm and relaxed and are able to cope with stress quite well. According to Costa and McCrae (1980), the neuroticism dimension has six facets: anxiety, hostility, depression, self-consciousness, vulnerability, and impulsiveness. In a study on the relationship between Eysenck and Eysenck's (1985) three dimensions of personality and verbal aggressiveness, Heisel, LaFrance, and Beatty (2003) measured neuroticism by asking individuals questions such as

> Do you ever feel "just miserable" for no reason? Do you often feel that life is very dull? Are you easily hurt when people find fault with you or your work? Would you call yourself tense, or "highly strung?" and, Are you an irritable person? (p. 8)

The extraversion dimension speaks to how social a person is, placed on a continuum from high to low extraversion. Outgoing, friendly, and gregarious individuals are typically high in extraversion. They are assertive and often emerge as leaders. Individuals who score low on extraversion tend to be shy and quiet. Low extraverts appear to others as reserved and formal, and prefer being alone. Extraversion has six facets: warmth, gregariousness, assertiveness, activity, excitement seeking, and positive emotions. Items designed to measure this dimension of personality include

> Do you enjoy meeting new people? Do you like mixing with people? Do you often make decisions on the spur of the moment? Do you like plenty of bustle and excitement around you? and, Can you easily adapt to new and unusual situations? (Heisel et al., 2003, p. 8)

As with the other dimensions of personality, openness (to experience) is on a continuum from high to low. People high in openness place much value on emotions. They tend to be more liberal and manifest an ability to communicate credibly on many topics. Individuals scoring low in openness tend to minimize the importance of emotions. They tend to be more conservative and somewhat dogmatic in their attitudes, beliefs and values. The six facets of openness to experience are fantasy, aesthetics, feelings, actions, ideas, and values.

Individuals also differ in the dimension of agreeableness. Agreeable people are easier to get along with and are more trusting of others. Highly agreeable individuals tend to be somewhat humble, see others in a very positive light, and when involved in a conflict situation, often defer to others (especially those with higher status and authority). Individuals scoring low on agreeableness tend to be more aggressive and competitive, especially in conflict situations. They find it more difficult to trust others and are often cynical and guarded. The six facets of agreeableness are trust, straightforwardness, altruism, compliance, modesty, and tender-mindedness.

Conscientiousness deals with how meticulous and persistent an individual is. Individuals scoring high in conscientiousness are organized, neat, and focused on tasks and task completion. Conversely, individuals low in conscientiousness are relatively unorganized and unprepared. They tend to procrastinate and are easily distracted. The six facets associated with conscientiousness are competence, orderliness, dutifulness/dependability, achievement orientation, self-discipline, and deliberation.

A final dimension of personality is psychoticism. While conventional usage suggests that being psychotic is when one's contact with reality is suspect, Eysenck and Eysenck (1985) suggested that psychoticism is better seen as emotional independence. Being high in the psychoticism dimension of personality does not suggest that you are psychotic, only that you may share some of the characteristics commonly found among psychotics. Eysenck and Eysenck described this dimension of personality as lacking in feeling and empathy, being somewhat unconcerned and possibly hostile to others, having a certain degree of disregard for common social conventions, and exhibiting a degree of inappropriate emotional expression. Some of the facets of psychoticism identified by Eysenck are cold, egocentric, impersonal, unempathic, creative, tough-minded, and aggressive. In the Heisel et al. (2003) study, psychoticism was measured by items such as

> Would you take drugs which might have strange or dangerous effects? Do you prefer to go your own way rather than act by the rules? Do you think that marriage is old fashioned and should be done away with? Do you think that people spend too much time safeguarding their future with savings and insurance? and, Would you like people to be afraid of you? (p. 8)

Although both models of personality have been employed in communication research, Beatty and McCroskey (2001) advocate the use of the Eysenck and Eysenck model. They argue for its superiority because (a) it has been in use for a longer period of time than the Costa and McCrae (1980) model, as Eysenck and Eysenck's research on dimensions of personality began in the 1950s; (b) it has a great deal of data to support it; (c) the factor structure of the model is stable and has been replicated across cultures; and (d) "the model aligns well with communication" (Beatty & McCroskey, p. 63). Beatty and McCroskey also suggest that "we believe that the fullest account of human communication will require research programs that pursue all posited models of communication" (p. 63).

The Relationship Between Temperament and Aggressive Communication Traits

Throughout this chapter we have suggested a relationship between the aggressive communication traits (i.e., assertiveness, argumentativeness, hostility, and verbal aggressiveness) and these other personality traits. As we have mentioned, assertiveness is one of the six facets of the extraversion dimension in Costa and McCrae's (1980) model, and argumentativeness has been related to the assertiveness facet of extraversion. Again, in Costa and McCrae's trait model of personality, hostility is considered a facet of neuroticism. Like hostility, verbal aggressiveness is considered part of the neuroticism dimension of personality (Costa and McCrae; Infante, 1987a).

Several studies have empirically examined the relationship between argumentativeness, verbal aggressiveness, and the personality dimensions described above. In one of the earliest studies, Blickle (1997) correlated Costa and McCrae's (1980) five dimensions of personality with trait argumentativeness. For a sample of male college students in Germany, argumentativeness correlated significantly and positively with extraversion and openness, and significantly and negatively with neuroticism and agreeableness. In a similar study with American students, Hamilton and Mineo (2002) examined the relationship between argumentativeness and Costa and McCrae's dimensions. They discovered positive relationships between argumentativeness and extraversion, openness to new experiences, and a negative relationship between trait argumentativeness and neuroticism.

As early as 1997, Beatty and McCroskey suggested that psychoticism and verbal aggressiveness should be positively related. To examine this speculation, McCroskey, Heisel, and Richmond (2001) examined the relationship between argumentativeness, verbal aggressiveness, and Eysenck and Eysenck's (1985) big three factors of personality. They found that argumentativeness correlated significantly and positively with extraversion and psychoticism. They also found that verbal aggressiveness was correlated significantly and positively with psychoticism. Indeed, substantial correlations between verbal aggressiveness and the psychoticism dimension of personality have been observed in other research (Beatty, Rudd et al., 1999; McCroskey et al., 2001; Valencic et al., 1998). These results suggest that "psychotics are non-responsive, and tend to report higher levels of verbal aggressiveness, argumentativeness and assertiveness" (McCroskey et al., p. 365).

In another study, Heisel et al. (2003) studied the relationship between Eysenck and Eysenck's three dimensions of personality and behavior patterns associated with verbal aggressiveness. The researchers wanted to examine whether the relationship between Eysenck and Eysenck's dimensions of personality and verbal aggressiveness would hold when observer measures were used in the place of self-report measures. The results supported that relationship in that "psychoticism predicted verbal aggressiveness" (Heisl et al., 2003, p. 10). In addition, an indirect relationship between extraversion and verbal aggressiveness was found, which the researchers suggest was mediated by affinity-seeking competence (i.e., verbal and nonverbal behaviors we use to get people to like us). Thus, individuals who are high in psychoticism and who lack affinity-seeking competence are more likely to engage in verbally aggressive behavior (Heisel et al., p. 11).

In summary, trait argumentativeness has been significantly and positively correlated with extraversion, openness, and psychoticism. That is, the higher one is in argumentativeness, the higher one is in extraversion, openness, and psychoticism. Trait argumentativeness has also been significantly and negatively correlated with neuroticism and agreeableness. That is, the higher one is in argumentativeness, the lower one is in neuroticism and agreeableness. Trait verbal aggressiveness has also been significantly and positively correlated with psychoticism and indirectly with extraversion, or, the higher one is in verbal aggressiveness, the higher one is in psychoticism and to some extent extraversion.

Conclusion

This chapter has served as an introduction to the study of argumentative and verbally aggressive communication. The development of both the argumentativeness and verbal aggressiveness constructs was derived not only from communication theory, but from psychology and social psychology as well. In this case, drawing from the literature on hostility as well as assertiveness, we are able to make a distinction between constructive or beneficial traits (i.e., assertiveness and argumentativeness) and destructive or detrimental traits (i.e., hostility and verbal aggressiveness).

As with most other communication and personality traits, the development and degree to which the traits affect behavior is constantly being debated. More specifically, we discussed the various ways in which researchers treat argumentative and verbally aggressive communication. These treatments range from the assumption that genetics and brain structure account for the vast majority of trait behavior (i.e., the communibiological perspective) to the assumption that the situation exerts a great influence on the trait (i.e., situational perspective). Between these two perspectives is the interactionist approach (Andersen, 1987), which holds that any trait is a joint function of both person (i.e., biological) and context (i.e., situational), which when combined are believed to account for most trait behavior.

An important concept discussed in this chapter was that of a supertrait or superfactor. More specifically, two types of approaches where highlighted. These approaches included the Eysenck and Eysenck (1985) three-factor model of psychotocism, extraversion, and neuroticism and the Costa and McCrae (1980) big-five model comprised of openness, conscientiousness, extraversion, agreeableness, and neuroticism. Regardless of which model you find more appealing, the assumption is that all personality and communication traits are subcategories of the three or big-five factor supertraits.

Now that we have introduced the concepts, discussed the different ways of conceptualizing argumentative and aggressive communication, and addressed the prevailing debate about which conceptualization is better, we turn to the measurement issues. You may recall from a past research methods class that an operational definition is the equivalent of a recipe (i.e., "argumentativeness is the tendency to . . ." and "verbal aggressiveness is the tendency to . . ."). Now, we move to the measurement phase or as we call it the operational phase. This is where we now must design ways to measure argumentative and aggressive communication based on some observable characteristics. The next chapter will address these measurement issues.

Discussion Questions for Chapter 1

1. Why do you think verbal aggression is so prevalent in today's society?

2. What does it mean when we say argumentative and aggressive communication can be good and bad? Are there situations in which verbally aggressive communication can serve a strategic purpose?

3. What is the social learning explanation for verbal aggressiveness? How does this explanation differ from the inherited trait explanation?

4. What is the argumentative skills deficiency explanation for verbal aggression? Do you think such an explanation is valid?

5. Based on the reading of the chapter, do you prefer a social learning explanation or a genetic explanation for the development of the argumentativeness and verbal aggressiveness traits? Why?

2

Measuring Individual Differences in Argumentative and Aggressive Communication

Communication researchers must be able to verify empirically (i.e., through observation) the presence and amount of a given communication trait or predisposition that individuals possess. Although there are several methods of assessing a person's communication predispositions, such as employing behavioral observation by a trained rater (see McCroskey, 1997), most communication traits have been measured by the use of self-report, paper-and-pencil instruments. That is, to identify and quantify the existence of a given communication predisposition, individuals are asked to respond to a series of items or statements about their cognitions (i.e., thoughts), behaviors, and affective states (i.e., feelings) that deal with the trait being assessed. Self-report measurement scales or instruments are carefully and systematically constructed to measure the dimensions of the given predisposition. For example, when assessing apprehension associated with communication, McCroskey (1982) asserted that the dimensions of communication apprehension consist of apprehension associated with speaking with another person, speaking in a group, speaking at a meeting, and giving a public speech. Further, self-report scales also endure much testing to ensure that they are both *reliable* (stable, consistent, and accurate) and *valid* (they measure what they say they measure).

After an individual responds to the items on the scale, he or she (or a researcher) may obtain a total score for the entire scale or a score for each separate dimension of the trait that the scale includes (if more than one dimension is measured). Respondents and researchers can then compare the total or dimensional score against the preestablished norms developed for the scale (i.e., scores found in previous research samples). Norms regarding what is considered high, moderate, and low scores on a given trait are established by the researcher and scale developer.

For example, to assess a person's level of trait *communication apprehension* (the fear or anxiety a person has about communicating with another person or person) an individual is asked to respond to the Personal Report of Communication Apprehension (PRCA) developed and refined by McCroskey (1970, 1978, 1982). Through this procedure, an individual or a researcher can determine whether the person who responded to the scale is considered high, moderate, or low in communication apprehension. A communication researcher can use these scores to identify a group of individuals who may be, for example, extremely high in communication apprehension, to solicit their participation for one of several programs designed to reduce levels of communication apprehension.

Measuring the Argumentativeness and Verbal Aggressiveness Traits

Like communication apprehension and other personality and communication traits, argumentativeness and verbal aggressiveness have been measured largely through the use of paper-and-pencil, self-report instruments. The use of self-report instruments is an efficient, inexpensive, and for the most part unobtrusive method of assessing the predispositions of large groups of individuals (McCroskey, 1997). Historically, for the measurement of argumentativeness and verbal aggressiveness, researchers have relied on the 20-item Argumentativeness Scale (Infante & Rancer, 1982) and the 20-item Verbal Aggressiveness Scale (Infante & Wigley, 1986). It is important to recognize that the content and scoring method for each scale are somewhat different.

The measurement instruments for argumentativeness and verbal aggressiveness evolved from the necessity to measure individuals' argumentative and verbally aggressive traits. Instruments were needed to measure both traits to facilitate research on argumentative and aggressive communication and to understand more fully individuals' orientations toward argumentative and aggressive forms of communication. Understanding how to measure these predispositions was a prerequisite to the development of methods of stimulating individuals' constructive conflict management orientations and reducing the tendency to engage in destructive forms of conflict management.

Infante and Rancer (1982) developed the Argumentativeness Scale as a way to measure the trait of argumentativeness in order to identify those high, moderate, and low in motivation to argue. Similarly, Infante and Wigley (1986) developed the Verbal Aggressiveness Scale in an effort to "facilitate research on the nature and control of (verbal) aggression" (p. 67).

As mentioned in the introduction of this book, the research program began as a way of understanding more fully the communication behaviors of individuals engaged in social conflict. The reasoning that one of the major components involved in social conflict was argumentative communication. That is, the primary interest was in situations where people hold different positions on controversial issues and exchange messages designed to present their position and attack verbally the positions held by their adversary. To study the behaviors and outcomes of those who seemed to enjoy and do well in an argument and those who seemed to dislike it and do not do well, a measure of people's general tendency to be argumentative was needed. Hence, the creation of the Argumentativeness Scale was begun.

The theoretical underpinnings of the Argumentativeness Scale were based on Atkinson's (1957, 1966) theory of achievement motivation. We will describe more fully how Atkinson's theory contributed to the creation of the Argumentativeness Scale in Chapter 3, but for now the notion of "trait argumentativeness" was conceptualized as "approach–avoidance motivational conflict" (Infante, 1987a, p. 171). In other words, individuals have competing approach and avoidance motivations when engaged in an argument. In situations where individuals hold different positions on a controversial issue, these competing tendencies are activated. When one argues about a controversial issue, for example, there is usually an expectation that one will be evaluated. The evaluation usually comes from the adversary in the argument, but at times, evaluation is also done by observers of the argument. During an argument, a highly argumentative individual experiences a sense of excitement and has a strong tendency to approach an argument while feeling little tendency to avoid an argument. Conversely, an individual low in trait argumentativeness would feel no such excitement and would probably experience strong avoidance tendencies. These competing motivations are based on both personality (trait) and situational (state) factors. We will discuss the interaction of these trait and situational factors in Chapter 3.

The Development of the Argumentativeness Scale

The Argumentativeness Scale is a measure of trait argumentativeness, that is, your general tendency to argue (also referred to as ARGgt). The scale was developed in a series of three studies reported by Infante and Rancer (1982). In the first study, 45 items were designed to measure the argumentativeness approach and the argumentativeness avoidance components of the argumentativeness model. In addition, several items designed to measure verbal aggressiveness were included in this first study. These 45 items were presented to college students who were asked to rate their agreement or disagreement with each statement using a Likert-type scale (e.g., 1 = Strongly Disagree, 2 = Disagree, 3 = Neither Agree nor Disagree, 4 = Agree, 5 = Strongly Agree).

After the data were collected they were subjected to a statistical procedure known as factor analysis that allows a researcher to discover which items on a scale are most closely related to each other. The results of a factor analysis produce a set of factors or clusters of the separate items. Each item receives a factor *loading* for each of the factors produced by the statistical procedure. Thus, on the basis of norms established in factor analytic research, items from the original 45 were either retained or discarded. On the basis of this first analysis, eight of the original 45 items were discarded. The remaining 37 items were presented to another group of students and again subjected to the statistical procedure of factor analysis. In this analysis, three independent factors (also called dimensions) emerged, one for ARGap (motivational tendency to approach arguments), one for ARGav (motivational tendency to avoid arguments), and a separate factor containing the verbally aggressive items. Based on these results, the best 20 items were selected, 10 for measuring ARGap and 10 for ARGav. These 20 items were presented to a final group of students who were asked to respond to them using the same response format. A clean factor solution was again produced, containing the 10 items for measuring ARGap and the 10 for ARGav. In addition, Infante and Rancer (1982) found that the two factors were not correlated with each other. As a consequence, motivational tendencies to approach and avoid arguments were considered "independent from one another" (p. 75).

The 20-item Argumentativeness Scale was then subjected to several tests for reliability (i.e., stability, consistency, accuracy) and validity (i.e., does the scale measure what it says it does?). For example, the stability of the scale was tested with a procedure known as test–retest reliability. That is, the scale was given to a group of students at the beginning of one week and then given again to the same group of students at the end of the following week. Then, the responses from time 1 and time 2 were compared. If the relationship between the two is strong, we can conclude it is stable over time. The correlation between time 1 and time 2 for ARGap scores was .87, while the correlation between time 1 and time 2 for the ARGav scores was .86. These results suggest that this measure of an individual's general trait to be argumentative is highly stable. This is important as researchers interested in assessing communication predispositions seek to have consistent measurement of a person's behavior over time.

The internal consistency of the scale was also examined by using a procedure called Cronbach's coefficient alpha. Cronbach's alpha is a reliability statistic that tells how consistent the subjects are in their responses to the scale and "more specifically, across all subjects in a study, [whether] subjects' responses across the instrument vary in the same manner as the subjects' scores" (Wigley, 2003, p. 2). Again, the stability, consistency, and accuracy of the scale were observed (alpha coefficients of .91 for ARGap and .86 for ARGav).

The validity of the scale was also examined in a series of studies. For example, it was reasoned that there should be a strong correspondence between an individual's score on the scale and how close friends perceive that person's argumentative behavior. To test this assumption, a different group of college students was asked to rate a close friend's argumentative behavior on a reworded version of the scale (i.e., the students rated their friend and not themselves). The close friends then rated themselves on the scale. A moderately strong and significant positive correlation was obtained between the subject's perceptions of his or her friend's scores on the scale and the friend's own self-report score. In other words, as the friend's report of the other person's argumentative behavior increases so does the friend's self-report of argumentative behavior.

Another validity study was conducted to assess the convergent and discriminant validity of the Argumentativeness Scale. Convergent validity asks, "How well does the scale relate with other scales that measure similar or related concepts?" Discriminant validity asks, "To what extent does the scale correlate with scales that measure very different concepts?" A sample of students was administered the scale. A week later, the students were told that they would be given a choice of four possible studies to participate in to fulfill a course research requirement. One of the studies required them to debate a controversial issue with a colleague, one asked them to watch and rate television programs, another asked them to converse with a fellow student about life goals, and a final choice asked them to deliver a public speech on a topic of their choice. The students then rated their desire to participate in each of these studies. If the Argumentativeness Scale indeed is a valid measure of argumentativeness, it was reasoned that their ARGap (argumentativeness approach) score would relate positively to their desire to participate in the debate, while their ARGav (argumentativeness avoidance) score would correlate negatively with this activity. It was also reasoned that desire to participate in the other studies would not be related to either

ARGap or ARGav, as they have little or nothing to do with arguing. These speculations were supported in that the only significant relationships found were with the debate study. ARGap correlated significantly and positively with desire to participate in the debate, and ARGav correlated significantly and negatively with desire to participate.

A final validity study on the argumentativeness scale was conducted to test the assumption that the more argumentative an individual is, according to the scale, the more favorable a person's attitude should be toward arguing in a specific situation. To test this speculation, another sample of students was administered the Argumentativeness Scale. A week later, the students were informed that they would be participating in a study to examine people's perceptions of an argumentative situation and how they would actually perform in that situation. They were told that they would be paired up with another student and were to engage in an argument with that student over a controversial proposal (i.e., converting the university from a quarter to a semester system). Participants were also told that their arguments would be observed by a student from an advanced argumentation class who would decide the winner of the argument. Before the argument was to take place, participants completed a set of scales measuring their attitudes toward the argumentative situation they were about to engage in. Once the scales were completed, participants were informed that the actual argument would not take place since the study was in fact only concerned about their perceptions of the argumentative situation. The results of this study supported the speculation; that is, attitudes toward the argumentative situation were significantly and positively correlated with their general tendency to be argumentative. This study again supported the validity of the Argumentativeness Scale. As a consequence of these procedures, the final Argumentativeness Scale was developed and was deemed both a reliable and a valid measure of trait argumentativeness (DeWine, Nicotera, & Parry, 1991; Infante & Rancer, 1982, 1996).

In terms of actual items that measure both tendencies to approach and avoid arguments, examples of items that measure ARGap (motivational tendency to approach arguments) include "I enjoy a good argument over a controversial issue" and "I am energetic and enthusiastic when I argue." Examples of items that measure ARGav (motivational tendency to avoid arguments) include "Arguing with a person creates more problems for me than it solves" and "I get an unpleasant feeling when I realize I am about to get into an argument." Appendix A of this book contains a copy of the Argumentativeness Scale, instructions for completing the scale, and the scoring norms that have been established for the instrument.

Trait argumentativeness scores can range from −40 to +40. The norms established during the development of the scale in 1982 had a mean ARGgt of 4.44, with a standard deviation of 9.83, with a normal distribution of scores. That is, approximately 68% of the people will score between −5.39 and +14.27 and will be considered moderate in their general tendency to argue. Approximately 16% of people scoring above 14.27 will be considered high in the general tendency to argue, whereas the 16% scoring below −5.39 will be considered low in the general tendency to argue.

The Argumentativeness Scale has been in use for almost 25 years and has been translated into numerous languages including Chinese, Finnish, French, German, Greek, Japanese, Korean, Romanian, Slovakian, and Thai. A discussion of argumentative communication in intercultural communication contexts will be presented in Chapter 7.

The Development of the Verbal Aggressiveness Scale

As presented earlier, aggressive communication is composed of four traits, assertiveness, argumentativeness, hostility, and verbal aggressiveness (Infante, 1987a). While adequate instrumentation existed for measuring assertiveness (e.g., Rathus, 1973), hostility (e.g., Buss & Durkee, 1957) and, as of 1982, argumentativeness (e.g., Infante & Rancer, 1982), a reliable and valid measure of trait verbal aggressiveness was now needed.

Recall that in the initial development of the Argumentativeness Scale, Infante and Rancer (1982) included some items designed to measure verbal aggressiveness (e.g., "I like poking fun at someone who does something I regard as stupid" and "I enjoy telling someone off who has insulted me"). This was done to test the speculation that argumentativeness and verbal aggressiveness are independent factors (and constructs). The results of the factor analysis on the items clearly supported this speculation, as it yielded three clearly interpretable factors, one for ARGap, one for ARGav, and a dimension or factor containing the verbally aggressive items.

The Verbal Aggressiveness Scale (Infante & Wigley, 1986) was developed in a similar fashion as the Argumentativeness Scale. Based on the conceptualization of verbal aggressiveness to a trait in which individuals attack the self-concept of others, instead of, or in addition to, their position on controversial issues, 30 items were developed and administered to college students. In addition to these 30 verbally aggressive items, the Argumentativeness Scale was also administered to these same respondents to again test the assumption that the two scales were measuring different dimensions of personality.

Given that verbal aggressiveness is not the most socially appropriate trait, people may not give true responses to the verbally aggressive items due to the possibility of defensiveness on the part of the respondents. That is, few people would want to come out and say "I am verbally aggressive!" To admit that you deliberately say things that attack a person's self-concept is not considered socially acceptable. To reduce this defensive tendency, Infante and Wigley (1986) designed the items with several safeguards. First, as the existence of verbal aggressiveness is assumed in the scale, respondents are asked where, how, and when it is expressed, rather than *whether* verbal aggression is expressed. Second, justification for engaging in verbal aggression was presented in several of the items that provided a legitimization for its use (e.g., "When people behave in ways that are in very poor taste, I insult them in order to shock them into proper behavior"). Finally, for some items, a verbally aggressive response was made to appear benevolent or kind (e.g., "I try to make people feel good about themselves even when their ideas are stupid").

As with the development of the Argumentativeness Scale, statistical analyses (factor analysis and item analysis) resulted in a 20-item Verbal Aggressiveness Scale consisting of 10 positively worded items (e.g., "I refuse to participate in arguments when they involve personal attacks," "When I try to influence people, I make a great effort not to offend them") and 10 negatively worded items (e.g., "If individuals I'm trying to influence really deserve it, I attack their character," "When individuals insult me, I get a lot of pleasure out of really telling them off").

These items were then administered to a different sample of students for further analysis. The results of a factor analysis produced two separate factors, consisting of positively worded aggressive items and negatively worded aggressive items. Although two separate dimensions emerged, Infante and Wigley (1986) suggested that the wording of the items (positive and negative) produced that result. As a consequence, they decided that the scale consisted of only one dimension and that respondents would receive only one score for verbal aggressiveness. Appendix A of this book contains a copy of the Verbal Aggressiveness Scale, instructions for completing the scale, and the scoring norms that have been established for the instrument. Verbal aggressiveness scores can range from 20 to 100. The mean for the scale when it was developed in 1986 was 49.10 and it had a standard deviation of 9.79. The distribution of scores also suggested the trait Verbal Aggressiveness Scale was normally distributed. That is, approximately 68% of the people will score between 39.31 and 58.89 and will be considered moderate in trait verbal aggressiveness. Approximately 16% of people scoring above 58.89 will be considered high in trait verbal aggressiveness, whereas the 16% scoring below 39.31 will be considered low in trait verbal aggressiveness.

This 20-item Verbal Aggressiveness Scale was then subjected to several tests for reliability (stability, consistency) and validity ("Does the scale measure what it says it does?"). The test–retest reliability of the scale was studied by having another group of students take the Verbal Aggressiveness Scale at the beginning of one week and then again four weeks later. Students' scores were highly correlated, suggesting the stability of the verbal aggressiveness trait. The internal consistency of this scale was also examined (using Cronbach's coefficient alpha) and the stability, consistency, and accuracy of the scale were observed.

The validity of the new Verbal Aggressiveness Scale was also assessed. First, the convergent validity (a type of validity that assesses the relationship of the scale to other scales that measure similar constructs) of the scale was investigated. In order to do so, Infante and Wigley (1986) administered the Verbal Aggressiveness Scale along with several other measures to students over three sessions. As hypothesized, verbal aggressiveness was significantly and positively correlated with the assault and verbal hostility subscales from Buss and Durkee's (1957) Hostility-Guilt Inventory. Again, no relationship was observed between the Argumentativeness and Verbal Aggressiveness scales, which again suggested that the two traits were conceptually and empirically distinct.

A final validity study tested the assumption that verbal aggressiveness scores would predict preferences for verbally aggressive messages in a variety of social influence situations (e.g., situations where we try to get people to do things for us). During one week, students completed the Verbal Aggressiveness Scale. Three weeks later, under the guise of a different study, the same students received a booklet containing various social influence situations. While six messages followed each situation, two of the messages were essentially verbally aggressive (e.g., "I would suggest my friend was simple-minded for not seeing my side of the issue"), while the other four were merely filler messages or messages that served to hide the verbally aggressive nature of the study. Students were asked to indicate the likelihood they would use each of these messages. The relationship between their scores on the Verbal Aggressiveness Scale and their likelihood of using the verbally aggressive messages was significant and strong. These findings suggest that the Verbal Aggressiveness Scale allows us to predict with precision the likelihood of a person using verbal aggression to secure compliance in social influence situations, again supporting the validity of the Verbal Aggressiveness Scale.

As a consequence of these procedures, the final 20-item Verbal Aggressiveness Scale was deemed both a reliable and a valid measure of trait verbal aggressiveness (Blickle et al., 1998; DeWine et al., 1991; Infante & Wigley, 1986). More recently, Chory-Assad (2002) supported the predictive validity of the scale by first having students complete the 20-item scale to obtain a measure of their trait verbal aggressiveness and then assessing the frequency of their use of verbal aggression during an interpersonal interaction. Those higher in trait verbal aggressiveness were found to exhibit more frequent use of aggressive communication behaviors. Finally, in a series of studies conducted using a German version of the Verbal Aggressiveness Scale, Blickle, Habash, and Senft (1998) concluded, "Considering all of this evidence, it may be justified to consider verbal aggressiveness as a personality trait, and the Verbal Aggressiveness Scale a valid tool of measurement" (p. 297).

The Verbal Aggressiveness Scale has been in use for almost 20 years and has also been translated into numerous languages, including Chinese, Finnish, French, German, Greek, Japanese, Korean, Romanian, Slovakian, and Thai. Again, a discussion of verbally aggressive communication in intercultural communication contexts will be presented in Chapter 7.

Challenges to the Scales

The Argumentativeness Scale and the Verbal Aggressiveness Scale have been used extensively since their development in the 1980s to measure their respective communication predispositions. These scales, along with McCroskey's (1970, 1978, 1982) measures of communication apprehension, have been cited as some of the most frequently used self-report scales in communication research over the past several decades (see McCroskey et al., 1998). The instruments with which we assess communication predispositions are always a prominent factor when discussing potential problems in assessment efforts. Both the argumentative and aggressive communication traits were initially operationalized through self-report measures (i.e., measurement scales in which respondents report on perceptions of their attitudes and behavior). As with most measurement instruments used in the social and behavioral sciences, researchers have attempted to identify potential limitations of these scales and have offered suggestions for their improvement. Indeed, most of the critiques that have been offered about the argumentative and aggressive communication traits have centered around measurement issues. In this next section, we will identify a few of the measurement concerns that have been suggested and provide responses to them.

Critiques of the Argumentativeness Scale

Issues With Item Wording

During the almost 25 years the Argumentativeness Scale has been in use, most research studies employing the scale have supported the reliability and validity of the original instrument (see Infante & Rancer, 1996). Although the original Infante and Rancer (1982) instrument is by far the scale of choice for researchers and practitioners wishing to assess an individual's general tendency to engage in argumentative communication, there have been some suggestions on how the original scale could be enhanced or modified.

Several years after the development of the original instrument, Dowling and Flint (1990) suggested that the wording of the items might pose some difficulty in assessing the overall trait. In particular, they suggested that the term *argument* could mean different things to different people. That is, when completing the scale, individuals might perceive the term argument as more "relationally based" than a "rational content-based discussions of issues" (p. 186). The items comprising the ARGap (argumentativeness approach) dimension of the scale "seem to test for willingness to engage in an argument as a form of communication that involves conflict over issues" (p. 186) and are thus consistent with the original conceptualization of argumentativeness. However, the items designed to measure ARGav (argumentativeness avoidance) do not use the term *issues*. As a consequence, there may be a tendency for respondents to perceive the avoidance items as referring to fights, bickers, or quarrels and not as arguments over issues. Dowling and Flint suggest that in our culture the concept of arguing may have a negative association for some individuals, consequently conjuring up unpleasant or punishing thoughts.

Dowling and Flint (1990) tested these speculations by creating four alternate versions of the original Argumentativeness Scale and by having students complete each of these new versions along with the original scale, the Verbal Aggressiveness Scale, and four semantic differential-type scales that assessed attitudes toward these new versions. Form 1 consisted of the original Argumentativeness Scale. In Form 2, they used the term *arguing over controversial issues* in all of the items. In Form 3, they used the term *argument* and deleted any reference to issues in all the items. In Form 4, they used the term *argument over controversial issues* in all of the items. In Form 5, they only used the term *arguing* and deleted any reference to issues in the items.

After comparing all versions of the scale, it was suggested that the wording of the scale items made some difference in how subjects responded to them, which might influence respondents' general tendency to be argumentative scores. Referring to "*arguing* over controversial issues" or "*argument* over controversial issues" might produce different scores on ARGap, ARGav, and ARGgt, and "respondents high in relational orientation and/or less familiar with academic meanings of argument seem to score significantly different from their counterparts" (Dowling & Flint, 1990, p. 196).

Dowling and Flint (1990) claim that the items to measure ARGav in the original scale do not contain the phrase *controversial issues* nor do the items use the product term *argument*. While their former assertion may be correct, the latter does not appear to be. An examination of the ARGav items in the scale (see Appendix A) reveals the use of the term *argument*. For example, Item 1 states, "While in an argument, I worry that the person I am arguing with will form a negative impression of me," and Item 10 states, "I get an unpleasant feeling when I realize I am about to get into an argument."

Nevertheless, Dowling and Flint's admonition that researchers and respondents must pay careful attention to the wording choices used in the scale is worthy of consideration. They advocate incorporating the term *argument over controversial issues* into each of the items of the original scale. While the ARGav items do not explicitly contain the phrase *controversial issues*, the instruction provided to respondents on the original Argumentativeness Scale is clear in that it specifies "This questionnaire contains statements about arguing controversial issues." To avoid this potentially confounding issue, it would be prudent for researchers who administer the scale to emphasize the instructions provided on the original version of the scale before having participants complete it.

Social Desirability

Social desirability bias is another concern often voiced when employing self-report measurement scales. Social desirability bias is defined as "the tendency for subjects to respond to personality test items in a manner that consistently presents the self in a favorable light" (Holden & Fekken, 1989, p. 181). When individuals are subject to a social desirability influence, they have a tendency to respond to scales or measurement instruments in a way that they think is "socially acceptable and desirable" (Sohlberg, 1976, p. 301). Critics suggest that if social desirability is present when individuals respond to scale items, their responses may be more indicative of this social desirability bias rather than their "actual behavioral tendency or predisposition" (Nicotera, 1996, p. 25). In this case, individuals who believe arguing is negative and socially undesirable might not be reporting their true responses because they do not want to look bad.

Social desirability has been examined as both a trait (Chen, 1994) and a bias (Nicotera, 1996) as it relates to the Argumentativeness Scale. For example, Chen cited research that suggested that Americans are "less aggressive, are less willing to talk, avoid social interaction, and are more persuasible and constrained" (p. 434). These findings led him to hypothesize that individuals who are high in trait social desirability would be lower in trait argumentativeness.

To test this speculation, Chen administered a 10-item short-form version of the Argumentativeness Scale along with a scale that measures trait social desirability orientation (Strahan & Gerbasi, 1972) to a group of students.

On the basis of their social desirability score, he divided the students into high and low social-desirability groups. Chen then compared the two groups on argumentativeness and found that the high social-desirability individuals scored lower on argumentativeness than did people reporting low social desirability. However, both Chen (1994) and Nicotera (1996) identify some problems with this study. First, since the study used only paper and pencil scales, "the results may not represent participants' real inclination toward social desirability (or) argumentativeness" (Chen, p. 436), suggesting a problem of validity with either or both instruments. Second, as the participants were all American students, the results may not be easily generalizable to other cultures.

Nicotera (1996) identified another potential and significant limitation to the study, the overwhelming presence of females in the sample Chen used. Nicotera suggests that "argumentativeness is traditionally seen as a male task" and hence might be "more socially desirable for men than for women" (1996, p. 27). Consequently, Nicotera makes the case that, with so many females in Chen's sample and with no reporting on gender differences in argumentativeness in the study, "Chen's study cannot be considered conclusive" (Nicotera, p. 27).

Nicotera also tested whether self-report scores on the Argumentativeness Scale and perceived social desirability of the scale are related. She wondered whether subjects are responding to the scale items on the basis of a true self-report of their behavior, are responding on the basis of the social desirability of the items of the scale, or are responding to the social desirability ratings based on judgments of themselves.

To test these questions, Nicotera (1996) administered the original Argumentativeness Scale to a group of male and female students, instructing them to "rate each item . . . indicating their own judgment of the statement's acceptability by society" (p. 28). A second sample of students was administered the original scale and the social-desirability version as just described. Participants were told to rate themselves on the one scale and to "use the social desirability rating on the other" (Nicotera, p. 28). The results of the study indicated that males perceived argumentativeness to be more socially desirable than did females. In addition, Nicotera found that self-report scores of argumentativeness and self-report judgment of the social desirability of the scale items were also related; "however, the relationship was not particularly strong" (p. 30); hence, the scales are not redundant. This finding led Nicotera to conclude that this was "a positive sign for those who wish to use the argumentativeness scale with confidence as a measure of trait argumentativeness" (1996, p. 30). Nicotera does recommend, however, that when administering the scale, respondents should be explicitly instructed that the term *argue* should be defined "as a discussion that focuses on a disagreement about a controversial issue and that an 'argument' is not to be equated with a fight or quarrel" (Nicotera, 1996, p. 33). While the instructions provided in the original scale are explicit and state that the instrument "contains statements about arguing controversial issues" (Infante & Rancer, p. 76), Nicotera's recommendation is sound.

Finally, in a cross-cultural examination of the social desirability of the Argumentativeness Scale, Blickle (1995) administered a German version of the scale to students from a technical college, a business college, and a college for special education in three cities in Germany. The students also completed a social desirability scale, also translated into German. Blickle found that social desirability scores were not correlated with trait argumentativeness scores, which Blickle suggests "may be interpreted as an indication of uncontaminated results" (p. 108).

The Dimensionality of the Argumentativeness Scale

Over the past few years, there appears to have been renewed interest in the dimensionality of both the Argumentativeness and Verbal Aggressiveness scales. Recall that Infante and Rancer (1982) argued that the argumentativeness scale contains two independent factors (also called dimensions): ARGap (motivational tendency to approach arguments) and ARGav (motivational tendency to avoid arguments). They based the scale on the approach–avoidance internal tension individuals experience when a conflict occurs between individuals who hold opposing positions on controversial issues.

Hamilton and Mineo (2002) questioned this assumption first offered 20 years earlier by Infante and Rancer (1982) regarding the dimensionality of the original scale. Using a research technique called meta-analysis, they examined whether the Argumentativeness Scale is best considered multidimensional (composed of two or more dimensions as suggested in the original instrument) or unidimensional (composed of only one dimension). Meta-analysis is a relatively newer technique used in communication research that "allows researchers to aggregate (combine) data and summarize existing reports" (Allen & Preiss, 2002, p. 3). Typically, meta-analysis is used when conflicting findings exist in a given area of research.

After conducting a series of meta-analytic studies, Hamilton and Mineo (2002) offered a few observations on the nature of the original scale. They concluded that the ARGap and ARGav dimensions are negatively correlated rather than independent as suggested by Infante and Rancer (1982) in the original scale development report. They take this finding as support for the unidimensionality of the scale (Hamilton & Mineo, p. 300). However, Hamilton and Mineo concomitantly suggest that the scale may contain as many as six or seven different content themes or dimensions. They suggest that the scale may actually be composed of the dimensions of argumentative skill (Items 16 and 18), hostility or guilt (Items 1 and 5), curiosity (Items 2 and 15), competitiveness (Items 4, 7, 9, 11, 13, 17, and 20), anxiety over consequences (Items 3, 6, 8, 10, and 12), and active avoidance or withdrawal (Items 14 and 19).

There is some additional support for the argumentative skill dimension. Blickle (1995) factor analyzed the original 20 items and observed an additional factor, also composed of Items 16 and 18, which he labeled "self-evaluation of argumentative skills" (p. 104). Blickle thus suggests that the Argumentativeness Scale may contain three factors, the original ARGap and ARGav dimensions along with the newly discovered argumentative skill dimension. Blickle reports that scores on self-evaluation of argumentative skill correlated strongly and positively with ARGap and negatively with ARGav and recommends that additional items be developed for this potential dimension of self-evaluation of argumentative skill "to have a broader basis for measurement" (p. 108).

Critiques of the Verbal Aggressiveness Scale

As with the Argumentativeness Scale, researchers have attempted to reassess the dimensionality of the Verbal Aggressiveness Scale. As you recall from our earlier discussion, Infante and Wigley (1986) suggested that in the development of the scale, two dimensions or factors emerged: a first factor with positively worded aggressiveness items and a second factor consisting of negatively worded aggressiveness items. However, Infante and Wigley decided that the scale should be treated as unidimensional and that researchers using the scale should add up the scores for all 20 items to obtain a total verbal aggressiveness score. They reasoned that two dimensions emerged due to the positive and negative wording of the items and not because there are two separate dimensions of verbal aggressiveness. They suggested that this "latent variable seemed to emerge, because, as would be expected, respondents tended to admit to the positively worded items . . . a little more than the negatively worded items" (Infante & Wigley, p. 65).

Recently, several communication researchers began to challenge the assertion of the unidimensionality of the verbal aggressiveness instrument. For example, Beatty, Dobos, Valencic, and Rudd (1998) and Beatty, Rudd, and Valencic (1999) suggested that disagreeing with the positively worded items does not necessarily mean that an individual endorses verbally aggressive behaviors or has a strong verbally aggressive predisposition. Beatty and his colleagues felt that the second factor that emerged, the positively worded or benevolent items, was not an artifact of the wording of the items but a true, legitimate, and important factor to be considered.

To test this speculation, Beatty and his colleagues (1999) administered the scale to students and again subjected the data to the statistical procedure of factor analysis. As they speculated, two dimensions emerged, one consisting of 10 aggressively worded items and a second factor consisting of eight benevolently worded items. Beatty et al. suggested that only the negatively worded items clearly measured verbal aggressiveness. They suggested further that the positively worded or benevolently worded items appear to measure concepts they labeled as "confirmation or interpersonal sensitivity" (Beatty et al., p. 15). Consequently, they recommended that researchers employing the Verbal Aggressiveness Scale should consider only scoring the negatively worded aggressive items to assess trait verbal aggressiveness and use the positively worded items as "distractor items" (Beatty et al., p. 16). They also suggested that additional testing needs to be conducted to develop a more appropriate scoring technique for the scale.

Another group of researchers recently heeded this call. Levine, Beatty, Limon, Hamilton, Buck, and Chory-Assad (2004) suggested that these benevolently worded items might not simply be a spurious dimension that should be included but then discarded when assessing an individual's level of trait verbal aggressiveness. Instead, they suggested these items might constitute a legitimate dimension related to "ego-supportive communication" (p. 246) and could be predictive of traits such as empathy and communicative responsiveness. To test these speculations, Levine and his colleagues conducted a series of studies to reexamine the factor structure of the Verbal Aggressiveness Scale. If a second benevolence factor emerged, the research team also intended to explore whether the items comprising this factor would measure not just a lack of verbal aggressiveness, but a distinct and legitimate dimension related to ego-supportive communication.

The results of these tests led Levine et al. (2004) to offer a few conclusions about the Verbal Aggressiveness Scale. First, they suggested that the 20 items on the Infante and Wigley (1986) scale actually measure two distinct dimensions: one that assesses trait verbal aggressiveness as conceptualized by Infante and Wigley and another dimension that measures a pro-social, supportive communication style. Again, these researchers recommend that those who want to obtain a single measure of trait verbal aggressiveness should use only the 10 aggressively worded items. Second, the other items do constitute a legitimate dimension that assesses a pro-social, supportive, and benevolent communication style. They again suggest that these items should not be scored, as they were not developed or ever intended to measure this pro-social communication style.

Levine and his colleagues (2004) do not offer an indictment of the original 20-item scale as a way of assessing trait verbal aggressiveness. They suggest, "Whereas reducing the scale to ten aggressively-worded items is recommended, the current evidence suggests that the negative consequences of scoring all 20 items as a unidimensional scale are minimal" (p. 260). Another possibility suggested is that the original 20-item scale may indeed be unidimensional as suggested by Infante and Wigley (1986) and that if a few problematic items are discarded, the scale might even be unidimensional. They recommend further that researchers should consider expanding the definition of verbal aggressiveness to go beyond just attacks on the self-concept. Rather, a more comprehensive conceptual definition of verbal aggressiveness could be offered with new items reflecting this broader conceptualization written and tested.

Alternative Methods of Assessing Argumentative and Aggressive Communication

Several years ago, Infante and Rancer (1996) acknowledged that the development of alternative measurement techniques for assessing argumentative and aggressive communication was a worthy goal of communication researchers when they stated, "It would be prudent to measure the argumentativeness and verbal aggressiveness constructs in various ways" (p. 325). Over the course of the past two and a half decades a few attempts have been made to introduce alternative methods of assessing trait argumentativeness and verbal aggressiveness. We shall identify a few of them in this section.

The Adolescent Argumentativeness and Adolescent Verbal Aggressiveness Scales

Prior to 1997, almost all research conducted on the argumentative and verbally aggressive communication traits investigated adult communication behavior. Since the development of the scales to measure argumentative and aggressive communication employed adults, using the original scales in these studies did not pose a difficulty. However, children are not immune from social conflict, argumentative discourse, and the sending and receiving of messages that attack the self-concept. Whether at home, at school, or at play, one of the most problematic issues facing today's adolescents is that of bullying and disrespecting one another. Prior to 1997, researchers had neglected to investigate argumentativeness and verbal aggressiveness in adolescent populations. To remedy this deficiency, a reliable and valid method of assessing these predispositions in adolescents was needed. In fact, equal care and design in measurement that went into the adult versions of argumentativeness and verbal aggressiveness was needed for instruments geared toward younger populations.

Roberto and Finucane (1997) argued that the language level used on the original Argumentativeness and Verbal Aggressiveness scales might be a barrier to the reliable and valid assessment of adolescents' argumentative and aggressive communication. In a pilot study, Roberto and Finucane found that eighth-grade boys had some difficulty understanding a few of the items on both scales. In addition, an analysis they conducted suggested that the Argumentativeness Scale had a 12th-grade readability level and the Verbal Aggressiveness Scale had an 11th-grade readability level. They concluded that this might compromise the ability of the scales to reliably and validly measure both traits. As such, they set out to develop measures that could be administered primarily to high school and junior high or middle school students.

One change involved adding more specificity to the directions of the Argumentativeness Scale, especially regarding the terms *arguing* and *controversial issue*. For example, the instructions for the adolescent Argumentativeness Scale state, "By arguing, I mean having a discussion or disagreement about a topic that has more than one side. For example, you might argue over who is the best basketball player or who is the best music group" (Roberto & Finucane, 1997, p. 24). The 20 items on both scales were rewritten to better reflect a readability level for an adolescent group and in a way that asks the respondents to complete the scales referencing an argument with a friend for the Argumentativeness Scale and changing a friend's mind for the Verbal Aggressiveness Scale.

The changes produced a 10-item ADARG–Adolescent Argumentativeness Scale and an 8-item ADVA–Adolescent Verbal Aggressiveness Scale. Appendix B contains both versions of these scales. Roberto and Finucane (1997) report satisfactory reliability (.81 for ADARG, .76 for ADVA) for both scales. In addition, each revised scale was subjected to a series of validity studies and the "results of the validity tests of each scale were encouraging, suggesting that the constructs originally formulated in the Argumentativeness and Verbal Aggressiveness scales can be validly applied to adolescent populations" (Roberto & Finucane, p. 31). The researchers caution, however, that while these new scales can be administered to children in the sixth grade, they should not be used with children younger than 10 or 11 years old. To assess trait argumentativeness and verbal aggressiveness in children younger than

10, they recommend either that the instruments be administered orally (which the researchers suggest may still pose the problem of understanding) or having an adult who knows the child quite well (i.e., parents, teachers) rate the child's argumentative and verbally aggressive communication behavior. Although the readability of the original instruments has been improved for use by an adolescent population, an examination of the wording of the adolescent and original versions of both scales suggests that they are still quite similar.

Another potential issue when assessing argumentative and aggressive communication in adolescents involves the association of the two traits. More specifically, the lack of association between the two traits identified in adult populations cannot be assumed in adolescent populations. This issue was also addressed by Roberto and Finucane (1997) in their study. Recall that in developing the Argumentativeness Scale and the Verbal Aggressiveness Scale, Infante and his colleagues suggest that the two scales are theoretically and empirically distinct. In fact, Infante and Wigley (1986) reported that the correlation between ARGgt and verbal aggressiveness was virtually negligible ($r = -.04$). More recent research using adolescent populations, including this study by Roberto and Finucane, suggests that argumentativeness and verbal aggressiveness may indeed be moderately and positively correlated. For example, Roberto and Finucane observed a moderate and significant correlation between the two traits ($r = .49$), as did Rancer, Whitecap, Kosberg, and Avtgis (1997) and Rancer, Avtgis, Kosberg, and Whitecap (2000) with correlations of .29 and .38, respectively. Anderson and Rancer (2003) reported a correlation of .47 between the two traits among a group of adolescents incarcerated for committing felony crimes. It should be noted, however, that these strong associations between the two traits have been observed with the adolescent versions of the measures. Such moderate correlations between argumentativeness and verbal aggressiveness have not been observed when employing the original instruments. Therefore, it is not yet conclusive as to whether these associations are based on the constructs of argumentativeness and verbal aggressiveness or occur as a result of the measurement of the constructs. This issue will be covered in greater detail in Chapter 10 when we discuss methods of modifying argumentative and aggressive communication.

Short-Form Versions of the Scales

To avoid the potential for error variance (generalized error in research associated with measurement) and subject fatigue, some researchers have employed shorter versions of both scales. This is particularly true in studies in which the respondents had to complete the Argumentativeness Scale, the

Verbal Aggressiveness Scale, and a number of other measures, questions, or items on a survey. Long surveys tend to overwhelm respondents and reduce the chances of them completing the entire questionnaire. For example, you may have participated in survey studies in which you have every intention of completing the survey but found the questionnaire to be too long. This may have resulted in your not responding to all of the items on the survey or not giving all the questions serious thought. A shorter-form 10-item version of the Argumentativeness Scale and a 10-item Verbal Aggressiveness Scale have been developed (see Appendix C for copies of the short-form versions of each scale). These short-form versions have been used successfully in research on argumentative and aggressive communication in the organizational context (e.g., Infante & Gorden, 1989, 1991), in the family communication context (e.g., Sabourin, Infante, & Rudd, 1993), and in the instructional communication context (e.g., Myers & Rocca, 2000a).

Measuring the Affective-Behavioral-Cognitive Dimensions of Argumentativeness: The ABCAS Instrument

In an early critique of the Argumentativeness Scale, DeWine et al. (1991) suggested that several of the 20 items on the Argumentativeness Scale seem to be assessing attitudes toward argumentative communication, especially the affective or feeling dimension toward argumentative communication. That is, they claimed that many of the items seem to measure respondents' like or dislike of argument (e.g., "I have a pleasant, good feeling when I win a point in an argument"). Hinkle (2003) suggests that the original scale, while a reliable method of assessing the approach–avoidance orientation toward motivation to argue, did not include items designed to measure individuals' cognitions (thoughts) or behaviors toward argument. Because attitudes are made up of affective, cognitive, and behavioral dimensions (Eagly & Chaiken, 1993), Hinkle suggested that it may be important to include all three dimensions of attitude in a scale that would measure "attitudes toward argumentative communication" (p. 12) and sought to create this more inclusive method of assessing attitudes toward argumentative communication.

Hinkle (2003) developed items designed to measure the three dimensions of attitudes toward arguing:

affective: emotional or feeling-based items about argumentative communication;

behavioral: action items dealing with argumentative communication; and

cognitive: fact-based items that deal with thoughts about argumentative communication.

In writing items for the new measure, Hinkle eliminated the use of all terms such as argue, arguing, and argument. Instead, words and phrases such as "discuss controversial issues, discussing controversial issues, and discussion of controversial issues" were used (Hinkle, p. 10).

After a series of factor-analytic studies, a 10-item, single-factor attitude toward argumentativeness measure was created that assesses how individuals feel about participating in controversial discussions (i.e., measuring the affective dimension), whether they actually engage in discussions over controversial issues (i.e., measuring the behavioral dimension), and what they think about when they are engaged in such discussions (i.e., measuring the cognitive dimension) (Hinkle, 2003, p. 13). The measure consists of two *affective* items (e.g., "When I think about having to discuss controversial issues with others, it bothers me"), five *behavioral* items (e.g., "My friends and I engage in controversial issues"), and three *cognitive* items (e.g., "Discussing controversial issues with another person sharpens my mind"). The reliability of Hinkle's measure was quite high (.83), and two studies supporting the convergent validity of this measure were also conducted. Appendix D contains a copy of this instrument.

Although conceptualized quite differently from the original Infante and Rancer (1982) Argumentativeness Scale, the Affective-Behavioral-Cognitive Scale (ABCAS) measure does provide researchers with an attractive addition to the original version for use in studies that attempt to assess trait argumentativeness. Hinkle (2003) suggests that the original Argumentativeness Scale and this new measure could be used in tandem, as "this cooperative approach could increase the scope of measuring an individual's tendency to engage in argument" (p. 14).

Assessing Argumentative and Verbally Aggressive Communication Activity

Another alternative to the self-report measurement of both traits has been developed by Infante and Rancer (1993). This method represents an extension of the notion that it may be productive to obtain some assessment of an individual's behavioral tendencies toward argumentative and aggressive communication in a more direct fashion. They reasoned that since trait argumentativeness was conceptualized in terms of motivation to argue, individuals should differ in their *argumentative activity,* that is, the frequency of engaging in advocacy and refutation on positions related to controversial issues. Similarly, individuals who differ in trait verbal aggressiveness should also differ in the frequency of their use of different types of verbally aggressive messages.

To test this and other related issues, Infante and Rancer (1993) needed to measure individuals' frequency of engaging in advocacy and refutation behaviors. Students were informed that a study concerned with how often they engaged in advocacy and refutation on different types of controversial issues was being conducted. The students were supplied with definitions of both advocacy and refutation. *Advocacy* was defined as occurring "when you state your position on a controversial issue and then defend your position when it is attacked by other individuals" (Infante & Rancer, p. 419). *Refutation* was defined as occurring "when you attack the positions that other people take on controversial issues" (Infante & Rancer, p. 419).

The students were provided with 11 types of controversial issues and given one or two examples of each issue, including

> *social issues* (e.g., welfare reform); *moral-ethical issues* (e.g., whether lying is sometimes justified); *family issues* (e.g., how money should be spent, family chores and responsibilities); *sports issues* (e.g., which football/baseball team is best); *entertainment issues* (e.g., whether a movie was good, whether to go to a concert); *educational issues* (e.g., whether a dormitory rule is necessary, whether an academic program is needed); *work issues* (e.g., whether a superior/ boss is fair); *personal behavior issues* (e.g., what you should or should not do); *others' behavioral issues* (e.g., what your friend, brother, neighbor, etc., should or should not do); *religious issues* (e.g., the value of religion); and *national, state, and local politics* (e.g., who should be elected to a particular office). (Infante & Rancer, 1993, p. 419)

Again, the students were asked to report the frequency of their advocacy and refutation behavior separately regarding these issues over the past 7 days (or any other typical week in their life) by specifying the number of discussions that they had on the issue for the week. The students also completed the Verbal Aggressiveness Scale.

In a second session 1 week later, the same students were presented with a measure of Verbally Aggressive Message activity (e.g., Infante, Riddle, et al., 1992). A list of 10 types of verbally aggressive messages was presented and students were asked how often they used each of these messages during the past week. The 10 types of verbally aggressive messages included character attacks, competence attacks, background attacks, physical appearance attacks, maledictions, teasing, ridicule, threats, swearing/profanity, and nonverbal emblems. These forms of verbal aggression were defined for you in Chapter 1. Again, the students were asked to report the frequency of use of these forms of aggressive message behavior separately over the past 7 days (or any other typical week in their life). In this session, the students also completed the Argumentativeness Scale.

As expected, highly argumentative individuals (assessed by their scores on the Argumentativeness Scale) reported engaging in more advocacy and refutation behaviors than either moderate- or low-argumentative individuals. In addition, and again as expected, individuals high in verbal aggressiveness (assessed by their scores on the Verbal Aggressiveness Scale) reported using more of the 10 types of verbally aggressive messages than did individuals moderate or low in verbal aggressiveness. These findings support the validity of the two constructs. In addition, the technique of asking individuals to report on how frequently they use argumentative and verbally aggressive message behaviors represents a productive alternative or complementary method to the use of the original self-report scales to measure both traits. Indeed, this technique may even have more validity in that individuals are "asked directly for the frequency of the very thing being measured" (Infante & Rancer, 1996, p. 326).

Indirect Interpersonal Aggressiveness

Beatty, Valencic, Rudd, and Dobos (1999) suggest that while a great deal of verbal aggressiveness is often exhibited during face-to-face interaction, perhaps even more verbal and nonverbal aggressiveness is manifest without face-to-face interaction. Indeed, Beatty, Valencic, et al. argue that while direct verbal aggressiveness is clearly hurtful and damaging, such episodes might soon blow over. In contrast, episodes in which indirect aggressiveness is exhibited may cause greater "long-term, substantive damage such as soiled reputation and lost professional opportunities" (Beatty, Valencic, et al., p. 104). Beatty and his colleagues provide several examples of indirect aggressiveness such as spreading rumors, withholding important information, failing to relay important messages, destroying personal property, betraying confidences, and undermining others by going behind their backs. Clearly, indirect interpersonal aggressiveness, like direct verbal aggressiveness, occurs when "people use messages as weapons" (Beatty, Valencic, et al., p. 104).

While a great deal of research has been conducted on direct trait verbal aggressiveness in the communication discipline, little research exists on indirect aggressiveness. Accordingly, Beatty and his colleagues offered a conceptualization of trait indirect interpersonal aggressiveness as well as a scale to measure this trait. Indirect interpersonal aggressiveness was defined as "a predisposition to harm other people without engaging in face-to-face interaction" (Beatty, Valencic, et al., 1999, p. 105). A 10-item scale designed to measure this trait was created and administered along with the 10 direct verbal aggressiveness items from the original Infante and Wigley (1986) scale to students. Using factor-analytic techniques, Beatty and his colleagues discovered that the 10 direct verbal aggressiveness items and the 10 indirect interpersonal aggressiveness items constituted two distinct dimensions. The new indirect aggressiveness items had high reliability and, as with the verbal aggressiveness trait, were also found to be correlated with Eysenck's psychoticism dimension of personality. A copy of the indirect Interpersonal Aggressiveness Scale can be found in Appendix E. While this scale needs to be subjected to more empirical testing, it does provide researchers with another tool to assess a person's predisposition to engage in a destructive form of communication.

Assessing Beliefs About Argumentative and Aggressive Communication

Another profitable avenue for understanding and measuring orientations toward argumentative and aggressive communication predispositions is to assess beliefs of people who differ in argumentativeness and verbal aggressiveness. Working from a theoretical model that suggests human behavior is directly linked to attitudes and beliefs (i.e., Fishbein & Ajzen, 1975), Rancer et al. (1985) identified several underlying beliefs that people have about arguing and argumentative communication.

The notion of a more complete understanding of an individuals' predispositions through knowledge of their beliefs was derived from Fishbein and Ajzen's (1975) theory of reasoned action (for more detail on this theory, see Chapter 9). That theory suggests that a predisposition (such as argumentativeness and verbal aggressiveness) is controlled by the set of beliefs that an individual learns to associate with the object of the predisposition. Thus, if you want to know why an individual is high, moderate, or low in motivation to argue (i.e., trait argumentativeness), then one way of knowing is to determine the beliefs that person has about arguing. Understanding or identifying the beliefs that individuals hold about argumentative and aggressive communication provides an additional and alternative approach to measuring these traits.

Researchers first had to identify a cluster of beliefs that individuals have about arguing and then determine the particular beliefs that differentiated the three major types of argumentatives (high, moderate, and low). Rancer et al. (1985) identified seven beliefs individuals have about arguing: (a) *hostility*—arguing perceived as a combative and aggressive communication encounter; (b) *activity/process*—arguing as a mode of social interaction, like having a conversation; (c) *control/dominance*—arguing perceived as a means of establishing, enforcing, or maintaining power, arguing perceived as a way of having one's opinions prevail; (d) *conflict/dissonance*—arguing perceived as a source of conflict or dissonance among or between antagonists; (e) *self-image*—arguing perceived as a communication encounter that overtly impacts a person's sense of self; (f) *learning*—arguing perceived as a way to gather or convey information about oneself or as a way to learn about one's self, others, or environment; and (g) *skill*—arguing perceived as a test or indicant of one's verbal and rhetorical skills.

These beliefs were found to distinguish individuals who vary in argumentativeness. For example, a greater proportion of high argumentatives had positive beliefs about activity/process, control/dominance, conflict/dissonance, self-image, learning, and skill. The proportion of low argumentatives was highest in terms of the negative beliefs of hostility, control/dominance, and conflict/dissonance. High argumentatives viewed arguing as a source for cultivating information while low argumentatives viewed arguing as a behavior that reveals their lack of argumentative and rhetorical competence. Moreover, while high argumentatives perceive arguing as a means of reducing conflict, low argumentatives view arguments as unfavorable and hostile acts that should be avoided at all costs (Rancer et al., 1985).

Understanding such beliefs about arguing is significant because it may help individuals function more effectively in compliance gaining, persuasive, and conflict management situations. Some spouses have difficulty managing their communication when they are trying to exert influence over each other. It may be that spouses' differing beliefs about arguing contribute to the marital tension they experience. The husband, for example, may possess a positive belief about arguing as learning (arguing as a way to gather information), and this belief is exhibited whenever he tries to understand his wife's position on an issue they disagree on. His wife, however, may possess a negative learning belief. As such, she may become agitated and uncomfortable when her husband begins arguing with her (i.e., when he asks her probing questions concerning the position she holds or continues to probe her position beyond what she feels is a reasonable amount of time).

Following this same vein, Rancer, Kosberg, and Baukus (1992) examined which beliefs best predict argumentativeness and which beliefs best discriminate between high and low argumentatives. To accomplish this, the researchers created a Beliefs About Arguing measure. A copy of this instrument is contained in Appendix F. Responses to this measure indicated that high argumentatives believe that arguing has enjoyable, functional, and pragmatic outcomes, as well as having a positive impact on their self-concept. Low-argumentative individuals tended to believe that arguing is a communication act that has a negative impact on the self-concept, creates dysfunctional outcomes, and has little to do with enjoyment or practical outcomes (Rancer et al.).

A related line of research has investigated beliefs about engaging in verbal aggression. For instance, Infante, Riddle, et al. (1992) found that those who vary in the trait verbal aggressiveness perceived differences in beliefs about verbal aggressive message behavior. Specifically, individuals high in verbal aggressiveness believed that competence attacks, physical appearance attacks, and threats are less hurtful to others than did individuals low in verbal aggressiveness.

Conclusion

Measurement issues associated with argumentative and aggressive communication have garnered as much attention and scrutiny from researchers as the actual traits themselves. The theoretical underpinnings of both argumentativeness and verbal aggressiveness have been readily accepted by the vast majority of researchers in the social sciences. This chapter addressed the issues surrounding the measurement associated with these traits. In this chapter, we addressed the question, "How do we quantify these communication traits?"

The contents of this chapter introduced you to the research program undertaken to develop reliable and valid measures of trait argumentativeness and verbal aggressiveness. Taken as a whole, the many studies conducted resulted in overwhelmingly conclusive evidence that the Argumentativeness Scale is a reliable and valid measure of trait argumentativeness. Similarly, the research provided the same degree of evidence for the Verbal Aggressiveness Scale as a reliable and valid measure of trait verbal aggressiveness.

The original measures of Argumentativeness (Infante & Rancer, 1982) and Verbal Aggressiveness (Infante & Wigley, 1986) have been the targets of some controversy with regard to measurement issues. One of the most significant issues is that of the dimensionality of the measures. As presented in this chapter, many research efforts that have made the claim that both the Argumentativeness Scale (which is comprised of approach and avoidance dimensions) and the Verbal Aggressiveness Scale (which is comprised of two dimensions) contain many factors have also suggested that treating the measures as originally proposed is acceptable.

The wording of both measures was also called into account. For example, several research efforts addressed the words *arguing* in the Argumentativeness Scale and the negative versus positive wording of items in the Verbal Aggressiveness Scale. In the majority of the research critiquing the wording of the scales, the conclusion suggests that impact on the measures, if at all, is modest.

Regardless of the trait we are measuring, all social science is concerned with the concept of social desirability. This is of special concern when we are addressing antisocial or unsavory behaviors. As presented in this book, verbal aggressiveness by nature is relationally destructive. Therefore, respondents may tend to not answer questions truthfully if they have a strong need to be seen as socially appropriate. Several studies have revealed that social desirability does not adversely impact either the Argumentativeness Scale or the Verbal Aggressiveness Scale. In the end, the measures originally proposed by Infante and Rancer (1982) and Infante and Wigley (1986) continue to be used in their original form to assess argumentative and aggressive communication. However, several promising alternative measurement tools have been developed and should be viewed as potentially viable for use in research and as diagnostic tools.

Discussion Questions for Chapter 2

1. What does it mean when we say that argumentativeness is conceptualized as an approach–avoidance motivational conflict?

2. What does it mean when we say that the factors of argument approach and argument avoidance are independent from one another?

3. What are some of the major critiques of the Argumentativeness Scale? Which critique do you see as most valid?

4. What does it mean when we say that social desirability may affect scores on the Argumentativeness Scale? Would you be influenced by social desirability if you had to complete the Argumentativeness and Verbal Aggressiveness scales?

5. What are some of the major critiques of the Verbal Aggressiveness Scale? Which critique do you see as most valid?

3

Trait, State, and Interactionist Approaches to Studying Argumentative and Aggressive Communication

In Chapter 1 we defined the term *communication trait* as a hypothetical construct that accounts for the way individuals behave when they are involved in communication-related activity. We presented the position, advanced by McCroskey et al. (1998), that "individual traits are a major force, if not the dominant explanation, for why people communicate the way they do" (p. vii). In Chapter 1 we also provided definitions of argumentativeness, a subset of the more global trait of assertiveness, and verbal aggressiveness, a subset of the more global trait of hostility. In this chapter we will review how personality and communication scholars perceive the influence of these and other traits and situational factors on determining why people engage in argumentative and verbally aggressive communication.

The Trait Perspective on Argumentative and Aggressive Communication

You may recall that in Chapter 1 we defined a communication trait as an abstraction that helps us account for the consistency in message sending and message receiving behavior (Infante et al., 2003, p. 77). We presented a model that suggests argumentative and aggressive communication is composed of four traits, two of which are considered constructive (assertiveness and argumentativeness) and two of which are considered destructive (hostility and verbal aggressiveness).

The trait perspective on argumentative and aggressive communication suggests that communication traits are relatively stable characteristics of individuals. Two personality researchers, Costa and McCrae (1980), argue rather convincingly for the stability of personality and suggest that one's personality is fairly set by the age of 30. As a consequence of that stability, scholars who advocate a trait perspective to understanding communication believe that individuals' communication across different situations will remain relatively consistent and that a person's behavior will not vary greatly from one situation to another (Infante et al., 2003; McCroskey et al., 1998; Nicotera, 1993, 1994; Rancer & Nicotera, in press).

According to the trait perspective, a person who is highly argumentative would be expected to exhibit this tendency across many different contexts and many different situations. An individual who has been identified as being highly argumentative would exhibit this orientation at home and at work, as well as in social situations. According to this perspective, the trait has such an influence on a person's communication behavior that highly argumentative individuals would be likely to argue a great deal with their spouses, relational partners, friends, and colleagues. The theory of independent-mindedness (see Chapter 5) suggests that highly argumentative individuals relish the opportunity to argue organizational issues even with superiors on the job (Rancer, 1995).

The trait perspective is exemplified in one of the earliest studies conducted on trait argumentativeness. In that study, Infante (1981) asked students to complete the Argumentativeness Scale in order to classify them as high, moderate, or low on the trait. The high argumentatives were then randomly paired with moderate argumentatives into same-sex dyads. Low argumentatives were also randomly paired with moderate argumentatives for an argumentive activity. A third student (a moderate argumentative of the same sex as the dyad) served as an observer of the argumentative discussion between the dyad members. One hundred dyads were created, each having a different, albeit same-sex, observer. Each participant was told that the goal of the argument was to persuade the other person over to his or her side on a controversial issue. Participants then selected one among a number of controversial topics to argue and agreed as to who would take the pro and con position on the issue. Before the arguments actually took place, each of the arguers indicated how much effort they intended to exert during the argument by completing a set of scales. The dyads then engaged in the argument that lasted, on average, about 12½ minutes. After the arguments were completed, the observers rated the communication behavior of each member of the dyad.

Overall, the study found that the communication behavior of high and low argumentatives differed a great deal when they argued with a moderate. Highly argumentative individuals, as compared with lows, were seen as more inflexible in the positions they took in the argument, appeared more interested in the argument, spoke more during the argument, exhibited more advocacy and refutation behaviors, seemed more dynamic and expert in their communication behavior, and appeared to be more skilled in argumentation (Infante, 1981). This study underscores the notion that differences in communication behavior emerge as a result of individuals varying in their trait of general tendency to argue and provides strong support for the influence of trait argumentativeness on a communicator's behavior.

The influence of verbal aggressiveness on an individual's communication behavior is similarly strong. A study by Infante, Riddle, et al. (1992) tested the speculation that individuals high in trait verbal aggressiveness have distinct reasons for engaging in that type of message behavior and that their behavior and reasons offered are different from people who are lower in trait verbal aggressiveness. The researchers first had students complete the Verbal Aggressiveness Scale to classify them as being either high or low in verbal aggressiveness (moderates were excluded from the study). In a follow-up session, the same students completed several scales that asked them about their verbally aggressive behavior. First, they were asked to indicate the type and frequency of verbally aggressive messages that they *received* during the past month. They also evaluated how much psychological pain and mental hurt they experienced when they were the recipients of verbally aggressive messages sent by others. Next, the students were asked to recall how many times during the past month they used 10 different types of verbally aggressive messages (e.g., character attacks, competence attacks, profanity) and were asked to estimate the percentage of their verbally aggressive behavior that involved those reasons (Infante, Riddle, et al., 1992, p. 120).

The results revealed that not only does the trait strongly influence the type of verbally aggressive messages people deliver, but it also influences reasons for using such messages. More specifically, it was found that high verbal aggressives, as compared to lows, used more competence attacks, teasing, swearing, and nonverbal emblems (e.g., flipping the bird, gritting the teeth, rolling the eyes). In addition, individuals high in verbal aggressiveness were also less aware than lows about the hurt that those messages caused others. Finally, those high in verbal aggressiveness differed from lows in reasons for using verbal aggression. Reasons given included wanting to appear tough and mean to their adversary, severe dislike for their adversary, or a belief that most argumentative encounters ultimately degenerate into verbal fights (Infante, Riddle, et al., 1992). Again, this study underscores the potency of the trait perspective by revealing how those who vary in verbal aggressiveness also vary in the behaviors and perceptions associated with the trait.

The Situationist Perspective on Argumentative and Aggressive Communication

A second perspective advanced by communication and personality scholars argues that factors in a given situation are largely responsible for the way an individual will behave and communicate in that situation. This position, referred to as the *situationist* position, maintains that an individual's behavior is likely to vary from situation to situation. As we mentioned earlier, personality theorist Mischel (1968) was an advocate for this situationist position. Mischel believed that the consistency of a person's behavior from one situation to another was quite low. Scholars who advocate the situationist position believe that each situation is relatively unique, and people adapt their behavior to fit each unique situation. Thus, situationists believe that behavior varies a great deal according to each situational demand. As such, a person who displays high levels of verbal aggression in one situation will not necessarily exhibit the same behavior in a different situation. Situationists believe that factors in the situation are a comprehensive and effective way to explain human communication and that there is little predictability of future behavior from past behavior. This perspective highlights the influence of situational factors on mediating the influence of a trait, and scholars who advocate this perspective believe that "personality is overwhelmed by the situation" (Infante et al., 2003, p. 80; Rancer & Infante, 1985).

Numerous situational factors can impact an individual's motivation to argue (Rancer & Infante, 1985). Some of the more obvious might include *characteristics and attributes of the person you are arguing with* (i.e., the attractiveness of the adversary, the age of the adversary, the degree of similarity between adversaries), *topical concerns* (i.e., the issue you are arguing about), *knowledge* (i.e., how much information and knowledge you have on the topic of the dispute), *saliency of the argument to the individuals involved* (i.e., how important the argument is to the participants), *environmental factors* (i.e., where the argument is taking place), and *relationship factors* (i.e., the type of relationship and degree of involvement between the participants).

Situational Factors: Topic and Topic Salience

The situationist perspective to understanding argumentative and aggressive communication has stimulated a number of research efforts. For example, two situational factors that might influence argumentative behavior are the topic and the saliency (importance) of the argument to the interactants. Does the topic of an argument and the relevance of the topic to those involved influence the argumentative behavior of individuals? It seems reasonable to suggest that people will argue more when the topic of the argument is more involving or important to them. What follows is the notion that when motivation to argue is increased, people will perform more effectively during the argument. For example, if the topic of the argument is very important (e.g., where to attend college, what type of automobile you should purchase, whether you should wait until after graduation to get engaged), motivation to argue should be greater. This increased motivation should then positively influence a person's argumentative behavior.

Onyekwere, Rubin, and Infante (1991) conducted a study in which they tested this speculation. They suggested that both high- and low-argumentative individuals would be perceived more favorably when they argued high versus low ego-involving topics. Ego involvement reflects the degree to which we perceive a personal stake on an issue. Students first completed the Argumentativeness Scale in order that they could be classified into high, moderate, or low categories on the trait. Several weeks later, high and low argumentative students were paired with a male and female opponent who scored moderate in trait argumentativeness. All students were then asked to indicate how important (i.e., ego involving) a set of topics were to them. Each group was then assigned to argue a topic that all three agreed was either high or low in ego involvement. The subject had to argue one side of the issue while the two opponents took the other side. The experiment was set up so that a high- or low-argumentative student always argued with two moderate-argumentative male and female opponents, one at a time. Following each argument, the opponents were asked to rate the student's appropriateness, effectiveness, expertise, trustworthiness, dynamism, perceptiveness, responsiveness, and attentiveness during the argument, as well as their own satisfaction with the argument.

Ego involvement in the topic of the argument was found to influence the behavior of high- and low-argumentative individuals (Onyekwere et al., 1991). First, and in support of the trait perspective, the overall communication behavior of high argumentatives was seen more positively than low argumentatives during the argument. Second, and in support of the situationist perspective, people who were more highly involved in an issue were more motivated to argue and their argumentative behavior was perceived more favorably. Additionally, ego involvement also affected perceptions of the high-argumentative person. When the topic was low in ego involvement, the high argumentatives were perceived less favorably than when they argued topics that were high in ego involvement (Onyekwere et al.). That is, the performance of high argumentatives during the argument declined when they were less motivated to argue and this decreased motivation was due their lower ego involvement with the topic. Interestingly, arguing topics of high ego involvement also benefited the low-argumentative students. Their communication behavior was perceived as equally favorable as the behavior of high argumentatives who argued low-involvement topics. The results of this study support some of the assumptions of the situationist perspective.

Situational Factor: The Adversary's Attributes

Another factor that can influence one's argumentative behavior is the characteristics and attributes of the person you are arguing with. One of the first factors that individuals become aware of as they approach an argumentative situation is who they are arguing with. The nature of one's adversary is probably the most critical factor in influencing one's motivation to argue. For example, you might be high in argumentativeness and, in almost all situations, you are very motivated to argue and enjoy arguing with others. However, you can probably think of a situation in which your usually high motivation to argue decreased because of the adversary you were arguing with (e.g., one of your parents, one of your teachers, your boss at work). Conversely, you may be someone who is low in trait argumentativeness but can think of a situation when your usually low motivation to argue increased because of who you were arguing with. For example, you may be highly motivated to argue with a sibling who you feel has taken advantage of you or with a close friend whose behavior or actions led to both of you getting in trouble.

Numerous attributes of adversaries could affect your desire to argue with them. One particularly potent factor might be how similar or dissimilar they are to you in personality. A great deal of research has been conducted in interpersonal communication that suggests similarity along personality dimensions increases interpersonal attraction (AhYun, 1999; Berscheid & Walster, 1978; Byrne, 1971; McCroskey, Richmond, & Daly, 1975). Applying this line of research on similarity and attraction to argumentative and aggressive communication, Rancer and Infante (1985) speculated that the trait argumentativeness of each individual would interact to influence motivation to argue in a given situation. Using the similarity–attraction framework, they hypothesized that high argumentatives would be more motivated to argue with other high argumentatives, and low argumentatives would be more motivated to argue with similarly low argumentatives. They reasoned that a high argumentative would really enjoy the challenge of arguing with another high argumentative, while a low argumentative would prefer someone like themselves who really dislikes arguing.

In order to test this speculation, Rancer and Infante (1985) had students at one public university complete the Argumentativeness Scale and classified them into high- and low-argumentative groups for the experiment. The students were told that the study would be conducted in two parts. First, they would be asked for their perceptions of an argumentative situation that they would be placed in. Next, they were told that they would argue informally with a student from a nearby, private college over a controversial issue (i.e., free tuition for all state college students).

The university students were supplied with an information booklet that contained, allegedly, information about their adversary that had been supplied by the other school. In addition to demographic information about the adversary, this information booklet also contained two Argumentativeness scales, one that they had completed several weeks earlier and another ostensibly completed by their intended adversary. Students were informed that the actual argumentative discussion was to take place in 2 weeks.

Participants were asked to complete a questionnaire that measured their attitude toward the upcoming argumentative situation, how much effort they intended to exert to succeed in the argument, and their perceptions of the probability and importance of success and failure in the upcoming argument. In addition, participants were asked to list each argument they would probably use in support of the proposal they were advocating. After collecting the questionnaires, the participants were told that the argument had to be canceled and were presented with a brief questionnaire that asked them to indicate how disappointed they felt now that the argument was canceled. After collecting this information, the participants were debriefed. In reality, there was no adversary and no arguments were ever actually scheduled. The opponent's Argumentativeness Scale was actually completed by the researchers to make it appear that the opponent was either similar or dissimilar to them in trait argumentativeness, the variable of interest in the study.

Rancer and Infante (1985) found that highly argumentative individuals were indeed more motivated to argue when they believed that the person was similar to themselves on argumentativeness (i.e., another high argumentative). However, low argumentatives' motivation did not differ regardless of whether they thought they were going to argue with a person similar or dissimilar to themselves. The findings of this study, however, identified another situational factor that influences motivation to argue, the similarity of the opponent's personality.

Stewart and Roach (1993) investigated how reactions to argumentative situations are influenced by trait argumentativeness, the religious orientation of the communicators, and another situational factor, argument topic. They speculated that when the topic of an argument evokes religious values and beliefs, individuals would react differently than if the topic evokes nonreligious values and beliefs. It was reasoned that high argumentatives who are low in religious conviction might not be highly motivated to argue a religious issue, while low argumentatives who are high in religious conviction might be very motivated to argue a religious issue "out of an expression or defense of faith" (Stewart & Roach, p. 28).

Religious orientation (another trait characteristic) was also examined as a factor that might affect motivation to argue. Two types of religious orientations, intrinsic and extrinsic, were examined in the study. Intrinsically religious individuals attend church regularly and tend to see religion as central to their lives, while extrinsically religious individuals see religion as more of a social convention and attend church on an irregular basis. Stewart and Roach (1993) speculated that intrinsically religious individuals might be more motivated to argue than extrinsically religious individuals when the topic of the argument invokes religion. They offered this question for examination: "Do reactions to an argument situation vary as a function of interactions among *levels of argumentativeness* (a trait characteristic), *type of religious orientation* (another trait characteristic), and *religious versus nonreligious nature of the topic* (a situational factor)?" (Stewart & Roach, p. 29).

First, they had students complete the Argumentativeness Scale to classify them into high-, moderate-, and low-argumentative categories. The students also completed a scale designed to measure their religious orientation (intrinsic, extrinsic, or nonreligious). Next, students were presented with one of two scenarios. The first dealt with the sale of condoms on campus and was deemed the religious issue by the researchers. The second, building new parking garages on campus in areas that were used for student recreation, was deemed the nonreligious issue. Each scenario informed the students to think about the issue in the following situations: "You happen to know that your good friend's opinion on the issue is opposite your own. Your friend raises the issue in a conversation over coffee, with the intent of changing your opinion and swaying your vote" (Stewart & Roach, 1993, p. 30).

After being presented with one of the issues, the students responded to a series of items that constituted a measurement of their reactions to the argumentative situation. One set of items asked them to indicate how willing they would be to argue with their friend over that issue and another asked for their perceptions of the perceived probability and importance of success and failure in that argument. A final set of items probed their emotional reactions to that particular argumentative situation.

Overall, the results demonstrated strong support for the trait position and only modest support for the potency of the situational factor, the topic of the argument. High argumentatives were more willing to argue than moderate or low argumentatives regardless of the religious or nonreligious argument topic. This finding supports the assumptions of the trait position and under-scores the potency of trait argumentativeness as a factor affecting one's motivation to argue. Religious orientation, the other trait, was also found to be an important factor in influencing students' motivation to argue. Extrinsically religious students were more willing to argue than were intrin-sically or nonreligious students. Willingness to argue was not affected by the argument topic, although modest support for the other situational factor, the religious orientation of the adversary, was found. This led Stewart and Roach (1993) to suggest "that religious orientation, a *characteristic of the proponent,* is a determinant of argumentative reactions that interacts to some degree with trait argumentativeness" (p. 38).

Argument Topic

The topic of an argument has been suggested as another situational factor that can affect argumentative behavior. Most arguments in interpersonal rela-tionships take either one of two forms, *public issue* arguments or *personal issue* arguments (Janan Johnson, 2003). Personal issue arguments involve controversial issues people disagree on regarding aspects of their interper-sonal relationships such as trust, jealousy, and how to spend leisure time. In their study of how advocacy and refutation behaviors differ between argu-mentative individuals, Infante and Rancer (1993) used topics such as how money should be spent by a couple, family chores and responsibilities, and whether to attend a given entertainment event as personal issue arguments.

Public issue arguments usually involve controversial issues people disagree on regarding aspects external to their relationship. These can include such topics as welfare reform, abortion rights, the environment, capital punish-ment, legalization of drugs, and local politics (Infante & Rancer, 1993; Janan Johnson, 2003). In her study, Janan Johnson speculated that regardless of their level of trait argumentativeness, people will view personal issue argu-ments more negatively and would seek to avoid these types of arguments, engage in less argumentative behavior, exhibit greater emotionality, argue less effectively, and be more prone to verbal aggression than they would when arguing public issue arguments. Conversely, it was also hypothesized that argumentative behavior would be higher when individuals argued public versus private issue topics. This study represents a direct test of the situationist perspective because the focus is primarily on the topic of the argument (a situational factor) and only secondarily on the trait in order to explain argumentative behavior.

To test these speculations, a questionnaire was provided asking students to think about an argument they recently had with a friend, romantic relational partner, or family member over one of the topics provided:

> abortion, death penalty, the environment, drug legalization, underage alcohol drinking, racial prejudice, sex discrimination, discrimination based on sexual orientation, religious issues, gun control, drug testing, increased military spending, animal experimentation, surrogate mothering, increased restriction of foreign products, sports, movies, etiquette/manners, race discrimination, and politics. (Janan Johnson, 2003, pp. 11–12)

These constituted the public issue argument topics. Participants were asked to describe the argument and then respond to questions about the argument.

The participants then received a list of personal issue argument topics and repeated this procedure. The personal issue argument topics included

> conflicts over romantic partners, how to spend leisure time together, other friends, how much time to spend together, household chores, roommate problems, one person's hurt feelings, money/bills, trust and jealousy, showing consideration for friend, use of alcohol, space in an apartment, broken plans, using each other's possessions, giving advice, doing favors for each other. (Janan Johnson, 2003, p. 12)

To counterbalance the distribution of the topics, half of the participants received the public issue topics first, while half received the list of personal issue topics first. The Argumentativeness and Verbal Aggressiveness scales were also completed, with items reworded to reflect the public issue or personal issue argument that the participant reported on earlier.

Some support for the situationist perspective was found in that the topic of the argument did influence argumentative behavior. Individuals reported less argumentative behavior when the topic consisted of personal (relational) versus public issues, and this finding did not vary regarding the sex of the participant. Participants did not report significantly different levels of verbal aggressiveness regardless of the personal or public nature of the topic. In the case of verbal aggressiveness, however, a sex difference did emerge with females reporting greater amounts of verbal aggression when arguing personal issue topics. This study provides further support for the notion that situational factors, such as the type of an argument, can impact argumentative behavior.

Context and Characteristics as Situational Influences

Other factors in the conflict situation have also been studied regarding their impact on argumentative communication. For example, Waggenspack and Hensley (1989) examined how the interpersonal context (socially oriented or conflict oriented) influenced preference for a partner who was either high or low in argumentativeness. They wondered whether preference for an interpersonal partner would vary contingent upon the type of situational demands. That is, if the situation calls for a person who is proficient in negotiations, bargaining, and advocacy, would people prefer someone who is high in argumentativeness? Conversely, if the situation is more socially oriented, calling for someone who is highly gregarious and disclosing, would people prefer a partner lower in trait argumentativeness?

Respondents were asked to indicate how much desire they had to associate with people who were high or low in argumentativeness in a social situation. When the situation is considered low in conflict and relatively nonaggressive (i.e., more social), respondents seemed to prefer a partner who is lower in argumentativeness. Surprisingly, there was no difference in preference when the situation was more conflict oriented, and this result did not vary by the sex of the respondent. That is, it did not matter whether the respondent was male or female, nor did it matter whether the situation required negotiation, bargaining, or advocacy. The Waggenspack and Hensley (1989) study supports the idea that people make decisions about whether to associate with argumentative or nonargumentative individuals based on whether the interaction is seen as primarily social-emotional or negotiator/ombudsman oriented. It also suggests that characteristics of a partner is another situational factor affecting one's argumentative behavior.

Is your preference for using verbal aggression dependent upon your level of argumentativeness and the stubbornness of your opponent? Infante et al. (1984) tested whether high-, moderate-, and low-argumentative individuals' intention of using verbal aggression was affected by another situational factor, the obstinacy or adaptability of the other person. Infante and his colleagues first administered the Argumentativeness Scale to students to classify them into high-, moderate-, and low-argumentativeness categories. The students were told that the purpose of the study was to examine what people would say in situations in which they were trying to influence another person and read one of two descriptions of an opponent that they would try to influence. In one description, the opponent was made to appear quite stubborn and difficult to persuade, while in the other, the opponent was made to appear quite adaptable and not very difficult to persuade. Participants then read a description of their persuasive goal in this hypothetical situation, "Your roommate has asked his/her friend to come live with the two of you indefinitely. You don't want to share the apartment with a new individual, so try and talk your roommate out of the idea" (Infante et al., p. 72).

Students were asked to indicate the likelihood of using 18 persuasive message strategies on their roommate in this situation. Four of the persuasive message strategies were comprised of verbally aggressive message behaviors (e.g., " I would tell my roommate his/her idea of having the friend stay is stupid" and "I would yell and scream at my roommate in order to get him/her to find another place for the friend to stay"). The results suggested that the stubbornness of an opponent does function, to a degree, as a situational factor that impacts argumentative behavior. High, moderate, and low argumentatives did not differ in their preference for using verbal aggression when their opponent was adaptable; however, there were differences when the opponent was portrayed as obstinate. Although high argumentatives did not differ in their use of verbal aggression toward both the stubborn and the adaptable opponent, moderate and low argumentatives reported a greater likelihood of using verbal aggression when confronted with the stubborn opponent than with the adaptable opponent (Infante et al., 1984). This study reinforces the notion that highly argumentative individuals are not as quick to employ verbal aggression perhaps because of their superior ability to generate arguments. However, it also suggests that the situational factor, obstinacy versus adaptability of an opponent, might actually determine whether moderate- and low-argumentative people will resort to using verbal aggression.

The Interactionist Approach to Argumentative and Aggressive Communication

Thus far, we have identified two positions that attempt to explain argumentative and aggressive communication behavior. On one end of the continuum lies the trait approach (i.e., traits primarily determine behavior) and on the other lies the situationist approach (i.e., situational factors primarily determine behavior). There is, however, a third perspective that attempts to unify these two extremes to explain argumentative and aggressive communication. Labeled the *interactionist position*, this view has received strong support (Andersen, 1987; Infante, 1987c; Magnusson & Endler, 1977). The interactionist position suggests that knowledge of both trait and situational factors is crucial in predicting a person's communication behavior in any given situation. According to this perspective, a person's communication behavior seems to be best understood as a joint product of situational factors and the trait characteristics of a person (Andersen; Atkinson, 1957; Epstein, 1979; Infante; Infante & Rancer, 1982; Magnusson & Endler).

Consistent with this approach, Infante's (1987a) theory of argumentativeness includes both trait and situational factors to more accurately predict how motivated people will be to argue in a given situation. The interactionist part of the theory suggests that a person's motivation to argue in a given situation is determined by the person's trait argumentativeness (ARGgt), as well as that person's perceptions of the likelihood of success and failure and the level of importance he or she places on succeeding or failing in the argument.

An example of this interactionist approach can be seen in the following illustration. Dale and his roommate, Lee, share an apartment off campus. So far, an unspoken pattern of household responsibility has been established. Lee's major contribution to this arrangement has primarily been the purchasing of food, while Dale's has been to clean and straighten up the apartment. Because Dale believes that cleaning the apartment is a more time-consuming and physically demanding task, he is beginning to resent this tacit arrangement and decides to approach his roommate to see if this pattern of domestic responsibilities can be changed. Because by nature he is a high argumentative, Dale prepares to confront his roommate by developing and writing down a few arguments in support of his position that all household chores should be shared by roommates.

In this scenario, how might situational perceptions influence Dale's motivation to argue with Lee? If Dale thinks his arguments will probably fail, and success is not very important to him, his motivation to argue might likely be low. If he thinks he will succeed, and success is very important to him in this situation, his motivation to argue might be high. Thus, according to the interactionist perspective, high motivation to argue in this situation, coupled with high-trait argumentativeness, should increase Dale's argumentative behavior even more.

This interactionist perspective on argumentative communication posits that people weigh their likelihood of success and failure in each argumentative encounter, and this judgment, along with the influence of their general trait, helps determine their motivation to argue in a given argumentative encounter (Infante, 1987c). That is, in conflict situations, individuals' responses are based on situational factors (i.e., their judgments of the importance and likelihood of failure or success in the given argumentative encounter), as well as due to the influence of their trait predisposition. In Atkinson's (1957, 1966) terminology this tension is labeled *excitation-inhibition*. Recall that the general trait of argumentativeness (ARGgt) is composed of two competing motivational tendencies, argumentative approach and argumentative avoidance. However, with respect to specific situations, there are also competing approach and avoidance motivations. These motivations are based on both personality (trait) and situational (state) factors (i.e., interactionist perspective).

Let us return for a moment to the trait-based conceptualization of argumentativeness. Based on this assumption of competing motivations to engage in argument (approach) and to withdraw from argument (avoidance), Infante and Rancer (1982) designed scale items to measure both motivations. Thus, general trait argumentativeness (ARGgt) equals the predisposition to approach argument (ARGap) minus the predisposition to avoid argument (ARGav). We can represent the general trait to be argumentative in this way:

$$ARGgt = ARGap - ARGav,$$

where ARGgt represents the general trait to be argumentative, ARGap represents the overall motivation to approach arguments, and ARGav represents the overall motivation to avoid arguments. The Argumentativeness Scale measures trait argumentativeness, the predisposition to engage in argument, which, according to trait theory and research, is a relatively stable and enduring personality orientation. You may recall that the original Argumentativeness Scale contains 10 items for measuring ARGap (motivation to approach arguments) and 10 items for measuring ARGav (motivation to avoid arguments).

To strengthen the predictability of argumentativeness as a trait, particular situational influences have to be accounted for. To do this, Atkinson's theory was again consulted to incorporate the situational factors. In a situation that might require argument, such as the one presented above, Infante's (1987a) theory suggests that motivation to argue is also impacted by the individual's feelings about the importance of success and failure in a particular situation. Thus, four situational factors were identified: *probability of success* (Ps), *probability of failure* (Pf), *importance of success* (Is), and *importance of failure* (If). Including these four situational factors should enhance our ability to predict how argumentative an individual might be in a given situation.

To accomplish this, we must be able to assess these situational factors, and Infante (1987c) provides a direction to do so. His theory states that an individual's tendency to approach an argument (Tap) in a situation is equal to his or her predisposition to approach argument (ARGap), multiplied by his or her perceptions of the probability and importance of success (Ps and Is) in that situation. This relationship can be expressed as

$$Tap = ARGap \times Ps \times Is,$$

where Tap represents the tendency to approach arguing in a specific situation, ARGap represents the motivational trait component to approach arguments, Ps represents the perceived probability of success in the given argument, and Is represents the perceived importance of success in the given argument.

Similarly, a person's tendency to avoid argument (Tav) is equal to his or her predisposition to avoid argument (ARGav) multiplied by perceptions of the probability and importance of failure (Pf and If) in that situation. This relationship can be expressed as follows:

$$Tav = ARGav \times Pf \times If,$$

where Tav represents the tendency to avoid arguing in a given situation, ARGav represents the motivational trait component to avoid arguments, Pf represents the perceived probability of failure in the given argument, and If represents the perceived importance of failure in the given argument.

Finally, the resultant motivation to argue (RMarg), which predicts the argumentativeness of an individual in a specific situation, can be represented as follows:

$$RMarg = Tap - Tav,$$

where RMarg represents the resultant motivation to argue in the particular situation, Tap represents the tendency to approach arguing in that given situation, and Tav represents the tendency to avoid arguing in that given situation.

Resultant motivation to argue (RMarg), the likelihood of argumentative behavior in a specific situation, is thus a combination of state (situational) and trait factors. The basic idea is that by adding these situational perceptions we can enhance the accuracy of our prediction of resultant motivation to argue in a given situation. Indeed, this speculation has been tested and supported. Infante (1987c) tested the hypothesis that greater precision in predicting that an individual's motivation to argue in a specific situation could be obtained if both the trait and situational variables inherent in the argumentative situation are measured.

To test this, the Argumentativeness Scale was administered to students to classify them regarding their general motivation to argue (i.e., high, moderate, or low). The students were informed that the study was "investigating the perceptions people have of a communication situation and how those perceptions relate to the person's behavior if he or she elects to participate in the situation" (Infante, 1987c, p. 312). Students were told that, if they agreed to participate, they would argue with another student on the topic of legalized wiretapping and that their potential opponent already had agreed to argue in favor of legalized wiretapping. The students were then informed that their adversary was given 25 pieces of evidence to aid in supporting the issue. Thus, the participants also received 25 pieces of evidence to help them prepare for the debate.

To make the experiment appear even more realistic and to stimulate their situational perceptions, a 3-minute pro speech on wiretapping, ostensibly created by their potential opponent, was then played for them. Following the playing of this tape, the students were presented with a questionnaire in which they were asked to indicate their perceptions of the potential argumentative encounter and then decide whether they wished to participate. A measure of their perceptions of probability and importance of success and failure in this forthcoming argument, and scales to measure their intended effort to win the argument, their attitude toward participating in the argument, their desire to participate in the argument, and their intentions to participate were administered to the students. In reality, there was no opponent, and no real arguments were ever actually scheduled. Following data collection, all participants were debriefed and informed that the study was really focused on their motivation toward arguing and not on their actual argumentative behavior.

The study supported all three perspectives on understanding and predicting argumentative behavior. First, and in support of the trait position, ARGgt (the general trait to be argumentative) was moderately and significantly ($r = .26$) related to the students' motivation to participate in the argument. Second, and in support of the situationist and interactionist positions, Infante found that by including the situational perceptions (Ps, Pf, Is, If) along with the trait, the relationship between argumentativeness and motivation increased substantially ($r = .64$). This study suggests that including both the individual's trait and situational perceptions of the given argumentative encounter enhances accuracy in predicting motivation to argue in that situation.

Let us provide an example of how this might work. Suppose you receive a paper back from a professor and you are not completely satisfied with the grade given. You ponder whether to ask your professor to change the grade. Because this professor has the reputation for not changing grades on papers, you recognize that this request may likely result in an argumentative encounter with him or her (i.e., you will need to provide data to support your request and the professor is likely to be stubborn and refute your arguments and may even provide some strong counterarguments to your assertions).

To more accurately predict your resultant motivation to argue (RMArg) in this particular situation, we would need to obtain data on several measures. First, we would need to assess your general tendency (i.e., trait) to argue. This can be obtained by administering the Argumentativeness Scale, which will provide us with a measure of your trait motivational tendencies to approach (ARGap) and avoid (ARGav) argumentative situations. Next, we would need to measure the situational factors that affect your decision to argue, that is, your perceptions of the probability and importance of success and failure (Ps, Is, Pf, If) for that particular argumentative encounter.

To measure Ps, we might ask you to respond to this item: "How likely is it that you will succeed when you argue with your professor about changing the grade on your paper" (likely–unlikely, probable–improbable, possible–impossible)? To measure Pf, we might ask you to respond to this item: "How likely is it that you will fail when you argue with your professor about changing the grade on your paper" (likely–unlikely, probable–improbable, possible–impossible)?

To measure Is, we might ask you to respond to this item: "How important is it for you to succeed when you argue with your professor about changing the grade on your paper" (important–unimportant, significant–insignificant, meaningful–meaningless)? Finally to measure If, we might ask you to respond to this item: "How important is it for you to fail when you argue with your professor about changing the grade on your paper" (important–unimportant, significant–insignificant, meaningful–meaningless)?

These perceptions would be measured on a seven-space response format using semantic differential scales and would presented in this way:

"How likely is it that you will succeed when you argue with your professor about changing the grade on your paper?" (Ps)

likely _____:_____:_____:_____:_____:_____:_____ unlikely

probable _____:_____:_____:_____:_____:_____:_____ improbable

possible _____:_____:_____:_____:_____:_____:_____ impossible

"How important is it for you to succeed when you argue with your professor about changing the grade on your paper?" (Is)

important _____:_____:_____:_____:_____:_____:_____ unimportant

significant _____:_____:_____:_____:_____:_____:_____ insignificant

meaningful _____:_____:_____:_____:_____:_____:_____ meaningless

We would use similar measures to obtain scores for your probability of failure (Pf) and importance of failure (If) in this specific situation. If we obtain your responses to all of these scales, a quantitative score for all components in the formula RMarg = Tap – Tav can be obtained, thus allowing us to predict your resultant motivation to argue in that situation.

Let us return again to the example of asking the professor to change the grade on your paper to see how these trait and situational factors might influence your resultant motivation to argue. Suppose that you score in the moderate range for both ARGap and ARGav, that is, you are neither high nor low in the general trait. Let us further presume that while your probability of success (Ps) for arguing with your professor is also in the moderate range (i.e., you think you have a 50–50 chance of winning), your perceived importance of success (Is) is quite strong (i.e., you see it as extremely important that you win the argument and get the grade on the paper changed). Further, while your probability of failure (Pf) is also moderate (i.e., you think you have a 50–50 chance of losing), your perceived importance of failure (If) is very strong (i.e., if you lose the argument and do not receive the higher grade on your paper you will need to get a grade of A on the final exam to get a passing grade in the course). In this case we would predict that your resultant motivation to argue (RMArg) would be higher than it would have been if we predicted it on the basis of your general tendency (trait) (ARGgt) to argue alone (which you recall was in the moderate range). Thus, adding situational perceptions can enhance the precision in our prediction of how motivated a person will be to argue in *a given situation*. This example supports the assumptions of the interactionist approach and suggests that both traits and situational factors are critical in understanding a person's argumentative communication.

Conclusion

This chapter presented a variety of ways in which scholars conceptualize argumentativeness and verbal aggressiveness. In fact, the development of any personality trait is subject to the same developmental discrepancies highlighted here. That is, the perspectives on behavior range from a primary emphasis on trait explanations to primary emphasis on situational explanations. In between these two perspectives lies a middle ground that assumes both trait and situational elements are needed to best account for behavior.

When concerned with trait explanations, it is assumed that whatever situation people find themselves in, the influence of that situation will have little to no impact on their communication behavior. For example, persons high in argumentativeness or high in verbal aggressiveness will tend to exhibit behaviors associated with these traits with little regard to specific situational characteristics. That is, regardless of topic, adversary, or other characteristics in the situation, these persons will most likely behave consistently due to their traits (i.e., be argumentative or verbally aggressive).

Other scholars have advanced the notion that only the situation should be considered when trying to explain behavior. The situationist perspective holds that while people do have predispositions, they are weak and it is primarily aspects of the situation that trigger a response. If you assume that people act uniquely and differently in every situation, there is little or no basis for predictability of behavior. In this light, a person can be high in verbal aggressiveness at the mall and low in verbal aggressiveness at the dinner table. It is important to recognize that there is a growing body of communication research arguing for the genetic, biological, and trait origins of verbal aggressiveness, but comparatively little research in communication indicating support for the situationist perspective. At this time prevailing conceptualizations of both argumentativeness and verbal aggressiveness support the interactionist perspective. This approach holds that human communication behavior is a joint function of the person and the situation. By accounting for both predispositional (i.e., trait) and situational factors (i.e., issue importance, probability for success, characteristics of the adversary, etc), scholars may be able to better explain and predict argumentative and verbally aggressive behavior.

The model of argumentativeness presented in this chapter assumes the two opposing motivations of approach and avoidance comprise a person's trait argumentativeness. In fact, the general tendency to argue is calculated by subtracting the motivation to avoid arguments from the motivation to approach arguments. Although a person may be high in his or her general tendency to argue, it is important to consider the situational factors of success probability, importance of success, failure probability, and importance of failure. These considerations coupled with the one's general trait comprise one's resultant motivation to argue. Although a growing body of research suggests a genetic basis for verbal aggressiveness, both argumentativeness and verbal aggressiveness continue to be seen as traits that can be influenced somewhat by situational factors.

Now that we have discussed the development of the traits, the next section of this book will be dedicated to the influence of argumentative and verbally aggressive communication in specific contexts. More specifically, there is an abundance of research on both traits that has been conducted in the family, in the workplace, in the classroom, between cultures, in the media, and in persuasive contexts. Part II of this book will highlight this research showing the constructive nature of argumentativeness and the destructive nature of verbal aggressiveness within those respective communication contexts.

Discussion Questions for Chapter 3

1. Given that trait theorists, situationists, and interactionists all offer explanations for behavior, which one do you think is the most comprehensive explanation? Why?

2. Which explanation for human communication behavior (trait, situationist, interactionist) do you think is most accurate?

3. What are some of the situational influences that studies identified as being important to argumentativeness and verbal aggressiveness? Have these situational influences ever affected you? How?

4. Why would researchers be concerned with perceptions of the probability and importance of success and failure in an argument when trying to explain a person's argumentative behavior in a given situation?

5. If we argue that traits are genetically influenced, what other possible influences do you think would serve to change a person's verbal aggressiveness?

PART II

The Function of Argumentative and Aggressive Communication

4

Argumentative and Aggressive Communication in Relational and Family Contexts

The study of argumentative and aggressive communication in interpersonal relationships has commanded more attention from scholars than other communication contexts. This chapter will focus on the influence that argumentative and aggressive communication has on a variety of interpersonal relationships. More specifically, we will discuss research on argumentativeness and verbal aggressiveness in (a) general interpersonal relationships, (b) friendships, (c) dating relationships, and (d) family relationships. The findings from studies that have been conducted within each of these relationships will be discussed and conclusions will be drawn.

Argumentativeness and Verbal Aggressiveness in General Interpersonal Relationships

Assessment of argumentative and aggressive communication at the interpersonal level has been primarily concerned with specific relationships (e.g., parent–child, marital, siblings). There are, however, a few studies that focused on more generic interpersonal relationships. For example, Myers and Johnson (2003) assessed the relationship between verbal aggression and liking in a variety of interpersonal relationships (e.g., friend, romantic partner, classmate, instructor, or colleague). Participants completed the 10 negatively worded items of the Verbal Aggressiveness Scale to assess the level of verbal aggressiveness as well as a measure of interpersonal liking. The results indicated that the more people are seen as verbally aggressive, the less liked they are. At first glance, you may think that these findings are intuitive. However, this type of research is critical for developing a body of knowledge and for theory building, as we cannot rely on anecdotal (i.e., "Because I said so!") kinds of evidence. We must rely on sound research methods to test important social scientific research questions.

In an attempt to assess argumentative prototypes and their willingness to engage in a relationship, Waggenspack and Hensley (1989) asked students to review either the 10 argument approach items or the 10 argument avoidance items contained in the Argumentativeness Scale. The respondents were asked to picture a person who exhibited either an argument approach or an argument avoidance profile. The participants were then asked a series of questions reflecting a variety of social situations, such as whether they would associate with this person in a (a) utilitarian-proponent situation (i.e., a task in which the other person is acting on your behalf), (b) utilitarian-opponent (i.e., a task in which the other person is acting as an opponent), (c) cooperative (i.e., joint goal orientation), and (d) judgmental (i.e., evaluative situation in which the other person gives an evaluation).

Among the most interesting findings of this study was that people prefer a nonargumentative person when in nonaggressive or nonconflict situations. The results suggest a moderating effect of the situation on the desirability of an argumentative person (see Chapter 3). That is, in situations that call for advocacy or conflict, highly argumentative people are seen as being desirable. However, in nonconfrontational situations or situations that require socioemotional support, there appears to be a preference for the low-argumentative person.

Friendship Relationships

The notion of friendship is often difficult to operationalize, as this definition rests on a myriad of factors including type of social support, amount of social support, frequency of contact, quality of contact, resources exchanged, and the amount and use of argumentative and aggressive communication. There is an old adage that states familiarity breeds contempt. This statement can be applied to just about any relationship where there is a bond between two people. Imagine driving down the street with your windows open. Suddenly and unknowingly, you run a stop sign. Another driver shouts out to you, "Nice going, idiot!" Most people would give little credence to this person's verbally aggressive message. However, it would be a different story if you walk into your home, accidentally knock over a vase, and the person with whom you share a relationship says "Nice going, idiot!" The difference in the reaction to the verbally aggressive message lies firmly in the expectations people have about these relationships.

One study explored the relational aspect of sending and receiving verbally aggressive messages. Martin et al. (1996) asked students to report their trait verbal aggressiveness and asked them to attend a presentation that defined and provided examples of different types of verbally aggressive messages. Referencing a friend, the students completed measures concerning justifications for sending verbally aggressive messages and indicated the degree of psychological hurt they feel from receiving these aggressive messages. The respondents then repeated this process while referencing an acquaintance. Martin and his colleagues believed that receiving verbally aggressive messages from friends would be seen as more hurtful than receiving them from acquaintances and the results supported this. Character attacks, competence attacks, background attacks, physical appearance attacks, maledictions, ridicule, threats, swearing, and nonverbal emblems were seen as more hurtful when delivered by friends. Further, and regardless of the relationship stage, people high in trait verbal aggressiveness also reported more justification in using verbal aggression. This study suggests that the closer or more developed the relationship, the greater the negative impact of receiving verbally aggressive messages.

The research discussed thus far has been concerned with people's perceptions rather than actual behavior. In an effort to link actual behavior to argumentativeness and verbal aggressiveness, Semic and Canary (1997) investigated argumentative and aggressive messages spontaneously exchanged between friends. Using a coding scheme developed in earlier research (see Canary, 1989; Canary, Tanita-Ratledge, & Siebold, 1982), Semic and Canary coded these messages as either starting points (i.e., assertions and propositions), developing points (i.e., elaborations, amplification, and justification), convergence markers (i.e., agreement and acknowledgment), prompters (i.e., objections, challenges, and responses), delimiters (i.e., framing, forestall/secure [stall the discussion by finding common ground], forestall/remove [stall the discussion by preventing conversation]), and nonargument (i.e., messages or behaviors that serve no function for the argument). The study, which used 31 dyads engaging in an argument, revealed that trait argumentativeness was not significantly related to argument behavior. However, verbal aggressiveness was found to be inversely related to proportion of arguments generated (i.e., the greater the verbal aggressiveness, the fewer the number of arguments generated). This study provides evidence contrary to the assumption of a linear relationship between argumentativeness, verbal aggressiveness, and actual interpersonal behavior, especially in arguments that are minimally rational (i.e., the way people give the appearance of logical argument as opposed to that of expert data, or specific argument forms).

Much of the research discussed in this text treats argumentativeness and verbal aggressiveness as independent or moderating variables in a variety of communication contexts. One exception is a study conducted by DiCioccio (2000) that sought to explain verbally and physically aggressive outcomes in friendship relationships. This model of friendship relationships focuses on how other factors contribute to an aggressive outcome. More specifically, DiCioccio argued that the perceived stage of the relationship, information processing, and the social skills of the friends will influence the degree of aggressiveness. Although this model awaits empirical testing, its utility lies in the novel way communication constructs such as social support are factored into the explanation of aggressive communication outcomes.

Although the next few studies do not exactly fit into the topic of friendship, it seems appropriate to include them here. Many of you reading this text will go home to someone with whom you are not romantically involved with and yet share the same living space. Having a roommate is a relationship that we, for the most part, willingly and legally (i.e., by lease or rental agreement) engage in for short periods of time. You may have had the pleasure of roommates seemingly from heaven and the pain of having roommates from somewhere much farther south. Some research has focused on the impact of argumentative and aggressive communication in the roommate relationship. Martin and Anderson (1995) assessed people from 15 to 57 years of age concerning communication competence, willingness to communicate, and verbal aggressiveness regarding their roommates. Both roommates agreed to complete the questionnaire. Comparisons of the roommates' self-reports revealed that the lower both roommates were in verbal aggressiveness, the more satisfied they were in the relationship and the more liking they expressed for their roommate. Argumentativeness, however, was not found to be related with communication satisfaction or social attraction toward a roommate (Martin & Anderson, 1997b).

Dating Relationships

For most dating relationships, we tend to use relational markers as indicators of the health or functionality of the relationship. One of these markers is the first fight. Interestingly, we often make judgments about our relational future by witnessing how our partner engages in interpersonal conflict. There is nothing more ugly than witnessing one partner swear or threaten another. In this section we will examine the use of argumentative and aggressive communication during and at the end of dating relationships.

Venable and Martin (1997) assessed young adults on both their own and their dating partners' verbal aggressiveness and argumentativeness. The results revealed that self-reports of both verbal aggressiveness and argumentativeness were positively related to reports of partner verbal aggressiveness and argumentativeness respectively. Further, only self-reported and partner verbal aggressiveness showed a significant and negative relationship with relational satisfaction. Argumentativeness, whether for self or partner, was not related to relational satisfaction in dating partners. Although the large body of research does advocate the constructive relational outcomes associated with argumentativeness, Venable and Martin suggest that "one should be careful in advocating the use of argumentation in interpersonal relationships until support is provided for the constructiveness of this type of communication" (p. 961). Other situational factors may temper the relationship between argumentativeness and constructive relational outcomes.

Focusing specifically on the disengagement process in dating relationships, Sutter and Martin (1998), using the same self- and dating partner report procedure used in the previously mentioned study, analyzed specific disengagement strategies and the use of verbal aggression. Results indicated that dating partners who were high in verbal aggressiveness were likely to use more relational disengagement strategies overall than people low in verbal aggressiveness. Further, relationships were observed between verbal aggressiveness and use of verbally aggressive messages during relationship termination and between reports of participants' perception of partner verbal aggressiveness and use of verbally aggressive messages during relationship termination. In addition, a reciprocity effect between self- and partner reports of using verbal aggression was observed. This suggests that the use of verbal aggression begets verbal aggression. This cycle of reciprocal escalation of verbally aggressive communication has been suggested by Infante and his colleagues for over 20 years.

Although there have been only a few studies conducted to investigate the role of argumentative and aggressive communication in dating relationships, the findings of these studies are not typical for other relational dyads and, as such, remain a unique and understudied area of research. Researchers interested in argumentative and aggressive communication have concentrated their efforts on relationships primarily in the marital realm. Given this, we will now turn attention to family communication and emphasize the role of argumentative and aggressive communication within specific familial dyads.

Family Relationships

One of the most socially compelling manifestations of argumentative and verbally aggressive communication is within the family unit. Every day we are bombarded with messages on how to raise our children, satisfy our mates, and regain our own identities. If you have any doubt about this focus on family interactions and marital relationships, simply turn on the television, read the newspaper, or speak with a neighbor. Whether it is Oprah, Dr. Phil, or your neighbor Pete, chatter about family and family interaction is ubiquitous.

One of your authors recalls numerous occasions of being in a public area such as a shopping mall or grocery store and hearing verbally aggressive messages being sent by "bad parents" to their "innocent and exploited" children. Hearing only one sentence from this stranger often conjured up the frightful image of (a) their home life, (b) the history of their relationship with their children, and (c) the broken child services department. After some thought about how these conclusions were derived, he realized that it was the use of verbal aggression, and more importantly, the severity of the verbal aggression that led to the creation of this perception of the bad parent.

Logic suggests that the more you study something, the better you can explain it. However, this logic might be best suited for inanimate objects. Scholars in all of the social sciences have struggled to explain the epidemic of dysfunctional family interaction. Yet, it seems that incidents of child abuse and domestic violence continue to increase. For example, Jacobson and Gottman (1998a) report that at least 1.6 million women in the United States are beaten by their husbands. According to the Centers for Disease Control's (n.d.) National Center for Violence and Control Web site, each year more than 10 million children witness interpersonal violence in their family. Shockingly, husbands, ex-husbands, and boyfriends perpetrated 30% of all female murders. On the face of it, our inability to alter these statistics seems illogical given the amount of resources government and institutes of higher learning expend on attempting to explain and reduce these sad and disturbing outcomes. However, when we are dealing with familial dynamics, there are so many facets and factors that influence dysfunctional and violent outcomes that there is probably no magic fix to all the social ills in the contemporary family.

Assisted by research, we feel comfortable asserting that within the family context, the consequences of verbal aggressiveness are most often destructive and the consequences of argumentativeness are most often constructive. The research, similar to most done on the family, focuses on specific family dyads. Part of this is due to the fact that most researchers have focused their investigation of argumentative and aggressive communication in the interpersonal realm. Another reason for this dyadic focus is the inability of the scholar to answer the question, "What is a family?" Galvin (2003) argued, "Families are defining themselves for themselves through their interactions at the same time that longevity, legal flexibility, personal choice, ethnicity, gender, geographic distance, and reproductive technology impact traditional biological and legal conceptions of family" (p. 676). Given the definitional difficulties of answering the question "What is a family?" we will present the research findings by the varied familial categories of the marital relationship, the sibling relationship, and the parent–child relationship.

Marital Relationships

As your authors can attest, marital communication is an art! Have you ever gone out to a restaurant with another couple only to witness that couple engaging in an embarrassing diatribe of verbal aggression directed at one another? If you have been unlucky enough to witness this you know it is not a pleasant experience. According to the Centers for Disease Control (2002), the probability that marriages will fail within 10 years is 48% for people under the age of 18, 40% for people 18–19 years old, 29% for people 20–24 years old, and 24% for people above age 25. Some of the major explanations and factors for the ending of marital relationships are communication related.

In this regard, researchers have asked the question, "What is the role of argumentativeness and verbal aggressiveness in marital satisfaction?" In one attempt to answer this question, Rancer, Baukus, and Amato (1986) studied married couples to examine the relationship between argumentativeness, verbal aggressiveness, and marital satisfaction. Their efforts were an attempt to see if symmetrical (i.e., balanced) traits of spouses' argumentativeness and verbal aggressiveness contributed to marital satisfaction. Each couple completed measures of argumentativeness and verbal aggressiveness as well as a measure of marital satisfaction. Surprisingly, verbal aggressiveness was not found to be a predictor of marital satisfaction, although argumentativeness was. More specifically, couples who were asymmetrical (i.e., complementary) in trait argumentativeness (e.g., one spouse high and one spouse low) reported significantly higher levels of marital satisfaction than couples who were symmetrical in argumentativeness (both reporting similar level of argumentativeness). They attempted to explain this by suggesting that since more husbands reported higher levels of argumentativeness than their wives, the participants may have been more reflective of traditional couples where marital roles are more prenegotiated (Fitzpatrick, 1977; Sillars, Pike, Jones, & Redmon, 1983). Interestingly, Fiztpatrick suggests that traditional couples are less likely to experience marital conflict.

In a similar study but with different results, Payne and Chandler-Sabourin (1990) used a known-groups comparison of nondistressed couples to examine the relationship between argumentativeness and marital quality. A known-groups comparison is when researchers go out and recruit a sample of people who have particular characteristics that are central to the research. In this case, they sought out couples who were nondistressed for participation in the study. Overall, the findings indicate that a wife high in argumentativeness (as assessed by self-report and other-report [i.e., her husband's report]) was the best predictor of marital satisfaction. In addition, verbal aggressiveness was also found to be a significant predictor of marital satisfaction. In short, husbands' self-report of verbal aggressiveness as well as the wives' report of the husbands' verbal aggressiveness were inversely related to marital satisfaction. That is, as the husband's level of verbal aggressiveness increases, marital satisfaction decreases.

The difference between these two studies might be attributed to several factors, including sample selection and the wives' level of argumentative skill. The Payne and Chandler-Sabourin (1990) study used only those couples who were in nondistressed relationships and focused on explaining the findings through the argumentative skill deficiency of the wife. The Rancer et al. (1986) study did not distinguish between distressed and nondistressed couples and chose to explain their findings through the marital relational typology and societal expectancies of marital roles that were gender based rather than through the argument skills deficiency model.

Those of you who have taken a few social science classes probably have drawn the conclusion that researchers are especially interested in discovering what makes people happy, in marriage and in life in general. However, communication scholars have recently begun to explore the dark side of interpersonal relationships. Instead of focusing on what makes us happy, some scholars have focused on what makes us miserable and even psychologically and physiologically threatened. Unfortunately, the ubiquity of verbally aggressive communication in marriage has served as a stimulus for researchers interested in the dark side of marriage. This line of research has commanded the majority of studies on argumentative and aggressive communication in marital interaction, and the reason for this will become clear as we discuss the destructive nature of verbally aggressive communication in marital relationships.

Most research focusing on argumentative and aggressive communication in married couples has, in one way or another, distinguished couples based on patterns of communication or the perceived volatility status of the relationships. For example, in a study investigating demand and withdraw patterns (i.e., a conflict pattern in which one spouse complains while the other spouse shuts down or withdraws), Caughlin and Vangelisti (2000) speculated that spouses who are high in argumentativeness will report greater levels of demand patterns, whereas spouses reporting lower levels of argumentativeness will report more frequent withdrawal patterns. The study found that argumentativeness is one factor that influences spousal conflict patterns. In fact, regardless of the model that these authors tested (i.e., the self-influence model or the relational influence model), argumentativeness (as well as several other predispositions) emerged as meaningful factors in conflict patterns.

When moving into more pathological or dysfunctional relationships, we find that argumentative and aggressive communication exerts a not-so-obvious influence in the marital dyad. In a study exploring verbal aggressiveness and depression, Segrin and Fitzpatrick (1992) assessed couples on the Relational Dimensions Inventory, a method used to classify couple types. In their sample, 62 couples were classified as traditionals (i.e., they held more conventional assumptions about marriage), 33 couples were classified as independents (i.e., they held more contemporary or individualistic assumptions about marriage), 12 were classified as separates (i.e., they held more conventional values toward marriage yet at the same time valued individuality), and 69 couples were classified as mixed (i.e., couples whose members defined their relationship differently from one another).

The results showed clear differences in verbal aggressiveness based on couple types. Verbal aggressiveness was most prevalent in separates, mixed, independents, and traditionals, respectively. Earlier we presented research that indicates men are higher in both argumentativeness and verbal aggressiveness than women (see Infante & Rancer, 1996). The results of the Segrin and Fitzpatrick (1992) study show that levels of verbal aggressiveness are also tempered by the type of marital relationship. More specifically, husbands' verbal aggressiveness was significantly lower for traditionals than for any of the other marital types (i.e., separates, mixed, or independents). Interestingly, wives' level of verbal aggressiveness was not influenced by marital type. In fact, across all marital types, wives' level of verbal aggressiveness was lower than that of husbands. Further, although there were significant relationships between verbal aggressiveness and depression for both marital partners, only husbands' depression was linked to the wives' level of verbal aggressiveness. The wives' level of depression was not related to the husbands' verbal aggressiveness.

The differing levels of argumentativeness and verbal aggressiveness based on couple types speak to the situational influences that affect predispositions toward argumentative and aggressive communication. To further exemplify this point, we will review a series of studies conducted to explain the role of these two traits in marriages in which physical aggression has occurred.

Argumentativeness, Verbal Aggressiveness, and Interspousal Violence

In one of the most comprehensive efforts designed to understand the role of argumentative and aggressive communication in marriage, Infante and his colleagues conducted a series of studies examining violent and nonviolent couples. Infante, Chandler, and Rudd (1989) proposed a model of inter-spousal violence that was based on the argumentative skills deficiency explanation. This model suggests that verbal aggression, along with other societal (e.g., socioeconomic status), situational (e.g., drug or alcohol use), and pre-dispositional characteristics (e.g., esteem and self-worth), can contribute to physical violence in marital and other intimate relationships. The model does not suggest that verbal aggression is a causal factor as much as a necessary one in promoting physical aggression in couples. That is, relationships in which verbal aggression is present will not necessarily lead to physically aggressive behavior; however, where physical aggression is present in marital relationships, verbal aggression is almost always present. This latent hostility is triggered by the multitude of factors mentioned above.

The concept of an argumentative skills deficiency is based on various social learning theories and assumes that a major cause of verbal aggression is the lack of effective conflict resolution skills and primarily weaker skills in arguing. That is, when one or both of the spouses are unskilled argumenta-tively, family conflict over even a relatively innocuous issue may result in physical aggression because the verbal attacks, rather than being directed toward the other's position on the issue, are misdirected toward the other person's self-concept. This inability to defuse potentially explosive situations serves to fuel the latent hostility and thus increases the probability of a phys-ically aggressive encounter.

When we cannot effectively invent and present arguments and offer an effective rebuttal during a conflict situation, whether because we are not motivated to or we simply do not have the ability to do so, we tend to pro-tect our position through other means. This may include first verbally, and then physically, lashing out at the other person (Infante, 1987a). It is believed that this type of behavior is reciprocal in that verbal aggression begets verbal aggression. This cycle, once engaged, is believed to bring out latent hostility (Infante, 1988).

Infante et al. (1989) surveyed women who were physically assaulted by partners and who were residing in a shelter, men attending group therapy for spousal battery, women in nonviolent marriages, and men in nonviolent mar-riages. The participants completed self-report measures of argumentativeness and verbal aggressiveness as well as other-report measures about their spouse's argumentative and aggressive communication. The findings indicated that there was more verbal aggressiveness reported in violent marriages than nonviolent marriages. Further, the spouses' level of verbal aggressiveness (as assessed through the other-report) accounted for the most variance whereas the participants' self-reported argumentativeness and verbal aggressiveness contributed, but to a lesser degree. Perhaps the most striking finding supporting the argumentative skill deficiency model comes from the results showing violent marriages more likely being comprised of one spouse lower in argumentativeness while perceiving the other spouse as being highly verbally aggressive. It was suggested that

> a communication model provides a basis for implicating one form of communication, verbal aggression, as a catalyst in the circumstances which surround interpersonal violence. It also suggests . . . that another form of communication, argumentation, may serve a constructive function in family conflict situations. (Infante et al., 1989, p. 174)

A series of related studies furthered this line of inquiry. Utilizing different samples, that were similar in composition (i.e., couples experiencing violent and nonviolent marital disputes), Infante, Chandler-Sabourin, Rudd, and Shannon (1990) examined the types of verbally aggressive messages used in marital verbal disputes (as opposed to only engaging in interpersonal violence). They hypothesized that people in violent disputes will not only perceive a greater amount of verbal aggression than those in nonviolent disputes, but will also be similar or more symmetrical in their reports of verbally aggressive behavior.

Instead of using the traditional Verbal Aggressiveness Scale (Infante & Wigley, 1986), the researchers had abused women and nonabused women provide written accounts of the most recent disagreement that resulted in physical aggression (for the abused sample) or the most recent important disagreement (for the nonviolent couples). All participants were then asked to indicate the frequency with which they used specific verbally aggressive messages during the dispute. This taxonomy (e.g., character attacks, competence attacks, threats, profanity, teasing, ridicule, maledictions, nonverbal verbal aggression) was developed by previous research (Infante, 1987a; Infante & Wigley). As expected, more verbal aggression was evident in the violent couple disputes (an average of 18.75 messages) as compared to nonviolent couple disputes (an average of 4.5 verbally aggressive messages). Further, the relationship between husband and wife verbal aggression in violent couples was strong and significant. Again, this finding speaks to the reciprocal nature of violent disputes. Another finding of this investigation is that wives in violent disputes categorically use character attacks and to a lesser degree swearing and competence attacks. Almost all of the explained variance in the violent marital disputes was accounted for through these three types of verbally aggressive messages. In terms of wives' reports of husbands' aggressive messages, the use of character attacks, profanity, and threats best distinguished violent and nonviolent couple disputes.

Efforts examining the role of verbal aggression in marital couples have also considered more strategic communication and more traditional relational outcomes. For example, Sabourin et al. (1993) expanded their distinction of marital couples to include violent, distressed but nonviolent (i.e., couples originally identified as nonviolent but determined via questionnaire to be violent), and nondistressed couples in their study of marital satisfaction. In their study, violent couples reported significantly more verbally aggressive messages than either nonviolent or distressed but nonviolent couples. Further, nondistressed couples reported higher levels of marital satisfaction than either the distressed but nonviolent, or the violent couples. These findings extend the Infante et al. (1989) study discussed earlier but at the dyadic level (i.e., self-reports from both husband and wife).

Reports of reciprocal message exchange also discriminated among the couple types. More specifically, reciprocal verbal aggression patterns differentiated violent couples from distressed nonviolent and nondistressed couples. The authors contend that the reciprocity and escalation of verbal aggression is a strong indicator of potential marital violence in relationships experiencing relational problems.

In Chapter 9 we will discuss the research concerning the influence of argumentative and aggressive communication on persuasion and compliance-gaining efforts. Persuasive messages have also been researched in relation to argumentativeness and verbal aggressiveness within the family context. Rudd, Burant, and Beatty (1994) studied women temporarily living in a shelter for battered women. Participants completed a measure of interpersonal compliance gaining (that was developed from a variety of previous compliance-gaining taxonomies) and measures of trait argumentativeness and verbal aggressiveness. Results indicate that battered women used *ingratiation* (e.g., "I said or did something nice"), *aversive stimulation* (e.g., "I did or said something that let him know how angry or hurt I was"), *explanation* (e.g., "I tried to give him an explanation or reason for accepting my ideas"), and *promise* (e.g., "I promise to do something") in disputes with their partner. Further, battered women who were higher in verbal aggressiveness and lower in argumentativeness use strategies of *guilt* (e.g., "I made him feel guilty"), *bargaining* (e.g., "I offered to make a trade or strike a deal with him"), *debt* (e.g., "I reminded him of all the things I have done for him"), *threat* (e.g., "I threatened that I might do something that he would not want me to do"), *aversive stimulation,* and *warning* (e.g., "I warned him that other people would criticize him").

Battered women who reported higher argumentativeness and lower verbal aggressiveness reported using strategies of *allurement* (e.g., "I explained how agreeing would make other people respect him or what he is doing"), *hinting* (e.g., "I hinted at what I wanted without really asking him"), *direct request* (e.g., "I asked him simply to agree with my suggestion or solution") and *aversive stimulation.* Overall, the authors suggest that battered women seem to rely heavily on indirect compliance-gaining strategies or strategies with an indirect power base. This may be attributed to battered women's sense of perceived helplessness, in which they feel the need to resort to secondary or indirect strategies to get the husband to comply.

In recent years, the flurry of research activity regarding argumentativeness and verbal aggression in the marital dyad has abated somewhat. However, Infante and his colleagues' efforts have provided a comprehensive framework from which training, counseling, and behavior modification strategies may be derived. Training programs such as those we will discuss in Chapter 10 will show how properly executed argumentative and aggressive communication modification programs could have meaningful and positive consequences for relationships in trouble.

Sibling Pairs

The sibling relationship is unique from other family dyads in that it has a greater probability of lasting longer than any other relationship (Fitzpatrick & Badzinski, 1994; Vangelisti, 1994). For some, this is an unfortunate fact of life; others, however, see this as a wonderful fact of sibling friendship. "Love 'em or hate 'em," there are few relationships over the course of a lifetime that undergo such dramatic changes and role negotiation as the sibling relationship. Although Noller and Fitzpatrick (1993) suggested that sibling dyads, when compared with other family dyads, had largely been ignored by family communication researchers, scholars have provided some findings regarding argumentative and aggressive communication between siblings.

One of your authors has two older brothers and one older sister. When they were young, he would often catch his brothers engaging in a variety of childhood shenanigans. Being the baby of the family, he put forth the most cogent argumentative message that he could muster: "I'm telling Mom!" His older brothers would respond with another potent but verbally aggressive message, "You do, and we'll kill you!" Needless to say, his sibling's verbally aggressive message prevailed and Mom never discovered what the brothers were up to. Today, as adults, the brothers rarely walk around threatening each other with those types of utterances. Instead they use other more strategic messages but with the same type of implications. As this stroll down memory lane indicates, sibling relationships can change over the life cycle. Researchers have long acknowledged the influence of time on the sibling bond (Newman, 1991). As we age, the sibling relationship becomes one of choice rather than one forced upon us and gives us the opportunity to increase or decrease the level of intimacy as well as the amount of interaction time with one another (Allan, 1977; Leigh, 1982).

There are a myriad of factors that influence our decisions to keep sibling relationships alive or not when we enter adulthood. One such factor is that of sibling violence. Some researchers suggest that sibling violence is reaching epidemic proportions and is more prevalent than any other form of intimate violence (Gelles, 1997). In fact, being antagonistic to our brothers or sisters is often seen as typical or normative behavior (Roscoe, Goodwin, & Kennedy, 1987). Recall the comprehensive studies into marital violence conducted by Infante and his colleagues that showed the level of verbal aggressiveness was far greater in violent marriages and often served as a catalyst for conflict escalation that eventually led to physical violence. Although research has yet to confirm this outcome in sibling relationships, several indicators suggest that these findings could emerge. The argumentative skills deficiency model contends that the better people can formulate and present arguments and refute the arguments of another person, the less likely that people will resort to messages involving personal attacks (i.e., verbal aggressiveness) and physical aggressiveness. The notion of ineffective communication patterns leading to physical violence is widely acknowledged by the social sciences and could hold true for any familial dyad (Cahn, 1996; Lloyd & Emery, 2000).

While research on aggressive communication between siblings is sparse, the research that has been conducted shows interesting patterns that support a conclusion presented throughout this book: Argumentativeness is constructive to relationships, whereas verbal aggressiveness is destructive to relationships. Martin, Anderson, Burant, and Weber (1997) investigated verbal aggression along with pro-social relational constructs such as interpersonal trust and relational satisfaction in sibling relationships. Students completed questionnaires while referencing a specific sibling. With researchers controlling for sex of the participant as well as sex of the sibling, the findings indicated a strong negative relationship between self-reported verbal aggressiveness and relational satisfaction (i.e., the higher sibling verbal aggressiveness, the lower sibling relational satisfaction). Further, perceptions of sibling verbal aggressiveness were also related to the participants' relational satisfaction. Another important finding of this study concerns the role of teasing, as those higher in verbal aggressiveness engage in more teasing of their siblings.

When sex was not held constant, female sibling dyads reported lower self-reported verbal aggressiveness than any other sibling sex combination. Further, females reporting on a male sibling reported higher levels of verbal aggressiveness than any other dyad. Female participants, regardless of the sex of the sibling, reported greater hurt from receiving verbally aggressive messages than any other sibling dyad. The findings of the Martin, Anderson, Burant, et al. (1997) study demonstrate the importance of accounting for sex differences even in specific family dyads, and the research indicates that females report males as being more verbally aggressive than themselves in both marital and sibling dyads.

Teven, Martin, and Neupauer (1998) extended the Martin, Anderson, Burant, and Weber (1997) study to include the specific verbally aggressive messages used in sibling pairs. This study provided participants with 14 verbally aggressive messages and behaviors and then asked respondents to record the frequency that their sibling engaged in these behaviors when interacting with the respondent. The verbally aggressive behaviors presented were (a) attack your intelligence, (b) make fun of your dating or lack of relationships, (c) make fun of your friendships, (d) call you uncomplementary nicknames, (e) make fun of your physical appearance, (f) threaten to get you in trouble, (g) threaten to hurt you physically, (h) make fun of your friends in front of you, (i) complain about something you have done, (j) attack your self-esteem, (k) threaten to abuse or destroy a possession of yours, (l) make fun of you in front of your friends, (m) tease you, and (n) swear at you. The findings revealed that the greater the sibling's use of verbally aggressive messages, the lower the relational satisfaction experienced by the respondent. Interestingly, the only sex difference observed was that women perceive more verbal aggression than men regardless of their sibling's sex.

Although other pro-social communication constructs in the sibling relationship have been studied, including perceived understanding (Avtgis, Martin, & Rocca, 2000), relational maintenance (Myers & Members of COMM 2000, 2001), and relational messages during conflict (Pawlowski, Myers, & Rocca, 2000), this review suggests that argumentativeness and verbal aggressiveness in the sibling relationship is still an underresearched area. Researchers have yet to fully explore the underpinnings of argumentative and aggressive communication on sibling relational dynamics. Consider, for example, the application of the argumentative skills deficiency model to aggression found in sibling dyads. Such an effort, in light of the fact that this relationship is believed to be of the most violent within the family (Gelles, 1997), might produce interesting findings that may lead us to a better understanding of this problem.

Parent–Child Dyads

Many contemporary magazines and current affair shows seem to be obsessed with telling American parents what they should be doing to best raise their children. The proliferation of these popular relationship gurus seems to be conspicuously related to the increase in dysfunctional family dynamics. The authors of this text are currently experiencing very different aspects and stages of parenthood. One author is experiencing the joys of a 19-month-old curious son and the other author is experiencing the joys of his teenage daughter beginning to date and move toward adulthood. Regardless of where we are in the parenting phase, similar questions are being asked. For example, should I use corporal punishment when reprimanding my child? What types of language should be used when I reprimand him or her? Where is the line drawn between using strong language to reprimand and verbal abuse? These types of questions are asked by most parents at various times during child rearing. In fact, pick up any one of the dozens of magazines targeted at new parents, old parents, and everyone in between and you will find at least one article concerning assertiveness and constructive criticism, aggressive and destructive criticism, and the difference between the two.

Few people might realize that the use of parental verbal aggression in other countries is not only considered socially inappropriate, but carries stiff legal consequences. Among the countries to pass laws banning the use of parental verbal aggression are Austria, Denmark, Germany, Israel, and Sweden. The passage of such laws stems from research indicating that verbal aggression is a form of violence that inflicts psychological injury to children.

In a highly publicized article in *U.S. News and World Report,* sociologist Murray Straus of the Family Research Lab at the University of New Hampshire surveyed parents on their use of verbal aggression toward their children. Shockingly, the findings revealed that one half of the parents shouted or screamed at their infants, and 98% of parents reported using verbal aggression with their children as young as age 7. Some of the most common types of verbally aggressive messages used were threats of physical violence and swearing. Recall Straus's earlier work that linked parental use of verbal aggression to a child's depression, antisocial behavior, and eating disorders. Although we are not suggesting that parental verbal aggression causes these maladies, we are suggesting that the relationship between parental verbal aggression and a child's negative relational, behavioral, and physical outcomes is undeniable.

This next section will dispel some anecdotal findings (e.g., like those presented in many popular parenting magazines) by focusing on social scientific investigations that present the problematic consequences of verbal aggressiveness and the productive outcomes of argumentativeness for parents and children.

Before we distinguish between moms and dads, we will examine the research focusing on parents in general. Bayer and Cegala (1992) investigated the impact of argumentativeness and verbal aggressiveness on parenting style. Utilizing the maternal behavior work of Schaefer (1959), three major parenting styles of *autonomy–love* (e.g., supporting and encouraging the individuality of the child), *control–hostility* (e.g., highly demanding and nonresponsive to the needs of the child), and *control–love* (e.g., give into the whims of the child, use ridicule, and love withdrawal) were identified. Parents who were high in argumentativeness and low in verbal aggressiveness reported an authoritative parenting style (i.e., autonomy–love behaviors), whereas parents reporting low argumentativeness and high verbal aggressiveness reported an authoritarian parenting style (i.e., control–hostility behaviors). The findings suggest that parental use of verbally aggressive communication is characteristic of potentially destructive parenting styles.

In an effort to capture the perspective of children with regard to parenting style, Prusank and Duran (1996) found that adult children who reported that their parents used an authoritative parenting style also reported less argument avoidance with their parents. This finding reinforces the influence of parents encouraging children to think independently and engage in debate, which can serve to increase the child's predisposition to engage in argument.

Moving from parenting styles to more patterned family communication, Booth-Butterfield and Sidelinger (1997) surveyed undergraduate students regarding one parent's traits and communication behaviors. The parent selected by the student was the one the student reported having the most communication with. The participants and the target parent completed the Verbal Aggressiveness Scale, a measure of affective orientation, and a measure of family communication patterns. The findings indicated that the more parents' verbal aggressiveness increased, the less open the family communication was perceive to be. Parents who rated themselves high on verbal aggressiveness had children who saw their family communication as being closed. That is, children growing up in families in which the communication climate was seen as closed were hesitant to discuss issues, hesitant to share opinions, and felt much less free to communicate in the family. This led the researchers to conclude that "verbal aggression closes the communication between the parent and child" (Booth-Butterfield & Sidelinger, p. 415).

In a self-report assessment of adult children and parents, Copstead, Lanzetta, and Avtgis (2001) investigated the relationship of adult childrens' perceived control over conflict with their verbal aggressiveness and argumentativeness toward parents. The results indicated that adult children with an internal conflict locus of control orientation (i.e., seeing outcomes of conflict as being under their control) also reported less verbal aggressiveness, less argument avoidance, and greater argument approach toward their parents. Thus, the perception of control over conflict may serve as a situational trigger influencing the use or nonuse of argumentative or verbally aggressive communication.

Comparing the traits between parent and child has also received attention from communication scholars. One effort examined the influence that parents' predisposition toward verbal aggressiveness has on children's development of the same trait. Recall from Chapter 3 that both biological and social learning factors influence the development of predispositions toward argumentative and aggressive communication. Martin and Anderson (1997a) compared the argumentativeness, verbal aggressiveness, and assertiveness of adult children to that of their parents. Young adults (78 daughters and 82 sons) and their parents (160 fathers and 160 mothers) participated in this study. The findings indicated both sons' and daughters' levels of argumentativeness and verbal aggressiveness were positively related with their mothers' level of these traits. No significant relationships were observed between sons and daughters with respect to fathers' argumentativeness and verbal aggressiveness. The researchers explain the lack of the father's influence on children's argumentative and aggressive communication by suggesting,

> Parents were not asked how much time they spent communicating with their children (either currently or during the children's childhood or adolescence). Sons and daughters may be more similar in communication patterns to the parent with whom they have spent the most time interacting, since frequency and length of exposure influence the modeling process. (Martin & Anderson, p. 310)

In a similar study, Roberto, McClure, and McFarland (2003) discovered that adult children's verbal aggressiveness was predicted by their perception of their same-sex parents' verbal aggressiveness. Further, sons' verbal aggression was actually predicted by mothers', and not fathers', self-reported verbal aggression. Again, research suggests that fathers, although higher in verbal aggressiveness than mothers, may play a diminished role in the development of the child's predisposition toward verbal aggression.

The influence of the maternal predisposition toward aggressive communication has even been found to be related to their children's future romantic relationships. Weber and Patterson (1997) found that as adult children's reports of mothers' verbal aggression increased, the less emotional support and interpersonal solidarity the adult children reported in their current romantic relationships. Thus, being the recipient of verbally aggressive messages from mothers may result in difficulties in interpersonal relationships in later life. In addition, children (both females and males) who were exposed to verbally aggressive messages from their mothers became more verbally aggressive themselves. As these children entered adult romantic relationships, they tended to use more verbally aggressive messages with their own romantic partners. Weber and Patterson suggest that maternal verbal aggression sets up a cycle of reciprocity that leads to less satisfying and less productive adult interpersonal relationships.

Rudd, Vogl-Bauer, Dobos, Beatty, and Valencic (1998) investigated the role of verbal aggressiveness, frustration, and anger in parenting behavior. Parents provided the researchers with written descriptions of a recent interaction they had with their child in which they were unsuccessful in getting their child to do something (or stop doing something). Then, the parents provided an estimate as to how angry and frustrated they were regarding this failed attempt. They found that parents' trait verbal aggressiveness was more strongly related to anger under highly frustrating conditions and that the higher the parents' level of verbal aggressiveness, "the more easily frustration is converted to anger" (Rudd et al., p. 7). This supports the notion that verbal aggressiveness can be triggered and moderated by situational cues.

A series of studies investigated father–son dyads and verbal aggressiveness by focusing on the influence of effectiveness and appropriateness of interaction plans when encountering an oppositional son (i.e., a son who will not behave as told to by his father; Beatty, Burant, Dobos, and Rudd, 1996; Rudd, Beatty, Vogl-Bauer, and Dobos, 1997). In the first study, large effects were observed in the predictability of fathers' trait verbal aggressiveness on interaction plan appropriateness. That is, the higher the fathers' verbal aggressiveness, the lower the social appropriateness of the fathers' interaction plans. This study relied on the sons' perception of fathers' appropriateness and effectiveness.

The second study sought to extend the findings to include the fathers' assessment of the appropriateness and effectiveness of their own interaction plans. In this study, fathers completed the Verbal Aggressiveness Scale and also evaluated the appropriateness and effectiveness of different tactics when interacting with an oppositional son. Results revealed that the higher the fathers' verbal aggressiveness, the lower the rating of appropriateness for fathers' influence tactics of stressing the importance of school and doing nothing. Further, highly verbally aggressive fathers gave higher ratings of appropriateness for the more aggressive tactics of corporal punishment. For effectiveness of tactics, fathers who were high in verbal aggressiveness also reported low effectiveness for influence tactics of doing homework with the son, talking about school, sending the son to his room, and turning off the television. These same fathers, however, reported that slapping their son was highly effective in gaining compliance. Again, we see that fathers' level of verbal aggressiveness, regardless of who is rating the appropriateness and effectiveness of tactics, is related to behaviors associated with corporal punishment.

Studying both father argumentativeness and verbal aggressiveness, Beatty, Zelley, Dobos, and Rudd (1994) found that fathers' argumentativeness contributed significantly less than fathers' verbal aggressiveness to the explanation of sons' reports of father sarcasm, criticism, and verbal aggressiveness. Fathers' self-reported verbal aggressiveness accounted for the largest amount in predicting sons' reports of their fathers' sarcasm, criticism, and verbal aggressiveness. Thus, a son's perceptions of his father's sarcasm, criticism, and perceived verbal aggressiveness is firmly based in the fathers' trait verbal aggressiveness. As fathers' use of criticism, sarcasm, and verbal aggression increased, so too did fathers' level of trait verbal aggressiveness.

A few studies have focused on parental use of physical tactics to bring about child compliance. When speaking with new parents, the topic often turns to the type of reprimands that are most effective in correcting behavior. Infante (2005) conceptualizes corporal punishment as communication targeted at social influence and that compliance is the ultimate goal of corporal punishment.

Conceptualizing corporal punishment as a form of compliance gaining has only begun to garner attention from communication researchers. Kassing, Pearce, Infante, and Pyles (1999) surveyed college students about their parents' use of corporal punishment, argumentative and verbally aggressive communication, assault tendencies, anger, and self-esteem and the students' tendency to use corporal punishment with their own children. Respondents were asked to recall examples from their childhood when responding about their parent's behavior. Students who reported that their parents used high levels of corporal punishment also reported their parents being high in verbal aggressiveness. Interestingly, argumentativeness did not emerge as a function of the recall of corporal punishment.

In a similar study focusing on the father–son dyad, Kassing, Pearce, and Infante (2000) measured levels of argumentativeness, verbal aggressiveness, and amount of corporal punishment used as an influence tactic. Results of this study offer support for the application of the theory of independent mindedness (see Chapter 5) to family communication. More specifically, fathers who were perceived as being low in argumentativeness and high in verbal aggressiveness recalled greater levels of corporal punishment and reported lower levels of affirming communicator style in the relationship. Basically, the higher the perceived levels of independent mindedness in the relationship, the lower the reports of corporal punishment used as an influence tactic. Again, we see the beneficial relational outcomes of parents and children who are high in argumentativeness and low in verbal aggressiveness in the reluctance to resort to physical violence as an influence tactic.

Although an abundance of research on aggressive communication has been conducted in the relational and family realm, the findings of these studies leave several questions unanswered. Research must continue to address both functional and dysfunctional family relationships and the influence of both argumentativeness and verbal aggressiveness on these relationships. Taken as a whole, the findings are compelling and show the negative relational outcomes associated with verbal aggressiveness and the positive relational outcomes associated with argumentativeness.

Conclusion

As evidenced throughout this chapter, much of the research investigating the dysfunctional outcomes associated with the use of verbal aggression has been focused on intimate and family relationships. A perusal of this research also reveals that the interpersonal communication context has produced the majority of the studies on argumentative and verbally aggressive communication, as the number of studies presented in this chapter exceeded those in other contexts discussed throughout this book. These research efforts have uncovered links between argumentativeness and constructive outcomes such as feelings of satisfaction, understanding, and support. They have also uncovered links between verbal aggression and destructive outcomes such as spousal abuse, sibling abuse, and overall interpersonal violence. Perhaps the most striking finding in this chapter can be summed up in the following sentence: *Verbal aggression is not necessarily a cause for physical violence, but it is always present when physical violence is present.* If we are to take this link between verbal aggression and physical aggression seriously, social scientists must continue their work toward finding and changing the conditions from which verbal aggression fosters violent and other destructive outcomes.

Regardless of the degree of intimacy (e.g., acquaintances, friends, lovers), length of relationship, or type of relationship (e.g., roommates, siblings, marital couples), the consistent link identified between relational satisfaction and higher levels of argumentativeness and lower levels of verbal aggressiveness remains constant. When considering the argumentative tendencies of both partners, the findings are somewhat inconsistent. Some research shows that interpersonal partners who are similar in their argumentative traits are more relationally satisfied, while other findings show interpersonal partners who are different in their argumentative traits are more relationally satisfied. More research into this issue needs to be conducted and should consider factors such as the partners' relational expectations, degree of involvement, and relational importance.

Future research must delineate further among the evolving definitions of family and relational partners. For example, do findings gleaned from research on heterosexual couples stand for homosexual couples in terms of interpartner violence, relational satisfaction, and parent–child interaction? Do cultural assumptions about family and marriage influence the appropriateness of verbal aggression and argumentativeness? Do Western concepts of romantic, platonic, parent–child, and sibling relationships apply only to people from individualistic cultures? These and other questions suggest the need for continued investigation into the impact that argumentativeness and verbal aggressiveness exert on interpersonal relationships of all types.

Discussion Questions for Chapter 4

1. Why do you think people who are high in verbal aggressiveness see using verbal aggression toward others as justifiable, whereas those people who are low in verbal aggressiveness see any use of verbal aggression as unjustified?

2. Why do you think married couples who are asymmetrical (one being high in argumentativeness and one being low in argumentativeness) report being more satisfied than couples who are symmetrical in argumentativeness?

3. What is the skills deficiency explanation of interspousal violence? Do you agree with this explanation? Why?

4. Why is the authoritative parenting style associated with parents who are lower in verbal aggressiveness and higher in argumentativeness? Do you think this is the most effective parenting style? Why?

5. What is the relationship between parental verbal aggressiveness and the use of corporal punishment? Do you think that there would ever be a situation in which parental verbal aggression would be warranted? When?

5

Argumentative and Aggressive Communication in Organizational Contexts

O rganizational life can be, and often is, fraught with worry, conflict, and controversy. Concerns about securing employment, losing a job, and getting along with colleagues and superiors can be overwhelming at times. We all know that one person who vacillates between "I love my job" and "I hate my job." The notion of the mean and hostile boss has pervaded many facets of American culture and folklore and comes to us through television, popular music, cartoons, and sharing stories with friends. We enjoy watching the television and movie programs and listening to the songs and stories that show the worker exacting some degree of revenge on the boss. Perhaps there was a time in your life that you had a strong desire to tell your boss off. This act, as well as other forms of argumentative and aggressive communication in the organization, will be addressed in this chapter.

The organizational context has provided a fruitful base for investigating the traits of argumentativeness and verbal aggressiveness. First, we will review the theory of independent-mindedness, a corporatist theory specifically developed for the organizational context and based on these traits. We will also discuss literature that examines the influence that argumentative and aggressive communication has on feelings of being satisfied with work, coworkers, supervisors, and subordinates. We will then present more general findings on the influence of argumentativeness and verbal aggressiveness in the organizational context.

The Theory of Independent-Mindedness

Since the development of organizational theory, scholars and practitioners have sought to find ways to motivate employees, to make employees more productive, and to uncover factors that lead to worker satisfaction. To those ends, a myriad of theories have been developed and tested. An example of this was corporate America's push in the late 1970s and early 1980s to emulate the mind-set and work structure of Asian cultures. During that time, a belief existed that worker collectivity was the ultimate answer for raising worker productivity. In the late 1980s and early 1990s a popular organizational theory was William Edwards Deming's total quality management (TQM), one of a number of participatory models of productivity. During that period, many resources were put into developing methods of changing organizational culture. Given that so many organizations adopted the TQM philosophy, it is interesting that few still subscribe to its principles. This has led us to ask questions such as why some theories of management are more effective than others and why the same theory does not work equally well when applied to different cultures and organizations operating within those cultures.

In an effort to address this latter question, Infante (1987d) developed a model of organizational communication based on the traits of argumentativeness, verbal aggressiveness, contemporary organizational theory, and cultural assumptions about America and Americans. He argued, "Management by consensus is possible in a homogeneous and implicitly hierarchical culture. Deference to seniority and authority is expected and respected in Japan. Subordinates (or associates as they are called) communicate in a very respectful, nonconfrontational style" (Infante, 1987d, p. 4). The assumption here is that both theory and practice developed through research should be compatible not only with the organization, but also with the larger society within which the organization operates.

In the United States, very different assumptions about organizational behavior exist. Employees desire self-determination, autonomy, and expressions of individualism and tend to be resistant to conformity (Infante, 1987b). In an effort to conceptualize a theory of organizational effectiveness that best represents the American culture at large, elements of individual freedoms and freedom of expression must not only be included, but also be fostered by the organization. According to the theory of independent-mindedness, employee dissatisfaction is a function of the differences that exist between American values (macrostructure) and the values of the organization (microstructure). Hence, bringing these two structures into alignment will result in greater employee satisfaction.

To do this, Infante (1987b) suggests that organizations emphasize a superior–subordinate dialectic; that is, Infante recognized that power and status differences do exist between organizational members. His model is in sharp contrast to the participatory models which deemphasize power and status differences in organizations. However, this emphasis should be done using a communication style that is affirming in nature (i.e., making people feel that they are respected and valued). Affirming communication promotes the exchange of ideas by encouraging organizational members to argue organizational issues. Allowing for argumentative behavior in the organization better reflects a society that values individual expression and diversity of opinion. This premise is in direct opposition with the collectivistic approach advocated by Japanese management models. The notion of encouraging functional and productive argumentative exchanges between superior and subordinate is also a rather radical departure from the traditional scientific management model (Infante & Gorden, 1987).

An important assumption of the theory of independent-mindedness is that optimal corporatist theory is the ideal for superior human performance in the organization. Given this, greater employee motivation, satisfaction, and productivity are believed to occur when the organizational culture is congruent with the culture of the larger society. If this congruity does not exist in the organization, employees can become disenchanted and feel disconfirmed. In effect, an organization that does not pursue this balance is asking employees to be someone else when at work, and to be themselves only when they go home. The logic here is that employees' sense of self is a derivative of the society within which they live. Employees cannot be satisfied when asked to be a different self on the job. When basic rights and values are congruent, there is little differentiation between the culture at large and the organizational culture, thus bringing about a self-validating organizational culture. Infante (1987d) believes so strongly in this that he argues that the organization is a microstructure of the society at large and the organization's core values should be a mirror reflection of the society's core values.

The ideal corporate theory would optimize human productivity, provide more profit for owners, and provide an effective way to achieve this through fostering independent-mindedness in their employees. Independent-mindedness "represents resistance to conformity, a will toward self-determination and autonomy, and is therefore an expression of individualism. Independent-mindedness is nurtured in organizations which extol freedom of speech by encouraging argument of corporate issues and discouraging verbal aggression"

(Infante, 1987d, pp. 6–7). A part of independent-mindedness includes the concept of promoting an *employee voice*. Employee voice refers to an employee's ability to generate good reasons and arguments for job modifications and organizational change rather than to continue performing exclusively under the dictates of one's job description (Gorden, Infante, & Graham, 1988, p. 102). An added element of this perspective is that employers and employees should display affirming styles that reflect relaxed, friendly, and attentive patterns of communication. This type of pattern is believed to be an essential condition for effective superior–subordinate communication (Infante, 1987b).

Argumentativeness in the organization is a key element in the theory of independent-mindedness. Not only does Infante believe that argumentativeness is beneficial, but he advocates that both superior and subordinate be trained in argumentative communication. More specifically, employers are encouraged to provide their employees with training in argumentation, affirming communicator style, freedom of speech, small-group communication, and effective conflict management. The assumption is that a focus on these communication factors will have the effect of tangible organizational outcomes such as increased production rates and other bottom-line enhanced production outcomes.

In an effort to provide empirical evidence for the theory of independent-mindedness, Infante and Gorden (1987) sought to identify communication profiles that represented an independent-minded employee. In order to do so, they assessed superior–subordinate dyads drawn from over 100 organizations through the eastern and mid-western United States. Supervisors who agreed to participate completed the Communicator Style Measure (Norton, 1983; consisting of the dimensions of impression leaving, open, dramatic, dominant, precise, relaxed, friendly, attentive, animated, and communicator image), a short-form version of the Argumentativeness Scale, a short-form version of the Verbal Aggressiveness Scale, and items assessing upward effectiveness. The supervisor was asked to respond to the items by focusing on one specific subordinate. That subordinate was then asked to complete the same measures with reference to the supervisor.

The findings provided empirical support for the theory of independent-mindedness. Superiors who were perceived as being high in verbal aggressiveness and lower in argumentativeness were seen as inattentive, unfriendly, and, to a lesser degree, lower in impression leaving, less relaxed, and lower in communicator image. In terms of supervisors' perception of subordinates, the more subordinates were perceived to be high in verbal aggressiveness, the more they were perceived as dramatic, dominant, and only somewhat open. These high-verbal-aggressive–low-argumentative subordinates were also seen as less relaxed, less friendly, and less attentive.

When subordinates were seen as being high in argumentativeness, they were also viewed as being higher in communicator image and more precise, with moderate ratings of attentiveness, animation, relaxed, impression leaving, dominant, and friendly styles. Infante and Gorden (1987) concluded,

> Positive profiles would entail expressions of independent-mindedness as represented by argumentativeness mediated by affirming characteristics such as friendly and attentive communicator styles. Negative profiles would entail expressions that demeaned the self-worth of others, as represented by verbal aggressiveness, and would be coupled with disconfirming communicator style dimensions such as inattentiveness. (p. 79)

Infante and Gorden (1991) also tested the theory from a subordinate's perspective. A model containing four quadrants of supervisor behavior was comprised:

1. high argumentative/high affirming style (hypothesized to be the optimal communication pattern for the supervisor);

2. high argumentative/low affirming style (hypothesized to bring about moderate levels of satisfaction and commitment);

3. low argumentative/high affirming style (hypothesized to also bring about moderate levels of satisfaction and commitment); and

4. low argumentative/low affirming style (hypothesized to bring about the lowest levels of satisfaction and commitment).

It was believed that if subordinates perceived a supervisor as highly argumentative and affirming in his or her communication, they will also report greater organizational commitment, greater satisfaction with their supervisor, and greater satisfaction with their work.

The results showed strong support that the low argumentative/low affirming supervisor was seen as the least favorable to subordinates and this combination was significantly different than the other three. However, the other assumptions of the model only received limited support. Subordinates reported the low argumentative/high affirming supervisor to be significantly more desirable than the high argumentative/low affirming supervisor. Thus, it was concluded that employee organizational commitment and satisfaction may be primarily the function of a superior's affirming communicator style, with argumentativeness contributing to a somewhat lesser degree.

In another effort along these lines, Edge and Williams (1994) studied how the affirming communicator style of a supervisor influences the upward influence tactics subordinates used with superiors. The study employed a typology of upward influence tactics that included ingratiation and exchange (labeled as *soft tactics* because "they involve acting nice and flattering others" [Edge & Williams, p. 203]), rationality (labeled as a *rational tactic* using logic and bargaining), and assertiveness, upward appeal, and coalitions (labeled as *hard tactics* because "they involve demanding, applying pressure, and making assertions" [Edge & Williams, p. 203]). Overall, subordinates who perceive their immediate supervisor as exhibiting an affirming communicator style (i.e., highly relaxed, highly friendly, highly attentive) were less likely to use hard influence tactics to exert upward influence on the superior. Interestingly, the theory of independent-mindedness has received only modest research attention in organizational communication studies. This concern is heightened given the amount of empirical evidence supporting the theory. The next section will focus on a variety of studies that have examined argumentative and aggressive communication from both the supervisor's and subordinate's perspectives and the influence on relational and work satisfaction.

Organizational Satisfaction

Social scientists have expended much effort attempting to discover what makes people satisfied. In fact, satisfaction is one of the most frequently examined dependent variables in the social sciences. Several studies have been conducted to explore the influence argumentativeness and verbal aggressiveness have on organizational satisfaction. The studies that have focused on satisfaction generally are restricted to studying dyads such as subordinate–subordinate, supervisor–supervisor, or supervisor–subordinate. We will first discuss research focusing on argumentative and aggressive communication on subordinate satisfaction and then discuss related research concerning supervisor satisfaction.

Argumentativeness, Verbal Aggressiveness, and Satisfaction

Several studies investigating the influence of argumentativeness and aggressive communication on employee satisfaction have been conducted. Infante and Gorden (1985b) investigated whether argumentativeness and verbal aggressiveness would be significant predictors of subordinate satisfaction. Employees from a variety of organizations completed the Argumentativeness Scale, the Verbal Aggressiveness Scale, and measures assessing their employee rights, satisfaction with supervisor, and satisfaction with upward communication.

The results indicated that the more a supervisor was perceived as higher in argumentativeness and lower in verbal aggressiveness, the greater the subordinate's satisfaction. Further, the gender of the supervisor did not affect the findings.

A series of studies have focused on subordinates' perceptions of organizational voice and rights. Gorden and Infante (1987) collected data from a diverse sample of employees in food service, education, retail, real estate, religious, financial, manufacturing, recreation, military, and construction organizations. The main speculation was that the more favorable or important employees feel their rights are, the more they will report their superiors as being higher in argumentativeness and lower in verbal aggressiveness and report being more satisfied.

Participants were assessed twice, 10 days apart. Overall, the results showed that employees value their organizational rights more when they perceive their supervisors as being lower in verbal aggressiveness. Although employee reports of superiors' argumentativeness was positively related to employee rights, supervisors' level of argumentativeness did not explain employee satisfaction as well as supervisors' level of verbal aggressiveness. As such, argumentativeness was not viewed as a significant predictor of employee satisfaction.

From these findings, Gorden and Infante (1987) concluded that the more subordinates perceive their supervisors to be higher in verbal aggressiveness, the less the subordinates report a sense of employee rights within the organization. The destructive nature of verbal aggressiveness, when displayed by a supervisor, creates an organizational climate that results in lower employee satisfaction and potentially greater damage to the subordinate's self-concept. In this case, "it seems likely that subordinates would infer that they are not respected as individuals. Such an inference would be a determinant for unfavorable perceptions of employee rights" (Gorden & Infante, p. 161).

In a study on employee voice, Gorden, Infante, and Izzo (1988) assessed superiors from a variety of organizations to explain what factors best distinguish satisfied supervisors, undecided supervisors, and dissatisfied supervisors regarding their subordinates. It was thought that supervisors would be more satisfied with subordinates who exhibit constructive disagreement styles (i.e., higher in argumentativeness and lower in verbal aggressiveness) than subordinates who exhibit apathetic (i.e., simply do not complain because it will not make a difference) or complainer styles (i.e., voice disagreement not to bring about change but to ruffle the feathers of the supervisor).

The findings revealed that the more satisfied supervisors are with subordinates, the more positive statements they make about the subordinates' dependability and attitude (i.e., the employee can be depended on and exhibits a positive attitude toward work), work quality (i.e., the employee is effective in completing the job), and interpersonal skills (i.e., the employee gets along well with other workers and can be a team player). Further, the subordinate who uses a complainer style was perceived as being higher in verbal aggressiveness than subordinates who exhibited an apathetic or constructive disagreement style. Subordinates who exhibit the constructive disagreement style were perceived as higher in argumentativeness than either the complainer or the apathetic styles respectively. Taken as a whole, subordinates who use the complainer style of disagreement are less argumentative and more verbally aggressive than the subordinate who uses the constructive style of disagreement. In effect, the employee who exhibits independent-mindedness in the workplace has the benefit of being viewed as a better employee than subordinates who are not seen as independent-minded.

Supervisor ratings of subordinates' communicator style, argumentativeness, and verbal aggressiveness were investigated by Infante and Gorden (1989). They asked superiors to rate subordinates with whom they were very satisfied, undecided, and very dissatisfied. These three levels of satisfaction, along with sex of superior and sex of subordinate, constituted the independent variables in the study. Argumentativeness, verbal aggressiveness, and the 10 communicator style variables (i.e., impression leaving, open, dramatic, dominant, precise, relaxed, friendly, attentive, animated, and communication image) were also examined.

The cluster of a subordinate being low in verbal aggressiveness and high in relaxed, friendly, and attentive styles thus exhibits an affirming communicator style. Supervisors who were satisfied with an employee's job performance reported the employee as being lower in verbal aggressiveness and higher in argumentativeness, more impression leaving, open, precise, relaxed, friendly, attentive, animated, and having a more favorable communication image. Superiors who were very dissatisfied with an employee's performance reported just the opposite. In addition, differences were observed regarding gender in that male subordinates, regardless of the gender of the superior, were viewed as more verbally aggressive than female subordinates. Conversely, female subordinates were viewed as being friendlier than their male counterparts.

The research program of Infante, Gorden, and their associates on argumentative and verbally aggressive communication in the organization is not limited to supervisor perceptions of good and bad subordinates. Indeed, a series of studies were conducted examining subordinates' perceptions of supervisors. For example, one study assessed subordinates' perceptions of their superiors' argumentativeness and verbal aggressiveness and the influence these traits have on subordinate satisfaction (Infante & Gorden, 1985b). Employees from a variety of organizations completed the short-form versions of the Argumentativeness and Verbal Aggressiveness scales, an employee rights measure, a measure of career satisfaction, and several demographic questions. The results showed that subordinates who reported their supervisor (regardless of sex) as being low in verbal aggressiveness and high in argumentativeness also reported higher levels of satisfaction with the supervisor. The relationships observed in this study did not depend on the subordinate and supervisor being similar in argumentativeness. In other words, regardless of subordinates' levels of argumentativeness and verbal aggressiveness, subordinates are more satisfied with a highly argumentative and low verbally aggressive supervisor.

Extending this line of research, Infante, Anderson, Martin, Herington, and Kim (1993) hypothesized that the more constructive communication traits a supervisor is perceived to possess (e.g., high in argumentativeness, low in verbal aggressiveness, and exhibiting an affirming communicator style), the higher the subordinate's threshold for negative affect. This suggests that subordinates will tend to not get upset as quickly if the supervisor is perceived as having a constructive communication orientation. Further, Infante et al. believed that subordinate satisfaction will also increase as the degree of perceived supervisor constructive communication increases.

To examine these speculations, respondents completed the Argumentativeness and Verbal Aggressiveness scales; the relaxed, friendly, and attentive dimensions of Norton's (1983) Communicator Style Scale Measure; and a modified version of Marwell and Schmitt's (1967) compliance-gaining strategies (altered to reflect the organizational context). The results demonstrated strong support for the hypotheses in that the greater the number of constructive traits the supervisor was perceived to have, the fewer compliance-gaining strategies the supervisor used and the more satisfied the subordinate. Subordinates also reported having an increased threshold for negative affect with supervisors who possess constructive communication traits.

These satisfaction studies point out the impact that argumentative and verbally aggressive communication have on superior and subordinate perceptions of quality of work-life. That is, constructive communication (i.e., argumentativeness) positively impacts and destructive communication (i.e., verbal aggressiveness) negatively impacts the quality of work-life as perceived by subordinates and supervisors alike.

Argumentativeness, Verbal Aggressiveness, and Gender Differences in the Organization

Gender differences regarding argumentativeness and verbal aggressiveness have been identified (Nicotera & Rancer, 1994; Rancer & Dierks-Stewart,

1985). These comparisons are especially important in the workplace due to the gender inequity that still exists regarding financial compensation and other organization benefits. The research on gender also indicates differences between men and women and the perceived appropriateness of argumentativeness and verbal aggressiveness in the organization.

In two studies concerning argumentativeness in the workplace, Schullery (1999) surveyed men employed full-time to determine whether their supervisory level was related to their level of argumentativeness. Respondents completed the Argumentativeness Scale and several demographic questions. The results indicated that those in supervisory positions reported having more moderate levels of argumentativeness than those in nonsupervisory roles. While these findings seem contrary to other studies that identified benefits of high argumentativeness in the organization, it may be that extremes of any trait (e.g., extremely high or extremely low levels of argumentativeness) could be viewed as potentially less desirable.

Schullery (1998) also sought to discover the optimal level of argumentativeness for women in the organization, given that argumentativeness has been linked to pro-organizational outcomes such as leadership and decision making. As such, there should be an optimal level of the trait reported by female supervisors. A sample of nonsupervisory females and female supervisors completed the Argumentativeness Scale and a series of demographic questions. A plot of their scores showed that moderate levels of argumentativeness were characteristic of women who hold higher-level positions. As with the male sample in Schullery's previous study (1999), extremely high or extremely low levels of argumentativeness may be more associated with nonsupervisory positions. While provocative, these findings do not suggest cause-and-effect relationships but indicate that for people who hold higher positions in the organizations studied, moderate levels of argumentativeness may be preferred. Given the preponderance of research cited in this chapter suggesting the value of being high or higher in argumentativeness, Schullery's findings should be subject to further examination.

In a study on gender bias in the organization, Infante and Gorden (1985a) speculated that women who exhibit what has been traditionally stereotyped as the male trait of being argumentative may also suffer from a negative bias. To test this, male and female supervisors completed measures of career satisfaction, perceived upward effectiveness, the Argumentativeness Scale, and a series of demographic questions. Although sex and age were strongly related with organizational success, argumentativeness was only slightly related. A profile emerged suggesting that a person who is younger and female, and to a lesser extent argumentative, reported a lower salary. Overall the findings show that there may be a bias toward women regarding organizational communication outcomes. However, this bias appears to be more gender based and not related to the argumentativeness of women. Further, the findings also suggested that older people in general (with a slight edge toward older males), and who are higher in argumentativeness, report greater perceived upward communication effectiveness, greater career satisfaction, and increased salaries.

Gender research in the workplace has been studied from many different perspectives. One central gender issue in contemporary organizations is that of sexual harassment. Argumentativeness has been found to influence perceptions of sexual harassment. Booth-Butterfield and Brusberg (1989) hypothesized that the more argumentative employees reported being, the less they would perceive sexually harassing communication. A sample consisting of males and females completed the Argumentativeness Scale, the Perception of Sexual Harassment Scale, and a job description index. The study revealed that as employees' level of argumentativeness increases, fewer messages and behaviors are perceived as being sexually harassing. One implication of this finding is "that high argumentative supervisors may not be responsive to complaints of any but the most severe or blatant harassment" (Booth-Butterfield & Brusberg, p. 8).

The investigation of the influence that argumentative and verbally aggressive communication has on gender and gender-related issues within the organizational context remains a rich area for empirical examination. As these studies reveal, there are still many unanswered questions that await organizational communication research efforts, and we will suggest a few of them in Chapter 12.

Argumentativeness, Verbal Aggressiveness, and Other Organizational Constructs

Although most research on argumentative and aggressive communication in the organizational context has had some form of satisfaction as an important outcome variable, studies have also focused on other communication factors. Kassing and Avtgis (1999) surveyed 192 full-time employees from a variety of organizations to investigate the influence that argumentative and aggressive communication has on how people express dissent. Organizational dissent is conceptualized as the various strategies that people use to voice their displeasure in the workplace. Kassing (1998) suggests that organizational dissent is comprised of three dimensions: (1) *articulated dissent* (i.e., expressing dissent openly to people who can bring about change); (2) *latent dissent* (i.e., expressing dissent to audiences within the organization, but who really cannot change the bothersome condition); and (3) *displaced dissent* (i.e., expressing dissent to audiences outside of the workplace such as friends and family). Kassing and Avtgis speculated that employees higher in argumentativeness would employ more articulated dissent and less displaced dissent than employees lower in argumentativeness. Conversely, they speculated employees reporting higher levels of verbal aggressiveness would employ more latent and less articulated dissent than employees with lower verbal aggressiveness.

Respondents completed short-form versions of both the Argumentativeness and Verbal Aggressiveness scales and the Organizational Dissent Scale. The results showed partial support for the hypotheses, in that both argumentativeness and verbal aggressiveness were significant predictors of articulated dissent use. The highly argumentative employee reported using the strategy of articulated dissent more, whereas the highly verbally aggressive employee reported using the strategy of articulated dissent less. Further, employee verbal aggressiveness was a significant predictor of latent dissent. Employee argumentativeness and verbal aggressiveness were not found to be significant predictors of the displaced dissent strategy use. Taken as a whole, the results suggest that the highly argumentative employee is more likely to employ dissent strategies that may bring about effective change in the work environment, whereas the highly verbally aggressive employee is more likely to enact strategies that serve as a complaint session to other organizational members who cannot bring about effective change (Kassing & Avtgis, 1999).

Martin, Anderson, and Sirimangkala (1997) investigated argumentativeness and verbal aggressiveness and their influence on employee conflict strategies. Subordinates were instructed to reference their supervisor while completing short-form versions of the Argumentativeness and Verbal Aggressiveness scales along with the Organizational Communication Conflict Instrument and a measure of socio-communicator style.

Control strategies, often used to intimidate another person, focus on verbal and nonverbal messages designed to get one's own way (Martin, Anderson, & Sirimangkala, 1997). Solution-oriented strategies involve actively working with another person by compromising one's own goals or collaborating with another to achieve a mutually beneficial resolution (Martin, Anderson, & Sirimangkala). Nonconfrontation strategies are strategies that do not directly address the nature of the conflict. The results indicated that subordinates who were high in argumentativeness tend to use control and solution-oriented strategies such as collaboration but do not use compromise and nonconfrontation strategies. The highly verbally aggressive subordinates reported using control and noncompromising strategies while also reporting using noncollaborative strategies. While these findings may seem somewhat similar in that highly argumentative employees reported using similar conflict strategies to those of the high verbally aggressive employee, one clear difference exists. Whereas highly argumentative employees tend to collaborate more with their supervisor in an attempt to achieve a mutually beneficial outcome, high verbally aggressive employees are not likely to use collaboration.

What is the effect of communication avoidance on organizational members' tendencies toward argumentative and verbally aggressive communication? In an effort to address this question, Cole and McCroskey (2003) assessed employees from a variety of organizations in the mid-eastern United States. Participants completed two measures of avoidance (i.e., communication apprehension and shyness) and measures of credibility, affect, and verbal aggressiveness. The results revealed a strong positive relationship between employee apprehension toward the supervisor and the use of verbal aggression toward the supervisor. That is, as employees' fear of communication with their supervisor increases, so does their predisposition to engage in verbal aggressiveness. Cole and McCroskey suggest that the employees' use of verbal aggression may be a lashing out response due to either the lack of communication skills or the perceived threat of the encounter.

The impact of argumentative and aggressive communication on the employment selection interview was studied by Lamude, Scudder and Simmons (2003). People seeking employment completed measures of communication apprehension (with regard to the employment interview), and the Argumentativeness and Verbal Aggressiveness scales. The results supported the findings of the Cole and McCroskey (2003) study in that interview apprehension was positively related with verbal aggressiveness. Further, apprehension about the interview was negatively related with argumentativeness. Thus, as apprehension toward the employment interview increases, the level of verbal aggressiveness increases and the level of argumentativeness decreases.

Anderson and Martin (1999) believed that small-group cohesion, consensus, and satisfaction would be positively related to argumentativeness and negatively related to verbal aggressiveness. Studying members of ongoing task groups, Anderson and Martin determined this speculation was partially supported in a study that revealed that group members who were somewhat argumentative, and not verbally aggressive, reported more group satisfaction, believed that their group was more likely to reach consensus, and had greater group cohesion. Studies like this that focus on situational aspects of organizational life highlight the need for further research in this area.

Argumentative encounters in the workplace are bound by different rules than arguments with family members or friends. Perceptions of the appropriateness of engaging in workplace argumentation is a complex issue addressed by Logue (1987), who asked employees from several different organizations to report on their organizational argumentativeness (via a modified version of the Argumentativeness Scale) and to respond to a series of questions as to whether arguing in the workplace is acceptable or appropriate, or both. The results suggested that employees reported taking workplace arguments seriously. They also reported that they are moderately effective in arguing and have generally positive feelings associated with winning an argument. However, the employees did express a preference to avoid arguments in the workplace, as well as a preference to associate with people who agree with their opinions.

This study highlights the commonly held belief that arguing in the workplace is bad and that harmony is preferred over argumentative discourse on the job. This belief, still pervasive throughout a number of American organizations, provides great challenges for the implementation of corporatist theories that advocate constructive, yet argumentative communication in the organization. As noted, the theory of independent-mindedness suggests that in order to be successful, both superior and subordinate should possess favorable beliefs about arguing organizational issues in the workplace. However, the Logue (1987) study was conducted during a time when Asian management theories that discourage open discussion of conflict were more popular. A replication of this study in today's corporate world may show marked differences in appreciation of workplace argument.

In a study comparing arguments at work with arguments in the home, Nicotera and DeWine (1991) found little difference in coworker and family member reports of a subject's argumentativeness when compared to the subject's self-report. This supports the notion of the consistency of the argumentativeness trait across several different contexts. Using a variation of this method, Infante, Myers, and Buerkel (1994) conducted an experiment to see if context had an effect on perceptions of constructive and destructive disagreements. They wondered whether the family and organizational contexts influence constructive and destructive disagreements. In the study, participants were randomly assigned to be either participants or observers and then randomly assigned to either the constructive disagreement condition (i.e., disagreements having very positive outcomes) or the destructive disagreement condition (i.e., disagreements having very negative outcomes). Participants were then asked to provide a written account of a recent disagreement with a family member and a coworker. Depending on the condition, participants provided either constructive or destructive accounts for each context. After completing the account, the participants were then asked to rate the account in terms of how constructive they thought it was.

Approximately 1 week later, the observers read an account of either a family or work disagreement that was either constructive or destructive. The results revealed that both participants and observers perceive greater levels of verbal aggression in family as opposed to organizational disagreements. The researchers concluded, "Our basic thinking was that verbal aggression is inhibited more in the organization because of the potential for social disapproval, especially from superiors, for a generally undesirable form of communication" (Infante, Myers, & Buerkel, 1994, p. 81).

In an attempt to extend the taxonomy of verbally aggressive messages, Infante, Rancer, and Ambler (1994) developed an enhanced classification system for coding verbal aggression that could be used profitably in assessing workplace aggressiveness. Additional types of verbally aggressive messages were identified, including *blame* (a verbal attack in which one person singles out another person as being solely at fault for a problem); *personality attacks* (a verbal attack in which one person demeans another person's personality or other traits); *command* (a verbal attack in which one person aggressively commands another person to do something); *physical appearance attacks* (a verbal attack directed at the physical characteristics of other people); *global rejection/disconfirmation* (a verbal attack in which one individual rejects or disconfirms another person without reference to any specific behavior); *negative comparison* (a verbal attack in which one person is unfavorably compared to another person); and *sexual harassment* (using some sort of sexual messages or comparisons to degrade another person). This taxonomy represents a more comprehensive one than was presented in Chapter 1 and may be especially productive for assessing argumentative and aggressive communication in the organizational context.

Conclusion

As evidenced in this chapter, our understanding of organizational communication has been enhanced by including knowledge of the traits of argumentativeness and verbal aggressiveness. The theory of independent-mindedness, truly a communication theory, focuses on the matching of cultural expectations regarding freedom of expression with the constructive expression of disagreement in the workplace. Put plainly, encouraging and even training employees to engage in argument is seen as a central component to productivity and satisfaction in organizations operating in the United States and other Western cultures. The evidence reported in this chapter supports such a notion.

Although some research suggests that too much of any personality trait (e.g., argumentativeness) may be seen as less appropriate or desirable, overwhelmingly the studies reviewed in this chapter endorse the idea that argumentativeness is a trait exhibited by satisfied and upwardly mobile employees, whereas verbal aggressiveness is exhibited by dissatisfied and disenfranchised organizational members. The future of argumentative and aggressive communication in organizations ranges from the continued validation and extension of the theory of independent-mindedness, to further examination of the influence gender exerts on perceptions of argumentative and aggressive communication at work, to the continued investigation of moderating variables (i.e., variables that influence argumentative and aggressive communication such as ethnic diversity and organizational complexity) unique to the organizational context.

Discussion Questions for Chapter 5

1. What are the basic assumptions of the theory of independent-mindedness? Do you agree with this theory? Why?

2. According to the theory of independent-mindedness, what is the ideal communication profile for supervisors and subordinates? Have you known a supervisor who exhibited this communication profile? Describe the quality of your relationship.

3. Do organizational gender studies support the notion that women high in argumentativeness are perceived differently than men? Why?

4. Regardless of how high the level of argumentativeness is, is it always beneficial in the organization? If not, when and how is it not beneficial?

5. Based on your experience, how does argumentative and aggressive communication in the organization differ from that found in the family?

6

Argumentative and Verbally Aggressive Communication in Instructional Contexts

Think about the best learning experience you have had. You might recall an example from elementary school, high school, or college or a time when you took some type of training program. Now, think of some factors that led you to consider this as one of the best. If your response is similar to most people, you will immediately focus on the instructor. The factors that made this learning experience so pleasurable are likely to include a cluster of instructor attributes such as being helpful, interesting, engaging, knowledgeable, and humorous. You may have had an instructor who learned your name and called on you by name. You may have had an instructor who challenged you in a positive way which resulted in you performing at the highest level or one who challenged your ideas but did so in a way that respected you and stimulated you to learn more about a topic. We are confident that a number of instructors you have experienced fit into this category.

Now, think of the worst learning experience you have had. Again, if you are similar to most people, you will first recall characteristics of the individual doing the instruction. This instructor may have also challenged your ideas, but did so in a way that made you feel ignorant or inferior. This instructor may have responded to you verbally with disdain and sarcasm or nonverbally with a demeaning tone of voice, smirks, or dirty looks. The instructor may have actually said something such as, "That's the most ridiculous answer I have ever heard," among other verbal put-downs. We hope that your experiences with this type of instructor have been few and far between.

Because our educational experiences have such a profound impact on our lives, researchers have investigated many aspects of teacher–student classroom interaction and especially the role teacher communication plays in student perceptions of classroom instruction. Several dimensions of what constitutes constructive and destructive teacher–student interaction have been identified. Much of this research has been produced by communication scholars who have focused on the impact of the instructor's communication behavior, especially in higher education contexts (see Chesebro & McCroskey, 2002; Kearney, Plax, & Allen, 2002; Vangelisti, Daly, & Friedrich, 1999). Some of this research has investigated teacher nonverbal immediacy behaviors (i.e., perceptions of the teacher's physical or psychological closeness; see Richmond, 2002b), teacher's predisposition to use humor in the classroom (Wanzer, 2002), teacher's use of power in the classroom (Richmond & McCroskey, 1992), and teacher socio-communicative style (i.e., focusing on how competent the teacher is as a consequence of the amount of assertive and responsive behavior; see Richmond, 2002a, p. 105). Research has even identified a cluster of teacher misbehaviors (what teachers say and do that students do not like; see Kearney, Plax, Hays, & Ivey, 1991).

Developing profiles of what makes a competent instructor based on communication behaviors and especially from a trait perspective has largely been accomplished by communication scholars. Ann Bainbridge Frymier, Joan Gorham, Dominic Infante, Matthew Martin, James McCroskey, Diane Millette, Timothy Mottet, Scott Myers, Patricia Kearney, Timothy Plax, K. David Roach, Virginia Richmond, and Melissa Wanzer have been especially instrumental in these efforts. Over the past several years researchers have begun to examine systematically the impact of teacher and student trait argumentativeness and verbal aggressiveness as factors that influence teacher–student classroom interaction and student learning outcomes.

Consistent with the focus of this book, in this chapter we will review and synthesize a growing body of research on the effects of argumentative and verbally aggressive communication in the instructional context. For the most part, this research has investigated students' perceptions of their instructors argumentative and verbally aggressive message behaviors in the college classroom. We will explore how these perceptions influence students' motivation to learn, their emotional reactions to learning, their ability to learn, and their satisfaction with instruction. Although few studies have examined characteristics of students' argumentativeness and verbal aggressiveness in the communication classroom, we will also review the findings and implications from those studies as well. We are encouraged that our understanding of instructor communication competence has been increased due to these efforts and that the argumentative and aggressive communication traits have been incorporated in these research programs.

The greatest number of studies investigating how argumentativeness and verbal aggressiveness functions in the instructional context have been conducted by Myers and his colleagues (e.g., Myers, 1998, 2001, 2002; Myers & Knox, 1999, 2000; Myers & Rocca, 2000a, 2000b, 2001). According to Myers (2003, p. 4), studies focusing on perceptions of instructor argumentative and verbally aggressive communication can be separated into four distinct areas: (1) studies exploring perceived instructor argumentativeness alone; (2) studies exploring perceived instructor verbal aggressiveness alone; (3) studies exploring both of perceived instructor argumentativeness and verbal aggressiveness; and (4) studies exploring instructor use of verbally aggressive messages. In this chapter we will utilize this taxonomy to review and discuss the research.

The Influence of Instructor Trait Argumentativeness

Throughout this book we have reviewed research that attempts to make the case that argumentativeness is a constructive communication trait. We have reported on research in both family and organizational contexts that argues convincingly that being higher in trait argumentativeness enhances communication outcomes. In this section, we will explore whether the positive outcomes of being argumentative also emerge in the instructional context.

Certain elements make the instructional context different and unique. For example, students constitute the inputs and outputs of the learning organization, whereas in more traditional business organizations, raw materials and goods and services usually constitute inputs and outputs. However, the instructional context is similar to other (i.e., organizational) contexts in some aspects. For example, in the classroom context the teacher–student relationship mirrors the superior–subordinate relationship observed in organizations. It is in this superior–subordinate relationship that the personality characteristics and trait orientations of the participants become especially potent for successful interaction. For example, in traditional superior–subordinate relationships important questions arise such as, "How open is a superior to feedback from subordinates?" "In what manner does the superior challenge the positions taken by subordinates on organizational issues?" and "How does the superior communicate when there is disagreement or conflict?" The personality and communication traits of teachers and students in instructional contexts also emerge as critical factors for the success, satisfaction, and productivity of that relationship. In the classroom, students are often influenced as much by the instructor as by what they learn from the course content. This has led Roach (1995a) to suggest, "Teacher argumentativeness, as a communication predisposition, may have great influence on teacher-student interactions and thus is likely to affect student learning" (p. 15).

Roach has been instrumental in investigating the impact of instructor argumentativeness in the teacher–student relationship. In one of the earliest studies on this topic, he examined the relationship between teacher argumentativeness and several instructor demographic characteristics. Given that argumentativeness is conceptualized as a positive and valuable trait that has been found to contribute to communication competence, Roach recognized that a teachers' level of argumentativeness is likely to impact their interactions with students, colleagues, principals, and parents, especially when those interactions involve disagreements, differences of opinion, and other interactions marked by conflict and controversy. If teachers are too low in argumentativeness, their communication competence may suffer, as they may not able to communicate as effectively and may be unable to challenge students' ideas and positions constructively.

In a seminal effort to understand the argumentativeness of teachers, Roach (1992) suggested that several teacher demographic variables (e.g., teacher gender, teacher age, teaching experience, grade level taught, and length of employment within a given institution) might influence a teacher's level of argumentativeness.

To address these relationships, Roach (1992) examined public school teachers who completed the Argumentativeness Scale (Infante & Rancer, 1982) and provided demographic data on themselves and their schools. A relationship between teacher gender, teacher age, teacher grade level, and teacher argumentativeness was observed. Consistent with previous research suggesting sex and gender differences in argumentativeness (Nicotera & Rancer, 1994; Rancer & Dierks-Stewart, 1985), male teachers reported higher levels of argumentativeness than female teachers. In addition, older teachers reported being more argumentative than younger teachers, and teachers of upper level grades (e.g., high school and university) reported being higher in argumentativeness than teachers of elementary school grades. As a consequence of these findings, Roach suggested that younger teachers, female teachers, and teachers of lower grades might profit from argumentative skills training. Further, he argued that school principals and other administrators should consider creating school climates conducive to freedom of speech and independent-mindedness (see Chapter 5).

A number of studies have examined teachers' use of power in the classroom. Hurt, Scott, and McCroskey (1978) define teacher power as "a teacher's ability to affect in some way the student's well-being beyond the student's own control" (p. 124). Teacher power use has been related to student cognitive (thinking) and affective (emotional) learning, as well as student motivation to learn (see McCroskey & Richmond, 1983; Richmond & McCroskey, 1992). Those who engage in argumentative activity to seek compliance from others are said to be exhibiting the use of *social power*. As such, students might perceive teacher argumentativeness as the exercise of teacher power (Roach 1995a, p. 17).

Five bases of teacher power have been identified. McCroskey and Richmond (1983) adapted French and Raven's (1959) taxonomy of power and identified the following five bases of teacher power: (1) coercive power refers to a student's expectation of being punished if he or she does not comply with the teacher's request; (2) reward power refers to the degree to which a teacher can provide a reward to a student for complying with the teacher's request; (3) legitimate power is based upon the student's perception that the teacher has the right to make requests and demands because of his or her position as the teacher; (4) referent power is based on the student's desire to identify with and please the teacher; and (5) expert power is based on the student's perception of the teacher's competence and knowledge (McCroskey & Richmond, 1983, pp. 176–177). Questions concerning the relationship between teacher use of power and teacher argumentativeness emerge and need to be researched.

Questions also emerge regarding the relationship between teacher argumentativeness and student affective learning. Affective learning is concerned with students' attitudinal and emotional reactions toward the course instructor and the course content. Research has found that when students have lower affect for instruction, they "learn less, engage in recommended (course) behaviors less often, are less responsive in the classroom, are less likely to comply with a teacher's request, and if not forced to attend class, will attend class less frequently" (Richmond & Gorham, 1996, p. 183). Roach (1995a) wondered whether highly argumentative instructors who engage and challenge students would engender more or less favorable reactions from them. Although previous research suggests that we might anticipate more favorable reactions from students who have highly argumentative instructors, Roach questioned whether a student might misinterpret a highly argumentative instructor's behaviors as an attempt to dominate or attack them personally and thus confuse the teacher's argumentative behavior with verbally aggressive behavior. As such, decreased student affective learning and a negative teacher–student relationship might result. In addition, a highly argumentative instructor might also be seen by students as too forceful in the display of teacher power.

Roach (1995a) investigated these issues by testing the effect of teacher argumentativeness on student affective learning and perceptions of teacher use of power. In his study, teaching assistants (i.e., typically graduate students with limited teaching experience) were the focus for the instructor portion of the study. Two reasons were offered for this choice: first, teaching assistants constitute a major portion of instructional personnel at colleges and universities, and second, as TAs often lack the experience of regular faculty, their communication behavior may be more trait driven and less flexible when they interact with students. Three research questions were tested in this investigation: (1) Does student affective learning differ by instructors who vary in trait argumentativeness? (2) Does student perception of instructor power use differ by instructors who vary in trait argumentativeness? and (3) To what extent are teacher argumentativeness and student argumentativeness associated with student affective learning and perceptions of instructor power use?

Roach used data from male and female teaching assistants who represented a wide range of academic disciplines, and information from over 900 college students from classes taught by these teaching assistants was obtained. The TAs completed the Argumentativeness Scale and a set of demographic questions. The students completed scales designed to measure their perceptions of TA power use (Roach, 1994), their attitudes toward the course content, attitudes toward the instructor of the course, and the likelihood of engaging in the behaviors recommended in the course (McCroskey, 1994). Finally, the students also completed a self-report scale on their own motivation to argue.

Teaching assistant argumentativeness was found to be a predictor of student affective learning and teaching assistant use of referent power. Surprisingly, the results revealed that student affective learning was higher in classes taught by low, versus high or moderate argumentative, TAs. Students with low-argumentative TAs reported more favorable attitudes toward the course content, had more favorable attitudes toward the course instructor, and had greater affect toward the recommended course behaviors than students who were taught by TAs seen as moderate or high in argumentativeness. Roach also found that student perceptions of TA power use were higher in classes taught by low-argumentative TAs. That is, low-argumentative TAs were seen as using more legitimate (i.e., assigned power), referent (i.e., likeable), and expert (i.e., knowledgeable) power than moderate or high argumentative TAs (Roach, 1995a).

While these results appear contrary to expectations, they suggest that moderate or high levels of instructor argumentativeness, or both, might be misunderstood by students. That is, students may perceive any attack, even one directed at their position on an issue, as an attack on their self-concept. In essence, the students may have been confusing TA argumentativeness with verbal aggressiveness. As such, this confusion could be responsible for their reports of lower affective learning with more argumentative instructors. In addition, the actual level of TA argumentativeness might not be stimulating these negative effects on affective learning as much as the students' perceptions of their teacher's argumentativeness (Roach, 1995a, p. 25). In contrast to these findings, the results of research by Myers and Knox (2000) showed that perceived instructor argumentativeness was positively related with student affective learning. These discrepant findings may be due to the nature of the target instructor used. While the Myers and Knox study had students report on an instructor's argumentativeness, Roach asked students to report on their TAs argumentativeness. Whether perceived credibility, instructor teaching experience, or instructor title are reasons for the different findings, further research is needed to sort out the influence of teacher argumentativeness on student affective learning.

These studies suggest that it may be profitable to train both students and beginning teaching assistants on what constitutes argumentative and verbally aggressive communication, as well as how to argue constructively. First, students should be taught the constructive nature of argumentative behavior, and distinctions between argumentativeness and verbal aggressiveness need to be made clearer. Second, beginning teachers and teaching assistants should learn the skills associated with how to argue constructively (see Infante, 1988). In Chapter 10 we will provide suggestions on how you can combine an affirming communicator style with higher levels of trait argumentativeness to create more favorable perceptions of an argumentative person.

In his first study, Roach (1995a) used students' perceptions of teacher argumentativeness and power use as a way of classifying the instructors. In a follow-up study, TA argumentativeness and power use were explored from the TA's own self-perception (Roach, 1995b). Again, beginning teachers from a variety of academic disciplines completed both the Argumentativeness Scale and an instrument designed to measure their use of the five bases of teacher power in the classroom. Sample items from the teacher power measure include "The student should comply to please the instructor," and "The student must comply because the instructor has the authority/right to direct students in this context" (McCroskey, 1994; Roach, 1995b, p. 98). In this study, TAs' self-report of argumentativeness and their perceived use of referent and expert power were positively related. That is, those instructors who saw themselves as higher in argumentativeness also saw themselves as using more referent and expert power in the classroom. TAs high in trait argumentativeness also indicated greater overall use of power than TAs low in argumentativeness. As referent and expert power are considered more effective and appropriate bases of teacher power, argumentative teachers may be more constructive in their use of power in the classroom.

The Influence of Instructor Trait Verbal Aggressiveness

Throughout this book, we have noted the many destructive outcomes associated with being high in trait verbal aggressiveness. For example, we have reported on the dysfunctional outcomes associated with the use of verbally aggressive messages in relational, family, and organizational communication contexts. In this section, we will review the outcomes associated with teachers' trait verbal aggressiveness in the instructional context.

The question, "How does a teacher's verbal aggressiveness affect students' liking of a teacher?" was one of several examined by Rocca and McCroskey (1999). Recall that one of the teacher behaviors mentioned in the beginning of this chapter is teacher immediacy. Teacher immediacy behaviors are defined as verbal and nonverbal messages that indicate warmth, involvement, and physical or psychological closeness (see Andersen, 1999; Richmond, 2002b). Examples of verbal immediacy include behaviors such as calling students by their name, using pronouns such as *we* or *us*, praising students' responses, and using encouraging verbal prompts such as, "I'd like to hear more about your thoughts." Nonverbal immediacy behaviors include closer physical space between teacher and student, greater use of gestures, increased eye contact, and greater smiling behavior. Research suggests that teacher immediacy can enhance trust of the teacher, favorably influence perceptions of the teacher's competence, positively influence liking for a teacher, and increase compliance with a teacher's requests (Richmond, 2002b, p. 66).

Rocca and McCroskey (1999) hypothesized that the more verbally aggressive teachers are, the less immediate they will be perceived. The method they used to test this relationship is the *teacher recall procedure*. In this procedure, students are asked to complete questionnaires on the teacher they had in the "course which meets prior to this class" (p. 311). Plax, Kearney, McCroskey, and Richmond (1986) recommend this procedure as it allows for a wide range of teachers to be included as targets of student perceptions. Students first completed a short-form version of the Verbal Aggressiveness Scale that was adapted to focus on the teacher's communication with the student (e.g., "My instructor makes students feel worthless and stupid"). Students also completed the Nonverbal Immediacy Measure (Richmond, Gorham, & McCroskey, 1987), the perceived Homophily (i.e. Similarity) Scale (McCroskey et al., 1975), and a measure of interpersonal attraction (McCroskey & McCain, 1974) regarding a target teacher.

The results supported Rocca and McCroskey's (1999) prediction. Teachers who were seen as more immediate (i.e., smiled more, stood closer to students, used more gestures and more eye contact) were seen as less verbally aggressive. Conversely, teachers who were seen as more verbally aggressive were also seen as less immediate, less similar, and less task, socially, and physically attractive by their students. Rocca and McCroskey suggest that teachers should attempt to increase their use of immediacy behaviors and reduce their verbal aggressiveness to enhance student perceptions.

In a related study, Rocca (2004) speculated that when students feel that they are not in a supportive classroom climate, they are less likely to attend class. Rocca reasoned that the higher the perceived verbal aggressiveness of the teacher, the less supportive the classroom climate, and the less supportive the classroom climate, the greater the number of class absences. Using the teacher recall procedure, students responded to a set of instruments including a nonverbal immediacy measure, a modified version of the Verbal Aggressiveness Scale, and three attendance measures (i.e., how frequently they missed the target class throughout the semester, how frequently they attended the target class, and how many days they missed during the semester; p. 189). Students who perceived their instructors to be highly verbally aggressive reported lower class attendance. As a result, Rocca offers prescriptive advice for classroom instructors: Use less verbal aggression (including put-downs and sarcasm) and you will likely see more students attend class.

While these research findings point to the negative influence of instructor verbal aggressiveness in the classroom, most of the studies have been based on student perceptions of instructor communication rather than on an examination of actual instructor classroom behavior. Findings based on the use of this methodological constraint stimulated Schrodt (2003a) to suggest that a students' own level of trait verbal aggressiveness might influence the perception of their instructor's use of verbal aggression. Recall that some students may tend to see any verbal attack by an instructor, even an attack on the student's position on an issue, as being verbal aggression. Schrodt speculated that this perception may be more likely to occur when the student is high in trait verbal aggressiveness and low in self-esteem. That is, students who are high in trait verbal aggressiveness and report low self-worth might be the ones who are more likely to interpret an instructor's challenge to their position as verbal aggressiveness.

To test this speculation, Schrodt (2003a) had undergraduate students complete a short-form, self-report version of the Verbal Aggressiveness Scale, a self-report Self-Esteem Scale (Rosenberg, 1965), and a 10-item perceived Instructor Verbal Aggressiveness Scale (Myers & Rocca, 2000a). Students were classified as high, moderate, or low in trait verbal aggressiveness by their scores on the self-report Verbal Aggressiveness Scale. The results revealed that students who were moderate in verbal aggressiveness saw their instructors as being more verbally aggressive than those students who were low in self-reported verbal aggressiveness. No differences were found in perceived instructor verbal aggressiveness between the moderate and high verbally aggressive student groups.

Students with high levels of self-esteem also perceived their instructors as being lower in verbal aggressiveness than students who were moderate or low in self-esteem. No differences were observed between the moderate and low self-esteem groups on perceived instructor verbal aggressiveness. In general, the alternative methodological approach taken in this study helps refine our understanding of how student perceptions of instructors' traits emerge. That is, Schrodt (2003a) suggests that it is important to take into account how students' own trait characteristics (in this case, their verbal aggressiveness and self-esteem) influence perceptions of instructors' verbal aggressiveness.

The Influence of Instructor Trait Argumentativeness and Trait Verbal Aggressiveness

Several studies have examined the influence of instructor argumentativeness and verbal aggressiveness together to better understand the influence they have on students' perceptions of teachers and on classroom outcomes. For example, Myers (1998) investigated argumentativeness, verbal aggressiveness, and instructor socio-communicative style. Socio-communicative style refers to a communicator's use of assertive and responsive behaviors as seen by other people. Assertiveness refers to being interpersonally forceful and dominant, that is, a person's tendency to stand up for him- or herself. Characteristics associated with assertiveness include being independent, willing to take a stand, competitive, and leader-like (Richmond & McCroskey, 1990; Wheeless & Dierks-Stewart, 1981). Responsiveness refers to how a person responds to others in a sympathetic, passionate, and sincere way and includes characteristics such as being helpful, responsive to others, compassionate, sensitive to the needs of others, sincere, and friendly (Richmond & McCroskey; Wheeless & Dierks-Stewart). A person can be classified into one of four socio-communicative styles. For example, a competent individual is high in both assertiveness and responsiveness. A noncompetent individual is low in both assertiveness and responsiveness. Aggressive individuals are high in assertiveness and low in responsiveness, whereas submissive individuals are high in responsiveness and low in assertiveness (Richmond & McCroskey, 1995).

Previous research found that competent and aggressive communicators are higher in argumentativeness than noncompetent and submissive communicators (Martin & Anderson, 1996). Myers (1998) speculated that this finding should also be evident among classroom teachers and thus predicted that competent and aggressive instructors should be rated higher in argumentativeness than noncompetent and submissive instructors. Similarly, as verbal aggression is seen as damaging and destructive, noncompetent and aggressive instructors should be rated higher in verbal aggressiveness than competent and submissive instructors.

To test this, students were asked to report their perceptions of a target teacher's argumentativeness, verbal aggressiveness, and assertiveness and responsiveness. The hypotheses were supported. Competent and aggressive instructors were seen as higher in argumentativeness than noncompetent or submissive instructors. However, there were no differences between competent and aggressive instructors on perceived argumentativeness. Noncompetent and aggressive instructors were also seen as higher in verbal aggressiveness than competent or submissive instructors. These findings led Myers (1998) to recommend that teachers foster a competent socio-communicative style, along with being high in argumentativeness and low in verbal aggressiveness, to maximize favorable student perceptions.

In Chapter 1 we discussed a class of communication traits identified as presentation traits. One of the most well-researched of these presentation traits is communicator style, defined as an overall impression people make when communicating (Norton, 1983). Perceptions of an argumentative individual are favorably influenced if they are also highly relaxed, friendly, and attentive when engaged in an argument (i.e., exhibit an affirming communicator style). Myers and Rocca (2000a) suggested that students' perceptions of a teacher's argumentative, aggressive, and presentational traits might be related and suggested a relationship between instructor communicator style and instructor use of verbal aggression.

Myers and Rocca (2000a) had students complete scales designed to measure their perceptions of a target teacher's trait argumentativeness, verbal aggressiveness, and use of verbal aggression in the classroom. The students were also given descriptions of each of the 10 communicator style dimensions (impression leaving, contentious, open, dramatic, dominant, precise, relaxed, friendly, attentive, animated) and were asked to indicate whether the target instructor used each type of communicator style (Montgomery & Norton, 1981). Myers and Rocca (2000a) found that when instructors are seen as argumentative, they are also seen as leaving a positive impression and being more open, relaxed, attentive, animated, precise, dramatic, and dominant. This suggests that students see these communicator style behaviors as being associated with competent communication. Further, competent instructors are seen as more argumentative. When instructors are seen as being verbally aggressive, they are also seen as being contentious (i.e., quarrelsome, belligerent, and hostile), unfriendly, inattentive, tense, nonanimated, and low on impression-leaving. These findings suggest that verbally aggressive instructors "may not appear open to student questions, inquiries, or interaction" (Myers & Rocca, 2000a, p. 8). Finally, verbally aggressive instructors do leave an impression, albeit a negative one. Communicating with a highly friendly communicator style, however, can make even verbally aggressive instructors appear less verbally aggressive.

Perceptions of a college instructor's competence, argumentativeness, and verbal aggressiveness have also been studied with two major conclusions emerging: (1) competent instructors are rated higher in argumentativeness and (2) noncompetent instructors are rated higher in verbal aggressiveness (Myers, 1998). Earlier, research was presented that found student affective learning was higher in classes taught by low versus high or moderate argumentative TAs (Roach, 1995a). Given the many favorable outcomes associated with being argumentative, this finding was unexpected and stimulated Myers and Knox (2000) to revisit this issue. Student affective learning was thought to be positively related with perceived instructor argumentativeness and negatively with perceived instructor verbal aggressiveness. In addition, a relationship was suggested between instructor argumentative and aggressive traits and student satisfaction.

Using the teacher recall procedure, students completed short-form versions of the Argumentativeness and Verbal Aggressiveness scales, an Affect Learning Measure (Mottet & Richmond, 1998), and a measure of student satisfaction on a target instructor (only instructors, no TAs were used in this study). The findings revealed that when instructors challenge students' ideas and responses with argumentative forms of communication, they promote higher levels of affect toward the course and themselves, and students report being more satisfied. Conversely, when instructors challenge students' ideas and responses with verbally aggressive communication, they engender lower levels of affect toward the course and themselves, and students are less satisfied. Thus, to improve college students' experiences in the classroom, "college instructors should cultivate argumentative behaviors and suppress verbally aggressive behaviors" (Myers & Knox, 2000, p. 305).

While classroom climate is a complex and multidimensional concept, research has suggested that the classroom can have a supportive or defensive tone (see Gibb, 1961). The classes students like are generally seen as being more supportive than defensive. As such, perceptions of an instructor's communication behavior should affect perceptions of classroom climate. Instructors who are seen as high in argumentativeness (i.e., those who encourage dialogue and the free exchange of ideas), might be seen as fostering a supportive classroom climate. Conversely, instructors who engage in competence attacks, threats, and forms of verbal aggression toward students may be seen as fostering a defensive classroom climate. These speculations led Myers and Rocca (2001) to predict that instructor argumentativeness will be positively related, and instructor verbal aggressiveness negatively related, to perceived classroom climate.

Further, classroom apprehension (a type of situational anxiety experienced when students are asked to respond to questions or enter into impromptu discussions during class sessions) may be triggered by both instructor argumentativeness and verbal aggressiveness. Students who may not have the skills to be able to argue effectively, or who confuse argumentativeness with verbal aggressiveness, might also experience classroom apprehension. Finally, student state motivation (e.g., motivation in a particular class) might be positively related to instructor argumentativeness and negatively related to instructor verbal aggressiveness (Myers & Rocca, 2001).

To test this, students completed modified versions of the Argumentativeness and Verbal Aggressiveness scales, a Communication Climate Questionnaire (designed to measure their instructors' supportive and defensive communication behaviors; Hays, 1970), a student self-report in the Classroom Apprehension Participation Scale (Neer, 1987), and the Student Motivation Scale (Christophel, 1990) that was targeted toward the instructor and the course.

A number of interesting findings emerged. Surprisingly, instructor argumentativeness was not related to classroom climate perceptions. Myers and Rocca (2001) suggest that students may see instructor argumentativeness as an appropriate, normative, and expected instructor communication behavior. As such, it may not be a significant factor influencing perceptions of classroom climate. However, students who reported that their instructor was argumentative also reported greater motivation to do well in the class. Instructors who were seen as highly verbally aggressive, however, were also seen as promoting a less supportive classroom climate than instructors who were rated as moderate or low in verbal aggressiveness, and students with verbally aggressive instructors reported being less motivated to learn. Neither perceived instructor argumentativeness nor verbal aggressiveness was related to student reports of classroom apprehension. Although it is highly desirable, Myers and Rocca suggest that student participation may not be a necessity for the successful completion of a number of college courses and subjects.

Throughout this book we have suggested that the most constructive combination of traits would be for an individual to be high in argumentativeness and low in verbal aggressiveness. In a test of this speculation in the instructional setting, Myers (2002) examined whether an instructor's level of argumentativeness and verbal aggressiveness jointly influences student state motivation, affective learning, and student satisfaction. Only those teachers who were seen as both high in argumentativeness and low in verbal aggressiveness were studied. He speculated that student state motivation, affective learning, cognitive learning, and satisfaction would be positively associated with this type of instructor (i.e., a teacher who is high in argumentativeness and low in verbal aggressiveness).

Students completed modified versions of the Argumentativeness and Verbal Aggressiveness scales on a target instructor, a Student Motivation Scale, an Affective Learning Measure (for affect toward the course and the instructor, see Mottet & Richmond, 1998), a Cognitive Learning Loss Measure (to assess how much they have learned from the instructor and how much they could have learned if they took the course from an ideal instructor; Richmond, McCroskey, Kearney, & Plax, 1987), and a measure of satisfaction with their instructors. Instructors who were seen with this combination of traits (high in argumentativeness, low in verbal aggressiveness) were seen more favorably and "have students who are highly motivated, evaluate their instructors highly, report cognitive learning, are highly satisfied, and to a lesser degree, have positive affect toward the course content" (Myers, 2002, p. 117).

Another factor related positively with student evaluations is perceived understanding, which is defined as an individual's perception of his or her success or failure when attempting to communicate with another person (Cahn, 1984). Students' value instructors more, and evaluate them more favorably, when they believe that an instructor understands them (Cahn). Schrodt (2003b) investigated the relationship between students' perceptions of an instructor's argumentativeness, verbal aggressiveness, and perceived understanding in the classroom. He tested whether an argumentative instructor (i.e., one who challenges the beliefs and opinions of his or her students) would bring about an increase in perceived understanding or perceived misunderstanding. He also predicted that when students perceive an instructor as verbally aggressive, perceived understanding with the instructor will be lower. Schrodt also hypothesized that instructor argumentativeness would be positively related with perceptions of instructor credibility, whereas perceived verbal aggressiveness would be negatively related with instructor credibility and instructor evaluations.

Students completed modified versions of the Argumentativeness Scale and Verbal Aggressiveness Scale on a target instructor, the Teacher Credibility Scale (McCroskey & Young, 1981), and an evaluation of instructor quality on a departmental teaching evaluation form. They also indicated the extent to which they felt understood and misunderstood by that instructor by completing Cahn and Shulman's (1984) Feelings of Understanding/Misunderstanding Scale.

Although perceived instructor argumentativeness was found to be unrelated to students' feelings of being understood or misunderstood, the more students' saw that target instructor as being verbally aggressive, the less they felt perceived understanding with that instructor. In fact, when instructors were seen as engaging in competence attacks, ridicule, and sarcasm they were also perceived as being more likely to foster feelings of misunderstanding. However, perceived instructor argumentativeness related positively with overall teacher credibility, especially teacher competence. This suggests that college instructors can engage in argumentative behaviors without negative outcomes and that "argumentativeness may be viewed by students as an instrumental (and positive) communication behavior, enhancing their perceptions of their instructors as intelligent, trained, and informed" (Schrodt, 2003b, p. 117).

Instructor argumentativeness was only slightly and positively related with instructor evaluations, whereas instructors seen as verbally aggressive had much lower student evaluations. Schrodt's (2003b) study underscores the findings of other studies reviewed in this chapter: Being argumentative is viewed positively regarding perceptions of instructor competence and being verbally aggressive can contribute to decreased credibility and increased perceptions of feeling misunderstood. These findings support Infante and Rancer's (1996) general conclusion about the influence of these traits in other contexts, that trait argumentativeness is constructive whereas trait verbal aggressiveness is destructive.

The Influence of Instructor Use of Verbally Aggressive Messages

Several types of verbally aggressive message behaviors have been identified, including competence attacks, character attacks, profanity, teasing, ridicule, maledictions, threats, personality attacks, physical appearance attacks, negative comparison, disconfirmation, and nonverbal verbal aggression (Infante, 1987a, 1995b; Infante, Riddle, et al., 1992). Although numerous negative consequences of instructor verbal aggressiveness have been presented, several important questions remained unanswered: "To what extent are instructors, as perceived by students, using verbally aggressive messages in the classroom?" "Do male and female instructors differ in students' perceptions in the use of verbal aggression?" and "Is instructor use of verbally aggressive messages related to student affective learning?"

Myers and Knox (1999) addressed these questions. Instructors' use of verbal aggression was assessed by having students indicate how often they thought the instructor used character, competence, background, and physical appearance attacks as well as maledictions, teasing, ridicule, threats, swearing, and nonverbal emblems (e.g., gritting the teeth, making snarling facial expressions). They also indicated their attitude toward the course instructor, affect toward the course content, affect toward the recommended course behaviors, and their likelihood of engaging in the behaviors recommended in the course (McCroskey, 1994).

Although instructors were perceived as rarely using any of the 10 verbally aggressive messages, character attacks were seen as being used most often and nonverbal emblems were used the least often by teachers. While this finding might be considered both desirable and positive, Myers and Knox (1999) explain it by suggesting that students may not be paying much attention at all to the communication messages of instructors, whether they contain verbal aggression or not. Further, students may also be giving college instructors more latitude in what is considered acceptable communication behavior compared with elementary and secondary school teachers (Myers & Knox, p. 40). However, Myers and Knox also discovered that when instructors are seen as using verbally aggressive message behaviors (e.g., character, competence, background, and physical appearance attacks, as well as teasing, ridicule, threats, and nonverbal emblems), students do report lower levels of affective learning. A gender difference was also observed: male instructors were seen as using more profanity, teasing, and ridicule than female teachers. Although instructor use of verbal aggression is rare, when it is exhibited it has a powerful negative and dysfunctional effect on student affective learning.

Does instructor verbal aggression also adversely influence student motivation? Myers and Rocca (2000b) addressed this question by examining the relationship between 10 types of verbally aggressive messages and the students' current feelings (i.e., state motivation) about a given course and instructor. They had students complete a Student Motivation Scale (Christophel, 1990) and a Recall of Verbal Aggression Instrument (Infante, Chandler-Sabourin, Rudd, & Shannon, 1990) on a target teacher. They also indicated how often that instructor used character, competence, background, and physical appearance attacks as well as maledictions, teasing, ridicule, threats, profanity, and nonverbal verbal aggression in class.

Not surprisingly, it was found that students reported lower motivation to learn when they saw their instructor using character, competence, and background attacks as well as threats, disparaging comments, and nonverbal verbal aggression (e.g., a grimacing face or demeaning tone of voice). Again, instructor use of profanity was not related to student state motivation. In a related study, Pearce and Berkos (2003) also found that teacher profanity use did not negatively impact either teacher credibility or teacher attractiveness, but only for those teachers who were seen as being highly verbally immediate. For teachers who were not seen as verbally immediate, less favorable perceptions of credibility and attractiveness resulted when teachers used profanity. Pearce and Berkos note, however, that "in no condition in our experiment did we find a benefit to teachers using profanity of any strength" (p. 21).

What influence, if any, does teacher trait verbal aggressiveness (and use of verbally aggressive messages) have on perceptions of teacher credibility? Myers (2001) speculated that when instructors are seen as verbally aggressive, they may be seen as less competent (i.e., less knowledgeable, expert informed), being lower in character (i.e., not being interested in whether students really learn the material, less trustworthy, selfish), and less caring (i.e., less understanding, less empathic, not concerned for students' welfare). Students completed a Recall of Verbal Aggression Instrument and a modified version of the Verbal Aggressiveness Scale and assessed the teacher's credibility on scales such as intelligent–unintelligent, cares about me–does not care about me, and untrustworthy–trustworthy (McCroskey & Teven, 1999). The more the instructor was perceived as being verbally aggressive, the lower his or her ratings were on the instructor credibility dimensions (Myers, 2001).

Additional studies have underscored the dysfunctional consequences of teachers' use of verbal aggression. Teven (2001) suggested that teacher verbal aggressiveness might be one of the most significant factors that "disrupt the students' perceptions of (teacher) caring" (p. 160). He found that the more a teacher was seen as being verbally aggressive, whether it was targeted toward an individual student or students in general, the less caring they were perceived as being. Does a teacher's use of slang (e.g., "What's up your ass, what's wrong") and use of verbal aggression (e.g., "Although from the looks of you, some of you do not date a lot") affect credibility and affect? Using an experimental design, Martin, Weber, and Burant (1997) had students listen to one of four audio-taped lectures that manipulated teacher use of slang and verbal aggression. The students then completed instruments designed to measure perceived teacher credibility (competence and character dimensions), teacher immediacy, teacher and lecture affect, and teacher use of appropriate language. Again, the teacher's perceived credibility, appropriateness, and teacher and lecture affect all suffered when the instructor used verbal aggression. These findings led Martin, Weber, et al. (1997) to state unequivocally, "Teachers should not use verbally aggressive messages" (p. 12). From the results of these studies, it is clear that verbal aggressiveness can now be added to the cluster of teacher misbehaviors identified by previous research.

Characteristics of the Argumentative Student

Most of the research in this chapter has focused on the effect a teacher's argumentativeness and verbal aggressiveness has on student perceptions. In this final section, we will review research relevant to the development of a profile of the argumentative and aggressive student.

Infante (1982) examined whether personality, family, and interpersonal factors could differentiate high versus low argumentative students. Several factors were examined for their potential relationship with students' trait argumentativeness including birth order, family size, liberal–conservative position on issues (called extremeness), amount of training in argumentation, college grade point average, class size, and high communication demands (i.e., as required for their job). Because argumentativeness is conceptualized as a constructive and desirable trait, Infante felt that students' satisfaction with their interpersonal relationships and their ability to relate to peers would not be negatively related to their level of argumentativeness.

Students completed the Argumentativeness Scale and then responded to a questionnaire that assessed the factors above. Students were classified into high-, moderate-, and low-argumentativeness categories by their scores on the scale. A profile of the argumentative student emerged: highly argumentative students, as compared with low argumentative students, received more prior high school training in argumentation, reported higher college grade point averages, were born earlier in the family birth order, preferred smaller-sized classes, and reported that they were more liberal.

Some speculation has suggested that being high in argumentativeness might create tension in interpersonal relationships. Infante's (1982) findings do not bear this out as satisfaction with interpersonal relationships and ability to relate to peers did not differentiate high argumentatives from moderate or low argumentatives. Being higher in trait argumentativeness does not seem to impair interpersonal relationships, at least as it is perceived by high argumentative students. A somewhat consistent sex difference did emerge, with males self-reporting higher scores on argumentativeness than females. Since higher levels of trait argumentativeness were found to be associated with higher grade point averages, it was suggested that "it seems reasonable to proceed in developing pedagogical techniques for increasing students' level of argumentativeness" (Infante, p. 146). Chapter 10 will provide some suggestions on how to enhance one's motivation and skill in argument.

Finally, studies have found that argumentativeness is positively related with level of higher education. Schullery and Schullery (2003) found that the higher the level of education reported, the higher the trait argumentativeness. This finding is not surprising as higher levels of education often require that students be able to present their positions on issues related to course content, argue in support of those positions, and attempt refutation of opposing positions.

Conclusion

In this chapter we reviewed the large body of research on the effects of argumentativeness and verbal aggressiveness in the instructional context. The bulk of this research has investigated students' perceptions of their instructors' argumentativeness and verbal aggressiveness in the college classroom. The results suggest that both of these instructor traits have an impact on student perceptions of the classroom climate as well as numerous student outcomes. In general, the findings extend Infante and Rancer's (1996) general conclusion that "the effects of argumentativeness are constructive and those of verbal aggressiveness are destructive" (p. 345) to the instructional context.

Classroom instructors seen as higher in argumentativeness are also seen as more competent and credible, using more constructive types of power, exhibiting more favorable communicator styles, promoting higher levels of student affective learning, and stimulating greater positive affect toward both course and teacher, as well as fostering a greater student motivation to learn. Conversely, instructors seen as higher in verbal aggressiveness are also seen as exhibiting less favorable communicator styles, fostering lower levels of student affect, fostering lower levels of student learning, creating less positive affect toward the course and instructor, creating a less supportive classroom climate, exhibiting less caring for students, fostering feelings of misunderstanding, and contributing to lower student motivation to learn.

Several implications and recommendations have been offered as a consequence of these findings. First, teachers should attempt to reduce or suppress verbally aggressive behaviors during teacher–student interaction. Although high levels of argumentativeness might be initially misunderstood (or even seen negatively by some students), instructors should attempt to develop or use more argumentative behaviors. In addition, it is important for instructors to try and make the distinctions between argumentative and verbally aggressive behavior clear to students. If these distinctions are made, students will be much less likely to misperceive a teacher's attack on their position as an attack on them. Teachers should also take into account their students levels of argumentative and aggressive traits as these student traits have been found to influence perceptions of the teacher. This is especially true regarding students' levels of verbal aggressiveness and self-esteem. That said, more research is needed on the impact of student traits in the teacher–student relationship.

Discussion Questions for Chapter 6

1. Can you think of a situation in your life when an instructor's use of verbal aggression was not only warranted, but possibly even appropriate? Explain?

2. Do you think that all students should be trained in argumentation? Why?

3. How or why do you think that a student's perceived understanding might be influenced by an instructor's level of argumentativeness and verbal aggressiveness?

4. What is the role of verbal immediacy in the effect of teacher's use of profanity?

5. Taking all the research findings cited in this chapter, what do you think is the optimal level of argumentativeness and verbal aggressiveness for a teaching assistant? An instructor? A student?

7

Argumentative and Aggressive Communication in Intercultural and Intracultural Contexts

The need to understand and appreciate other cultures has never been more important. Due to technological advancements, the global community is shrinking. A culture once thought of as far away can be accessed easily by flight or with one click of the mouse on your computer. Unfortunately, the world has also become more volatile with lines of division drawn from religious, sociopolitical, cultural, and racial origins. Thus, the study of argumentative and aggressive communication within and between cultures holds important and perhaps profound consequences for enhancing communication within and between cultures. Recall that in Chapter 4 we discussed research that suggested verbal aggression in abusive marriages was not a cause, but a catalyst, of physical aggression. In light of the many global conflicts we have observed, understanding the role of argumentativeness and verbal aggressiveness in intercultural discourse could potentially enhance effective intercultural dialogue and promote greater diplomacy. In fact, by understanding which behaviors constitute aggression in any given culture (as they are as varied as the cultures themselves), a person can avoid employing any given behavior that may appear overly aggressive in nature. Further, the ability to create cogent and persuasive arguments may inhibit potentially incendiary rhetoric that might lead to physically aggressive encounters.

This chapter will present the research on argumentative and verbally aggressive communication that has focused on people who are from different cultures and from co-cultures within the same culture (i.e., United States' co-cultures based on regional and racial differences). We will then discuss studies focusing on these traits in comparisons of the United States with similar Western cultures such as those of Australia and New Zealand. We will then present research that compares Eastern and Western cultures regarding the argumentativeness and verbal aggressiveness predispositions. As we will see, the comparison of Eastern and Western cultures has generated the largest attention from intercultural scholars interested in argumentative and aggressive communication. The chapter will conclude with some suggestions for future research and a discussion of methodological concerns that are especially salient when conducting intercultural communication research.

Co-cultural Differences in Argumentativeness and Verbal Aggressiveness

To say that the United States is a *patchwork quilt, vegetable soup,* or *tossed salad* of people from different cultural origins is more than a cliché; it is a very accurate description of the increasing diversity of the nation. Before we discuss how Americans may be different from other cultures regarding argumentative and aggressive communication, we will first present research showing differences among Americans themselves. In one of the first efforts along these lines, Sanders, Gass, Wiseman, and Bruschke (1992) tested for differences in argumentativeness, verbal aggressiveness, and need for cognition (i.e., a predisposition to enjoy critical thinking) among the United States's co-cultural groups of Asian Americans, African Americans, European Americans, and Hispanic Americans. Several hundred respondents representing those co-cultural groups completed measures of argumentativeness, verbal aggressiveness, need for cognition, and a set of demographic questions. Because only a very small percentage of the respondents were African American, the African American sample was dropped from the analyses. However, the results found no difference among the remaining three groups (i.e., Asian Americans, European Americans, and Hispanic Americans) on level of trait argumentativeness. Contrary to conventional cultural assumptions, Asian Americans self-reported higher levels of verbal aggressiveness than either European Americans or Hispanic Americans.

Sanders, Wiseman, and Gass (1994) also investigated differences in individuals' perceptions of arguing based on argument style, trait argumentativeness, and trait verbal aggressiveness. The researchers manipulated arguments in terms of warrant type (e.g., use of analogy or cause and effect), argument potency (i.e., weak arguments versus strong arguments), and attitudinal orientation of the issue (i.e., pro-elective abortions and capital punishment were deemed controversial issues whereas a hypothetical construction contract was deemed a neutral issue). These arguments were then judged by the participants as convincing or unconvincing, persuasive or unpersuasive, and effective or ineffective.

The results showed that European Americans were more critical of weaker arguments in comparison with Hispanic Americans and Asian Americans. A further analysis of the data revealed that European Americans high in verbal aggressiveness rated the weaker arguments more favorably, while European Americans who were high in argumentativeness rated the weaker arguments less favorably than the other co-cultural groups. Argumentativeness and verbal aggressiveness were not found to be predictors of argument quality for either Hispanic Americans or Asian Americans. One of the most interesting findings that emerged from this set of studies was the influence of co-culture on the relationship between communication traits (e.g., argumentativeness and verbal aggressiveness) and judgment of argument quality. That is, the Hispanic American and Asian American co-cultures appear to minimize the influence of trait argumentativeness and verbal aggressiveness on judgment of argument quality, whereas trait argumentativeness and verbal aggressiveness in the European American co-culture has a much greater influence on judgments of argument quality. This suggests that it is more difficult to predict the quality or arguments from the trait argumentativeness and verbal aggressiveness of Hispanic Americans or Asian Americans. There is a greater predictability of the argument quality of European Americans based on the knowledge of their trait argumentativeness and verbal aggressiveness.

In another comparison of Americans, Nicotera, Rancer, and Sullivan (1991) investigated differences in argumentativeness, verbal aggressiveness, and beliefs about arguing between European American and African American college students. The students completed self-reported measures of trait argumentativeness and verbal aggressiveness, as well as an altered other-report version of the Argumentativeness and Verbal Aggressiveness scales to reflect the other race. Beliefs about arguing were assessed through the Beliefs About Arguing Scale (Rancer, Kosberg, & Baukus, 1992; see Appendix F for a copy of this scale).

The results indicated that, regardless of the race of the respondents or their beliefs about arguing, African Americans scored higher and were seen as higher in argumentativeness than European Americans. Furthermore, African Americans also stereotyped themselves as higher in argumentativeness than

European Americans. Regardless of the respondents' race, those with positive beliefs about arguing stereotyped themselves as higher in argumentativeness. Similar findings were obtained with regard to verbal aggressiveness. Regardless of the respondents race or beliefs, African Americans were stereotyped as being higher in verbal aggressiveness. European American respondents, regardless of the target person's race, stereotyped others as being higher in verbal aggressiveness than did African American respondents. European Americans were found to stereotype other people in general (regardless of race) as being higher in verbal aggressiveness than African Americans. A link between high verbal aggressiveness and the tendency to stereotype others as high in verbal aggressiveness was suggested. In light of the verbally aggressive stereotype observed, the need for training in argumentativeness may be important given a verbally aggressive encounter could, under certain conditions, evolve into a physically aggressive one. And, as we have already discussed, the evidence of the destructive nature of verbal aggressiveness is undeniable.

Regional Differences in Argumentativeness and Verbal Aggressiveness

Observable and stereotyped dialect and regionally based language differences between people who live in the various regions of the United States seem to exist. As such, it would not be a stretch to suggest that if people were asked to identify a region in the United States where the phrase "foggetaboutit" is more prevalent, they might likely identify it as New York City. Similarly, the utterance "Dude, let's catch some tasty waves" might be more likely to be identified as native to southern California. Do these stereotypes and differences observed in dialect and regionalism extend to the traits of argumentativeness and verbal aggressiveness? One line of inquiry has offered some insight into this question. Media portrayals and other anecdotal data may lead you to conclude that people from the northeastern United States are more verbally aggressive than people from other parts of the country. Having grown up in New York City and Boston, respectively, your authors might be inclined to agree with this stereotype! There have been, however, a few systematic investigations attempting to provide empirical evidence of regional differences in argumentative and verbally aggressive communication.

Before we address the question of potential regional differences in argumentativeness and verbal aggressiveness, a few meaningful distinctions between regions of the United States need to be made. Researchers in other disciplines have used agricultural or geological maps as guides for making regional distinctions. In a review of regional patterns of communication in the United States, Andersen, Lustig, and Andersen (1987) found differences based on dialect patterns, ethnic and foreign background, racial minorities, religious affiliations, political affiliations, voting behavior, economic regions, quality of life, degree of educational attainment, physiography, climate, influence of southern culture, and general geographic regions. Given the variation in regional identification, it is difficult to identify regions of the United States to explore for potential differences in the traits of argumentativeness and verbal aggressiveness. In one of the seminal efforts, Geddes (1990) distinguished between the northern and southern United States simply by using state guidelines. More specifically, she operationally defined northern states to be New York and Pennsylvania and the southern states as South Carolina, Tennessee, and Kentucky.

Geddes (1990) posed a research question to see if any regional differences exist in argumentativeness and verbal aggressiveness. Participants were 113 Southerners and 90 Northerners who completed the Argumentativeness and Verbal Aggressiveness scales. Contrary to what stereotypes might suggest, the results indicated that no regional differences existed between Northerners and Southerners on argumentativeness and verbal aggressiveness. Geddes noted, however, that the sample for this study consisted of college students and that homogeneity of age and educational level may have suppressed any regional effects that may otherwise have been present. In addition, since college-age students exhibit higher levels of geographic mobility than other age groups, it was also suggested that some participants might have grown up in one region, yet now live in another region. As such, these conditions may have been confounding factors in the study.

In a follow-up study, Geddes (1992) attempted to more accurately distinguish between regions of the United States. Using the seven regional categories put forth by the American Institute of Public Opinion (AIPO), the 48 contiguous states were divided into South, New England, East Central, West Central, Mountain States, Middle Atlantic, and Pacific Coast. The study also used Elazar's (1972) regional nominal taxonomy, which classifies regions of the United States as traditionalistic (e.g., Georgia, Kentucky, and South Carolina), individualistic (e.g., Illinois, Indiana, Ohio, New York, and Pennsylvania), and moralistic (e.g., California, Oregon, and Washington) regions. In addition, a criterion that participants had to have lived in the region since childhood and also be attending college in that region was imposed. Within those parameters, Geddes surveyed 333 people who met the AIPO criteria and 390 people who met the Elazar criteria.

Using the Elazar taxonomy, Geddes (1992) found that students from the individualistic states scored higher on verbal aggressiveness than those from either the moralistic or traditionalistic states. Using the AIPO taxonomy, Northerners were found to score higher in verbal aggressiveness than Midwesterners, Southerners, and people from the Western United States. There were no significant regional differences observed for argumentativeness with either taxonomy. Recall the theory of independent-mindedness (see Chapter 5), which suggests that the American culture as a whole (macro-structure) values individualistic expression and the debating of ideas (Infante, 1987d). This macro-structural assumption regarding argumentativeness may have over-whelmed any regional influence (micro-structural) regarding trait argumenta-tiveness. That is, the overall American cultural assumptions about the benefits of arguing may have overwhelmed any potential regional differences in trait argumentativeness that might have existed.

West Meets West

Researchers studying differences in argumentative and verbally aggressive communication between cultures often utilize Hall's (1976) high- and low-context cultural distinction as the basis for making comparisons. Hall sug-gests that people from high-context cultures (e.g., Japan) rely on contextual cues for giving meaning to messages. People from low-context cultures (e.g., the United States) look directly to the message content to derive meaning. Most studies have used this conceptualization even when comparing other low-context cultures to American culture.

Avtgis and Rancer (2002) investigated differences in argumentativeness and verbal aggressiveness across three low-context cultures: the United States, New Zealand, and Australia. The participants were 184 American, 243 New Zealand, and 280 Australian college students. Given that all three cultures speak English as their native language and are considered Western cultures, there was little concern for conceptual (i.e., how we define argu-mentative and aggressive communication) and operational (i.e., how we measure argumentative and aggressive communication) inconsistency across cultures. To test for differences in these traits, all respondents first com-pleted the Argumentativeness and Verbal Aggressiveness scales. Because Australians have been evaluated as more outgoing or have a self-concept that is independent of their culture (see Callan & Gallois, 1983; Kippax & Brigden, 1977; Markus & Kitayama, 1991), Australians were hypothesized to be higher in both argumentativeness and verbal aggressiveness than either Americans or New Zealanders.

The results supported that speculation. Australians reported higher levels of trait argumentativeness and trait verbal aggressiveness than both the United States and New Zealand samples. One of the more interesting findings was that the U.S. sample reported significantly lower trait argu-mentativeness and trait verbal aggressiveness than the Australians and

New Zealanders. This result was surprising because it was assumed that New Zealanders, being a derivative of the collectivist Maori society and agricultural in nature, would be lower in both argumentativeness and verbal aggressiveness than the U.S. participants. However, the findings suggested otherwise. Perhaps there was an underestimation of the influence of Maori society on New Zealanders' levels of argumentativeness and verbal aggressiveness. That is, there may have been a naive assumption that all low-context cultures are individualistic in nature and that all high-context cultures are collectivist in nature. The findings of this study suggest that researchers should not assume that because a culture is considered low context, it is necessarily high in individualism. Indeed, these findings suggest that there is a combination of context (i.e., low) and culture (collectivistic vs. individualistic) that is influencing the results. America and Australia, while individualistic in nature, could be less individualistic cultures whereas New Zealand might be considered a lower-collectivist culture.

In another study involving two low-context cultures, Rahoi, Svenkerud, and Love (1994) compared Norwegians and Americans for differences in trait argumentativeness. The Argumentativeness Scale was translated into Norwegian and validated before administering it to the participants. Norwegians were found to be higher than Americans in their tendency to approach arguments, but lower in their tendencies to avoid arguments. Thus, Norwegians' general trait to be argumentative was found to be significantly higher than that of the U.S sample. Rahoi et al. attempted to explain these results by suggesting that a priori differences in the two samples may have contributed to the differences observed in motivation to argue. That is, the data for the United States sample were gathered at a public university, whereas the Norwegian sample consisted of students from a more selective and competitive higher educational system. Thus, the Norwegian student sample may have already been composed of more skilled and argumentatively motivated communicators than those constituting the United States sample.

Klopf, Thompson, and Sallinen-Kuparinen (1991) compared levels of trait argumentativeness between Finnish and American students, and again, Americans were thought to possess higher levels of argumentativeness. Contrary to this speculation, the findings suggested that Finnish students reported significantly higher levels of argumentativeness than the American students. Although there were no significant differences in the tendency to approach arguments, American students reported greater levels of ARGav (argument avoidance) than the Finnish sample. Klopf et al. suggested that another reason for these differences may be that the Finnish students are especially enamored with arguing and the intellectual challenges associated with it. Further, American students, and Americans in general, may have a more difficult time distinguishing between arguing and fighting. As such, Americans may have reported higher levels of argumentative avoidance than their Finnish counterparts. Future research investigating belief structures of the Finnish regarding arguing may reveal more meaningful distinctions between these two cultures regarding what arguing means to them. Utilizing observational studies may further elucidate the findings.

East Meets West

An examination of the literature on intercultural communication reveals that an abundance of research has focused on comparing Asian cultures with Western cultures on a variety of communication predispositions and practices. Whether a matter of researcher interest, ethnocentrism, or because some Asian cultures are seen as more exotic than some Western cultures, researchers have spent considerable effort comparing these two cultures. Indeed, several efforts have compared Asians and Americans regarding beliefs about arguing, measurement validation across cultures, and differences between the cultures on the trait predispositions.

One common critique of research on intercultural comparisons involves measurement and concept equivalency issues. Cultures are bound by their idiosyncratic language, belief, and value systems. Too often, intercultural scholars have utilized concepts and measures that were conceived and validated in one culture and applied them to a very different culture without checking for concept and measure equivalence. Researchers have operated with the assumption that these concepts and measures will be equally valid in other cultures. While it may be safe to conclude that a measure might yield similar evidence of dimensionality and validity when those cultures are similar in structure, what about measurement validity when examining very different (i.e., high-context) cultures?

One response to this question was provided by Suzuki and Rancer (1994), who tested the conceptual and measurement equivalence of the Argumentativeness and Verbal Aggressiveness constructs and scales across two different cultures. Using a large sample of students from two countries, they assessed Japanese and American students in terms of their trait argumentativeness and trait verbal aggressiveness. First, both scales were translated into Japanese by trained language experts for both meanings and phrasing to convey similar interpretations for both cultures. Next, participants in both cultures were asked to complete their respective-language version of the scales. Results revealed that both the Argumentativeness Scale and the Verbal Aggressiveness Scale demonstrated, with the exception of a few items on each, evidence of cross-cultural validity. Further, construct validity for the model of argumentativeness (i.e.,

ARGgt = ARGap − ARGav; see Chapter 3) for the Japanese sample was supported. Similar evidence of construct validity was obtained for verbal aggressiveness among the Japanese. This suggests that researchers interested in comparing trait argumentativeness and verbal aggressiveness between these two cultures can utilize existing conceptualizations and measures across these cultures with confidence.

In light of the conceptual and measurement consistency found between the two cultures on argumentativeness and verbal aggressiveness, Suzuki (1998) hypothesized that any differences between those cultures might also be influenced by gender. Using the same sample as the Suzuki and Rancer (1994) study, Suzuki also found evidence for conceptual and methodological validity regarding gender differences within and between Japanese and American cultures. Both American and Japanese males scored higher than American and Japanese females on tendency to approach argument, general tendency to argue, and verbal aggressiveness. American and Japanese females scored higher than American and Japanese males in tendency to avoid argument and verbal aggressiveness. These results extend our understanding of gender differences in argumentative and verbally aggressive communication to high-context cultures as well. That is, males, regardless of the cultural distinction, seem to be more argumentative and verbally aggressive than females.

In other studies, Americans, regardless of gender, reported higher levels of argument approach (ARGap) and general tendency to argue (ARGgt) than the Japanese (Prunty, Klopf, & Ishii, 1990a, 1990b). No significant differences were observed between Americans and Japanese with argument avoidance (ARGav). Regarding verbal aggressiveness, Harman, Klopf, and Ishii (1990) found no differences between American men and Japanese men as well as American women and Japanese women. However, Suzuki (1998), who delineated between positively worded and negatively worded verbal aggressiveness items, did show gender by culture differences. This treatment of the Verbal Aggressiveness Scale with a positively worded dimension and a negatively worded dimension was at the time unique in the measurement of verbal aggressiveness. Recall that Infante and Wigley (1986), in the original development of the Verbal Aggressiveness Scale, also found two dimensions based on positively and negatively worded items but concluded that these differences were an artifact of the scale and not a meaningful distinction. While most research on verbal aggressiveness has treated the scale as unidimensional, recent research may suggest otherwise (see Chapter 2).

The research reviewed here suggests that males are more verbally aggressive and report greater tendencies to approach arguments and less tendency to avoid arguments than females. Regardless of the context (e.g., intracultural, intercultural, organizational), gender differences in argumentativeness and verbal aggressiveness tend to hold constant across all research areas.

In a study comparing reaction to criticism among American, Japanese, and Chinese cultures, Bresnahan, Shearman, Lee, Ohashi, and Mosher (2002) studied Americans, Japanese, and Chinese who were randomly assigned to one of three experimental conditions. The first condition consisted of receiving a complaint from an aggressive neighbor (e.g., "Turn down that music! You are really rude and inconsiderate of others! You don't have any manners!"). The second condition consisted of receiving a complaint from an assertive neighbor (e.g., "Could you turn down your music? It's very loud!"). The third condition consisted of receiving a complaint from a nonassertive neighbor (e.g., "I am sorry to disturb you. I am trying to study for a big exam. I can kind of hear your music in my room. It's a little loud, I hope you understand."). Participants were asked to indicate in writing how they would respond to the complaint.

The researchers used the Alberti and Emmons (1970) taxonomy as a way to classify the responses into four conditions: a verbally aggressive response, an assertive response, simple agreement with the criticism, and a nonassertive or apologetic response. Raters from the three countries ranked the responses from the most aggressive to the least aggressive in the following order: verbally aggressive response, assertive response, agreement with criticism, and nonassertive or apologetic response, respectively. The raters also completed measures of trait argumentativeness, verbal aggressiveness, and assertiveness. The results confirmed previous research suggesting that men tend to be more verbally aggressive and display greater argument approach and less argument avoidance tendencies than women. Regardless of the condition, Americans were also more assertive than both Japanese and Chinese in responding to the criticism. Further, Japanese women who were high in verbal aggressiveness, high in argument approach, and low in argument avoidance also reported being more assertive. The findings of this study further highlight the influence that gender exerts on intercultural comparisons of argumentative and verbally aggressive communication.

People from Western cultures tend to view the Asian culture as a monolithic entity. As evidenced in the research discussed thus far, there are distinctions within Asian culture that demand further delineation by intercultural communication researchers. Long-held assumptions that people from collectivist cultures value harmony over conflict have recently been challenged (Cai & Fink, 2002). Scholars interested in testing for differences in argumentative and verbally aggressive communication have recognized this issue by broadening their perspective as to what constitutes Asian culture. To that end, one study examined the Korean culture as a basis for investigation and comparison with American culture. Kim, Aune, Hunter, Kim, and Kim (2001) compared Korean, Hawaiian American, and mainland American cultures on cultural and self-construals (i.e., the way people view themselves in relation to their culture, which ranges from independent to interdependent) of argumentativeness and communication apprehension.

Korean, Hawaiian American, and mainland American students completed items from the Ego-Task Analysis Scale (Breckler, Greenwald, & Wiggins, 1986), the Self-Construal Scale (Singelis, 1994), the Argumentativeness Scale (Infante & Rancer, 1982) and the Communication Apprehension Scale (McCroskey, 1982). The findings suggest that people who report individualism at the cultural level also possess self-construals that lead to increased levels of argumentativeness. Conversely, people who report interdependence at the cultural level possess self-construals that lead to decreased levels of argumentativeness. These results lend support to the interactionist perspective regarding the traits. Culture, a situational factor, influences peoples' self-concepts, which in turn affects the degree to which they report levels of trait argumentativeness.

Focusing on American Korean comparisons, Jenkins, Klopf, and Park (1991) compared the argumentativeness of students in Korea with that of students from the United States. The results revealed that Americans, as a whole, were higher in argumentativeness than the Koreans. Consistent with previous research, no differences were found between Korean and American males. However, across both cultures, males were found to be more argumentative than females. Although Korea is considered an Eastern and high-context culture, it has its own unique cultural norms regarding relationships, the nature of conflict appropriateness, and the appropriateness of various forms of communication during disagreement. As such, more research is needed before we can generalize findings from one Eastern culture to another.

Conclusion

Argumentative and verbally aggressive communication in the intercultural context still remains relatively understudied, at least as compared with the other contexts discussed in this book. To correct this imbalance and to generate more and more reliable research findings, several concerns should be addressed. Clearly, the number of studies on argumentativeness and verbal aggressiveness within and between cultures as well as across diverse interaction settings needs to be increased before any definitive conclusions can be drawn.

One of the most significant concerns is the assumption that conceptualizations and measures of traits developed in the United States and from a Western perspective can be applied to other cultures with conceptual and methodological equivalency. Issues of beliefs about arguing and of distinguishing between the types of utterances that constitute constructive and destructive communication (i.e., semantic aspects of messages), as well as the translation of items from one language symbol system to another (i.e., syntactical aspects of messages) are major issues still facing intercultural researchers. Efforts must address these validity concerns before final conclusions about argumentativeness and verbal aggressiveness across cultures can be derived. With the exception of the Suzuki and Rancer (1994) study, few studies have addressed the need for appropriate cultural conversion of the method of conceptualizing and measuring argumentativeness and verbal aggressiveness. Addressing these concerns before investigating cross-cultural differences in argumentative and verbally aggressive communication can only enhance the validity of the findings.

There is also a need to delineate further among factors that contribute to intracultural differences. As discussed in this chapter, race and regional differences in argumentativeness and verbal aggressiveness have been studied, but only to a small degree. There are a plethora of other intercultural factors (e.g., age, religion, political, and socioeconomic systems) that may work in tandem with trait argumentativeness and verbal aggressiveness to influence communication behavior. As technology makes the world seemingly smaller and more accessible, the influence of different cultural orientations on the world becomes more important. This speaks to the need for continually updating and extending the research cited in this chapter. In short, the intercultural context is one that offers some of the greatest research challenges and opportunities for scholars interested in argumentative and verbally aggressive communication.

Discussion Questions for Chapter 7

1. Why do you think it is important to study intercultural differences in argumentative and aggressive communication?

2. How do you think argumentative and verbal aggressiveness research focusing on ethnic and racial differences could help to explain interracial relationships?

3. What do you think are some possible reasons intercultural researchers have expended so much time comparing American and Asian cultures?

4. Why do you think there would be conceptual concerns when applying the argumentativeness and verbal aggressiveness constructs to Eastern cultures?

5. What arguments do you think can be made for including sex differences when investigating intercultural differences in argumentativeness and verbal aggressiveness?

8

Argumentative and Aggressive Communication in Mass and Mediated Communication Contexts

M ass communication is one of the best researched and influential of all the communication contexts. It is also the context that has stimulated the most controversy by both scholars and practitioners alike. Sending potentially millions of people the same message at the same time assumes some degree of responsibility. Messages containing profanity, indecency, and obscenity have been of concern since the earliest days of broadcasting. Since its inception in 1934, the Federal Communications Commission (FCC) has monitored the content of broadcast communication and has levied fines for stations that broadcast content deemed to contain offensive messages.

Entertainers who employ verbal aggression often find themselves the center of controversy. In the 1970s, comedian George Carlin developed a routine titled "Seven Words You Can't Say on Television," which directly addressed this issue. In the name of good taste we will refrain from identifying the seven words, but will point out that broadcasting messages deemed profane, obscene, or indecent can carry significant monetary consequences.

Over the years, corporations that broadcast radio shock jock Howard Stern's program have been fined several times for using obscene, graphic, explicit, and verbally aggressive language. In 2003, the FCC received numerous complaints from individuals about the broadcast of the Golden Globe Awards program, during which the rock performer Bono used an obscene word in violation of the FCC's rules restricting the broadcast of indecent material. The complainants maintained that such language was obscene and/or indecent and requested that the commission levy sanctions against the licensees for broadcasting the subject material under the assumption that profane and verbally aggressive messages are destructive to the public.

If you were to look at popular television and radio programs, you might notice the relationship between a program's popularity and the use of verbally aggressive communication. A consistent theme overheard today is that entertainment has become more verbally aggressive and that earlier generations were not exposed to such content. However, one could point to programs such as *The Three Stooges, The Honeymooners, All in the Family, The Jeffersons, Roseanne, Murphy Brown, Cheers, The Simpsons, Seinfeld, South Park,* and *Married . . . With Children* to demonstrate that verbal aggression has been a mainstay on television at least throughout the past five decades.

This chapter will address research on argumentative and aggressive communication in the mass media and in other mediated channels. We will begin by presenting some research on the possible link between media messages and aggressive behavior followed by a discussion of other types of verbally aggressive messages conveyed between two or more people using other forms of technology.

Social Learning, the Media, and Aggression

Recall in Chapter 1 we discussed potential causes for the development of trait verbal aggressiveness, such as disdain, psychopathology, genetics, and the argumentative skill deficiency explanation. Another cause that was mentioned, and one that has also been implicated in the development of trait verbal aggressiveness, is social learning. Although a complete discussion of social learning theory (Bandura, 1977) is beyond the scope of this book, a few essential tenets of the theory will be presented to help understand the utility of the theory as an explanation for argumentative, and especially verbally aggressive, communication.

Social learning theory suggests that we learn to behave a certain way by modeling the behaviors we observe. Thus, social learning theory has also been referred to as observational learning (Perse, 2001). Social learning is considered a complex process that is further subdivided into four subprocesses: attention, retention, production of the learned behavior, and motivation to perform (associated with the perceived rewards or punishments associated with the learned behavior; Perse, p. 191). If an individual is to model a given behavior, he or she must first pay attention to it and understand its components. Tan (1986) suggests that behaviors that are prevalent and perceived as useful will more likely be attended to. The second step in social learning is retention, the mental learning and commitment of the behavior to memory. The third step is the actual production of the learned behavior. For this step to be accomplished, individuals must have the ability to, or the belief that they can indeed, enact the behavior that has been learned. Step four of the theory involves determining whether the learned behavior will actually be enacted. According to Perse, "If a behavior is rewarded, it is more likely to be produced; if it is punished, it becomes less likely to be produced" (p. 191).

What are some of the sources that contribute to our observational learning? Family and friends, which are our primary and secondary social groups, are sources that contribute to social learning. According to Bandura (1978), another principle source of social learning is the mass media or the tendency of people to model the behaviors they observe in the media. Over the years, the media have become a very important source of information for symbolic modeling, including behaviors that are physically and verbally aggressive. As early as 1978, Bandura recognized the power of the media to influence behavior modeling:

> The advent of television has greatly expanded the range of models available to a growing child. Both children and adults today have unlimited opportunities to learn the whole gamut of violent conduct from televised modeling within the comfort of their homes. (p. 15)

Well before the development of the argumentativeness and verbal aggressiveness constructs, Bandura and a host of other scholars invested considerable time and effort studying the effects of media content on violent and aggressive behavior of both adolescents and adults. One general conclusion reached is that a relationship exists between television viewing of aggression and aggressive acts against others (Johnson, Cohen, Smailes, Kasen, & Brook, 2002; Slater, Henry, Swaim, & Anderson, 2003). Tan (1986) underscores this relationship by stating,

> For example, if a television viewer observes and learns that a specific aggressive act is a preferred and effective means of resolving interpersonal conflict, he or she may accept the principle that aggressive behavior in general (as a class of behaviors) is an acceptable and effective means of solving problems. (p. 49)

It follows that if the media are a source of physically aggressive cues that stimulate symbolic modeling, then the media's presentation of verbal aggression may help stimulate the enactment of that behavior as well in some people. Indeed, research suggests that the amount, type, and frequency of verbal aggression in prime-time network television programs are increasing. For example, Kaye and Sapolsky (2004) analyzed offensive language broadcast on network television programs. They found that in the sample of prime-time programs they examined, "profane words and phrases were heard about once every eight minutes" (Kaye & Sapolsky, p. 921). In addition, about three quarters of the cursing and profanity used in these shows was directed at another character, clearly constituting verbal aggression designed to hurt, embarrass, and humiliate another. One consequence of this increase in television's use of verbal aggression is that viewers may become desensitized to this form of communication. As such, this desensitization "may lead to more tolerance of mediated verbal vulgarities and increased use of aggressive words in everyday conversation" (Kaye & Sapolsky, p. 914).

One study investigated the relationship between exposure to mediated physical and verbal violence and self-reported verbal aggression. Whaley (1982) assessed students' self-reported use of verbal aggression, the intensity of verbal aggression used, the amount of exposure they had to television programs with verbal and physical violence, and their predisposition toward verbal aggressiveness. Whaley used the contentiousness dimension of Norton's (1983) Communicator Style Measure as a method of assessing predisposition toward verbal aggressiveness. Although no significant relationship was observed between contentiousness and the viewing of verbal and physical violence, "the most efficient model for predicting verbal aggression, as revealed in the regression analysis, included exposure to real verbal aggression as a predictor of verbal aggression" (Whaley, p. 496). This finding is supportive of the social learning framework because observing real verbal aggression was an important predictor of the students' self-reported use of verbal aggression.

Television Situation Comedies

Ratings show that situation comedies (sitcoms) are among the most popular genres of television programs. The impact of situational comedies on society is undeniable. On any given day, non-task-related messages in the workplace, at the dinner table, in schools, and in coffee shops are filled with references about an episode of *Will & Grace*, *Scrubs*, or a *Seinfeld* rerun. We are just beginning to understand the effect these shows have on the development and use of verbally aggressive messages. Most of the research conducted has focused on verbally aggressive communication contained in situation comedy television programs. When examining the genre of program (e.g., dramas, situation comedies, reality shows), Kaye and Sapolsky (2004) found that one type of verbal aggression (i.e., profanity) occurred in situation comedies more than in any of the other television genres.

In a series of studies, Chory-Assad and Tamborini (2003) provided evidence linking exposure to situation comedies with increased levels of verbal aggressiveness. The authors speculated that people who have positive regard for a sitcom will react with verbal aggression toward a TV critic's negative review of a program and that the more people watch sitcoms (regardless of the degree of liking for the show), the greater the tendency to engage in verbal aggression. To test this, students completed the Verbal Aggressiveness Scale and scales to measure exposure to sitcoms and the degree to which they like sitcoms. Sitcom exposure was measured by providing respondents with a list of prime-time sitcoms on all the major networks and asking them to indicate the number of times that they viewed the show in the preceding 8 weeks. In that study, *Friends*, *Frasier*, *Will & Grace*, and *Just Shoot Me* emerged as the most frequently mentioned sitcoms. Respondents then indicated their degree of liking for the sitcom and were also interviewed about how they would respond to a television critic who had the opposing opinion about the sitcom.

The results indicated that as the participants' liking for the sitcom increased, their tendency to use verbal aggression when discussing the sitcom decreased. Tendency to engage in verbal aggression toward the critic, however, was not associated with the degree of liking for the sitcom. The researchers also examined whether the amount of exposure to a sitcom results in increased verbal aggression toward the show. Interestingly, the more people were exposed to these four situation comedies (regardless of whether they liked them), the less they engaged in verbal aggression toward the show. The researchers speculated that as sitcoms are generally funny and pleasurable to watch, they may not trigger aggressive thoughts or tendencies in viewers, but instead may stimulate more playful communication tendencies.

Chory-Assad and Tamborini (2003) suggested that another explanation for this finding may lie in the method in which the data were collected. Interviews were used to solicit the respondents' level of verbal aggression about the sitcom. Thus, when faced with reporting a negative behavior (e.g., being verbally aggressive), people may distort the truth to appear more socially appropriate or to provide a more socially desirable response as to not seem as verbally aggressive (see Chapter 2 for a discussion of social desirability response bias). Thus, the findings may be due more to this bias and not represent the true relationship between verbal aggressiveness and sitcom viewing.

In a study investigating viewing frequency and enjoyment of situation comedy television shows, Martin, Mottet, Weber, Koehn, and Maffeo (1998) believed that there would be differences between people who are high and low in trait verbal aggressiveness, length of viewership, and enjoyment of situation comedies. As indicated by Kaye and Sapolsky (2004), situation comedies contain some of the most verbally aggressive content. Too often, people mistakenly assume that verbal aggression is evident only in violent or dramatic programs. However, on the receiving end of every joke there is often a person, with the brunt of the joke being the recipient of character attacks, competence attacks, teasing, and ridicule. In fact, sarcastic and biting humor represents an understudied form of verbally aggressive messages.

Martin, Mottet, et al. (1998) assessed college students' trait verbal aggressiveness, the specific situation comedy show they watched, and the degree of entertainment they received from the program. Thirty-three situation comedies were included in the analyses. The results indicated that people high in trait verbal aggressiveness reported watching *The Fresh Prince of Bel Air*, *The Simpsons*, *Married . . . with Children*, *The Jeff Foxworthy Show*, and *Martin* significantly more than people low in trait verbal aggressiveness. All of these programs, while clearly humorous, contain instances of verbal aggression. Conversely, people low in trait verbal aggressiveness reported watching *Caroline in the City*, *Mad About You*, *Hope & Gloria*, and *Sister-Sister* significantly more than people high in verbal aggressiveness. In terms of entertainment value, people high in verbal aggressiveness rated *Seinfeld*, *The Simpsons*, and *Married . . . with Children* as being more entertaining than people low in verbal aggressiveness. People low in verbal aggressiveness reported that *Frasier*, *The Nanny*, *Mad About You*, *Wings*, *Ellen*, *Hangin' With Mr. Cooper*, *In the House*, and *Sister-Sister* were more entertaining than did high verbally aggressive viewers.

Martin, Weber, and Mottet (2003) sought to determine whether people who report the world as a mean place also report higher levels of verbal aggressiveness. Along with the measures already completed by the respondents in the previous study, students also completed the Mean World Index (Gerbner, Gross, Eleey, Jackson-Beeck, Jeffries-Fox, & Signorelli, 1977). People who report a high mean world index score tend to see other people as being self-centered and untrustworthy. The measure has been primarily used to link television viewing to perceptions of violence in the world. Given this, people who have a greater tendency to say hurtful things to others might also see the world as an untrustworthy and violent place. The results supported this speculation in that trait verbal aggressiveness and perceptions of a mean world were found to be positively related (Martin et al., 2003).

Focusing specifically on family-oriented situation comedies, Martin, Koehn, Weber, and Mottet (1997) investigated the frequency of verbally aggressive messages in these programs. More specifically, they coded verbal aggression delivered by the specific family dyads on the television show (e.g., sibling to sibling, mother to child, child to mother, father to child, child to father, husband to wife, and by other family members such as grandparents, cousins, in-laws, and divorced spouses). The researchers were interested in the amount of verbally aggressive messages, the types of messages that were used, the response to the verbally aggressive message, the sex of both the sender and the receiver of the messages, and the number of verbally aggressive messages that involve family members.

During the spring of 1996, four episodes of each prime-time sitcom from ABC, NBC, CBS, and Fox were recorded. Of the 37 situation comedies recorded, only those that featured a family member character under the age of 18 were included in the analyses. This resulted in 13 sitcoms consisting of *The Nanny, Family Matters, Step by Step, Hangin' With Mr. Cooper, Home Court, Hope & Gloria, Boy Meets World, Married . . . With Children, The Simpsons, Grace Under Fire, Roseanne, Home Improvement,* and *Coach.*

A category system was developed in which to code the content of each situation comedy. In addition to coding the name of the show and the episode title, the categories also included the actual verbally aggressive message(s) delivered, the sex of the source and the receiver of the message, the type of verbally aggressive message (e.g., character attacks, competence attacks), whether the receiver actually received the message, how the receiver responded to the message, whether the verbally aggressive messages involved family members, the relationships between the family member sending the message and the family member receiving the message, and whether there was audience laughter after the verbally aggressive message.

The findings indicated that the most verbally aggressive family-oriented sitcoms were *The Nanny* (averaging about 23 verbally aggressive messages per episode) and *Married . . . With Children* (averaging about 25 verbally aggressive messages per episode), with the least verbally aggressive shows being *Grace Under Fire* and *Coach* (each averaging about 6 verbally aggressive messages per episode). Taken as a whole, 782 messages were coded as verbally aggressive for all shows combined. Of these, 332 were considered as character attacks, 152 were competence attacks, 69 were physical appearance attacks, 75 were threats, 128 were teasing, and 9 were examples of nonverbal verbal aggression (they also identified 17 instances of physical aggression).

The most common response to verbally aggressive attacks was passivity (or no response to the verbally aggressive attack), and the least common response was the use of physical aggression. Male characters sent 58.8% of the messages and received 58.8%, whereas female characters sent 41.2% of the messages and received 38.2%. Worth noting were the verbally aggressive messages sent between family members. Of the 782 messages coded as verbally aggressive, 301 were exchanged between family members, where 98 were between siblings, 68 were between spouses, 31 were from father to child, 27 were from mother to child, 21 were from child to father, and 28 were from child to mother. The remaining 28 messages were exchanged between various extended family dyads (e.g., inlaws, grand parents, etc.)

Clearly the most significant findings of the study lie in the sheer number of verbally aggressive messages contained in situation comedies as a whole. Indeed, family-oriented sitcoms contained as much verbal aggression as those shows targeted toward adults. The power dynamics between family members and incidents of verbal aggression is also worth mentioning. The greatest amount of verbal aggression was exchanged by family members with relatively equal power (i.e., between siblings and among marital couples). Fewer verbally aggressive messages were exchanged between family members with great power and status differences (i.e., father to child, mother to child, child to father, child to mother). This decrease in aggressive communication between those characters dissimilar in power could be due to the notion that verbal aggression between people of similar power may be considered more appropriate and humorous, whereas verbal aggression exchanged between people where there are clear power differences may not be humorous and might even be seen as socially inappropriate.

Martin, Anderson, and Cos (1997) assessed trait verbal aggressiveness and affect toward verbally aggressive television shows. The researchers were interested in the interaction between the viewer's trait verbal aggressiveness and the degree of psychological pain experienced by verbally aggressive messages. Psychological pain was assessed using the Infante, Hartley, Martin, Higgins, Hur, and Bruning (1992) instrument, which measures the degree of psychological pain associated with verbally aggressive messages. A measure of television show affinity (i.e., the degree of liking of the television show) and a measure of realism (i.e., the degree to which people in the show are similar to people in real life) were also completed. The participants were then shown a 7-minute segment of the Fox situation comedy *Daddy Dearest*. The researchers believed that people who are high in trait verbal aggressiveness would not only like the show, but would report the show as being realistic. Further, they believed that people high in verbal aggressiveness would report the verbal aggression in the show to cause little psychological harm. It was further hypothesized that people who report being psychologically harmed by verbally aggressive messages will also report less affinity (i.e., liking or attraction) for the television show. These speculations were supported, with one exception. People who reported being hurt by verbally aggressive messages did not report lower affinity for the show. That is, even though the viewers reported increased levels of psychological pain experienced from the aggressive messages in the show, the level of liking for the sitcom did not differ from those who reported that they were not hurt by the messages.

Comparing Sitcoms to Other Television Genres

In a comparison of sitcoms and crime drama shows, Chory-Assad (2004) used the general aggression model (Anderson & Bushman, 2002) as a theoretical framework for this study. The general aggression model assumes that a person's personality and the factors in the specific situation combine to influence behavior based on that person's thoughts, feelings, and arousal levels. It was reasoned that because there is a considerably greater amount of verbal aggression contained in sitcoms, there would be more aggressive thoughts recalled from sitcom viewers. To test this, two conditions were created. In one condition, participants were exposed to a crime drama (NYPD Blue) whereas in the other condition, participants were exposed to a situation comedy (Titus). Similar to earlier studies described, the participants completed the Verbal Aggressiveness Scale and then viewed the respective show and were asked to record their thoughts after viewing the program (i.e., by listing the things they were thinking), their feelings about the show (i.e., items concerning the like or dislike of the show and the characters), and the degree of arousal they felt (i.e., ranging from low arousal, "dull," to high arousal, "sharp").

The results revealed that participants in the sitcom condition produced significantly more verbally aggressive thoughts (approximately 16%) than those in the crime drama condition. These aggressive thoughts were primarily character and competence attacks. One of the most interesting findings of the study is that level of trait verbal aggressiveness predicted the number of aggressive thoughts recalled during the sitcom viewing but not in the crime show viewing. The findings provide support for the general aggression model in that individual differences (i.e., levels of trait verbal aggressiveness) appear to have the greatest influence on aggressive thoughts when the level of media violence is moderate. The finding that more aggressive thoughts were generated during the viewing of the sitcom (moderate media violence) than the crime show (high media violence) speaks to this notion. Apparently, verbal aggressiveness has the greatest influence on thoughts when media violence is not extreme (i.e., either extremely high or extremely low).

Differences between situation comedies and television dramas regarding gender and racial differences and use of verbal aggression has been investigated (Glascock, 2003). Glascock sampled 1 week of prime-time television consisting of 39 shows totaling 27 hours of programming (i.e., 15 one-hour dramas and 24 half-hour comedies). Of the 556 total television characters identified in these shows, females comprised 36.7% whereas men comprised 63.3%. In addition, African American characters comprised 15.3% of all characters, Asians represented 2.3%, and Hispanics comprised 1.6%. Because the percentage of Asian and Hispanic characters was so low, only the African American category was retained in the analyses. Results revealed that African American characters initiated and received verbal aggression far more than their total representation on television (approximately 20% more). In terms of gender, male characters in both comedies and dramas initiated and received significantly more verbal aggression than female characters. Recall that this gender effect was also reported by Martin, Mottet, et al. (1998) in their study of verbal aggression and sitcoms. Glascock (2003) reported 17 verbally aggressive acts per hour for television dramas and 26 verbally aggressive acts per hour for situation comedies. This finding further supports that verbal aggression is more prevalent in comedies than in dramatic television shows. Comedic television programs are saturated with verbally aggressive messages that constitute a large portion of the humor represented on the shows. Although some explanations have been offered as to why something so potentially damaging (i.e., verbal aggression) can be seen as humorous and enjoyable, more research still needs to be conducted to better understand this relationship.

Would individuals who are high in verbal aggressiveness (and who presumably might also use one type of verbal aggression, profanity) be less likely to attend to and be offended by profane language on a broadcast program? That was the focus of a study by Krcmar and Sohn (2004), who investigated the effects of viewer trait verbal aggressiveness, warning labels, and bleeping (self-censoring) on a variety of viewer attitudes. An ESPN-produced movie about the legendary and controversial basketball coach Bobby Knight called *A Season on the Brink* was edited down to 30 minutes. This segment contained 76 incidents of curse words being spoken or bleeped out, depending on the experimental condition. The four experimental conditions were (1) warning label (i.e., "Due to strong adult language, viewer discretion is advised") with no censorship (i.e., swear words were actually spoken), (2) no warning label and censorship (i.e., bleeps were inserted instead of the actual swear word), (3) warning label with censorship (i.e., bleeps were inserted instead of the actual swear word), and (4) no warning label and no censorship (i.e., swear words were actually spoken).

Participants completed a short-form version of the Verbal Aggressiveness Scale and measures assessing how much they enjoyed the movie, the perceived realism of the movie, the movie's offensiveness, familiarity with the movie's story (i.e., if they viewed it prior to the study), and perceived frequency of profanity use (an estimate of the number of times they heard either swear words or bleeps).

Among the findings, it was revealed that viewers liked the movie more when it contained a warning label and there was censorship. Viewers who heard the curse words reported liking the movie less. Interestingly, the bleeping out of the profanity actually increased the viewers' estimates of profanity use. The researchers believed that the bleeps actually called attention to, rather than diffused, the effect of profanity. Further, as viewer trait verbal aggressiveness increased, the report of offensiveness of the profanity use decreased. Perhaps level of trait verbal aggressiveness serves as a threshold for offensiveness. That is, as viewers' level of trait verbal aggressiveness increases, their tendency to interpret profanity as offensive decreases. This study underscores the relationship between aggressive communication traits and cognitive processing, a relationship found to be important in persuasion (see Chapter 9).

Televised Wrestling

Before the advent of reality television, there was what arguably could be termed *quasi-reality* television. A popular genre of quasi-reality TV is the world of professional wrestling. From the earliest days of Chief Jay Strong Bow to the more contemporary wrestler The Rock, these athlete-actors have come into our homes for decades. Most adults understand that professional wrestling is a form of entertainment with staged verbal and physical aggression. When these athlete-entertainers take the microphone, they verbally attack their opponents, the live audience, and even the television viewers. In the wrestling world, "the more you hate them, the more you love them."

Accounting for aggressive messages used in this quasi-reality television genre, Tamborini, Chory-Assad, Lachlan, Westerman, and Skalski (2005) investigated the use of verbal aggression by professional wrestlers and their motivations for doing so. Attendance at and television viewing of professional wrestling matches are extremely popular, especially among children. Tamborini, Chory-Assad, et al. cite the 2003 Nielson ratings, which stated that "822,000 children age 2–11 watched Smackdown, and 483,000 watched Raw every week from Fall 2002 through Summer 2003. The numbers are even larger for children 9–14, with an average of 847,000 for Smackdown, and 627,000 weekly for Raw" (p. 4).

In their study, both physical aggression and verbal aggression were coded using the categories developed by the National Television Violence Study for categorizing the types of aggression (Wilson, Kunkle, Linz, Potter, Donnerstein, Smith, et al., 1997). An interaction was defined as verbally aggressive if there was an aggressive exchange between a perpetrator (i.e., the person sending the message) engaging in the behavior (i.e., the specific aggressive utterance) toward another person. Data collection consisted of 10 weeks of televised wrestling programming and two teams of coders were used to categorize the content. The results indicated that 833 verbally aggressive exchanges were observed averaging 30 verbally aggressive exchanges per hour. Profanity and swearing, competence attacks, and character attacks were most prevalent in the sample of programs. These types of verbal aggression were followed by a combination of any two types of the following verbally aggressive utterances: mocking, background attacks, physical appearance attacks, demands, sarcasm, threats, dislike, maledictions, rejections, and a combination of any three types of verbal aggression.

Going beyond the frequency of verbally aggressive messages, motivations or perceived reasons for using aggressive messages were also studied. Reasons identified included verbal aggression being used for amusement, in anger, as mandated (i.e., aggressive interactions that occur as a necessary part of the show), for personal gain, for protection of life (i.e., verbal aggression used to save a victim from a physical attack), in retaliation, by accident, and for a combination of these reasons. The categories were then condensed again into three supercategories, which included unsanctioned reasons (i.e., amusement, anger, personal gain, or a combination of these reasons), sanctioned reasons (i.e., mandated, protection of life, retaliation, or a combination of these reasons), and neutral reasons (i.e., unknown, other, accident). After condensing the categories, the findings revealed that verbal aggression in professional wrestling is employed overwhelmingly for unsanctioned reasons (Tamborini, Skalski, Lachlan, Westerman, Davis, & Smith, 2005).

Perpetrators of verbal aggression tended to be male and acted as an individual as opposed to part of a group. Surprisingly, over half of the verbal attacks were attributed to the announcers, with verbal attacks by other wrestlers coming in second. Other perpetrators only accounted for a small amount of the verbal aggression used. The receivers of the verbal aggression shared similar characteristics in that they were predominately male and were individual targets as opposed to being part of a targeted group. Although the recipients of the verbally aggressive messages included people such as the announcers, the crowd, and the referees, the targets of these messages were primarily other wrestlers.

Taken as a whole, the findings that professional wrestling contains high levels of verbal aggression is not surprising. What is unique to these studies is the finding that, unlike other genres of television, in professional wrestling there is no clear good or bad guy. The use of verbal aggression is prevalent in characters of all dispositions (i.e., good, bad, and in-between). This blurring of dispositions led Tamborini, Chory-Assad, et al. (2005) to suggest the need to revisit traditional assumptions concerning outcomes associated with verbally aggressive television effects and to reconsider the disposition on the part of both the perpetrator and the victim. It is important to remember that in situation comedies there is little ambiguity as to the disposition of the character, as they generally have a clearly good disposition and in relatively few cases a clearly bad disposition. Few, if any, characters in sitcoms have ambiguous dispositions.

The consequences of the verbal (and physical) aggression gleaned from these televised wrestling programs on individuals' behavior again are suggested by social learning theory. When an adolescent (usually male) exposes himself to a daily or weekly dose of the verbal aggression contained in the World Wrestling Entertainment's *Raw* and *Smackdown* and observes functional consequences and outcomes of using these behaviors (e.g., becoming champion, getting one's way, encouraging submissiveness in others) they are often modeled and can become part of his behavioral repertoire.

Music

Thus far, we have reviewed studies concerning the verbally aggressive content of television programming. What about the influence that music exerts on the development and use of verbal aggression? For decades we have heard the direct-effects argument (i.e., music directly influences an individual's thoughts, feelings, or behavior). Whether it is Ozzy Osborne's "Suicide Solution" or the lyrics of rapper DMX, critics indict music and music artists for negative societal consequences (e.g., suicide attempts, sexist and misogynistic attitudes toward women). Among contemporary adolescents who grew up in the MTV culture, music is just as, if not more, influential than television. As such, we would expect that scholars interested in argumentative and aggressive communication would put forth great effort in investigating this medium.

Of all the studies presented in this chapter, only one has focused on the influence of music on verbal aggressiveness. Examining a myriad of factors that might contribute to adolescent verbal aggression, Atkin, Smith, Roberto, Fediuk, and Wagner (2002) asked, via questionnaire, 2,300 adolescents about verbally aggressive messages. The media (i.e., television radio, music), demographic predictors (i.e., gender, age, race, size of school, grades in school, and family income), and social predictors (i.e., trouble with police and peer substance use) were measured as potential factors influencing the use of verbal aggression. In terms of music's influence, a relationship between use of verbal aggression and preference for listening to heavy metal and gangsta rap was observed. Atkin et al. (2002) concluded, "The more intense verbally aggressive language and the hostile expressions of the performers may provide an influential novel input to adolescents" (p. 264). As music plays a central role in many people's lives, especially among adolescents and teenagers, the influence of music content on verbal aggression is not completely known and is in need of more study.

Other Mediated Communication Research

The term *mediated communication* encompasses any medium that comes between the sender and the recipient. Given this rather global definition, mediated communication can take a variety of forms and functions. In light of the vastly changing and ever-growing number of communication technologies, this area of study will continue to intrigue and attract more attention from communication scholars. Cellular phones, e-mail, and instant messaging, for example, can have effects on the feelings, thoughts, and actual behaviors associated with argumentative and aggressive communication. As research has and will investigate, technology does influence the degree of aggressive communication a person displays.

For example, Cicchirillo and Chory-Assad (2005) were interested in studying the relationship between trait verbal aggressiveness and the frequency and length of violent video-game play. Using the general aggression model as the theoretical framework for the study, the researchers suggested that playing video games serves a type of social learning in which "aggression-related knowledge structures" (p. 6) are reinforced. In other words, beliefs and attitudes toward aggression as well as perceptions and expectancies of aggressive behavior become part of the knowledge structure and, as such, become part of a person's personality and behavioral repertoire. College students were asked to indicate the frequency per week that they play video games and the duration of play during any one session. The participants also completed the Verbal Aggressiveness Scale.

The results reinforced many findings regarding verbal aggressiveness and sex differences highlighted throughout this book and extended our knowledge about video-game play and trait verbal aggressiveness. Males reported playing video games for more total hours and also reported higher levels of verbal aggressiveness than males who play for a shorter time and females regardless of video-game play time. Overall hours of game play for both sexes was found to be significantly related to verbal aggressiveness. Thus, the more video game play reported, the higher the verbal aggressiveness.

An experiment investigating the influence of argumentativeness and verbal aggressiveness on computer-mediated decision making was conducted by

Martin, Heisel, and Valencic (2001). They hypothesized that people who communicate with a verbally aggressive stranger through e-mail will view both the stranger and the task less favorably, while those who interact with another stranger who used arguments would be perceived more favorably. The researchers created two conditions for the experiment. In the first condition, participants interacted via e-mail with a verbally aggressive confederate (i.e., a person who was instructed by the researchers to be verbally aggressive toward the participant) for 5 minutes on the topic of a foreign language requirement in college. The second condition required the participants to interact with an argumentative confederate via e-mail (i.e., a person who was instructed by the researchers to be argumentative toward the participant). After the interaction, participants completed measures of social attractiveness and task attractiveness on the partner. The results revealed that participants in the verbally aggressive condition rated the stranger as significantly less socially attractive than the stranger in the argumentative condition. This finding emerged as expected and supported the hypothesis. However, regarding the task (i.e., discussion of the foreign language requirement), no significant differences were observed. In this case, the participants were able to separate the person from the task. In addition, although the argumentative condition influenced interpersonal perceptions in a positive way, the findings did not carry that positive feeling over toward the task.

The ability to distinguish between the task and the person may be a derivative of the computer-mediated environment. Earlier we highlighted the link between verbal aggressiveness and negative outcomes for both person and task. However, this link between verbal aggressiveness and negative affect toward the task seems to be buffered by the technology (i.e., computer mediated communication). Given that the researchers did not test this explanation, future research on computer-mediated decision making will have to address such questions.

Conclusion

In the digital age we continue to see the proliferation of media outlets and entertainment choices. The explosion in the adoption and use of the Internet and subscription radio provides us with yet even more channels for consuming mass media. Despite the enormity of research conducted on violence, aggression, and media effects, a paucity of research exists on argumentativeness and verbal aggressiveness in mass and mediated communication contexts. This is especially unfortunate given the potency of the mass and mediated communication contexts.

As is evidenced by the research in this chapter, the television situation comedy has been the genre of choice for researchers interested in argumentative and aggressive communication. This may be due to the fact that the sitcom remains one of the most popular types of shows and one replete with verbal aggression. Character analysis and use of aggressive messages has revealed some intriguing findings regarding the disposition of a character and the perceived appropriateness of the verbal aggression. When a character is clearly a bad person, we tend to interpret the use of aggressive communication in a different way than when the character has a clearly good disposition. To further complicate this, many television characters do not possess clearly good or bad dispositions, but are portrayed ambiguously regarding disposition. The impact of this ambiguity has been studied especially regarding professional wrestling characters.

The effect of verbal aggression should continue to generate interest from scholars, especially when coupled with the increase in programs containing verbal and other forms of aggression. There is another trend, however, concerning viewer affect and interpretations of aggressive communication. We have witnessed the impact that viewer affinity toward the show and characters and aggressive thought generation have on the interpretation of character verbal aggression use. However, there are a host of other affective (i.e., emotion-based) and cognitive (i.e., thought-based) dimensions that remain to be studied.

From pagers to cell phones and video phones, these mediated devices are becoming increasingly prevalent as the medium of interpersonal communication. In a world where a growing percentage of people's communications are mediated through devices, the impact of verbal aggression will invariably affect interpersonal relationships. For each new technology, there may be different implications for the constructive or destructive outcomes associated with argumentative communication or aggressive communication. The research in this area has yet to fully emerge. Too often people assume interpersonal research findings at the face-to-face level (e.g., married people who report high levels of verbal aggression also report lower levels of marital satisfaction) will translate equally to interpersonal research that is mediated by technology. Clearly, there is a difference between saying something to someone's face and saying it on the phone or in a text or e-mail message. There are appropriateness issues as well as impact issues that should be studied. Future research needs to account for new media technology and its impact on argumentative and aggressive communication.

Discussion Questions for Chapter 8

1. Why do you think that most verbal aggression research in mass communication has focused on situation comedies?

2. What does it mean to say that verbal aggression in situation comedies, when used by characters who are equal in power, is perceived as funny, whereas verbal aggression used by characters who have unequal power is perceived as not humorous? Has this ever happened to you in your life? Explain.

3. Do you think there are differences in the use of verbal aggression by characters of different races as portrayed in television situation comedies? Explain.

4. Do you think it is important to consider the disposition of the source and the disposition of the receiver when researching the effect of verbal aggression in the media? How can source–receiver disposition ambiguity affect how we think about verbal aggressiveness?

5. What is the link between argumentative and aggressive communication with social and task attraction in the mediated communication environment?

9

Argumentative and Aggressive Communication in Persuasion and Social Influence Situations

A rguably, many if not most communication interactions involve some type of persuasion. Whether asking your parents if you can borrow the car, asking the boss for a raise, trying to close a sale, persuading a professor to allow you into a course that is closed, convincing your doctor that your upper respiratory distress is severe enough to warrant prescribing an antibiotic drug, or convincing a relational partner that you are worthy of a long-term commitment, the persuasive dimension is ubiquitous in human communication.

It seems apparent, then, that being a competent communicator involves the ability to engage in successful persuasive efforts. Competence in persuasion is considered an essential element in a number of career paths as well. The ability to craft and deliver persuasive messages is a skill necessary in professions such as marketing and sales, teaching, legal communication, public relations, publishing, journalism, the ministry, training and development, human resources, management, counseling, health, and political communication, to name just a few.

In this chapter, we will review the work on the impact of argumentativeness and verbal aggressiveness in persuasive and compliance-gaining efforts. First, we will describe a transactional approach to persuasion that focuses on how one individual's trait argumentativeness combines with the trait argumentativeness of another individual to affect persuasive outcomes. We will then review work highlighting the influence of argumentative and aggressive communication in the processing of persuasive messages. Next, a review of the research on how argumentativeness and verbal aggressiveness function in compliance-gaining efforts will be presented. A summary and review of a test of two competing theoretical frameworks for determining a person's intentions to argue follows. Finally, we will conclude the chapter with a discussion of how the argumentativeness and verbal aggressiveness traits function in resisting persuasive efforts.

Understanding the process and products of persuasion has long been a goal of researchers and theorists from the disciplines of communication and social psychology. The formal study of persuasion is often traced back to the days of the ancient Greeks and especially to the teachings of Aristotle. In *The Rhetoric,* Aristotle states that rhetoric (or communication) is "an ability, in each case, to see the available means of persuasion" (Kennedy, 1991, p. 36). In addition to the guidance we have received from the ancient scholars and philosophers, several contemporary persuasion scholars have developed models and theories of persuasion (see Gass & Seiter, 2003; Perloff, 2003).

In the communication discipline, contemporary persuasion research seems to be marked by two distinct periods (Infante, Rancer, & Womack, 2003). In the first period, roughly from the 1950s to the early 1970s, the focus was on what has been called traditional persuasion research. This line of research investigated how message (e.g., use of fear appeals, language intensity) and source (speaker) variables (e.g., credibility, attractiveness) influenced large groups of people. During this period, a linear or one-to-many model of persuasion was dominant. The major concern of persuasion scholars was on how a speaker delivering a speech could use a variety of source and message variables to alter the attitudes of an audience.

From the mid-1970s to the present, the focus of persuasion research has changed considerably, moving away from the formal one-to-many models to scholarly interest on social influence in less formal, and more interpersonal or one-to-one contexts (see Miller, Boster, Roloff, & Seibold, 1977). Early in this transition period, Miller and Burgoon (1978) noted that "most social influence attempts take place in one-to-one or one-to-few situational contexts" (p. 33). Today, questions such as, "How do we convince someone to do something we want them to do?" "How can we get people to like us?" "What are effective methods of resisting the persuasive attempts of others?" and "What is the role of argumentative and aggressive communication in the process of interpersonal relations and social influence attempts?" now occupy with greater frequency the scholarly pursuits of persuasion theorists and researchers (Infante et al., 2003, p. 102).

An Orientation to Persuasion

Being persuasive demands several competencies, including the ability to invent and deliver well-constructed arguments in support of the position you are advocating. It also demands that you are able to refute or pick apart the arguments others present to support their position. As we have suggested throughout this text, being motivated and skilled in argumentation suggests that a person possesses a higher level of trait argumentativeness. Before we focus on how argumentative and verbally aggressive communication affects persuasive and compliance-gaining efforts, a few important terms should be defined.

Over the years, numerous definitions and conceptualizations of persuasion have been offered; however, we shall mention only a few. Bettinghaus and Cody (1994) defined *persuasion* as "a conscious attempt by one individual or group to change the attitudes, beliefs, or behavior of another individual or group of individuals through the transmission of some message" (p. 6). Gass and Seiter (2003) suggested, "Persuasion involves one or more persons who are engaged in the activity of creating, reinforcing, modifying, or extinguishing beliefs, attitudes, intentions, motivations, and/or behaviors within the constraints of a given communication context" (p. 34). Infante et al. (2003) stated, "At its most basic level, persuasion may be thought of as attitude change toward a source's proposal that results from a message designed to alter beliefs about the proposal" (p. 102). A *proposal* is defined as "a recommended course of action" (Infante et al., p. 102). It is apparent that there are some similarities among these definitions, with the focus being on attitude, belief, and behavior creation, reinforcement, or change.

Although many of us may inherently understand the notion of behavioral change, we might not understand the concepts of attitudes or beliefs. *Attitudes* can be defined as "how favorably we evaluate something" (Infante et al., 2003, p. 102). For example, what is your attitude toward the proposal, "In order to lose weight we should go on a low carbohydrate diet"? A *belief* is defined as "a perception of how two or more things are related" (Infante et al., p. 102). An example of a belief would be, "Diets low in carbohydrates are critical to effective weight loss efforts." Thus, beliefs are conceptualized as individuals' perceptions of the consequences of a proposal (Infante et al., p. 102). Therefore, a person's belief system, for the most part, will influence his or her attitude toward any object.

Persuasion often involves the creation and dissemination of messages (both verbal and nonverbal) aimed at creating favorable attitudes toward an object, person, or event. While persuasion researchers caution against accepting the notion of a direct relationship between attitudes and behavior (also referred to as attitude–behavior consistency), our behavior very often does correspond with our attitudes. For example, if you have an extremely unfavorable attitude toward operatic music, it would be highly unlikely to find you attending a concert featuring The Three Tenors, unless you were coerced into attending by the use of physical or verbal aggression or by some of the compliance-gaining strategies we will identify in this chapter.

If you can persuade a person to endorse a proposal, you might be confident that a person's behavior regarding the object of the proposal will follow in the direction of the persuasive effort. For example, if you can persuade an individual to accept the proposal "We should abandon our current low-fat diet plan in favor of adopting a low-carbohydrate diet plan," then you may be reasonably confident that this person will change eating behaviors by cutting out carbohydrate-laden breads, cakes, rolls, pasta, rice, and potatoes.

As we have suggested, argument is inherent in the process of persuasion. Thus, from a source perspective, argumentativeness should be related to persuasion. Research on this trait has established that high argumentatives generate more arguments (Rancer & Infante, 1985) and that their arguments are of higher quality (Infante, 1981; Onyekwere et al., 1991) than low argumentatives. From a receiver perspective, high argumentatives have been found to be more inflexible regarding their position when others try to persuade them (Infante, 1981). In this chapter we report results of research that, among other things, examines speculations regarding whether high argumentatives use a greater diversity of persuasive strategies, are more persistent in their persuasive attempts, generate more counterarguments when considering persuasive messages, and invent more arguments favorable to a persuader.

An Orientation to Compliance Gaining

Compliance-gaining attempts are ubiquitous in human communication. Although persuasion is thought of as primarily concerned with changing attitudes, beliefs, intentions, and behaviors (see Fishbein & Ajzen, 1975; Ajzen & Fishbein, 1980), compliance gaining has focused primarily "on what people do when they want to get something" (Gass & Seiter, 1999, p. 205). Compliance-gaining efforts involve a variety of people, including strangers, friends, and intimates, and a variety of issues ranging from something major (requesting that your parents pay your college tuition for this academic year) to more minor issues (asking a friend to let you borrow their car for the evening). It should be noted, however, that a minor issue to one person may be seen as a major issue to another, and vice versa. Recall that compliance gaining involves the use of persuasive strategies designed to get someone to perform some desired behavior that they may be reluctant to do (Wilson, 1998, p. 273). An assumption in compliance-gaining research is that persuaders are generally aware of the choices they make.

The manner in which partners communicate during compliance-gaining efforts can help determine whether a relationship will be seen as satisfying or unsatisfying or whether a compliance-gaining attempt will be successful or unsuccessful. A person who communicates in a verbally aggressive manner to secure compliance from a partner would likely damage the relationship and end up being less successful as a result. Accordingly, an understanding of argumentativeness and verbal aggressiveness can facilitate a better understanding of persuasion and compliance gaining in one-on-one settings. With this in mind, interpersonal (or informal) persuasion as it is exhibited via argumentative and aggressive communication will be the focus of this section.

Although a great deal of scholarly attention has been directed at understanding compliance-gaining message behavior, the psychology and communication disciplines have not abandoned interest in more traditional persuasion approaches and theories. The major difference appears to be in the focus of these research efforts. Gass and Seiter (1999) suggest that while traditional persuasion research "has concerned itself with identifying what strategies are more effective, studies on compliance gaining have attempted to identify which strategies are most likely to be used by a persuader" (p. 205).

Both persuasion and compliance-gaining attempts involve the use of argumentative and verbally aggressive behavior. That is, when attempting to persuade others, people try to present arguments supporting the position(s) they are advocating, while attempting to refute the position(s) of others. This is the essence of being argumentative, a constructive form of communication. It is not uncommon, however, for people to use destructive methods when attempting to persuade or obtain compliance from others. For example, the use of physical aggression is routinely employed by misguided and psychologically unhealthy people as a method of getting what they want from others. The use of physical aggression to gain compliance has been examined by scholars studying spousal abuse (Jacobson & Gottman, 1998b), sexual violence in dating (Andonian & Droge, 1992), violence between siblings (Simonelli, Mullis, Elliot, & Pierce, 2002), and corporal punishment of children (Infante, 2005; Kassing, Pearce, & Infante, 2000; Kassing, Pearce, Infante, & Pyles, 1999). Unfortunately, the use of threats and other forms of verbal aggression is also employed as a compliance-gaining strategy (see Rudd, Burant, & Beatty, 1994).

Persuasion and Compliance-Gaining Research: A Focus on Traits

For quite some time, communication and personality scholars have investigated how individual difference factors (i.e., traits and predispositions) function in persuasion and compliance-gaining situations. In their seminal book *Personality and Persuasibility*, Hovland and Janis (1959) suggested that a personality trait, *persuasibility*, exists, which is defined as how susceptible a person is to the persuasive efforts of others. This trait allows us to predict how much an individual will be predisposed to persuasive efforts regardless of who is doing the persuading, what the topic is, or what situational factors are present. Similarly, a great deal of persuasion research was conducted by Rokeach (1960) on the personality trait of *dogmatism*, defined as how open or closed an individual's belief system is. Research has revealed that highly dogmatic (or closed-minded) people are more difficult to persuade, *unless* the source of the persuasive effort is seen as highly credible and the topic is less important to them. In this case, dogmatic individuals tend to be more easily persuaded. Another personality trait, *Machiavellianism*, has been studied extensively by persuasion researchers (see Christie & Geis, 1970). Machiavellianism "refers to an orientation in which people believe manipulating others is a basic strategy of social influence" (Infante et al., 2003, p. 108). High Machiavellian personalities have a strong need to influence others and use whatever tactics they can in order to do so.

Several traits and personality predispositions have also been studied with regard to compliance-gaining efforts. For example, O'Keefe and Delia (1979) studied the influence of *cognitive complexity* (a trait referring to the number and abstractness of constructs we use to perceive the world). Koper and Boster (1988) explored the relationship of *communication apprehension* and compliance gaining. Neuliep (1986) examined use of compliance-gaining messages by high- and low-dogmatic individuals, and Boster and Stiff (1984) studied compliance-gaining message selection behavior among Machiavellian individuals. More recently, a body of research that examines the interaction of the traits of argumentativeness and verbal aggressiveness on persuasion and compliance-gaining efforts has begun.

A Transactional Approach to Argumentativeness and Persuasion

Levine and Boster (1996) expanded our understanding of argumentativeness and persuasion by developing a transactional perspective to studying argumentative behavior. They argue that a fundamental tenet of human communication is that one person's message behavior affects another person's message behavior, and vice versa. This transactional approach to personality suggests that a person's personality may influence others' behavior as well as one's own behavior (p. 346).

Drawing from this transactional perspective, Levine and Boster (1996) hypothesized that when interacting in pairs, highly argumentative individuals should generate a greater number of arguments in support of their positions and be less yielding to others' positions than low argumentative individuals (p. 350). These results were expected due to the interaction of the argumentativeness of both individuals, rather than from either person's trait alone. In other words, the level of argumentativeness of each interactant was predicted to influence the number of arguments generated and to determine which partner would be most likely to yield to the other.

Levine and Boster (1996) also offered three hypotheses pertaining to the transactional nature of interpersonal argument. First, they suggested that a dyad composed of low argumentatives would present fewer arguments and show greater yielding of positions. Second, they predicted that a dyad composed of high argumentatives would present a greater number of arguments and show lower levels of yielding than any other combination. Finally, they predicted that a high argumentative paired with a low argumentative would generate a greater number of arguments and exhibit less yielding than any other dyad combination.

To test these speculations, Levine and Boster (1996) had students complete the Argumentativeness Scale, and a total of 60 (only male) students were selected for the study (30 high and 30 low argumentatives). A number of controversial issues were selected for the arguments, including gun control, increased military spending, drug testing, the death penalty, legalization of drugs, and surrogate mothering. Individuals were paired with a person who was either similar or dissimilar to themselves in trait argumentativeness (i.e., a high argumentative with a high argumentative, a low argumentative with a low argumentative, and a high argumentative with a low argumentative). Each dyad received one of the controversial issues and was told to discuss it with their partners for 5 minutes. The experimenters then assigned each participant to another debate with a different partner on a different issue.

Videotapes of each argument were made and the impact of both actors' argumentativeness on the number of arguments and the type of resolution generated in these arguments was examined. Coders were asked to identify the number of arguments generated by each participant in order to obtain a measure of willingness to yield.

The results provided support for the transactional perspective regarding trait argumentativeness and argumentative behavior. First, both conversational partners' levels of argumentativeness interacted to influence the number of arguments generated and the extent to which one person yielded to the position advocated by the other. The "high argumentative subject–low argumentative partner" dyad emerged as the one that generated the greatest number of arguments and showed the most resistance to yielding to the other. That is, highly argumentative individuals were more argumentative when paired with a low, rather than high, argumentative partner. It was also revealed that the argumentativeness of the adversary did not affect the argumentative behavior of low argumentatives. Thus, the findings support the transactional perspective to argumentative interaction.

To explain these findings, Levine and Boster (1996) speculated that when paired with a low argumentative partner, high argumentatives seize this opportunity to demonstrate their superior argumentative skill. When paired with an equally argumentative adversary, the high argumentative may experience frustration in his or her inability to dominate the adversary, which is then reflected in less assertive behavior. These findings are somewhat different from earlier research by Rancer and Infante (1985), who discovered that highly argumentative individuals report more motivation to argue when paired with a similar adversary. A reason for differences in the results of these studies may be that Rancer and Infante used both males and females, whereas in Levine and Boster's study only males were included. The reaction of the frustrated male participants could be a function of their inability to dominate each other during the argument. Further, in Rancer and Infante's study, participants never actually argued with each other; they simply provided predictions about how motivated they would be to argue. Thus, Levine and Boster's study underscores the value of using a transactional approach to studying argumentative communication and persuasion, in that individuals' levels of trait argumentativeness function *interactively* to influence the amount of argumentative behavior and the amount of yielding (i.e., persuasion) in conflict situations.

Processing Persuasive Messages: The Influence of Argumentative and Aggressive Communication

Research has also explored how argumentativeness and verbal aggressiveness affect peoples' processing of persuasive messages. Hample and Dallinger have conducted several studies designed to enhance our understanding of individuals' argumentative behavior in the interpersonal context. In one effort, they examined how people edit their own arguments before they actually deliver them. The tradition of *argumentative invention* suggests there are two parts to the process of argumentation. First, people create or invent arguments, and then they select certain arguments to present during a persuasive or compliance-gaining attempt. Hample and Dallinger (1987) investigated the second part of this inventional process by asking "why is one argument offered, and another suppressed, during an argumentative encounter" (p. 124).

Hample and Dallinger (1985a, 1985b) identified four general categories of *cognitive editing standards* (i.e., criteria people use in deciding whether to present or suppress a given argument). These general categories are defined as follows:

1. *effectiveness*, in which people reject certain arguments because they feel the argument will not work well or might backfire;

2. *principled objections*, in which people reject arguments because they have a severe dislike for the type of argument strategy it represents (e.g., the use of threats or bribes);

3. *person-centered issues*, in which an argument may be rejected because it violates the arguer's image of him- or herself, might injure their adversary, or, if presented, might do irreparable harm to the relationship;

4. *discourse competence,* in which people might reject an argument because the argument is judged to be false, too easily refuted, or irrelevant to the conflict.

The influence of argumentativeness and verbal aggressiveness on cognitive editing of arguments was investigated by Hample and Dallinger (1987). In addition, gender and *interpersonal orientation* (defined as how sensitive, responsive, and tuned into the personal characteristics of a partner you are; see Swap & Rubin, 1983) are said to influence this processing of arguments. Previous research has revealed that high argumentatives generate and plan to deliver more arguments (Infante & Rancer, 1982; Rancer et al., 1997), are more willing to argue, and have more skill at arguing (Infante, 1981). It was speculated that high argumentatives would differ from low argumentatives in their cognitive editing such that highs would offer more arguments, would make more use of the *discourse competence* category to reject the delivery of arguments, and would make less use of the *principled objections* category to reject the delivery of arguments (Hample & Dallinger, p. 125).

Previous research has also revealed that people high in verbal aggressiveness are more likely to present messages designed to damage another person's self-concept (Infante & Wigley, 1986). As such, Hample and Dallinger (1987) speculated that high verbally aggressive individuals would differ from low verbally aggressive individuals in their cognitive editing standards. They predicted that those high in verbal aggressiveness would deliver more arguments (i.e., they would not reject some arguments even if they cause damage to the other or the relationship), would make more use of the effectiveness criterion (i.e., their lack of concern for interpersonal outcomes makes effectiveness their primary objective in cognitive editing), and make less use of the principled objection criterion (i.e., high verbal aggressives may feel that any message or argument, even if it involved threats or bribes, is fair). They also suggested that those high in verbal aggressiveness would make less use of the harm-to-other and relationship preservation criteria of the person-centered issue category (Hample & Dallinger, 1987, pp. 126–127).

Students were told that the study was concerned with "how people go about trying to persuade others to do something" (Hample & Dallinger, 1987, p. 129). First, they were administered the Argumentativeness and Verbal Aggressiveness scales. Next, they were given one of three different compliance-gaining situations (e.g., "You want your friend to go jogging with you," "You want your roommate to buy some typing paper for you," "You want to have your roommate begin the job search process by writing a resume, and getting placement papers together"). Each compliance-gaining strategy was accompanied by three arguments, and participants' were asked to indicate whether they would endorse or reject each argument (responses included, "I would use this one," "No, this is too negative to use," "No, this argument is irrelevant").

Overall, the study demonstrated that people who vary in argumentativeness and verbal aggressiveness do use different cognitive editing standards in suppressing arguments. First, individuals high in argumentativeness and high in verbal aggressiveness expressed a greater tendency to endorse compliance-gaining arguments. In addition, females and individuals low in verbal aggressiveness were less likely to use the effectiveness category or to endorse arguments in general, but were more likely to use principled objections and person-centeredness (e.g., harm to others) to suppress the use of persuasive appeals.

The argumentativeness and verbal aggressiveness traits do influence cognitive editing of arguments, with those people high in both traits being less willing to suppress arguments, even when those arguments might be considered harmful to the adversary and to the relationship. Although these results are consistent with what was already known regarding the person high in verbal aggressiveness, it was a surprising finding regarding those high in argumentativeness. That is, we have previously believed that individuals who are high in argumentativeness would not resort to delivering harmful or hurtful messages. These results, however, suggest that under certain circumstances even high argumentatives may resort to verbally aggressive communication.

Mongeau (1989) studied how argumentativeness and another predisposition, the need for cognition, impact persuasive message processing and the attitude–behavior relationship. To explore this, Mongeau utilized the elaboration likelihood model (Petty & Cacioppo, 1986) of persuasion. This model proposes that people process information in two ways, centrally and peripherally. In central processing, individuals carefully scrutinize the message content and engage in a great deal of issue-related thinking. At other times, people process messages through the peripheral route where the receiver decides to follow a principle or decision rule derived from the persuasive situation (e.g., "This source is a real expert so I can believe in and trust what she is saying").

Mongeau (1989) offered hypotheses regarding the relationship between the two traits (i.e., argumentativeness and need for cognition) and the processing of persuasive messages. First, people high in the *need for cognition* (defined as "enjoyment individuals derive from engaging in effortful information processing"; Cacioppo, Petty, Kao, & Rodriguez, 1986, p. 1033) were thought to be more likely to scrutinize messages than those who were low in the need for cognition. Mongeau also speculated that those individuals high in need for cognition and high in argumentativeness would be able to differentiate between strong and weak arguments more effectively, base their attitudes on message quality more strongly, and exhibit stronger attitude–behavior relations than individuals low in need for cognition or low in argumentativeness (p. 2).

An experiment was conducted to explore whether argument quality (i.e., high-quality argument versus low-quality argument), need for cognition (high, low), and argumentativeness (high, low) influenced attitudes toward a proposal ("the adoption of comprehensive exams for undergraduate students" (Mongeau, 1989, p. 3) and behavioral intentions (intentions to work for or against that proposal). Students were administered both the Need for Cognition measure (Cacioppo, Petty, & Kao, 1984) and the Argumentativeness Scale (Infante & Rancer, 1982) and their scores were used to create the high and low need for cognition and high and low argumentativeness groups.

The participants were also given a packet of materials that contained items designed to measure perceived argument quality, scales designed to measure attitudes toward the proposal (to adopt comprehensive exams for undergraduates), measures of behavioral intention (e.g., "Do you intend to attend a meeting to discuss the proposal?" "Do you intend to work for a group that supported or opposed the proposal, or for neither group?"). They were also asked how many hours they intended to work for the group they had chosen, then participants read the written proposal and completed the scales.

While low- and high-argumentative participants did not differ in their perceptions of the higher-quality arguments, high argumentatives did perceive the lower quality messages as weaker. High argumentatives also exhibited greater attitude–behavioral intention consistency than did low argumentatives.

That is, those who expressed favorable attitudes toward the proposal of adopting comprehensive exams for undergraduates also expressed greater intentions of attending a meeting to discuss the proposal, greater intentions to work for a group that supported the proposal, and greater intentions to work longer hours as well. Thus, trait argumentativeness influenced persuasive message processing and the relationship between attitudes and behavior in a very similar fashion as did need for cognition. This finding suggests that argumentativeness has a cognitive as well as behavioral component and underscores the importance of trait argumentativeness as a critical factor in persuasive efforts (Mongeau, 1989, p. 5).

Reacting to Verbal Aggression: The Role of Self-Esteem and Information Processing

Throughout this book we have suggested that being the recipient of verbal aggression causes damage to one's self-esteem due to the psychological pain, hurt, and embarrassment associated with it. Kinney and Segrin (1998) investigated factors that might influence the way individuals react to receiving verbal aggression from others. Why is it that some people are especially sensitive to verbal aggression from others, whereas others are more resilient to it? What Kinney and Segrin discovered is that people's ability to process information, their sensitivity to feedback, and their beliefs about themselves can make them more or less susceptible (and possibly even impervious) to the negative effects of verbally aggressive messages. That is, the way individuals see themselves and the way they process and react to information contribute to the way people react to verbal aggression from others.

According to Kinney and Segrin (1998) one's *sensitivity to feedback* is defined as "the ability to classify correctly incoming information as beneficial or detrimental to self" (p. 51). *Self-discrepancies* are people's self-perceptions formed when they deviate from what they and others expect of them. *Dysfunctional attitudes toward self* have been implicated as sources of either positive or negative reactions to verbal aggression delivered by others. To test these relationships, Kinney and Segrin designed a study in which students listened to a persuasive message (i.e., a public service announcement on sexually transmitted disease). The message was manipulated to either attack the participants' self-concepts by including their group membership (e.g., "you college students") and their intelligence (e.g., by calling them "stupid") or was supportive of their self-concepts (e.g., "being the smartest segment of society you can set an example for others"). Contrary to speculations, the aggressiveness of the message did not have a direct effect on participants' reports of self-esteem. However, a stronger relationship was found between sensitivity to feedback and self-esteem in the aggressive message than in the nonaggressive message. Kinney and Segrin speculated that perhaps only when a socially significant other (e.g., friend, family member, roommate) delivers a verbally aggressive message does it impact self-esteem and emotional state. Recall that in this study, the person delivering the verbal aggression was a stranger.

To test this, Kinney and Segrin (1998) modified the procedures and conducted another study in which the participants were exposed to verbally aggressive messages from someone they knew well and had actually interacted with. Contrary to this prediction, friends' verbal aggressiveness was not associated with positive or negative affect. However, participants' self-discrepancies and sensitivity to feedback along with their friends' use of verbal aggression combined to predict the participants' negative affect, their self-esteem, and their level of depression. Collectively, these findings led Kinney and Segrin to conclude that people who are less certain about themselves are more likely to experience negative emotions when friends who are usually supportive behave in verbally aggressive ways. Further, these results were explained by expectancy violations theory (Burgoon & Hale, 1988). That is, when friends who are usually supportive act in an unsupportive and verbally aggressive way, the emotional effects are significant because these friends have violated expectancies. They also noted that being sensitive to feedback may be a characteristic that can protect individuals from verbal aggression and may be another cognitive moderator when receiving verbal aggression (Kinney & Segrin, p. 66).

Argumentativeness, Verbal Aggressiveness, and Compliance-Gaining Behavior

A persuader's choice of compliance-gaining message strategies depends, in part, on the anticipated emotional impact on the target. Hunter and Boster (1987) presented a model suggesting that "the more negative the emotional impact of a compliance-gaining message on the listener, the less any given persuader will want to use the message" (p. 65). For example, suppose you want your roommate to contribute more money to the living expenses of the apartment you share. You might say, "If you don't contribute more money, I'll look for another roommate." If you use a potentially negative compliance-gaining strategy such as this threat, your roommate (the target of your compliance-gaining effort) may become angry or resentful, and your attempt to persuade may fail. It might be better for a persuader to avoid using compliance-gaining messages that elicit negative emotional reactions in targets (Hunter & Boster, p. 65).

Although this model might describe most people's selection of compliance-gaining strategies, what if the person selecting a strategy is argumentative or verbally aggressive? Whether a person is high or low in these traits may play a role in the amount and types of compliance-gaining strategies used (Hunter & Boster, 1987, p. 82). Some individuals might not care about the feelings or the emotional reaction of the target of the compliance-gaining request. Might a person high in verbal aggressiveness, who exhibits little concern over the feelings of another, use fewer compliance-gaining strategies, but more negative ones? This question has led to several studies testing the influence of argumentativeness and verbal aggressiveness on compliance-gaining behavior. An early study conducted by Reynolds (1987) examined whether an individual high in argumentativeness (i.e., a more skilled persuader) would use more compliance-gaining strategies or only avoid using the more negative strategies that punish and repel an opponent (Reynolds, p. 6). To address this question, Reynolds studied the effects of argumentativeness, assertiveness, and need for cognition on the selection of compliance-gaining strategies.

Students completed the Need for Cognition Scale (Cacioppo et al., 1984), the Argumentativeness Scale (Infante & Rancer, 1982), and the Assertiveness Measure (Bakker, Bakker-Rabdau & Breit, 1978). Participants were also presented with a list of compliance-gaining messages and were asked the likelihood of using each. Surprisingly, the approach dimension of argumentativeness (ARGap) was not related to compliance strategy use. However, the tendency to avoid arguments (ARGav) and proactive assertiveness (e.g., being forceful and ascendant in support of self)

> were associated with the use of *fewer* compliance-gaining strategies. An example of proactive assertiveness would be: "When standing in line and a person pushes in front of me, I tell them to go to the back of the line." Thus, as an individual's tendency to avoid arguments increases, their use of compliance-gaining strategies decreases. This suggests that assertiveness and the tendency to avoid arguing may be associated less with overt compliance-gaining strategies, and more with subtle or nonverbal suasory message strategies. (Reynolds, 1987, p. 15)

To try and make sense of these findings, Boster and his colleagues replicated and extended this line of research. A series of studies was conducted examining how argumentativeness and verbal aggressiveness relate with compliance-gaining message choices. First, Boster and Levine (1988) speculated that high argumentatives and high verbal aggressives would produce higher compliance-gaining message ratings than low argumentatives and low verbal aggressives. To test this, the Argumentativeness and Verbal

Aggressiveness Scales were administered to students to classify them into the high and low conditions of each trait. Next, two compliance-gaining situations were presented. The first situation dealt with trying to get the best trade-in value on a used car and was considered a "non-interpersonal situation with short-term consequences" (Boster & Levine, p. 117). The second dealt with trying to get a relational partner to move to the southwest United States and was deemed an "interpersonal situation with long-term consequences" (Boster & Levine, p. 117). Participants were presented with 32 compliance-gaining messages and were asked how likely it was that they would use each of them. High argumentatives reported that they would use a greater variety of compliance-gaining strategies and were generally more persistent than low argumentatives in their compliance-gaining attempts, although both expressed an equal concern with the emotional impact of their messages. In contrast, high-verbal aggressives were unconcerned with the emotional impact of their compliance-gaining messages regardless of whether the target was an intimate or nonintimate other (Boster & Levine, p. 117).

This line of research was further extended by measuring two dimensions of actual compliance-gaining behavior, diversity and persistence (Boster, Levine, & Kazoleas, 1993). *Diversity* refers to the number of different message strategies used in a compliance-gaining effort, whereas *persistence* is the total number of compliance-gaining attempts. Students participated in a negotiation game in which they sent written messages to each other to buy and sell a used car. Points were awarded based on the purchase price of the vehicle during this negotiation, with the goal of accumulating the most points. The researchers measured persistence by summing the total number of messages used, and diversity was measured by computing the total number of different compliance-gaining message types.

The findings revealed a difference between high and low argumentatives regarding diversity of messages used. High argumentatives used more diverse compliance-gaining strategies than low argumentatives. In addition, verbally aggressive individuals used more negatively-oriented compliance-gaining messages. They reportedly did so because their lack of skill in arguing impedes their ability to create and use compliance-gaining strategies that are more positive in nature (Boster et al., 1993).

What is the role of argumentative and aggressive traits in refusing a compliance-gaining effort? What type of follow-up message appeals will people use in response to a refused request, and does the argumentative and aggressive nature of the person influence this? To address these questions, Ifert and Bearden (1998) explored whether argumentativeness and verbal aggressiveness influence the types of appeals individuals say they would use when responding to refusals of requests. They suggest that in persuasive situations, individuals usually respond to refusals with two types of appeals, evidentiary and nonevidentiary. *Evidentiary* appeals are referred to as rational appeals because they contain information to support a claim (e.g., "I can't help you study for your geometry test because I haven't taken the geometry course yet" (see Cody, Canary, & Smith, 1994; Ifert & Bearden; Reardon, 1991). As such, evidentiary appeals are seen positively and judged more favorably and effectively. *Nonevidentiary appeals* are arguments (claims) that contain little or no supporting material, but instead rely on simple assertions (e.g., "I can't help you study for your geometry test because I'm too tired"). This type of appeal tends to be more emotional and is seen less favorably than evidentiary appeals (Ifert & Bearden).

The influence of argumentativeness and verbal aggressiveness on the types of messages people enact after the refusal of a request was examined by Ifert and Bearden (1998). They suggested a positive relationship would be observed between argumentativeness and use of evidentiary appeals, and a negative relationship would be found between verbal aggressiveness and use of evidentiary appeals. Conversely, they also predicated a positive relationship between verbal aggressiveness and use of nonevidentiary appeals and a negative relationship between argumentativeness and use of nonevidentiary appeals.

Participants were asked to imagine themselves trying to either persuade a professor to change a low grade or convince a security officer to refrain from ticketing their car. Participants were then given a hypothetical statement that the professor or security guard might give to reject their persuasive request. They responded to various refusal statements (e.g., "The law says I have to ticket you" for the ticketing scenario or "You didn't fulfill the assignment guidelines" for the changing-grade scenario) by writing out what they would say in response to the refusal statement. Participants also completed both the Argumentativeness and Verbal Aggressiveness scales. The results showed that both argumentativeness and aggressiveness influenced choices of appeals to the refused requests. People high in trait argumentativeness reported constructing more evidentiary appeals in response to the refused requests whereas people high in verbal aggressiveness reported constructing a greater number of nonevidentiary appeals. Ifert and Bearden's (1998) results support the notion that verbal aggressiveness may be the result of an argumentative skill deficiency, an explanation we covered earlier in this book. That is, individuals who are predisposed to employ verbal aggression as a (compliance-gaining) message strategy may do so because they lack the ability and skill in inventing arguments.

Determining Intentions to Argue: Testing Two Frameworks

Several theoretical or explanatory frameworks that have guided our understanding of individuals' motivation to argue have been presented throughout this book. For example, in developing the argumentativeness construct, Infante and Rancer (1982) relied on Atkinson's theory of achievement motivation (see Chapter 2) and the interactionist approach (Infante, 1987a; see Chapter 3) to help understand intentions to argue. Stewart and Roach (1998) speculated that another often cited persuasion theory, the theory of reasoned action (Ajzen & Fishbein, 1980; Fishbein and Ajzen, 1975), might also be a valuable framework for helping us to understand individuals' intentions to argue. As such, they tested two competing theoretical frameworks (the interactionist perspective versus the theory of reasoned action) to determine which would be more efficacious for predicting whether people will, or will not, argue an issue. Recall that the interactionist perspective maintains that people's motivation to argue is determined by the interaction of traits (i.e., argumentativeness) and situational factors (the perceived probability and importance of success and failure of arguing) to predict motivation to argue in a given situation.

The theory of reasoned action maintains that a person's decision to engage in a purposeful activity depends on several factors, of which some are situational and some are mediated by personal dispositions or traits. At the core of the theory is the idea that when people engage in a given behavior it is because they formed an intention to do so and have reasons for their decision to actualize their intentions. Because of this, much of our behavior can be characterized as "reasoned action" (Infante et al., 2003, p. 129). Fishbein and Ajzen (1975) suggested that behavioral intentions are controlled by two factors: attitude toward an act and the normative component. Attitude toward an act is influenced by the beliefs that people have about the consequences of performing an act. The normative component is controlled by our beliefs about what valued others (i.e., people important in our lives) expect us to do. For some behaviors we rely more on our attitude toward an act, whereas for other behaviors we may rely more on the normative component for guidance on how to behave.

Stewart and Roach (1998) speculated that the theory of reasoned action might have greater explanatory power than the interactionist framework for understanding intentions to argue because it takes into account a greater number of situational factors such as people's beliefs about arguing (e.g., Rancer et al., 1985, 1992), the importance placed on the issue of the argument (e.g., Infante & Rancer, 1993; Onyekwere et al., 1991), the effects of other dispositional factors (such as religious orientation; see Stewart & Roach, 1993), and the influence of other people. They reasoned that all of these factors might combine to influence a person's intentions to argue in a given situation. Because arguing is an intentional behavior under the control of the arguer, it can legitimately be called a form of reasoned action (Stewart & Roach, 1998). Several hypotheses were advanced pertaining to the components of the theory of reasoned action, including intentions to argue, attitude toward arguing an issue, the subjective norm, emotional reactions to arguing, and ego involvement with the issue.

First, Stewart and Roach (1998) had students complete the Argumentativeness Scale and a scale to measure religious orientation (Allport & Ross, 1967). A few weeks later, another questionnaire was administered that asked the same students to provide their "thoughts and feelings" about arguing the issue of "distributing free condoms on campus" (Stewart & Roach, 1998, p. 182). The questionnaire also contained scales to measure the components of the theory of reasoned action, including their perceived ego involvement, intentions to argue the issue, beliefs about the value of outcomes of arguing the issue of free condom distribution, and normative beliefs (or what they thought valued others would think about whether they should or should not argue the issue), as well as items designed to measure their motivation to comply with those normative beliefs.

Recall that Stewart and Roach (1998) speculated that components of the theory of reasoned action would be better predictors of intentions to argue than the interactionist perspective. The results showed that the theory of reasoned action was no better and perhaps even a little less powerful than the interactionist model in predicting intentions to argue. They did find, however, that the theory of reasoned action has some utility in predicting intentions to argue. That is, individuals' attitudes toward arguing in a particular situation, coupled with their beliefs about what people who are important to them think about arguing, are the primary determinants of intentions to argue. In addition, although high argumentatives had a more positive attitude toward arguing than did low argumentatives, the direct effect of those attitudes on intentions to argue came from the normative component and the perceived behavioral control portions of the theory of reasoned action. The normative component concerns societal expectations of what is appropriate or inappropriate, whereas perceived behavioral control reflects the degree to which a person sees an outcome as being under his or her control.

These findings are in opposition with the assumption that the trait alone influences intentions to argue and suggest that beliefs about arguing and motivations to argue may be more socially driven than individually determined. Stewart and Roach (1998) speculated that because high argumentatives are more competent communicators, they may be more open to normative pressures in deciding whether to engage in an argument and that high argumentatives experience strong social pressure to perform well in an argumentative situation. Assessing the outcome of this test of the two competing theories prompted Stewart and Roach to conclude, "As such, the interactionist model warrants further use as a framework for the study of trait versus situational determinants of argumentative intentions" (p. 191).

Argumentative and Aggressive Communication and Resistance to Persuasion

Throughout this book we have suggested that highly argumentative individuals, as compared with low argumentatives, are more competent in a variety of communication contexts (Rancer, Kosberg, & Silvestri, 1992; Richmond, McCroskey, & McCroskey, 1989). Some research suggests that high argumentatives may enjoy an advantage over low argumentatives in persuasion and compliance-gaining efforts. Argumentative people may have characteristics that make them more resistant to persuasion, and a few studies have investigated the influence of argumentativeness (and verbal aggressiveness) on *resistance to persuasion*.

Research by Kazoleas (1993) suggests that high and low argumentatives may differ in the ability to generate or construct counterarguments. An experiment was conducted in which respondents watched a 1-minute TV commercial advocating moderation in drinking and promoting the necessity to avoid drinking and driving. They also read two printed messages, one an advertisement from *USA Today* presenting arguments against the Clear Air Act and another consisting of a 1-page pamphlet from the American Cancer Association that advocated abstaining from sunbathing and using tanning booths. After watching the TV commercial and reading the printed material, respondents were requested to write down "any important thoughts they might have had during the message" (Kazoleas, 1993, p. 125). Following this, they completed a questionnaire that asked about their attitudes toward each topic (i.e., alcohol moderation, the Clean Air Act, and sunbathing and tanning), perceptions of the source's trustworthiness and expertise, and degree of involvement with each topic. Participants also completed the Argumentativeness Scale.

Kazoleas (1993) found high argumentatives were more resistant to persuasion and exhibited less agreement with each message's recommendations. In addition, high argumentatives generated more counterarguments when presented with a counterattitudinal message (i.e., a message inconsistent with one's existing attitude). Counterattitudinal activity was thought to be more enjoyable for high argumentatives than for low argumentatives, and as such, counterattitudinal activity can be thought of as another message in the persuasion context.

This line of reasoning led Infante, Step, and Horvath (1997) to speculate that high argumentatives might possess a greater tendency to persuade themselves, even if they initially disagree with a particular position (p. 80). They examined responses to intrapersonal argument by manipulating the extent to which high and low argumentatives were required to argue counterattitudinally (that is, arguing with themselves and against their existing position). They reasoned that high argumentatives should not only generate more arguments when asked to argue against a position they believed in, but should like the task more than low argumentatives. The counterarguments they generate, in turn, should function as intrapersonal persuasive messages.

Infante and his colleagues (1997) created an experiment in which participants completed the Argumentativeness Scale and were asked to create either a proattitudinal or counterattitudinal message on a proposal (i.e., registration of all firearms in the United States). After encoding these messages, attitudes toward the proposal were measured. Infante et al. found that argumentatives who created a counterattitudinal message (a message inconsistent with their existing attitudes toward the proposal) were no less favorable toward the task than people who provided a proattitudinal message. Thus, for high argumentatives, enjoying an argument extends even to situations when the opponent is oneself. This willingness to construct arguments that oppose one's currently held positions may help explain why argumentativeness has been associated with numerous positive outcomes (Infante et al.; Johnson & Johnson, 1979). Moreover, the findings support the notion that high argumentatives behave distinctively from others, both cognitively and affectively during arguments.

Levine and Badger (1993) were also interested in whether being high or low in argumentativeness makes one more or less resistant to persuasion. They utilized the cognitive response model, which suggests that people's thoughts (referred to as cognitive responses) explain their receptivity to persuasive messages, as the framework of their study. If a message stimulates pro-message thoughts in a person, the person will be more likely to support the position advocated in the message. Conversely, if a message stimulates irrelevant or unfavorable thoughts, it is likely to be counterargued and the person will be less likely to support the position advocated in the message. Because highly argumentative individuals engage in more counterargumentation, Levine and Badger predicted that highly argumentative individuals would be more resistant to persuasion than low argumentatives.

To test this assumption, Levine and Badger (1993) first classified individuals as high or low in argumentativeness and then asked them to indicate their opinions on a series of issues (e.g., forest conservation, organ donation, preventing heart attacks, abortion, voting, better eating habits). Participants were also asked to develop a persuasive speech on one of the topics. Later, they made and listened to several persuasive speeches on these topics and then completed the opinion survey a second time. The results were surprising in that they were opposite of what was expected. High argumentatives demonstrated significantly greater attitude change in the direction of the message than did low argumentatives. This finding was consistent across the different message topics. Levine and Badger offered several explanations for these unexpected and contradictory findings. First, since the participants were allowed to choose their own topics, they may have selected topics or positions that they were already in favor of. As such, they may have actually heard only pro-attitudinal persuasive messages. Second, high argumentatives may have also generated more pro-messages when faced with an acceptable message. It was also suggested that highly argumentative individuals may be more open-minded and less dogmatic. However, Levine and Badger continue to suggest that high argumentatives would be more resistant to persuasion, but only for positions that they oppose. If the message is pro-attitudinal, high argumentativeness may lead to less resistance to the position advocated in the message.

Of course, not all persuasive efforts are successful. What types of follow-up messages would a persuader choose to deliver if a receiver was resistant to the persuader's initial compliance-gaining attempt? How might that resistance affect a persuader's verbal aggressiveness in subsequent persuasive efforts? In an effort to address these issues, Lim (1990) studied whether receivers' resistance to compliance-gaining efforts led persuaders to be more verbally aggressive in subsequent persuasive efforts. The study examined whether the friendliness (the extent of liking toward the receiver) and intensity of the receiver's resistance affected persuaders' verbal aggressiveness. Lim predicted that when confronted with unfriendly and strong resistance from a target, persuaders will engage in consistently higher levels of verbal aggressiveness and will become verbally aggressive earlier in the subsequent compliance-gaining attempt with the target (p. 176).

To test this, Lim (1990) had six confederates (individuals who are part of the study) act as resisters of the persuasive attempts of others. The persuaders (i.e., the participants in the study) attempted to convince the confederates to redo some group project coursework that was done poorly and that could, if not corrected, jeopardize the group's grade on the assignment. The confederates were trained to exhibit different types and levels of resistance. For example, in the unfriendly and strong resistance condition, confederates were told to act in an unfriendly manner to the persuader, to shake their heads, and to say "I can't do it again." In the unfriendly and weak resistance condition, confederates again disagreed with the persuader, shook their heads, but said things like "If you promise to help me, I'll think of doing it again." In the friendly and strong resistance condition, confederates were told to act in a friendly manner, nod their heads, and say, "I can't do it again." Finally in the friendly and weak resistance condition, confederates were told to act in a friendly manner to the persuader, nod their heads, and say things like "Uh-huh" and "If you promise to help me, I'll think of doing it again."

The results demonstrated that persuaders who encountered strong resistance to a persuasive attempt exhibited verbally aggressive behavior more quickly than those facing weaker resistance. In addition, persuaders engaged in more verbal aggression when encountering unfriendly targets (confederates). Indeed, an outright rejection of a persuasive appeal by the target made persuaders the most verbally aggressive of all. This study supports the transactional nature of interpersonal persuasion by showing that persuaders decide on a persuasive course of action not only because of situational and personal preferences, but also as a result of the responses that they receive from the targets of their persuasive attempts (Levine & Boster, 1996; Lim, 1990).

Conclusion

In this chapter we have examined the role of argumentative and aggressive communication traits in the persuasion and compliance-gaining context. The research discussed in this chapter demonstrates that argument and arguing play a major part in persuasion and compliance-gaining efforts. As such, a trait perspective on argumentative and aggressive communication is useful to understanding the process and products involved in persuasion and compliance-gaining efforts.

Research on argumentativeness and verbal aggressiveness has also examined how persuasion and compliance gaining influence, and are influenced by, these traits. For example, research has found that high argumentatives discover more arguments in persuasion situations and use different criteria in deciding which arguments to use and which to suppress in a persuasive situation. In addition, high argumentatives use a greater diversity of influence strategies and are sometimes more persistent. They also generate more counterarguments and thus tend to be less susceptible to persuasion. Highly argumentative individuals also tend to display more attitude-behavior consistency in response to persuasive messages. Finally, a transactional approach to persuasion was advanced, suggesting that the combination of the interactants' levels of trait argumentativeness determines persuasive outcomes. As interpersonal persuasion is a more common form of persuasion, incorporating an understanding of argumentative and aggressive communication traits helps us understand persuasion and compliance gaining more fully.

Discussion Questions for Chapter 9

1. What is meant by the transactional approach regarding argumentativeness in the persuasion process? Do you agree with this approach? Why or why not?

2. Given that a person's level of argumentativeness and verbal aggressiveness influences how that person processes persuasive messages, do you notice the influence of these traits when trying to persuade your friends? How do your messages differ when trying to persuade friends who are high or low in argumentativeness? How do your messages differ when trying to persuade friends who are high or low in verbal aggressiveness?

3. It is argued that people who are high in verbal aggressiveness use fewer compliance-gaining strategies. Do you agree with this? If so, what types of compliance-gaining messages do you see your verbally aggressive friends using?

4. Some scholars believe that the theory of reasoned action is a better explanation for explaining intentions to argue than the interactionist explanation. Which explanation do you think best explains intentions to argue? Why?

5. What does it mean to say that people who are high in argumentativeness also have a greater tendency to persuade themselves? Based on your own level of argumentativeness, do you agree or disagree with this assertion?

PART III

Enhancing Communicative
Outcomes Through Improved
Understanding of
Argumentative and Aggressive
Communication Processes

10

Modifying Argumentative and Aggressive Communication

As most people have experienced firsthand, skills training is something that is part of our personal and professional lives. Examples include training for *hard skills* such as learning new software programs, driver education programs, and organizational procedure training. In contemporary society we have also seen a dramatic increase in the training of *soft skills*. Unlike hard skills where there is a mechanistic outcome (e.g., "I can effectively create and save a file in Microsoft Word"), soft-skill training reflects material focused largely on communication in human relationships. Some examples include effective decision making, assertiveness, public speaking skills, leadership, listening and empathetic skills, negotiation, and conflict management techniques. The goal of these programs are enhanced skills designed to bring about more satisfying relationships with family members and coworkers, among others.

Soft-skill training has occasionally been viewed as warm and fuzzy, but with little substance. However, research indicates that effective soft-skill training does affect the bottom line for people and organizations (Seibold, Kudsi, & Rude, 1993). For example, the more effective the communication between superior and subordinate, the more satisfied the employee. The more satisfied the employee, the more motivated he or she is. The more motivated the employee, the more productive he or she will be.

Argumentativeness and verbal aggressiveness are traits developed as a function of both inherited personality and environmental influences. If we assume that biology is solely responsible for these traits, then no amount of training would be effective in altering these predispositions. However, even advocates of the inherited trait explanation recognize that some communication behavior is the result of social learning and thus may be modified through training. In this chapter, we will highlight several efforts that have resulted in some meaningful and lasting changes to individuals' levels of argumentativeness and verbal aggressiveness.

The Call for Training

Inherent in the human condition and present throughout the life cycle is the need and desire to learn. From the time we enter the world we are continually acquiring the skills necessary for survival and enhanced existence. Recall the manners training provided by our parents through utterances such as, "What do you say when someone gives you something?" "We do not speak like that in this house!" and "Don't use that tone of voice." As we age, this training is often provided by our friends, coworkers, supervisors, and spouses. Just as we train people in constructive communication (e.g., argumentativeness), there is also a need to train people in the management or reduction of behaviors that are deemed destructive (e.g., verbal aggression).

The notion that people should be trained in argumentation can be traced to antiquity. Whether in ancient Greece or Rome, the ability to argue effectively was considered an invaluable skill. For example, in *The Rhetoric*, Aristotle presented rhetorical *topoi*, or lines of argument that could be used to enhance persuasion.

The Inventional System

In Chapter 4 we presented the argumentative skills deficiency model of interpersonal violence. The basic premise of this model is that people who lack the motivation and skill to invent arguments have a greater tendency to resort to verbal aggression, which can result in an escalated potential for physical aggression. Therefore, training people to argue is thought to bring about a decreased tendency to resort to verbal aggression. To this end, Infante (1988) proposed the inventional system for developing or generating arguments. The assumption here is that through training in how to invent arguments, people can enhance argumentative behavior. Regardless of the nature of the conflict or the proposition being argued, the inventional system is thought to be effective in helping individuals generate arguments to use when they are needed. That is, whether arguing propositions of policy (e.g., the government should legalize marijuana), fact (e.g., adding fluoride to water supplies results in better dental health), or value (e.g., people who are considered medically brain dead should not be kept alive by artificial means), the inventional system should work to improve one's ability to invent arguments.

The inventional system (Infante, 1988) is composed of four main topics and several subissues. The main topics are problem, blame, solution, and consequence. The problem and blame components reflect the need for the proposal whereas the solution and consequence components reflect how the proposal will satisfy the need. The problem component contains three subissues of "What are the signs of the problem?" "What is the specific harm?" and "How widespread is the harm?" The blame component contains three subissues of "What causes the problem?" "Is the present system at fault?" and "Should the present system be changed?" The solution component contains two subissues of "What are the possible solutions?" and "Which solution best solves the problem?" The consequence component also contains two subissues of "What good outcomes will result from the solution?" and "What bad outcomes will result from the solution?"

The questions posed by the inventional system prompt people to think in a methodical and structured way. Infante (1988) contends that once a person commits this system to memory and uses it appropriately, it will have lasting effects on a person's thinking about any issue. Although primarily used to help generate arguments, the system can also be used to determine whether a person has enough knowledge to even argue in the first place. Given the series of questions posed by the inventional system, a person may quickly realize he or she does not have enough information to argue in a knowledgeable and successful fashion, which might result in the person actually refraining from arguing.

The development of argumentative skills has been part of several training efforts aimed at both adults and adolescents. A few of these efforts have focused on helping people increase their argumentative behavior while concomitantly dampening or diminishing their use of verbal aggression. One assumption inherent in these programs is that the teaching of argument (a constructive behavior) should decrease the likelihood of an individual to resort to verbally attacking another person (a destructive behavior).

Training Adults to Argue Constructively

How would one go about designing training aimed at increasing argumentative communication while simultaneously reducing verbal aggression? The most comprehensive effort along these lines was advanced by Infante (1995a). Infante proposed teaching a unit designed specifically toward understanding and controlling verbal aggression in the undergraduate class-room. The training has three fundamental goals:

1. understanding the nature of verbal aggression,

2. developing strategies for controlling verbal aggression, and

3. engaging in activities designed to internalize the knowledge and behaviors learned in the training.

The first goal focuses on understanding the following: (1) distinctions between constructive and destructive communication (i.e., that assertiveness and argumentativeness are constructive traits, whereas hostility and verbal aggressiveness are destructive traits), (2) the nature of verbal aggressiveness which concerns the potency and types of verbally aggressive messages (e.g., character and competence attacks, teasing, ridicule, maledictions, profanity, nonverbal verbal aggression), (3) the reasons or origins of verbal aggression (i.e., psychopathology, disdain, social learning, genetics, and argumentative skill deficiency), and (4) the effects of verbal aggression (i.e., self-concept damage and the potential escalation of aggression). Understanding this model constitutes the knowledge portion of the training.

The second goal concerns the development of strategies for controlling verbal aggression and conflict situations. Infante (1995a) proposed using three approaches to achieve this goal. First is the ability to create inter-personal situations that do not contain verbal aggression by employing communication skills such as positiveness, supportiveness, empathy, and confirming the position of the other person. This, in effect, will reflect a sup-portive communication climate as opposed to a defensive communication climate (Gibb, 1961).

The second approach focuses on the individual as opposed to the situation. As the level of verbal aggressiveness varies among people, Infante (1995a) recommends that we try to avoid being in relationships with people who are high in verbal aggressiveness. Training people to identify verbal and nonverbal behaviors that are indicators of verbal aggression early in a relationship make it easier for people to terminate a potentially destructive relationship. These behaviors can include a person shaking his or her head in disgust or a person's reaction to other aggressive people. Further, once identified, relational disen-gagement strategies (i.e., break-up strategies) should also be taught.

The third approach in achieving the ability to control verbal aggression involves training in argument skills. Recall the research that revealed the probability of verbal and physical aggression is reduced when people possess the ability to formulate arguments when they need to advocate positions on issues and use arguments to attack the positions of others. One of the most effective ways of generating arguments is through the use of Infante's (1988) inventional system.

Preventing the escalation of an aggressive situation is part of the second goal of this training unit. As several of us have experienced, when one person resorts to personal attacks, the other person generally responds in kind. That is, verbal aggression begets verbal aggression. There are, however, strategies that can be used to deescalate or diffuse an otherwise potentially explosive situation. Infante (1995a) offers three approaches for neutralizing an aggressive situation. The first is an adaptation of Margoline's (1979) treatment model for abusive couples. More specifically, this involves training people in the following seven phases of aggressive situations:

1. identifying factors that stimulate anger in the situation (e.g., topic, time of discussion, etc.),

2. developing tactics to interrupt the angry reaction (e.g., the person tells the other that they are getting angry),

3. developing tactics to discuss the issue later when the angry person has calmed down,

4. eliminating the behavior that provokes anger (e.g., rolling of the eyes, interruptions),

5. changing incorrect thoughts about the relationships (e.g., we fight, therefore you do not love me anymore),

6. sharpening the skills to resolve or solve problems, and

7. developing strategies to improve the climate of the relationship.

The second approach offered by Infante (1995a) is the development of skills to protect the self from abusive situations by dismissing the attack. These strategies can be targeted at the situation, the victim, or the attacker. Using Wagner's (1980) strategies for dismissal, Infante offers the following strategies for the dismissal of attacks due to the situation: misinformation (i.e., claiming that the attack was based on faulty information) and coercion (i.e., claiming that the information used to attack the person was obtained by the threat of force). Dismissal strategies consist of personal growth (i.e., the belief that the person who is attacked has changed and, as such, is no longer worthy of the attack), the unconscious (i.e., agreeing with that attacker but blaming the characterization on the subconscious and, as such, being beyond control), and excuse (i.e., claim that the characterization is unwarranted because the victim is not to blame). Strategies toward the source consist of ignorance (i.e., the person who is making the attack has no idea what he or she is talking about), the dark side (i.e., the person doing the attacking is motivated by jealousy, resentment, envy, or a general tendency to be cruel), and unacknowledged motives (i.e., the person making the attack has ulterior motives). All of these dismissal strategies are believed to neutralize an aggressive situation.

Infante's (1995a) final approach focuses directly on interaction between the victim and the attacker and is known as the argumentative approach. This involves the following five types of communication: (1) refuting the verbally aggressive claim (i.e., counterarguing the premise of the personal attack), (2) distinguishing argument from verbal aggression (i.e., speaking of how the argument turned into a personal attack and suggesting that the attacker get back to the argument), (3) taking a position of nonreciprocity (i.e., acknowledging to the attacker that the attack has occurred but you will not reciprocate and that the topic should be turned back to the issue at hand), (4) appealing to rationality (i.e., telling the attacker that the personal attack is not a rational behavior and that having a rational discussion involves staying on topic), and (5) threatening interaction termination (i.e., telling the attacker that you will cease to discuss any issues until the personal attacks cease).

The final goal proposed by Infante (1995a) involves the development of activities that serve to have trainees internalize the knowledge and behaviors acquired in the unit. These activities range in scope from individually focused to group focused. At the individual level, people are asked to write a position paper or deliver a message on a particular aspect of verbal aggression (e.g., Are there situations where verbal aggression would be warranted?). A second individual activity concerns having the person conduct a brief research project on verbal aggression and write a paper or give a speech on the results. For the final individual activity, people are asked to keep a diary of the situations in which they encounter verbal aggression. These encounters should include the type of message, the situation around which the message was sent, whether they were the sender or receiver of the message, and whether the verbal aggression escalated.

For activities at the group level, Infante (1995a) proposes giving each group a problem such as "Can genetics explain verbally aggressive behavior?" The group then conducts a study and presents it in a panel format to the others in the training session. A variation of this would be to have group members take a subset of the data the group has collected and do a series of individual papers based on that data (e.g., one person focuses specifically on comparing men and women in verbal aggression use while another focuses on comparing young people and older people in verbal aggression use). A second group activity concerns charging the group with an issue such as

"Should spouses ever use verbal aggression with each other?" The group then discusses the issue and comes to a decision. That decision is then reported to the rest of the trainees. The final group activity uses a role-playing technique. A situation is assigned to the group and each group member is given a role (e.g., your teacher calls you stupid in front of the class). Each group member plays both the aggressor and the victim role. The group then discusses the different experiences.

The curriculum presented by Infante (1995a) represents a comprehensive matrix for decreasing verbal aggression. At this time, few if any attempts at integrating the entire curriculum have been made. This program, if performed as specified, holds exciting possibilities in teaching the knowledge and skills necessary to control verbal aggression. This is not to say that parts of the curriculum have not been utilized. The next section of this chapter will address specific efforts geared at increasing argumentative behavior and decreasing verbal aggression. Although Infante's curriculum was written with undergraduate college students in mind, he believes that it is applicable to numerous other situations including family communication, political communication, and organizational communication, as well as with different age groups.

Training in Argument

An effort to train adults in argumentation was conducted by Anderson, Schultz, and Courtney-Staley (1987), who investigated the impact that argumentation training has on assertiveness. More specifically, the training was based on the following assumptions: (a) effective conflict management assumes that a person is willing to engage in a conflict situation, (b) cognitive data (i.e., knowledge) about argument and conflict is needed to change negative stereotypes about arguing and conflict, and (c) when perceptions have been altered by knowledge of effective arguing, theories of argumentation as well as persuasion can be taught.

Ninety-six participants (45 men and 51 women) were assigned to the experimental condition (i.e., they received the training) and 89 (32 men and 57 women) were assigned to the control group (i.e., they received no training). The training included lecture, discussion, and small-group role playing. During the 3-hour training, the trainers highlighted the negative perceptions that people have of conflict and arguing as well as the constructive nature of being high in argumentativeness and having effective conflict-management skills. This was achieved by the sequence of training proposed by Schultz and Anderson (1984). The curriculum for the training included determining the perceptions of conflict and argumentativeness, determining individual goals, and determining the most effective strategy to achieve those goals (which may include argument, persuasion, agitation or avoidance, diffusion, and confrontation).

The results revealed that women showed the greatest amount of positive change from the training, which prompted the researchers to focus on the female trainees. Therefore, with this particular conceptualization of argument and conflict management content, a viable curriculum for the training of females in argumentative communication was offered. An ancillary finding of this study is as equally important as the sex differences observed. Anderson et al. (1987) report that the most dramatic change as a result of the training was found in the moderate argumentative group. That is, more pretraining moderate argumentatives (as identified by a pretest) were higher in argumentativeness (on the posttest) after the training than any other group. The percentage of females who moved from moderate to high in argumentativeness increased from 8% to 22% (a 14% increase as a result of the training). This is in contrast to a 3% increase for the low-argumentative group moving into moderate argumentativeness. One of the implications of this study is that we might expect more posttraining change in argumentativeness to occur among those moderate in the trait. Avtgis and Rancer (2005) suggest that individuals with extremely low or extremely high levels of a trait (e.g., argumentativeness and verbal aggressiveness) might be less influenced by situational factors (i.e., training programs) and may not benefit as much from training as would those more moderate in the traits. The results of the Anderson et al. study offer some support for this speculation.

Training Adolescents to Argue Constructively

The need to minimize the use of verbal aggression in adolescent populations is obvious. Among adolescents, the presence of verbal aggression seems ubiquitous as we hear it in their popular music and echoing throughout the streets where they play. We have all heard terms such as *bullying* and *abusive* when describing contemporary middle and high school life. Many school systems throughout the United States have instituted conflict management programs designed to minimize students' use of verbal abuse and physical aggression. Over the past several years, we have seen the devastation of Columbine (Colorado) High School and more recently the Red Lake (Minnesota) High School shootings in which verbal abuse has been implicated as a possible cause (Leary, Kowalski, Smith, & Phillips, 2003). Aggression has both a verbal and a physical component. As stated earlier, the goal of verbal aggression is to humiliate, embarrass, and hurt another person. The argumentative skill deficiency explanation for verbal aggression suggests that when a person lacks the skill and motivation to engage in argument, there is a greater tendency to resort to verbal aggression. This explanation has spawned efforts to develop training to encourage argumentative behavior and, as a result, to potentially decrease the use of verbal aggression.

One of the most comprehensive efforts to train adolescents in argument skills was conducted by Rancer et al. (1997), who sought to enhance motivation to argue and increase skill in argument by training adolescents how to use the inventional system. By teaching adolescents the system, the following objectives were included in the training program: (1) helping students understand the role that trait argumentativeness and trait verbal aggressiveness play in our conflict behavior, (2) teaching them the difference between argumentativeness and verbal aggressiveness, (3) providing them with a working knowledge of the inventional system, and (4) having them actually put the inventional system into practice by having them argue with an opponent.

To review, Infante's (1988) inventional system is based on the following argumentation premise: the status quo is in need of change and any given proposal will satisfy the need. The components of the system consist of a problem (e.g., what does the problem look like?), blame (e.g., who or what is responsible for the problem?), solutions (e.g., what possible solutions exist for the problem?), and consequences (e.g., what are the benefits and drawbacks from adopting the proposed solution?).

Because teaching adolescents to use such a system may seem a daunting task, Rancer et al. (1997) used a restaurant menu analogy in an effort to make components of the inventional system easier to memorize and learn. As a result, The Peanut Butter and Soda Crackers Diner Menu was created. The problem component was now the Peanut Course, the blame component was known as the Butter Course, the solution component was known as the Soda Course, and the consequence component was known as the Crackers Course. Each of these components also has subtopics that were also taught using pneumonic devices. For example, under the Peanut Course (problem component) there was swiss (i.e., sign of the problem), ham (i.e., harm being done by the problem), and wheat (i.e., how widespread the problem is). All of the subtopics of the other components were described in a similar manner (see Rancer et al.).

Seventh-grade students in a Pennsylvania middle school participated in the training program and study. During the first week of the school year, students were administered the adolescent versions of the Argumentativeness and Verbal Aggressiveness scales (see Roberto & Finucane, 1997). Students were placed into groups, with some of the groups receiving the training (i.e., the experimental group) and other groups not receiving the training (i.e., the control group).

The program consisted of 7 days of instruction. The first day consisted of learning the different types of arguments common in middle school, the distinctions between argumentative and verbally aggressive communication, and the importance of being able to argue effectively. The second day students were trained to identify constructive versus destructive arguments. In an effort to measure argument behavior, students were asked to generate arguments in support of the following proposition: "All students should be fluent in a foreign language in order to graduate from high school." The students then provided written arguments to support the proposition. This measure of argument behavior served as the pretest for the study.

The third and fourth days of training consisted of learning the components of the inventional system. On the fifth day, students were trained to use the system to generate arguments. The sixth day was used for posttraining argument behavior. The students were asked to develop arguments to the following proposition: "Crowding should be considered the most serious problem in cities today." The seventh and final day of training served as a posttest of student trait argumentativeness and verbal aggressiveness (again using the adolescent versions of both scales).

The results of the training were encouraging. When the experimental and control groups' posttest results were compared, adolescents in the experimental group reported a significant increase in their general tendency to argue (ARGgt). That is, their motivation to argue was significantly higher after the training. The training appears to have functioned effectively to enhance adolescents' motivation to argue.

Recall that the subjects in both conditions were also asked to generate as many arguments as they could on the proposition both prior to and after the training program. The results revealed that, on average, the experimental (trained) group generated almost four more arguments than the control group. Thus, the effects of the training also appear to have significantly influenced their ability to generate actual arguments.

The adaptation and use of the inventional system seem to have functioned successfully for increasing trait argumentativeness and argumentative behavior in adolescents. Another interesting finding was the confidence that the adolescents reported in their perceived mastery of the inventional system and the usefulness of the arguing skills they had learned. Sixty-one percent of the students reported feeling very confident, whereas only 4.4% of the students reported feeling confused or very confused with the skills acquired during the training. In terms of the usefulness of the training, 69% of the students also reported the skills as being very useful, useful, or somewhat useful to them.

An unexpected finding also emerged in the study. When predictions derived from the argumentative skill deficiency explanation were used, it was thought that increasing adolescents' motivation and skill in arguing would concomitantly reduce their level of verbal aggressiveness. However, the findings did not support this. In fact, students in the experimental condition actually increased their level of verbal aggressiveness from the pretest to the posttest. Several explanations were offered. Could the training, which exposed students to the concept of verbal aggression, stimulate the students to more accurately reflect on their own predispositions in the posttraining assessment? Did the training fail to successfully distinguish between a verbal attack on the person and an attack on the issue? Do adolescents see distinctions between constructive and destructive communication as meaningless? Is a separate training unit on verbal aggression (alone or in tandem with argument training) necessary to help adolescents further distinguish between argumentativeness and verbal aggressiveness? These and other questions need to be considered in the development of future training programs.

Whenever people experience change as a result of training, the question arises as to how long the change will last. The effect of training is only meaningful if the skills learned are integrated in one's behavioral repertoire and not just exhibited immediately after training. In an effort to examine this, the experimental group was revisited 1 year later to see if the training had an longitudinal effect on their trait argumentativeness and verbal aggressiveness. In this study, Rancer et al. (2000) re-examined the same students who underwent the training during the previous school year. Again, students were administered the adolescent versions of the Argumentativeness and Verbal Aggressiveness scales (Roberto & Finucane, 1997). The results indicated that the students' general tendency to argue (ARGgt) scores did not change significantly from their posttraining scores approximately 1 year before. These findings suggest support for the longitudinal effects of training regarding argumentativeness.

However, a significant increase in students' level of verbal aggressiveness was observed from 1 year earlier. Again, reasons were offered for this surprising finding. One explanation was that the training program did not contain content on teaching adolescents how to control for verbal aggressiveness. Other explanations for the increase in verbal aggressiveness included adolescents' inability to distinguish between argumentative and aggressive communication and the maturation process adolescents go through from seventh to eighth grade. It may be that adolescents become more verbally aggressive between seventh and eighth grades. Whether they are influenced from mass media, popular culture, or some perceived positive relational outcome for the use of verbal aggression, as adolescents mature, there seems to be an increase in their tendency to be verbally aggressive. A final explanation concerns the genetic inheritance explanation. You may remember that Beatty and

McCroskey (1997) suggest that an individual's trait verbal aggressiveness is in his or her nature and largely determined by genetics. Perhaps the influence of this temperamental expression is so strong that it is not easily altered by a week-long training program.

This is not to suggest that researchers and practitioners should become resigned to this. On the contrary, the application of Infante's (1995a) recommendations for controlling verbal aggression should be incorporated in future training programs. In addition to intervention training specifically geared at promoting argumentative behavior, what other educational experiences might contribute to or detract from constructive communication? Does participation in sports teams, student club memberships, or other activities serve to enhance or subvert levels of argumentativeness and verbal aggressiveness?

One effort revealed some interesting evidence that participation in competitive academic debate does influence both traits. Colbert (1993) believed that students who engaged in competitive debate would be lower in verbal aggressiveness and higher in argumentativeness than students who did not participate in competitive debate. High school students participating in a large competitive speaking tournament served as subjects for Colbert's study. He distinguished between those with debate experience (i.e., those reporting 1 year or more of debate experience) and no debate experience (i.e., beginning forensic students). Students completed the Argumentativeness and the Verbal Aggressiveness scales at the beginning of the school year. The results revealed that the experienced debate students reported significantly lower levels of verbal aggressiveness than those having no debate experience. Further, students with debate experience also reported higher levels of trait argumentativeness than students having no debate experience.

The types of debate activity that students engage in also appear related to their argumentativeness and verbal aggressiveness. More specifically, students with value debate experience reported significantly lower levels of verbal aggressiveness than students without this experience. Students without policy debate experience reported significantly lower levels of argumentativeness than experienced policy debate students (Colbert, 1993). These findings suggest that debate experience may serve as a co-curricular activity for enhancing constructive communication (i.e., argumentativeness) as well as an inhibitor of destructive communication (i.e., verbal aggressiveness). It is important to note that competitive debate involves not just knowledge, but also behavior. By knowing how to and actually engaging in debate, students realize the benefits associated with argumentative behavior and this pattern appears to influence their levels of argumentativeness and verbal aggressiveness.

Sanders et al. (1994) investigated the effect of teaching argumentation on the ability to engage in critical thinking. Critical thinking is defined as thinking that "is reflective and reasonable that is focused on deciding what to believe or do" (Ennis, 1985, p. 45). The researchers were interested in how argumentation training affects trainees' perceptions of arguing, their self-reported levels of arguing skill, and their self-reported levels of arguing-related traits.

In their study, the content used in the training consisted of a noncontroversial or attitudinally neutral topic, arguments that varied in warrant type (e.g., cause and effect and analogy), and arguments that varied in strength (i.e., strong versus weak). Each argument was measured by scales consisting of convincing–unconvincing, persuasive–unpersuasive, and effective–ineffective. Students also completed the Need for Cognition Scale, the Argumentativeness Scale, the Verbal Aggressiveness Scale, and five questions assessing the respondents' level of self-perceived arguing skills. College students were assigned to either the experimental group or the control group.

The results of the Sanders et al. (1994) study showed that although the teaching of argumentation had no effect on the trainees' trait argumentativeness or need for cognition, there were statistically significant differences between the experimental and the control group regarding verbal aggressiveness. That is, people who received the argumentation training reported significantly less verbal aggressiveness than those who did not receive the training. Other findings indicated that the experimental group reported increased levels of self-perceived arguing skills, rated weaker examples more negatively, and judged weak causal arguments as less cogent (less well argued) than people in the control group.

These results are consistent with those of Colbert (1993), which showed that training in argumentation does positively affect reducing verbal aggressiveness. The evidence provided by these studies suggests that when students are put into situations (e.g., argumentation classes or participating in debate) requiring critical thinking and arguing skills, some dampening of trait verbal aggressiveness ensues.

As a result, efforts are underway to provide mini-instructional units for high school students geared toward the reduction of both physical and verbal aggression. Meyer, Roberto, Boster, and Roberto (2004) tested the efficacy of the "Get Real about Violence" curriculum. The curriculum was developed by the Comprehensive Health Education Foundation (1997) and was geared toward the reduction of adolescent verbal and physical violence. The program consists of 12 lessons targeting the aggressive behaviors of fighting, watching a fight, spreading rumors about a fight, and verbal aggression. The lessons are presented in a multimedia format that includes handouts, posters, audiocassettes, worksheets, panel discussions, class discussions, videos, and role playing.

To assess the efficacy of the program, Meyer et al. (2004) chose a pretest–posttest control group design (seventh-grade students in one school received the training and students in another school did not). Both the experimental and the control group participants came from moderately sized public schools from the midwestern United States. The curriculum was taught to students in the experimental group during a required social studies class. Before the training, all participants completed several measures assessing a variety of violent behaviors (i.e., watching a fight, telling a friend about a fight that is about to happen, and fighting), beliefs, and attitudes. Verbal aggression was conceptualized as consisting of four behaviors (i.e., making fun of someone, swearing at someone, yelling at someone, and insulting someone).

The results of the study revealed that the group who received the training reported significantly less verbally aggressive behavior than students in the control group. Further, the experimental group reported a decreased tendency to engage in verbally aggressive behavior in the future. When using any preexperimental design, there are concerns as to whether the training was responsible for the observed effect or whether the outcome can be attributable to something else. Thus, questions arise from this study as to whether the decrease in the experimental group's verbally aggressive behavior is a function of the training or a function of social desirability (i.e., the tendency to answer in appropriate ways to be socially acceptable). Is there the possibility that a combination of the pretest and the training is responsible for the outcome and not the training alone? Although these concerns apply to most experimental designs, the results do show that some modification in verbal aggressiveness can be made.

Conclusion

The evidence provided in this chapter clearly shows the impact that training has on modifying both argumentativeness and verbal aggressiveness. Given the prevalence of verbal aggression in our society, it is recommended that required courses in argumentation be implemented for middle school, high school, and college students. The studies reviewed indicate that the specific type of training may be secondary, as several of the studies showed a significant impact on enhancing the constructive communication skills of the participants.

One goal of research is to attempt to improve people's lives. Anecdotal data provided by both students and their parents suggest that several of these argumentativeness training programs have made a meaningful impact on the quality of people's lives. The longitudinal impact of the training conducted by Rancer and his colleagues will hopefully serve those students well into the future. The studies and training programs reviewed here constitute the existing evidence accumulated by communication scholars to date. Given the significance of these efforts, it becomes imperative for scholars and practitioners to put forth even greater efforts to design, implement, and assess other training programs.

A good place for such efforts to begin would be to implement the Infante (1995a) curriculum for understanding and controlling verbal aggression. As indicated earlier, successful efforts utilizing various aspects of the curriculum have been conducted. However, no one has instituted the curriculum in its entirety. This comprehensive training plan appears to have great potential for reducing the increasing use of verbal aggression found throughout society.

Another important point garnered from the programmatic training efforts and the research cited here deals with the assessment of training outcomes. Based on decades of personality variable research, people who are high or low in any trait tend to be more influenced by their inherent predisposition to behave with only a limited amount of influence coming from the situation. Given this, and some evidence provided by Anderson et al. (1987), the greatest amount of change regarding any trait modification training program might be found in people who are moderate in the trait and not in those who are in the high or low groups. Therefore, efforts that may initially appear to be only marginally successful may have been artificially suppressed by only testing people who are at the extremes of the trait. Future training outcome assessment should build into posttraining analyses a comparison of changes, especially among those moderate in argumentativeness and verbal aggressiveness (see Avtgis & Rancer, 2005).

Taken as a whole, programmatic efforts and the research on training in argumentativeness and verbal aggressiveness hold great promise. The efforts show the effectiveness that quality training can have on the lives of people. It remains for researchers and instructors to continue to expand such efforts.

Discussion Questions for Chapter 10

1. Of the various types of strategies used to control verbal aggression, which strategies do you think are most effective? Why?

2. Why do you think training in argumentation would serve to reduce verbal aggressiveness?

3. Given the many training methods for increasing argumentativeness and decreasing verbal aggressiveness, which method do you like the best? Why?

4. In light of the existing research, do you think that high school or college students should be required to take a formal debating class? Why or why not?

5. Provide your answer to the following question: "Where should we target our training efforts?"

11

Relating Argumentative and Aggressive Communication With Apprehension, Adaptation, and Personality Traits

S uppose you were asked to describe a person you know well to someone else. What would you say? What kind of information would you provide? Your description of this person would probably include personality and communication traits you believe he or she possesses. One of your authors recalls a phone conversation during which he was asked to provide a reference for a former student who was applying for a university teaching position. The person on the search committee said, "Please describe this person's communication and teaching style." Without hesitation, the response provided was, "He's friendly, open, conscientious, dynamic, and assertive." This description helped paint a picture of the candidate for the interviewer, who revealed that this set of attributes was appropriate for the position being filled. It also underscores that "an individual's personality includes a collection of traits which are characteristic of that individual" (Richmond, McCroskey, & McCroskey, 2005, p. 71). Describing individuals in terms of their traits and predispositions is often quite helpful in that it provides "a basis for what to expect from others in various situations" (Infante et al., 2003, p. 78).

Chapter 1 outlined the assumptions of the trait approach to understanding communication behavior. You'll recall that trait theorists believe that in order to understand how people communicate (and behave), knowledge of the traits that individuals possess is essential. Scholars who advocate the trait perspective suggest that individuals will act in predictable and relatively stable ways across situations as a consequence of the cluster of traits they possess. This stability in behavior due to the influence of traits has been referred to as cross-situational consistency.

Individuals possess a cluster or constellation of traits that function interactively to influence a person's communication behavior and communication-based perceptions (Daly & Bippus, 1998). Indeed, we often think of people in terms of a cluster of central traits we believe they possess. In the previous example, the former student was described as friendly, open, conscientious, dynamic, and assertive. However, another person might be described as shy, reserved, unfriendly, passive, and careless. All of the traits that a person possesses are not equally important in the makeup of that person's total personality, as one or two of them might overwhelm the others (Infante et al., 2003, p. 81). That is, a person might consistently be assertive, but might not always exhibit the characteristics of friendliness, openness, and conscientiousness.

Researchers and theorists have identified a number of communication traits or predispositions that influence a person's perception and behavior and developed a classification system to organize them (Infante et al., 2003). This classification system includes apprehension traits (e.g., communication apprehension, receiver apprehension, willingness to communicate), presentation traits (e.g., communicator style and disclosiveness), adaptation traits (e.g., rhetorical sensitivity and self-monitoring of expressive behavior), and aggressive traits (e.g., argumentativeness and verbal aggressiveness). Although the focus of this book has been on the traits of argumentativeness and verbal aggressiveness, other communication and personality traits interact with them to influence behavior.

Argumentativeness and verbal aggressiveness have been conceptualized as communication traits that exist within a person's personality structure. In Chapter 1 we took a macrolevel view and described how argumentativeness and verbal aggressiveness are associated with an array of individual traits in a person's personality, as articulated by Costa and McCrae's (1980) big five personality traits and Eysenck and Eysenck's (1985) three-factor model of personality. Argumentativeness and verbal aggressiveness were found to be related, positively and negatively, with several traits emerging from these superfactors. In this chapter, we take a more microlevel view and look at the relationship of argumentativeness and verbal aggressiveness with other apprehension, adaptation, and personality traits.

Throughout this text, we have reviewed a large body of research that profiles individuals who vary in trait argumentativeness and verbal aggressiveness. This research has identified several communication behaviors of individuals who are high, moderate, and low in argumentativeness and verbal aggressiveness in interpersonal (including marital and family), organizational, intercultural, and mass and mediated communication contexts, as well as in social influence and persuasive situations. We have discovered much about the influence of argumentativeness and verbal aggressiveness in these contexts, although we have yet to describe the relationship between the argumentative and aggressive traits and other communication and personality traits. Research reviewed in this chapter will rectify this. Understanding the association between argumentativeness, verbal aggressiveness, and an array of other communication and personality traits may allow for the development of personality profiles of highly successful communicators. That is, along with being high in argumentativeness and low in verbal aggressiveness, what combination of other traits might make for an especially effective salesperson, manager, teacher, or public relations consultant? By the end of this chapter, we hope that you will be able identify a cluster of other traits, along with argumentativeness and verbal aggressiveness, that would enhance the communication effectiveness of these professionals.

The Relationship of Argumentativeness, Verbal Aggressiveness, and Apprehension Traits

The relationship between the argumentative and aggressive communication traits and apprehension traits was first investigated during the development of the Argumentativeness Scale. Recall that Infante and Rancer (1982) reasoned that argumentativeness should be related to other communication predispositions, including communication apprehension (i.e., the fear or anxiety associated with real or anticipated communication with others). To test this speculation, the then-newly-developed Argumentativeness Scale, along with the Personal Report of Communication Apprehension (McCroskey, 1970) was administered to students enrolled in introductory-level communication courses and a correlation between students' scores on both instruments was obtained. The prediction of a moderate, negative relationship between argumentativeness and communication apprehension was supported. Tendency to approach arguments (ARGap) was moderately and negatively related with total scores on communication apprehension, and scores on the avoidance dimension of the trait (ARGav) were moderately and positively related with total scores on the Personal Report of Communication Apprehension. This finding suggests that the higher a person's tendency to approach arguments (ARGap), the lower that person is in communication apprehension. Conversely, the higher a person's tendency to avoid arguments (ARGav), the higher that person is in communication apprehension.

Building upon previous research on communication apprehension (i.e., fear of sending messages), Wheeless (1975) speculated that some people experience a cross-situational fear of receiving messages sent by others. He labeled this trait *receiver apprehension* and defined it as the "fear of misinterpreting, inadequately processing, and/or not being able to adjust psychologically to messages sent by others" (Wheeless, p. 263). Being motivated and skilled in argumentative communication requires a person to be able to carefully listen to, comprehend, and understand an adversary's position on an issue in order to present arguments challenging the position taken by the adversary. Any anxiety associated with listening should thwart individuals from being able to receive, comprehend, and thus refute an adversary's arguments. Thus, Wigley (1987) hypothesized a negative relationship between argumentativeness and receiver apprehension. To test this, the Argumentativeness Scale and the Receiver Apprehension Test (Wheeless, 1975) were administered to students. A significant and negative relationship between the two traits was observed. That is, as a person's receiver apprehension increases, his or her overall tendency to argue (ARGgt) decreases. One implication of this finding is that training in argument might help reduce one's level of receiver apprehension because "as a person reaps the rewards of effective arguing, his or her motivation to become an effective arguer and, therefore, an effective listener, would be enhanced" (Wigley, p. 52).

The relationship between receiver apprehension and the argumentative and aggressive communication traits was furthered examined by Schrodt and Wheeless (2001). They speculated that both argumentativeness and verbal aggressiveness should be related to this receiver apprehension trait, which was expanded and called *informational reception apprehension*. According to Wheeless, Preiss, and Gayle (1997), informational reception apprehension is a trait associated with cognitive deficiencies that hinder a person's ability to receive, process, interpret, and adjust to information. This reconceptualization of receiver apprehension contains three factors: listening anxiety, reading anxiety, and intellectual inflexibility (Wheeless et al.).

Schrodt and Wheeless (2001) suggested that two of these factors, listening anxiety and intellectual inflexibility, would be related with argumentativeness and verbal aggressiveness. More specifically, individuals who have higher levels of informational reception apprehension (i.e., listening anxiety and intellectual inflexibility) were thought to be lower in argumentativeness. Because informational reception apprehension is thought to be negatively related with argumentativeness and because some research shows argumentativeness has been negatively associated with verbal aggressiveness, Schrodt and Wheeless reasoned that "IRA [informational reception apprehension] would be positively related to verbal aggressiveness" (p. 58).

To test these speculations, undergraduate students were asked to complete the Argumentativeness Scale, the Verbal Aggressiveness Scale, and the Informational Reception Apprehension Test. Overall, the findings suggested that receiver apprehension is a trait factor that distinguishes argumentativeness and verbal aggressiveness. As a person's informational reception apprehension increases, a person's trait argumentativeness decreases. Although informational reception apprehension was negatively related with trait argumentativeness, a very small relationship was found between receiver apprehension and verbal aggressiveness. This suggests that "IRA is a greater factor in argumentative behavior than in verbally aggressive behavior" (Schrodt & Wheeless, 2001, p. 62). It was suggested that efforts designed to train people to increase their motivation and skill in argumentative communication and reduce their tendency toward verbal aggression, such as those discussed in Chapter 10, might be enhanced by including a section on reducing informational reception (i.e., receiver) apprehension.

The Relationship of Argumentativeness, Verbal Aggressiveness, and Adaptation Traits

Adaptation traits influence how we adapt to the people we are speaking with to maximize communication success. In this section, we will describe the research focusing on the relationship between argumentativeness, verbal aggressiveness, and the adaptation traits of self-perceived communication competence, self-monitoring of expressive behavior, conversational sensitivity, and cognitive flexibility.

Communication competence is seen as how appropriate and effective a person is in communication behavior (Infante et al., 2003; McCroskey & McCroskey, 1988). A trait approach to communication competence suggests that there are some people who are such good communicators that they almost never communicate with others inappropriately or ineffectively. Conversely, some people low in communication competence always seem to come up short in their ability to communicate appropriately and effectively. Self-perceived communication competence is defined as a person's self-perception of the "ability to pass along or give information; the ability to make known by talking or writing" (McCroskey & McCroskey, p. 109). Self-perceived communication competence is measured by the Self-Perceived

Communication Competence Scale (McCroskey & McCroskey). The scale contains items used to assess an individual's self-perception of communication competence in four contexts (public speaking, talking in a large meeting, talking in a small group, and talking one-on-one) and with three common types of receivers (strangers, acquaintances, and friends). A global self-perceived communication competence score is obtained as well as individual scores for each context and type of receiver.

The relationship between self-perceived communication competence and argumentativeness was examined by Richmond et al. (1989). Students completed a battery of scales including the Self-Perceived Communication Competence Scale (McCroskey & McCroskey, 1988) and the Argumentativeness Scale. Trait argumentativeness was found to be positively related with total self-perceived communication competence, as well as with self-perceived competence in public speaking and speaking in groups, one-on-one, in meetings, and with strangers, acquaintances, and friends. Although cause-and-effect relationships cannot be assumed, these results do suggest that the higher the level of argumentativeness, the greater a person's self-perceived communication competence.

Self-monitoring of expressive behavior is a trait identified by social psychologist Snyder (1974, 1979). Self-monitoring refers to the way people monitor, control, and regulate their verbal and nonverbal self-presentations in social situations and in interpersonal relationships (Allen, 1986). A score on the Self-Monitoring Scale (Snyder, 1974) classifies a person as either a high or a low self-monitor. People who score high in self-monitoring exert control over the public image they project to others. That is, they use information gleaned from the environment to alter their self-presentation in an attempt to fit in with people they are communicating with. According to Snyder (1979), high self-monitors are like polished actors who can act in reserved, withdrawn, and introverted ways when the situation calls for it, and in another instance, they can appear quite friendly, outgoing, and extraverted. Conversely, individuals low in self-monitoring tend to exhibit much more cross-situational consistency in their self-presentation. They verbally and nonverbally express exactly what they think and feel rather than altering their self-presentation, attitudes, and behavior to fit the given social situation.

Chory-Assad and Cicchirillo (2005) suggested that high self-monitors might be more effective communicators. They reasoned that as verbal aggressiveness has been related with several characteristics of ineffective communication (i.e., more apprehension, less argument production, less flexibility), verbal aggressiveness should be negatively related to self-monitoring. Recall that in Chapter 2, we presented research by Levine and his colleagues (2004) that suggested the Verbal Aggressiveness Scale may actually measure two distinct dimensions: a dimension of aggressiveness as originally conceptualized by Infante and Wigley (1986), and a pro-social, benevolence dimension (i.e., a person's tendency to be supportive and cooperative with others during conflict communication). According to Chory-Assad and Cicchirillo, items tapping this benevolence factor seem consistent with the communication strategies employed by high self-monitors. Based on this, they hypothesized that the benevolence factor of the Verbal Aggressiveness Scale should be positively related with self-monitoring and will be more strongly related to self-monitoring than will the aggressiveness dimension of the Verbal Aggressiveness Scale.

To test these speculations, undergraduate students completed several self-report measures including the Verbal Aggressiveness Scale, a hostility measure (e.g., "Other people always seem to get the breaks," see Buss & Perry, 1992), and a revised Self-Monitoring Scale (e.g., "In conversations, I am sensitive to even the slightest change in the facial expression of the person I'm conversing with," "I have the ability to control the way I come across to people, depending on the impression I wish to give them," see Lennox & Wolfe, 1984). In addition to computing verbal aggressiveness scores as originally suggested by adding up all 20 items (Infante and Wigley, 1986), Chory-Assad and Cicchirillo (2005) created an aggression and a benevolence score for each participant from the original 20 items. The results showed that neither dimension of self-monitoring (sensitivity to the expressive behavior of others or ability to modify self-presentation) was related to the total verbal aggressiveness score as measured by the 20-item scale. However, the benevolence factor of verbal aggressiveness and the "sensitivity to the expressive behavior of others" (Chory-Assad & Cicchirillo, 2005, p. 16) dimension of self-monitoring were modestly related. Sensitivity to the expressive behavior of other scores was not related to the aggressive score of verbal aggressiveness. The researchers concluded that the benevolence dimension of verbal aggressiveness was "somewhat associated with having the capacity to alter, control, and regulate behavior to appropriately suit the situation" (Chory-Assad & Cicchirillo, p. 19), which are characteristics of the high self-monitor.

A study of the effects of both verbal aggressiveness and self-monitoring on responses to an adversary in a conflict situation was conducted in Japan. Ohbuchi and Fukushima (1997) speculated that when an opponent in a conflict situation behaved in an impolite manner, verbally aggressive participants would engage in more confrontational tactics than less aggressive participants. However, Ohbuchi and Fukushima hypothesized when the opponent behaved in a polite manner, no differences in responses would be observed. They also speculated that high self-monitors (whose behavior depends more on situational factors) would produce milder responses than low self-monitors when they were not requested to respond quickly to the opponent. Further, no differences would be expected between high and low self-monitors when asked to respond very quickly.

To test these speculations, Ohbuchi and Fukushima (1997) first assessed Japanese students (all male) on verbal aggression and self-monitoring. For their study, a Japanese version of the Buss and Durkee (1957) Verbal Aggression Scale was used to assess trait verbal aggressiveness, and a Japanese version of Lennox and Wolfe's (1984) Self-Monitoring Scale was used to measure self-monitoring. After completing both scales, participants were randomly assigned to one of four experimental conditions: opponent's manner of communicating (polite or rough) and time pressure to respond (immediate or delayed). The participants were asked to interact verbally with a female confederate in one of three hypothetical conflict situations (i.e., pay an extra fare for a train ticket, come into work on a day previously scheduled as their day off, provide compensation for a damaged bicycle). For each conflict situation, the confederate expressed the request in either a polite or a rough (i.e., rude) manner. In addition, the participant's response to the request was either demanded by the experimenter immediately ("please respond immediately") or slightly delayed ("wait and think for 30 seconds and then speak").

The results revealed that both verbal aggressiveness and self-monitoring interacted with the situational variables (opponent's manner of communicating and time pressure of response) to influence participants' responses to the conflict. As expected, when they were subjected to the rude opponent, high verbally aggressive participants responded with more hostility and verbal aggression than they did with the polite opponent. The results also revealed that high self-monitors produced more integrative (i.e., less hostile) and more cooperative responses than low self-monitors, but only when there was no time pressure to respond. Apparently, high self-monitors can control their social behavior better but only when their cognitive functions are not impaired, in this case by the possible stress of responding immediately to an opponent.

Conversational sensitivity, another adaptation trait, is defined as a person's predisposition to interpret and attend to the many subtle verbal, paraverbal, and nonverbal cues of conversation (Daly, Vangelisti, & Daughton, 1987). Like high self-monitors, conversationally sensitive communicators tend to be more adaptive during communication encounters and are able to recognize conversational alternatives. As such, conversational sensitivity has been positively related with other traits such as self-monitoring of expressive behavior and self-esteem, and negatively with communication apprehension, receiver apprehension, and rhetorical sensitivity.

Wigley, Pohl, and Watt (1989) explored the relationship between conversational sensitivity, verbal aggressiveness, and laudativeness (the predisposition to verbally praise others, see Wigley & Graham, 1986). Wigley and his colleagues speculated that those high in conversational sensitivity would be more likely to engage in conversations in which compliments and praise of others were evident. Conversely, those low on conversational sensitivity are less favorable to conversations and may even find conversations to be somewhat unpleasant. As such, one method low conversationally sensitive people could use to end conversations would be to engage in verbal aggressiveness. Thus, Wigley et al. suggested a negative relationship between conversational sensitivity and verbal aggressiveness.

Students completed the Conversational Sensitivity Scale (Daly et al., 1987), the Verbal Praise Scale (Wigley & Graham, 1986), and the Verbal Aggressiveness Scale. As hypothesized, a significant negative relationship was found between verbal aggressiveness and laudativeness. That is, the higher the person's verbal aggressiveness, the lower their tendency to praise others. However, virtually no relationship was observed between conversational sensitivity and verbal aggressiveness. This finding led Wigley and his colleagues to speculate that individuals low in conversational sensitivity might use verbal aggressiveness to avoid conversations, whereas those high in conversational sensitivity might use verbal aggressiveness for the purposes of persuasion (Wigley et al., 1989, p. 94). These results were supported by Chesebro and Martin (2003), who also predicted a negative relationship between conversational sensitivity and verbal aggressiveness, but, like Wigley et al., found none. Chesebro and Martin speculated that although conversationally sensitive communicators "may effectively recognize important meanings in conversations, the ways in which they respond to those meanings may vary considerably, most likely depending on other personality or situational variables" (p. 148).

Two studies investigated argumentativeness, verbal aggressiveness, and cognitive flexibility. Cognitive flexibility is similar to self-monitoring and conversational sensitivity in that cognitively flexible communicators "are able to adapt their communication to meet the demands of the situations, and perhaps more importantly, to consider options and alternative ways of behaving in different situations" (Martin, Anderson, & Thweatt, 1998, p. 531). As such, cognitive flexibility has also been positively associated with self-monitoring and negatively related to unwillingness-to-communicate (Martin & Rubin, 1995).

Extending this research, Martin, Anderson, and Thweatt (1998) speculated that cognitive flexibility would be positively related to argumentativeness and negatively related to verbal aggressiveness. Students completed the Argumentativeness and Verbal Aggressiveness scales and the Cognitive Flexibility Scale (which measures how cognitively aware people are that behavioral alternatives exist in communication interactions; Martin & Rubin, 1995). The researchers' speculations were supported: argumentativeness was positively related with, and verbal aggressiveness negatively related with, cognitive flexibility. Thus, the greater the trait argumentativeness, the greater the cognitive flexibility (i.e., those people who are higher in argumentativeness recognized that they had more behavioral options in communication situations). A profile of the adaptive and flexible communicator was suggested as one who is willing to argue and disagree, but is not likely to use verbal aggression (Martin, Anderson, et al., 1998, p. 537). Conversely, the greater the verbal aggressiveness, the lower the cognitive flexibility. People high in verbal aggressiveness perceived fewer behavioral options in communication interactions. Interestingly, the most frequent option perceived by individuals low in cognitive flexibility is verbal aggression.

Recall that in Chapter 2 we introduced the notion of indirect interpersonal aggressiveness. Beatty, Valencic, et al. (1999) defined indirect interpersonal aggressiveness as the "predisposition to harm other people without engaging in face-to-face interaction" (p. 105). Examples of indirect interpersonal aggressiveness include spreading rumors, withholding important information from others, betraying confidences, and failing to relay important messages. Chesebro and Martin (2003) tested the relationship between cognitive flexibility and the use of indirect interpersonal aggression. They speculated that while cognitively flexible people may not resort to verbal aggression due to their awareness of alternatives to verbal aggression, one strategy they might employ is indirect interpersonal aggression. While verbal aggression is a direct verbal attack on another person, indirect aggression is still within the parameters of an aggressive personality.

To test this potential relationship, students completed the Cognitive Flexibility Scale (Martin & Rubin, 1995) and a measure of indirect interpersonal aggressiveness (e.g., "I might 'forget' to relay information to a person who has been hostile or unfair to me," see Beatty, Valencic, et al., 1999, in Appendix E for the complete scale). The results indicated that cognitive flexibility was negatively related with indirect interpersonal aggressiveness such that the higher the cognitive flexibility the lower the reported use of indirect interpersonal aggression. Apparently, the cognitively flexible person recognizes the harm that both direct and indirect forms of aggression can cause and has a greater behavioral repertoire of more constructive strategies to choose from during interpersonal conflict episodes.

The Relationship of Argumentativeness, Verbal Aggressiveness, and Personality Traits

A number of studies have investigated the relationship between argumentativeness, verbal aggressiveness, and other personality traits. In this section, we will review findings from studies that explored interrelationships between argumentativeness, verbal aggressiveness, and the personality traits of self-esteem, self-handicapping, self-defeating personality, compulsive communication, locus of control, and need for cognition.

An individual's self-concept occupies a central position regarding communication behavior, and one's self-esteem is a pervasive component of the self-concept (Rancer, Kosberg, & Silvestri, 1992). Self-esteem has been defined as an "individual's overall feelings of personal worth, usefulness and degree of liking for self" (Glauser, 1984, p. 117). Individuals high in argumentativeness have been found to feel better about themselves, perhaps due to the benefits they enjoy from being more successful in arguments and in social conflict episodes (Rancer et al., 1985). Thus, self-esteem and argumentativeness should be positively related. Conversely, the many negative outcomes associated with verbal aggressiveness suggest a negative relationship between self-esteem and verbal aggressiveness. These speculations were tested in a study on the relationship between self-esteem, argumentativeness, and verbal aggressiveness conducted by Rancer, Kosberg, and Silvestri.

Students completed the Argumentativeness and Verbal Aggressiveness scales, as well as the Multidimensional Self-Esteem Inventory (O'Brien & Epstein, 1988). This scale consists of items designed to assess both global (i.e., dispositional) self-esteem and eight subdimensions of self-esteem. The personal power dimension of self-esteem emerged as the strongest predictor of argumentativeness. This dimension is associated with feelings of power, success at leadership, being assertive, and having a strong impact on others. The strongest predictor of verbal aggressiveness was the defensive self-enhancement (i.e., defensiveness) dimension of self-esteem. That is, individuals high in verbal aggressiveness tend to be less open, more defensive, and less modest and tend not to acknowledge their mistakes. To some degree, individuals higher in verbal aggressiveness also saw themselves as less capable of influencing others (Rancer, Kosberg, & Silvestri, 1992).

The tendency to protect one's self-esteem has also been described as a trait and has received attention from personality and communication researchers alike. Labeled *self-handicapping*, this trait has been defined as "the adoption or advocacy of impediments to success in a situation where the person anticipates failure. By assuming a self-handicap, the person has an excuse for the impending failure and thereby may maintain self-esteem and the illusion of competence" (Harris, Snyder, Higgins, & Schrag, 1986, p. 1191). Thus, self-handicapping is a face-saving strategy used to maintain the perception of competence, as self-handicappers can blame factors outside of their control for their failed performances. Self-handicaps can also be used to accentuate a success. That is, if a person can overcome a self-handicap, the person might be seen as even more competent.

Avtgis, Rancer, and Amato (1998) predicted a relationship between this type of esteem-protection behavior and the use of verbal aggression. Recall that research by Rancer, Kosberg, and Silvestri (1992) found that the defensive self-enhancement dimension of self-esteem emerged as a predictor of verbal aggressiveness. Individuals high in verbal aggressiveness may be less open and more defensive and tend to avoid acknowledging their mistakes. This suggests a relationship exists between verbal aggressiveness and the self-handicapping orientation in that this type of esteem-protection behavior (i.e., self-handicapping) may be used differently by people who differ in verbal aggressiveness. To that end, Avtgis and his colleagues suggested that those high in self-handicapping orientation would be higher in verbal aggressiveness than those low in self-handicapping orientation.

To test this hypothesis, students completed the Self-Handicapping Scale (Jones & Rhodewalt, 1982) and were classified as either high, moderate, or low in self-handicapping orientation by their scores on the scale. They also completed the Verbal Aggressiveness Scale. The results supported the hypothesis that people who reported higher levels of self-handicapping orientation (the highs and moderates) also reported higher levels of verbal aggressiveness than those lower in self-handicapping orientation. This suggests that verbal aggression thus may be another esteem-protection strategy self-handicappers can use to thwart perceived attacks on their competence. For example, one spouse who does not know the answer to a question posed by the other spouse might use verbal aggression as a response in order to protect the illusion of competence (e.g., "That's a stupid question, any idiot knows that!").

Another trait related closely to self-esteem is the *self-defeating personality*. People who possess this trait often choose situations that lead to personal disappointment and failure even when other options are available to them. The self-defeating personality "incites anger or rejecting responses from others and then feels hurt, defeated, or humiliated (e.g., they may make fun of spouse in public, thus provoking an angry retort which then makes them feel devastated)" (American Psychiatric Association, 1987, pp. 373–374). As such, the self-defeating personality has been found to be negatively correlated with self-esteem (Yelsma, 1993) and positively correlated with self-handicapping (Schill, Morales, Beyler, Tatter, & Swigert, 1991).

Because prior research suggested that the self-defeating personality lacks assertiveness (Schill, 1995) and that argumentativeness has been related with higher levels of self-esteem (Rancer, Kosberg, & Silvestri, 1992), Schill (1996) wondered whether individuals high in self-defeating personality would be lower in argumentativeness. Participants completed the Self-Defeating Personality Scale (Schill, 1990) and the Argumentativeness Scale. Using separate scores on the two dimensions of the Argumentativeness Scale (ARGap and ARGav), a positive and significant relationship was found between self-defeating personality and tendency to avoid arguments (ARGav), but only for females. This suggests that females who score higher on self-defeating personality also score higher on tendency to avoid arguments. Schill (1996) states that while the self-defeating personality "may invite anger and rejection from others, it is unlikely that arguing is one of the main reasons why this occurs" (p. 1128). It was suggested that this sex difference in the relationship between self-defeating personality and argumentativeness may be due to differences between males and females on belief structures about arguing (Schill, 1996). Recall that women saw arguing as a more hostile, aggressive, and combative communication activity than men did (see Rancer & Baukus, 1987).

Have you ever encountered someone who talks too much? While apparently rare, some individuals have a compulsion to communicate to excess. McCroskey and Richmond (1993) label these overcommunicators as compulsive communicators or *talkaholics*. *Talkaholism* does not refer simply to those who are low in communication apprehension and high in extraversion and assertiveness. Rather, talkaholism is considered a distinct and separate trait. Indeed, McCroskey and Richmond (1995) state that the opposite of the talkaholic is the person who talks within the normal range of talking quantity. They developed a scale, the Talkaholic Scale, in which people are scored only as talkaholics (high scores) or not being talkaholic (all other scores).

Several characteristics of the talkaholic have been identified, including compulsiveness (e.g., they acknowledge they cannot stop communicating), awareness that others' see their communication as excessive, consistency in their excessive communication, and awareness that their compulsive communication can be detrimental to them. Talkaholics have been known to "talk themselves into trouble when all they would have to do to stay out of it would be to keep quiet" (McCroskey & Richmond, 1993, p. 109).

Studies have investigated the relationship between talkaholism and argumentativeness and verbal aggressiveness. In a seminal study, Hackman, Johnson, and Barthel-Hackman (1995) studied the relationship between talkaholism and argumentativeness among New Zealand college students. Students completed several self-report measures including the Talkaholism

Scale (McCroskey & Richmond, 1993) and the Argumentativeness Scale. A moderate and positive relationship was observed between these two traits in that compulsive communication was associated with increased levels of argumentativeness (Hackman et al., 1995, p. 58).

Do compulsive communicators differ in communication competence? This question was addressed by Ifert, Long, and Fortney (1997). They reasoned that while compulsive communicators might be competent, it may also be that incompetent communicators are also compulsively communicative. Further, Ifert and her colleagues suggested that compulsive communicators who see themselves at different levels of competence might engage in different communication behaviors. One of the behaviors that might differentiate compulsive communicators who see themselves as competent from those who do not involves argumentative communication. Compulsive communicators who see themselves as competent were thought to be higher in argumentativeness as they are likely to possess the motivation and skill to do well in argumentative situations. Conversely, compulsive communicators who see themselves as less competent should be lower in trait argumentativeness. This led to the prediction that among compulsive communicators, there will be a positive relationship between self-perceived communication competence and trait argumentativeness.

Verbal aggression might be another behavior that differentiates high and low competent compulsive communicators. Compulsive communicators who see themselves as competent might avoid engaging in verbal aggression, as it has been shown to be related to a host of negative outcomes such as embarrassment, relationship damage, and physical aggression (Infante et al., 1984). Thus, Ifert et al. (1997) also predicted a negative relationship between self-perceived communication competence and verbal aggressiveness among compulsive communicators.

To test these relationships, students completed the Talkaholic Scale (McCroskey & Richmond, 1993), the Self-Perceived Communication Competence Scale (McCroskey & McCroskey, 1988) and the Argumentativeness and Verbal Aggressiveness scales. The relationship between argumentativeness and self-perceived communication competence for talkaholics was supported. Compulsive communicators (i.e., talkaholics) who saw themselves as highly competent communicators were higher in argumentativeness, while those who saw themselves as less competent were lower in argumentativeness. The prediction regarding the relationship between communication competence and verbal aggressiveness among compulsive communicators was not supported. Ifert et al. (1997) speculated that as compulsive communicators are more adaptive to situational factors, they might choose to employ either argumentative or verbally aggressive messages depending on situational factors. Thus, "talkaholics are not a monolithic group" (Ifert et al., 1997, pp. 12–13), and the strategies you should employ with a talkaholic depend in large part on their self-perceived level of communication competence and level of argumentativeness.

Another predisposition associated with successful interaction behavior is locus of control. Derived from social learning theory, locus of control is conceptualized as the amount and type of control individuals believe they have over their own behavior (Brenders, 1987; Lefcourt, 1982; Rotter, 1954). In general, people have either an internal or an external locus-of-control orientation (Avtgis & Rancer, 1997). Those with an internal locus-of-control orientation believe that they alone exert control over their environment and lives. Individuals with an external locus-of-control orientation believe that luck, chance, fate, and powerful others control their lives. Previous research suggests differences in the communication behavior of internals and externals. For example, internals reported greater likelihood of using rationality (i.e., providing reasons) than externals (Canary, Cody, & Marston, 1986), and externals, who perceive interactions as less personally controllable, tend to employ more aggression and coercion in influence attempts (Brenders).

Some research has investigated the relationship between argumentativeness, verbal aggressiveness, and locus-of-control orientation. Canary, Cunningham, and Cody (1988) found that the effort and ability dimensions of the Conflict Locus of Control Scale (which are more indicative of an internal locus-of-control orientation) were positively related with the tendency to approach (ARGap) arguments. The dimensions of powerlessness, chance, and situational contingencies (which are indicative of an external locus-of-control orientation) were positively related with the tendency to avoid (ARGav) arguments.

Based on this previous research, Avtgis and Rancer (1997) conducted a direct test of the relationship between argumentativeness, verbal aggressiveness, and locus-of-control orientation. They predicted that individuals with an internal control orientation would be higher in tendency to approach arguments (ARGap) and lower in tendency to avoid arguments (ARGav) than individuals with an external control orientation. Further, the lack of control over interpersonal interaction might lead externals to use more destructive communication tactics. As such, individuals with an external control orientation were predicted to be higher in verbal aggressiveness than those with an internal control orientation.

Students completed the Argumentativeness and Verbal Aggressiveness scales, and a modified version of Levenson's (1973) Locus of Control Scale (Rubin, 1993). This scale consists of three factors: powerful others control, chance control, and internal control. Items measuring each dimension include powerful others control, "I feel like what happens in my life is mostly determined by powerful people"; chance control, "To a great extent my life is controlled by accidental happenings"; and internal control, "I can pretty much determine what will happen in my life."

The results found significant differences on tendency to avoid arguments (ARGav) between externals, moderates, and internals. Those with an external locus of control orientation were significantly higher on tendency to avoid arguments than were internals. There were no differences between internals, moderates, or externals on tendency to approach arguments (ARGap). In addition, individuals with an external locus of control orientation were significantly higher on verbal aggressiveness than either moderates or internals. Overall, this study found that individuals with an internal control orientation report being less verbally aggressive and less likely to avoid arguments. Avtgis and Rancer (1997) speculate that externals, sensing that many communicative interactions are simply beyond their control, may be more likely to engage in destructive forms of communication (i.e., use verbal aggression) during conflict.

One of the most popular instruments used to assess personality types is the Myers-Briggs Type Indicator (MBTI). This instrument is frequently used as a diagnostic tool in the job recruitment, hiring, and promotion processes in organizations. The MBTI asks for responses to a large set of questions (e.g., "Are you inclined to value sentiment more than logic, or value logic more than sentiment?") from participants who are then classified along four basic areas of personality: introversion (I) versus extraversion (E); sensing (S) versus intuition (N); thinking (T) versus feeling (F); and judging (J) versus perceiving (P). The introversion–extraversion continuum assesses whether individuals get their personal energy from interacting with others or through reflecting on ideas. The sensing–intuition continuum assesses how much attention people pay to their five senses when they obtain and process information. The thinking–feeling continuum assesses whether people make decisions based on more objective or subjective criteria. The judging–perceiving continuum assesses the processes people go through in dealing with the world and how well-planned out or spontaneous they are when making decisions (see Lorr, 1991, for an evaluation of the MBTI typology).

Loffredo and Opt (1998) examined the relationship between MBTI preferences and argumentativeness. They speculated that trait argumentativeness would be related to the extraversion (E) and introversion (I) preference types. In particular, it was suggested that introverts would be expected to score low in argumentativeness, while extraverts would score higher. They also speculated that thinkers (T) would score higher than feelers (F) on argumentativeness because thinkers have a preference for competing in conflict situations while feelers prefer more social harmony (Loffredo & Opt).

Students ranging in age from 21 to 60 years old were administered the MBTI (Form G, Self-Scoring) and the Argumentativeness Scale. As expected, those identified as introverted on the MBTI were lower in argumentativeness than those identified as extraverted. However, no differences were observed between thinkers and feelers on argumentativeness. Loffredo and Opt suggest that "these findings may indicate that argumentativeness is more reflective of the way a person externalizes mental processes (the E-I dimension) as opposed to the thinking processes themselves" (pp. 25–26).

How would you respond to the following questions: "How much genuine motivation and enjoyment do you have for thinking?" and "Are you the type of person who enjoys solving complex problems which require much deliberation and thought, or would you rather avoid issues and problems which require thinking in depth about something?" These questions tap into the predisposition labeled "need for cognition" or the "enjoyment individuals derive from engaging in effortful information processing" (Cacioppo et al., 1986, p. 1033).

It seems logical that relationships, both positive and negative, should exist between need for cognition and argumentativeness and verbal aggressiveness. Because argumentative behavior requires deliberation, thought, and careful scrutiny of issues and positions, these traits were thought to be related to each other (Mongeau, 1989). After administering scales to measure both traits (the Argumentativeness Scale and the Need for Cognition Measure; Cacioppo et al., 1984), a moderate relationship was observed between trait argumentativeness and need for cognition, with the higher the argumentativeness, the greater one's need for cognition. Thus, although both traits involve the predisposition to argue cognitively, they are apparently not measuring the same thing. Mongeau's study also revealed that although those low in need for cognition might be persuaded by either strong or weak arguments, those high in need for cognition need more compelling arguments and reasons to accept an advocate's position on an issue.

Is need for cognition also related with verbal aggressiveness? Sanders et al. (1992) tested this relationship. First, based on the notion that arguing calls for much cognitive activity, Sanders and her colleagues also hypothesized a positive relationship between argumentativeness and need for cognition. Second, they predicted a negative relationship between verbal aggressiveness and need for cognition "because an individual who enjoys grappling with ideas and issues might be less likely to become angry or frustrated (i.e., verbally aggressive) during argumentative encounters" (Sanders et al., p. 51).

Students completed the Need for Cognition Scale (Cacioppo et al., 1984) and the Argumentativeness and Verbal Aggressiveness scales. A positive relationship between argumentativeness and need for cognition was again supported in this study, suggesting that individuals higher in argumentativeness are also higher in need for cognition. Conversely, a negative relationship was observed between verbal aggressiveness and need for cognition, with the lower individuals' need for cognition, the higher their trait verbal aggressiveness. This led them to suggest that individuals who "prefer less cognitive rigor appear more likely to resort to the use of ad hominem (i.e., personal attacks) rather than focusing verbal battles on substantive issues" (Sanders et al., 1992, p. 54). Thus, argumentativeness, verbal aggressiveness, and need for cognition are three predispositions that have been found to influence the amount and type of behavior exhibited during conflict.

Another factor that has been associated with need for cognition is called epistemological beliefs, which are defined as "beliefs about the nature of knowledge and knowing" (Chan & Elliott, 2004, p. 123). Five dimensions of epistemological beliefs have been identified: simple knowledge (i.e., knowledge consisting of specific facts), certain knowledge (i.e., knowledge is certain, avoid ambiguity), omniscient authority (i.e., depend on authority for knowledge), innate ability (i.e., the ability to learn is inborn), and quick learning (i.e., learning occurs quickly or not at all).

Nussbaum and Bendixen (2003) suggested a relationship between students' argumentativeness and their epistemological beliefs. They suggested, for example, that individuals who possess certain knowledge or quick-learning epistemological beliefs would have a lower tendency to approach arguments. To test this, students completed the Argumentativeness Scale, the Need for Cognition Scale (Cacioppo et al., 1984), and the Epistemic Beliefs Inventory (EBI; Schraw, Bendixen, & Dunkle, 2002). The EBI measures beliefs about the nature of knowledge and knowing (e.g., "What is true today will be true tomorrow," "If you don't learn something quickly, you will never learn it").

Contrary to the hypothesis that predicted a relationship between epistemological beliefs and tendency to approach arguments, the results revealed that certain knowledge or quick learning epistemological beliefs were related to an individual's tendency to avoid arguments (ARGav). As with previous research, the need for cognition was related with the tendency to approach arguments. The contribution of this study is the identification of two fairly stable epistemological beliefs that appear related to a person's tendency to avoid arguments. Nussbaum and Bendixen (2003) suggest that these findings indicate that as people's desire to "maintain warm relationships with others" (p. 591) increases, their tendency to avoid arguments decreases. This supports the constructive nature of argumentativeness, a conclusion that has been advanced throughout this text. In addition, "students with less well-developed epistemological beliefs, specifically in the certainty or simplicity of knowledge, tend to avoid arguments" (Nussbaum & Bendixen p. 591). As such, these findings broaden our understanding regarding why some people might choose to avoid arguments.

In this chapter, we have described relationships between numerous communication and personality traits with the argumentative and verbally aggressive predispositions. Table 11.1 presents a summary of the relationships observed in this corpus of research.

Table 11.1   Apprehension, Adaptation, and Personality Traits Related to Argumentativeness and Verbal Aggressiveness

Argumentativeness	*Verbal Aggressiveness*
Traits Positively Related	
Self-Perceived Communication Competence (Richmond, McCroskey, & McCroskey, 1989; Ifert, Long, & Fortney, 1997)	Self-Esteem-Defensiveness (Rancer, Kosberg, & Silvestri, 1992)
Cognitive Flexibility (Martin, Anderson, & Thweatt, 1998)	Self-Handicapping (Avtgis, Rancer, & Amato, 1998)
Self-Esteem-Personal Power (Rancer, Kosberg, & Silvestri, 1992)	Locus of Control-External (Avtgis & Rancer, 1997)
Talkaholism-Compulsive Communication (Hackman, Johnson, & Barthel-Hackman, 1995)	
Extraversion-MBTI (Loffredo & Opt, 1998)	
Need for Cognition (Mongeau, 1989; Sanders, Gass, Wiseman, & Bruschke, 1992)	
Traits Negatively Related	
Communication Apprehension (Infante & Rancer, 1982)	Laudativeness (Wigley, Pohl, & Watt, 1989)
Receiver Apprehension (Wigley, 1987)	Cognitive Flexibility (Martin, Anderson, & Thweatt, 1998; Chesebro & Martin, 2003)
Informational Reception Apprehension (Schrodt & Wheeless, 2001)	Need for Cognition (Sanders, Gass, Wiseman, & Bruschke, 1992)

Conclusion

Individuals possess clusters or constellations of traits that function interactively to influence communication and behavior. Numerous traits or predispositions that influence an individual's perceptions and behavior have been identified by researchers in communication and psychology. Taking a microlevel view, the chapter reviewed the relationship of argumentativeness and verbal aggressiveness with a number of apprehension, adaptation, and personality traits.

An understanding of other traits and predispositions found to be related with trait argumentativeness and verbal aggressiveness allows us to develop a profile of a competent communicator. We begin that process by addressing the question, "What combination of other communication and personality-related traits might produce the greatest potential for interpersonal influence, interpersonal satisfaction, and communication success?"

The following cluster of traits seems to have the greatest positive consequences for successful communication. As we have suggested unequivocally throughout the text, being high in argumentativeness and low (or lower) in verbal aggressiveness should produce the most favorable communication outcomes in a variety of contexts. Along with trait argumentativeness and verbal aggressiveness, research suggests that avoidance of indirect interpersonal aggression should be added to this cluster. In addition, and while controversy still exists regarding the dimensionality of the Verbal Aggressiveness Scale (see Levine et al., 2004), it is suggested that higher scores on the benevolence dimension of verbal aggressiveness and lower scores on the aggression dimension of verbal aggressiveness might contribute to more favorable communication outcomes.

What other combination of traits should be added to this mix? Greater communication competence should be seen with lower levels of communication apprehension and receiver apprehension. The fear and anxiety associated with both of these apprehension traits should weaken one's success in social and personal influence attempts.

A number of adaptation traits should interact with higher levels of argumentativeness and lower levels of verbal aggressiveness to produce more favorable outcomes. For example, high levels of self-perceived communication competence, being a high self-monitor, and possessing higher levels of cognitive flexibility might provide enough adaptability to enhance the chances of being successful in many communication encounters.

Possessing higher levels of personal power and lower levels of defensiveness (two dimensions of self-esteem found positively and negatively related to argumentativeness and verbal aggressiveness, respectively) might be especially productive to enhance communication competence and communicative outcomes. Lower levels of self-handicapping and self-defeating personality orientation should be beneficial. Perhaps an internal locus-of-control orientation (but clearly not an external orientation) and a high need for cognition constitute companion traits that would enhance a person's communication outcomes. Of course, these suggestions were stimulated by the findings reported in this chapter. We await the results of research that will empirically examine the combination of traits we have suggested here.

Discussion Questions for Chapter 11

1. Explain why someone who is high in argumentativeness and low in verbal aggressiveness would be perceived as more competent?

2. Why do you think someone who is less flexible in the communicator style would be high in verbal aggressiveness?

3. How do you think indirect interpersonal aggression differs from verbal aggressiveness?

4. What influence do you think self-concept has on trait argumentativeness and verbal aggressiveness? Can you provide an example?

5. What does it mean when we suggest that argumentativeness and verbal aggressiveness should be used in the development of a trait profile for determining a competent communicator? How similar or dissimilar is your own trait profile to that of the competent communicator?

12

Advancing Research and Theory-Building Efforts on Argumentative and Aggressive Communication

T hroughout this book we have chronicled the development of the argumentative and verbally aggressive communication traits from their genesis to the most recent research. A question that remains to be asked is "Where do we go from here?" While we will offer our ideas for future inquiry, obtaining the views of several prominent scholars in argumentative and aggressive communication seems fitting. Given this, we invited several researchers whose work appears multiple times throughout this book to offer their vision of future research directions.

We will begin this chapter with a discussion of what has been called a problem-centered approach to research in communication. This approach argues the need for research to address important problems for which enhanced communication may provide solutions. Next, we will present the contributions of these leading scholars who graciously responded to our query. Finally, we will conclude this chapter and this text with a few of our own thoughts.

A Problem-Centered Approach
to Communication Inquiry

Infante (1995a) contends that the communication discipline must continue to create its own identity, stand on its own two feet, decide what is important to study, and then develop theories which guide research. Infante believes that identifying important problems that involve communication is essential for their solution. This focus on problem-centered or applied communication research has been called for by other scholars as well. Miller and Sunnafrank (1984) suggested that applied communication research meant conducting theoretically important studies on issues of real world concern. Boyer (1990) urged academia to "reconnect the academy more vitally to the larger society" by conducting research aimed at solving pressing social problems.

For more than two decades scholars and researchers interested in argumentative and aggressive communication have attempted to more fully understand communication during disagreement and conflict by developing a theory of argumentative and aggressive communication. Over the past several years that theory has been applied to important communication problems and in several communication contexts. At its core, the theory posits that argumentative and aggressive communication are controlled mainly by a cluster of four traits that interact with factors in the situation that serve to increase or decrease message behavior. Those traits include assertiveness, argumentativeness, hostility, and verbal aggressiveness. Factors in the situation that interact with these traits can consist of inhibitors for the behavior (e.g., being seen as inappropriate or having the possibility of destroying a relationship) or disinhibitors for the behavior (e.g., alcohol or drug consumption). The most fundamental tenet of the theory however, and the one that has been supported by much of the research reviewed in this text, is that most outcomes of argumentativeness are constructive, whereas outcomes of verbal aggressiveness are destructive.

In this regard, researchers must continue to investigate the dark side of relationships. Dysfunctional relationships associated with verbal aggressiveness are found in all contexts of communication. Communication scholars suggest that how we communicate in the family shapes much of how we communicate in many other contexts and influences how we communicate on the job and with romantic partners (Infante et al., 1994). The research reviewed in this book underscores the destructive nature of verbal aggression in family communication and suggests that more constructive and positive family outcomes may result when people have higher motivation and greater skill in argumentative communication and lower levels of verbal aggressiveness. We are hopeful that the results of this research continue to stimulate the development of programs designed to help ameliorate major social problems.

The effect of argumentative and aggressive communication in the workplace is well documented, yet still needs to focus on relational problems that result from verbally aggressive encounters. Perhaps the most obvious solution, yet one that has not been incorporated to date, is that superiors and subordinates should be taught the skills associated with arguing and should engage in argument with an affirming communicator style. The research reviewed in Chapter 5 demonstrates that this is likely to result in more committed organizational members at all levels.

Within the classroom, we reviewed an abundance of research showing that verbal aggressiveness displayed by the teacher is never seen as appropriate and is often compounded by other issues, such as teacher status (e.g., teaching assistant versus a professor), and teacher communication style. We are encouraged that understanding of instructor communication competence has been increased now that the argumentative and aggressive communication traits have been incorporated in several research programs. We look forward to additional efforts along these lines.

In the intercultural context, we have reviewed studies concerning the comparison of different cultures and co-cultures based on argumentative and aggressive communication with other characteristics such as the cultural context, comparison of Eastern and Western cultural characteristics, and regional comparisons within the United States. We believe that future research efforts taking this problem-centered approach should focus on destructive and damaging forms of verbal aggression observed in different cultures. A related issue that deserves attention is, "When should one engage in argumentative communication in these different cultures?" In the American culture, it is not only acceptable but normative and often required that we engage in argument with others. This behavior, however, may be seen as inappropriate in other cultures. Thus, we need to discover when it is acceptable to argue and when is it unacceptable to argue in different cultures. What values in a given culture serve to foster the argumentativeness trait? For example, the Australian and Finnish cultures have been found to be especially argumentative, warranting further study as to how and why varying degrees of culture influence trait argumentativeness. In addition, what sanctions are imposed in other cultures to dampen an individual's motivation to argue? What types of cross-cultural training in argumentation would increase the likelihood of successful conflict management between members of different cultural or different ethnic groups?

Since antiquity, the communication discipline has advanced the notion that individuals can enhance their ability to argue. To that end, training programs and methods for enhancing motivation and skill in argument have been developed, including the inventional system (Infante, 1988), a topical system of argument invention (Wilson & Arnold, 1983), and cognitive training in interpersonal conflict (Anderson et al., 1987). Although these programs utilize different methods and procedures, all of them appear helpful in providing participants with some tools necessary to enhance motivation to argue and argumentative skill in adult populations (Kosberg & Rancer, 1991). As reported in Chapter 10, we have more recently seen the application of these programs in adolescent populations. These efforts include the training of middle school students in argument generation as well as increasing trait argumentativeness (Rancer et al. 1997; Rancer et al., 2000), training aimed at reducing adolescent verbal and physical aggression (Meyer et al., 2004), and efforts designed at understanding conflict management orientations among incarcerated youth (Anderson & Rancer, 2003).

We must revisit the curriculum of these training programs to expand their content. Additional distinctions regarding argumentativeness and verbal aggressiveness must also be stressed. Longitudinal assessments (i.e., measuring over long periods of time) regarding adolescents' predispositions and use of argumentative and verbally aggressive communication should continue after modifications, additions, and enhancements to the existing curricula are made. However, it appears clear from the findings that training adolescents to argue can enhance their motivation to argue and actual argumentative behavior. Programs designed to reduce verbal aggression await further research and development, and the efficacy of these programs needs to be studied.

We concur with Infante (1995b) that the need for research that addresses practical problems and the development of a problem-centered research agenda are pressing. When applied to the situations mentioned above (i.e., intrafamily violence, training teachers to be more competent in the classroom, enhancing organizational life, having better understanding of intercultural conflict, and providing communication skills in an effort to reduce the use of verbal and physical aggression), the research program described in this text suggests some viable options available to enhance conflict management behavior.

The Research Contributions

We have identified some directions in which future research efforts might be focused. Now, let us turn to suggestions from several leading scholars whose names you have encountered throughout this book on their perceptions of the future of argumentative and aggressive communication research. In an effort to ensure that the researchers were addressing the same question, we developed a scenario and asked each scholar for a response. The scenario was as follows:

You are teaching an undergraduate seminar course titled Argumentative and Aggressive Communication. You have spent the last 14 weeks reviewing all aspects of these traits including measurement issues and research in specific contexts (e.g., family, organizational, training). A student raises her hand and asks, "Professor, we have read and studied all about argumentativeness and verbal aggressiveness, yet there seem to be some unanswered questions. In your opinion, what issues and research efforts need be addressed regarding these traits in the future?"

Much to our delight, our invited scholars provided what we believe are visionary responses that we attempted to group by common themes. This process resulted in the following research foci: (a) message and individual focus, (b) cultural influence focus, (c) theoretical foundation and meta-theory focus, and (d) measurement and theoretical-refinement focus.

A Focus on the Message and Individual

Four scholars submitted responses that focused on verbally aggressive messages. These suggestions explore the influence of communication competence, paralinguistic differences, thresholds and tolerances for engaging in debate, and situational triggers that motivate people to be verbally aggressive.

Name:	Charles J. Wigley III, Ph.D., J.D.
Title:	Professor
Institution:	Canisius College
Major Area of Research:	The role of verbally aggressive communication in the jury selection process

Future research can improve our understanding of these two traits by answering five main questions: (1) how stable are these traits (there is almost no evidence of test re-test reliability)? (2) under what circumstances is aggressive communication ordinarily considered justified (a common reason people offer to excuse their own aggressiveness)? (3) to what extent are the people who engage in verbal aggression hurt by their own aggressiveness (does it hurt them more than their intended victims)? (4) what is the role of chemical influences (e.g., medicines or alcohol) in causing argumentative or aggressive communication to be expressed (do barroom brawls start early or late in the evening)? and (5) what role do verbal trigger events (VTEs; i.e., statements that lead to explosive verbal responses) take in serving as a catalyst for an aggressive response (i.e., secondary aggression)?

If we could answer that last question, we might gain a lot of insight as to why ordinarily pleasant people go off the deep end. If a person feels verbally attacked by another person because of something that person said (a VTE), he or she might feel justified in using aggression for self-protection. Would that lead to more problems or, possibly, greater problems? An old friend of mine said, "The pen is mightier than the sword." Although most people would choose the sword over the pen in a physical duel, the reality seems to be that some people rely on strong and aggressive language when they feel put down by others. This secondary aggression might account for more than half of the negative exchanges between people! To date, only a few research studies (see the studies reported in this book on reciprocal aggression) have even begun to explore this problem. A first step (by you) toward investigating this issue might involve recalling a personal conversation that went badly. Was there a VTE? If so, did the response to the VTE help smooth things over or was it a case of conversations gone wild?

Name:	James C. McCroskey, Ed.D.
Title:	Professor
Institution:	West Virginia University
Major Area of Research:	Human communication (instructional, organizational, interpersonal, intercultural, nonverbal, health, trait orientations)

There is another line of research which appears to be similar to that which deals with argumentativeness and verbal aggression. This research focuses on tolerance for disagreement. The theory upon which this research is based holds that communication that involves disagreement (engaging in argument) on substantive issues is a positive factor in reaching better decisions, but when the interaction includes personal attacks (verbal aggression) the communication becomes conflict, which is a negative factor in reaching better decisions. The theory suggests that each person has a threshold for moving from disagreement to conflict. This threshold is based on the strength of the disagreement (low to high) and the affect (negative to positive) the person has for the other person(s) involved in the communication. Hence, when the disagreement is higher and/or the affect is less positive, the likelihood of conflict (verbal aggression) is increased. Although for many people the threshold is very flexible, depending on the levels of disagreement and negative affect in any given context, it is also theorized that there is a trait (tolerance for disagreement) that impacts the threshold also. This is a tendency (at least partially genetically based, ranging from very low to very high) to approach or avoid dealing with disagreement. Those at the low end, therefore, are people who are more able to deal with more severe disagreement or negative affect, and people at the high end who are less able to do so. Efforts are needed to study how these theories blend (or conflict) with theories of argumentativeness and verbal aggression and to test the predictive power of these theories.

Name:	Carolyn M. Anderson, Ph.D.
Title:	Professor
Institution:	University of Akron
Major Area of Research:	Interpersonal and small group communication

Barge (2001) reminds us that communication is a practical discipline. Hence, researchers must build and unify aggressive-based theoretical models useful for people. First, inspiration for models may come from acknowledging that communication contexts are fluid and not static isolates. Just imagine in one day that a verbal aggressor may confront people in interpersonal, group, organizational, and public settings. Researchers should couple these ideas with any number of factors influencing outcomes. For example, one factor might be the aggressor's competence in sending messages in a variety of settings from face-to-face contact to use of technology.

Second, if a lofty research goal is advancing understanding of competent and not so competent communication and communicators, researchers must delete obstacles that cloud thinking by blending trait and state methodologies and by seeking a broader range of recurring issues to investigate. For example, a verbal aggressor engages in decision making processes and practices with people in various contextual settings. One practical research question might be, How does the use of aggressive communication impact decision-making processes and practices of verbal aggression in everyday life? It makes intuitive sense that by seeking answers to practical questions, researchers will contribute data that will enrich people's understanding of aggressive communication and clarify ways to enhance competence in communication across contexts.

Name:	Scott A. Myers, Ph.D.
Title:	Associate Professor
Institution:	West Virginia University
Major Area of Research:	Instructional communication

One area that has received scant attention is the composition of the verbally aggressive message. Although research has found that an individual's perceived level of trait verbal aggressiveness can have a detrimental impact on his or her relational partner and various relational outcomes, researchers have not yet identified the linguistic and vocalic devices associated with verbally aggressive messages and how these devices contribute to the detriment of the relationship. For example, does the choice or use of a particular word or phrase make a message seem verbally aggressive? Does the use of inflection, rate, or pitch alter whether a message sounds verbally aggressive? If so, how? By studying the linguistic and vocalic devices associated with verbally aggressive messages, particularly in the context of a specific relationship, it might be possible to determine more accurately not only the extent to which verbal aggressiveness is present in relationships, but also the extent to which the verbal aggressiveness is perceived as detrimental by the relational participants.

Cultural Influence Focus

Three scholars highlighted the influence of culture on the interpretation of argumentative and aggressive communication. More specifically, there is an emphasis on intercultural or co-cultural interpretations as well as global interpretations as to the appropriateness and effectiveness of argumentative and aggressive communication.

Name:	Anne M. Nicotera, Ph.D.
Title:	Associate Professor
Institution:	Howard University
Major Area of Research:	Intercultural communication

Aggressive communication predispositions is one of the most well-researched areas in the field of communication. Hundreds upon hundreds of studies have examined this set of phenomena in dozens of contexts. How can there still be questions? The answer is that there **must always** be new questions. Human communication is enormously complex, with layer upon layer of meaning to be dissected by researchers, each layer yielding only more questions. And this is the mark of excellent research: it is heuristic—it generates more questions. The more knowledge we amass, the more we become aware of how much more there is that we do not know.

In my mind, one of the greatest untapped areas of study in this research tradition is the extent to which aggressive communication predispositions, namely argumentativeness and verbal aggressiveness, are linked to culture in all its myriad of forms. Although several researchers have compared members of two or more cultures to one another, this is not the same as studying culture—but it is a good start. The problem with what we have done when comparing members of American culture to members of other cultures is that we have been guilty of ignoring America's multiculturalism. Most research in the field of communication has been conducted with respondents who are predominately white, middle-class Americans.

So, any conclusions drawn about Americans are actually conclusions about middle-class Americans of European descent. We know little about argumentativeness and verbal aggressiveness for Americans of African, Latino, Asian, Native American, or Middle Eastern descent. And all American cultural groups (including European Americans) have vast internal diversity.

Moving to forms of culture beyond ethnicity and race, we know nothing about how aggressive communication predispositions can be linked to socioeconomic class and level of education, occupation, or age. There has been limited study of geographic region. Are New Yorkers really more aggressive than Californians? How might one or more of these other factors combine with ethnicity? For example, how might Italian American New York construction workers compare to Scandinavian American Minnesota farmers? Math teachers? History professors? Bankers? Dancers?

We do have some understanding of age, but there is a long way to go here, as well. And I have some current data on African American urban teenagers that challenges what we thought we knew. We have long thought that argumentativeness and verbal aggressiveness were related in adolescent populations. But, as I explained, the research this knowledge was based upon was conducted with white middle-class samples. In the current data, which are still undergoing analyses, the two traits are **not related** for African American urban teenagers. What is the explanation? Is it race? Socioeconomic class? Region? Some combination of these? I don't yet know, but I do know that it points to the importance of carefully defining not only **what** we study, but **who** we study. We must become more sensitive to the cultural makeup of our samples and the multicultural nature of the American population. And we must understand that America is multicultural by many factors.

And, finally, once we've exhausted what can be done by comparing groups to each other we can begin exploring the mechanisms by which cultural values are acted upon to create aggressive communication. The field of intercultural communication has begun a tradition of examining links between cultural values and individual behavior that has much to offer by way of example.

Name:	Jill E. Rudd, Ph.D.
Title:	Associate Professor
Institution:	Cleveland State University
Major Area of Research:	Aggressive communication and dispute resolution

Many areas remain for the study and advancement of argumentativeness and verbal aggressiveness research. Future studies should focus on global negotiations and intercultural conflicts. Given that approximately four out of five jobs are a result of global trade and that international trade is climbing dramatically (approximately 120%) the knowledge and ability to communicate effectively is critical. The 21st century is a period of movement from an international community to a global community. How we resolve our differences, whether in the workplace, at home, or in our communities, will be affected by the vastly changing world of intertwined cultures.

Name:	Matthew M. Martin, Ph.D.
Title:	Professor
Institution:	West Virginia University
Major Area of Research:	Communication traits and interpersonal relationships

Dominic Infante (1987a) talks about how aggressive communication can be viewed by studying the source, the receiver, and the content of the message or by considering how aggressive a society or a culture would perceive a message. I believe that there is evidence that American culture has become more overtly aggressive and that it is becoming more culturally appropriate for both men and women to communicate aggressively; thus, more attention will be paid to what type of messages are considered to be destructive aggressive messages. Messages that at one time might have been considered inappropriate might now be considered acceptable, as well as effective.

Additionally, I believe more attention will also be given to the potential instrumental use of verbally aggressive messages. As we know, overwhelmingly, verbally aggressive messages are related to negative consequences and relational outcomes. No one enjoys being on the receiving end of verbally aggressive messages, especially when these messages are received on a regular basis. However, can there be particular situations, possibly with certain individuals, when using verbally aggressive messages might be the most effective strategy and possibly even appropriate?

Theoretical Foundation and Meta-Theory Focus

The next two contributions focus on the way we think about theory and human nature. They address human nature and whether we are destined for self-destruction or are able to make profound changes in an effort toward self-preservation.

Name:	Dominic A. Infante, Ph.D.
Title:	Professor Emeritus
Institution:	Kent State University
Major Area of Research:	Argumentativeness and verbal aggressiveness

There are numerous unresolved issues concerning aggressive communication that appear important and would benefit from research. I will comment briefly on two that I think are particularly significant. The first is we need to determine which aggressive communication traits are biologically determined and which are learned. The communibiological model by Professors James McCroskey and Michael Beatty would provide a useful approach for such an inquiry. This knowledge would provide a basis for developing methods for modifying any given behavior. If a trait is genetically determined, a pharmacological rather than an educational approach might be more effective. For example, some research has found that there is a biological basis for verbal aggressiveness. Because we also know that increased levels of male hormone testosterone are associated with hyper-aggressiveness, it might be determined that extreme forms of verbal abusiveness can be modified by injections of the drug Lupron, which reduces the production of the hormone. However, if a trait is primarily determined by social learning, an educational or training approach might be effective. Professor Andrew Rancer and colleagues have conducted some useful preliminary research in this area with schoolchildren. The communication discipline can have the most favorable effect on society if training methods are developed for reducing aggressive behaviors and enhancing constructive aggressive communication.

The second issue is related and also socially significant. The study of history reveals that perhaps a hundred million people have been killed in wars. Physical aggression is a form of communication and countries have turned to it thousands of times to resolve conflict. I do not believe, despite the efforts of the United Nations, that argumentation has been used very extensively to resolve international conflict. Instead, typically after limited argumentative exchange, physical aggression or the threat of physical aggression is employed. More research is needed to determine what increases the attractiveness of debate as the primary method used for resolving differences between nations. How to enhance attitudes toward debate is a research focus that could find success in the communication field if an intensive effort is made. Although humans have been characterized as the "killer apes," it is possible that if argumentative theory is encouraged to evolve further, "debating apes" will emerge as a most welcomed replacement.

Name:	Michael J. Beatty, Ph.D.
Title:	Professor
Institution:	University of Missouri–St. Louis
Major Area of Research:	Biological aspects, especially brain-related dimensions of interpersonal communication

I would say, first, we need to discover why some people are aggressive, assertive, or argumentative whereas others are more passive and congenial. There is a great deal of speculation—and I've done a lot of it myself—but not much solid, direct evidence regarding the issue. Studies of identical twins seem to suggest that most of our orientation toward others is inherited, but these studies have their share of critics. Right now the question of whether we are born to communicate as we do, or whether it is our upbringing and childhood experiences, a combination of the two, or something else entirely still needs to be answered. Second, why does aggressiveness exist at all in humans? We certainly do not seem to be a peaceful species. Why aren't we passive, peaceful, and cooperative? What evolutionary purpose, if any, does our aggressiveness serve? Once we know more about those questions, I think it would be important to know whether we can change, if we want to, and if so what would we need to do to effect the change? Can aggressive people become less aggressive? Can passive people become more assertive? I don't mean a little more peaceful or assertive. I mean, can we change our basic approach to relating to others in a profound way?

Measurement and Theoretical Refinement Focus

Our final contribution offers some important measurement questions about both the Argumentativeness and Verbal Aggressiveness traits. Novel ways of assessing argumentative and aggressive communication are suggested that may allow for more accurate assessment of the true interdependent nature of both constructs.

Name:	Timothy R. Levine, Ph.D.
Title:	Professor
Institution:	Michigan State University
Major Area of Research:	Interpersonal, persuasion, research methods

In my opinion, there are two main issues that need to be addressed in future theory and research on trait argumentativeness and verbal aggressiveness. First and probably most pressing, the scales measuring both constructs are in need of refinement. The conceptual definition of trait verbal aggressiveness needs rethinking and updating, and both the Verbal Aggressiveness Scale and the Argumentativeness Scale have validity problems (e.g., see Levine, Beatty, Limon, Hamilton, Buck, & Chory-Assad, 2004). For example, the factor structures of both scales are unstable and whereas both scales are typically scored as if they are unidimensional, both are often found to have two orthogonal factors. The existing scales are useful and have led to many new insights, but both could be improved. So, I hope that new scales will be constructed and validated in the near future.

The second issue is related to argumentativeness and verbal aggressiveness research, but also to the study of all communication traits. Communication is fundamentally an interdependent activity characterized by mutual respect. Yet most research on how traits affect communication focuses on the individual or on the impact of only one person's personality. Studies show how certain traits affect a person's communication patterns and how a person's traits affect other people. Research is needed on how the combination of people's traits interrelate to affect their joint communication. So, if you and I are talking, how does the combination of my trait argumentativeness and your argumentativeness combine to determine how we interact? This is an issue Professor Boster and I wrote on nearly a decade ago (Levine & Boster, 1996), but little research has followed up on this idea of a transaction approach to personality. I think the idea has merit, and I hope it catches on in the future.

Conclusion

The journey for better understanding of argumentative and verbally aggressive communication started over two decades ago. We have reviewed scores of research studies that have revealed interesting and useful findings regarding a variety of outcomes in a number of different communication contexts. Researchers have spent thousands of hours in the pursuit of understanding these traits. However, more research is needed into the measurement and consequences of argumentativeness and verbal aggressiveness.

As our society continually grows more splintered and diverse, research conducted over 20 years ago may need to be revisited as perceptions of argumentative and aggressive communication may have changed. Would research findings concerning the beliefs about arguing conducted in the mid-1980s reveal the same findings today? We continue to witness the blurring of distinctions between argument and verbal aggression. For example, many people in our culture cannot distinguish between having a fight (i.e., exchange of verbal aggression) and having a disagreement (i.e., exchange of arguments). This trend, if not countered, may lead to a culture that believes any disagreement requires strategic verbal aggression where the destruction of the other person supersedes the need to resolve the issue.

This book has served as a chronicle of evidence on the impact of argumentative and aggressive communication research amassed in the fields of communication studies, psychology, social psychology, and sociology over a relatively short period of time. We believe, and sincerely hope, that in another two decades the chronicling of studies on argumentativeness and verbal aggressiveness research will fill several additional volumes. It is also our hope that the information in this book has served to inform you, and for the hopes of a world often mired in verbal and physical aggression, inspired you to examine your own behavior. Our greatest satisfaction, however, would be that you might even decide to conduct some research yourself with the goal of producing an even better understanding of the nature of argumentative and aggressive communication.

Discussion Questions for Chapter 12

1. Which of the message and individual focus responses best reflects your feelings about future research? Why?

2. How do you think focusing on verbal trigger events aids our understanding of verbal aggression? Why?

3. Why do you think future researchers, when investigating the cultural influence of argumentative and aggressive communication, should consider specific subsets within a culture such as location, age, education level, race, vocation, ethnicity and so forth when conducting intercultural research?

4. Of the theoretical foundation and meta-theory focus, which best reflects your feelings about future research? Why?

5. Based on your readings of the previous 11 chapters of this book, how would you respond to the scenarios presented to the leading scholars?

Appendix A: The Argumentativeness and Verbal Aggressiveness Scales

The Argumentativeness Scale

Instructions: This questionnaire contains statements about arguing *controversial issues*. Indicate how often each statement is true for you personally by placing the appropriate number in the blank to the left of the statement. Use the following scale:

1 = almost never true

2 = rarely true

3 = occasionally true

4 = often true

5 = almost always true

_____ 1. While in an argument, I worry that the person I am arguing with will form a negative impression of me.

_____ 2. Arguing over controversial issues improves my intelligence.

_____ 3. I enjoy avoiding arguments.

_____ 4. I am energetic and enthusiastic when I argue.

_____ 5. Once I finish an argument I promise myself that I will not get into another.

_____ 6. Arguing with a person creates more problems for me than it solves.

_____ 7. I have a pleasant, good feeling when I win a point in an argument.

_____ 8. When I finish arguing with someone I feel nervous and upset.
_____ 9. I enjoy a good argument over a controversial issue.
_____ 10. I get an unpleasant feeling when I realize I am about to get into an argument.
_____ 11. I enjoy defending my point of view on an issue.
_____ 12. I am happy when I keep an argument from happening.
_____ 13. I do not like to miss the opportunity to argue a controversial issue.
_____ 14. I prefer being with people who rarely disagree with me.
_____ 15. I consider an argument an exciting intellectual challenge.
_____ 16. I find myself unable to think of effective points during an argument.
_____ 17. I feel refreshed and satisfied after an argument on a controversial issue.
_____ 18. I have the ability to do well in an argument.
_____ 19. I try to avoid getting into arguments.
_____ 20. I feel excitement when I expect that a conversation I am in is leading to an argument.

Scoring Instructions for the Argumentativeness Scale

1. Add scores for items 2, 4, 7, 9, 11, 13, 15, 17, 18, 20

   (A) Total = _____

2. Add scores for items 1, 3, 5, 6, 8, 10, 12, 14, 16, 19

   (B) Total = _____

3. Subtract your (B) total from your (A) total

Interpretation of Argumentativeness Scores

If the result is any number between 14 and 40, you may have a high motivation to argue.

If the result is any number between 4 and 13, you may have a moderate motivation to argue.

If the result is any number between 5 and 25, you may have a low motivation to argue.

Errata for *Argumentative and Aggressive Communication: Theory, Research, and Application by* Andrew S. Rancer and Theodore A. Avtgis, 2006, Sage.

Page 256, *Interpretation of Argumentativeness Scores* should read as follows:

If the result is any number between +14 and +40, you may have a high motivation to argue.

If the result is any number between −4 and +13, you may have a moderate motivation to argue.

If the result is any number between −5 and −25, you may have a low motivation to argue.

The Verbal Aggressiveness Scale

Instructions: This survey is concerned with how we try to get people to comply with our wishes. Indicate how often each statement is true for you personally when you try to influence other persons. Use the following scale:

1 = almost never true

2 = rarely true

3 = occasionally true

4 = often true

5 = almost always true

_____ 1. I am extremely careful to avoid attacking individuals' intelligence when I attack their ideas.

_____ 2. When individuals are very stubborn, I use insults to soften their stubbornness.

_____ 3. I try very hard to avoid having other people feel bad about themselves when I try to influence them.

_____ 4. When people refuse to do a task I know is important, without good reason, I tell them they are unreasonable.

_____ 5. When others do things I regard as stupid, I try to be extremely gentle with them.

_____ 6. If individuals I am trying to influence really deserve it, I attack their character.

_____ 7. When people behave in ways that are in very poor taste, I insult them in order to shock them into proper behavior.

_____ 8. I try to make people feel good about themselves even when their ideas are stupid.

_____ 9. When people simply will not budge on a matter of importance I lose my temper and say rather strong things to them.

_____ 10. When people criticize my shortcomings, I take it in good humor and do not try to get back at them.

_____ 11. When individuals insult me, I get a lot of pleasure out of really telling them off.

_____ 12. When I dislike individuals greatly, I try not to show it in what I say or how I say it.

_____ 13. I like poking fun at people who do things which are very stupid in order to stimulate their intelligence.

_____ 14. When I attack a person's ideas, I try not to damage their self-concepts.

_____ 15. When I try to influence people, I make a great effort not to offend them.

_____ 16. When people do things which are mean or cruel, I attack their character in order to help correct their behavior.

_____ 17. I refuse to participate in arguments when they involve personal attacks.

_____ 18. When nothing seems to work in trying to influence others, I yell and scream in order to get some movement from them.

_____ 19. When I am not able to refute others' positions, I try to make them feel defensive in order to weaken their positions.

_____ 20. When an argument shifts to personal attacks, I try very hard to change the subject.

Scoring Instructions for the Verbal Aggressiveness Scale

1. Add your scores on items 2, 4, 6, 7, 9, 11, 13, 16, 18, 19

2. Add your scores on items 1, 3, 5, 8, 10, 12, 14, 15, 17, 20

3. Subtract the sum obtained in step 2 from 60

4. Add the total obtained in step 1 to the result obtained in step 3 to compute your verbal aggressiveness score

Interpretation of Verbal Aggressiveness Scores

If you scored between 59 and 100, you may be considered high in verbal aggressiveness.

If you scored between 39 and 58, you may be considered moderate in verbal aggressiveness.

If you scored between 20 and 38, you may be considered low in verbal aggressiveness.

From "Verbal Aggressiveness: An Interpersonal Model and Measure," by D. A. Infante & C. J. Wigley, 1986, _Communication Monographs, 53_, pp. 61–69. Copyright 1986 by National Communication Association, Taylor & Francis.

Appendix B: The Adolescent Argumentativeness and Adolescent Verbal Aggressiveness Scales

The Adolescent Argumentativeness Scale (ADARG)

Instructions: This survey contains statements about arguing. By "arguing," I mean having a discussion or disagreement about a topic that has more than one side. For example, you might argue over who is the best basketball player or who is the best music group. Indicate how often each statement is true for you personally when you argue *with your friends*. Use the following scale:

1 = Almost never true

2 = Rarely true

3 = Sometimes true

4 = Often true

5 = Almost always true

_____ 1. I have a great time when I argue.
_____ 2. I feel good when I am winning an argument.
_____ 3. When I finish arguing with someone, I feel nervous and upset.
_____ 4. I enjoy a good argument.
_____ 5. I get a bad feeling when I am about to get into an argument.
_____ 6. I am happy when I keep an argument from happening.
_____ 7. I do not like to miss the chance to argue.

_____ 8. Arguments are a fun challenge.

_____ 9. I feel refreshed and satisfied after an argument.

_____ 10. I have the ability to do well in arguments.

Scoring Instructions for the Adolescent Argumentativeness Scale

1. Reverse the scoring for items 3, 5, and 6. Use the following conversions: (5 = 1) (4 = 2) (3 = 3) (2 = 4) (1 = 5). That is, for Items 3, 5, and 6, if you scored a "5" change the score to a "1"; if you scored a "4" change the score to a "2" and so on.

2. Sum the scores on the ten items after this reverse scoring.

The Adolescent Verbal Aggressiveness Scale (ADVA)

Instructions: This survey is concerned with how we try to get people to do what we want. Indicate how often each statement is true for you personally when you try to change *a friend's* mind. Use the following scale:

1 = Almost never true

2 = Rarely true

3 = Sometimes true

4 = Often true

5 = Almost always true

_____ 1. When people are very stubborn, I use insults to soften their stubbornness.

_____ 2. When others do things I think are stupid, I try to be very gentle with them.

_____ 3. When I want my way and someone won't listen, I will call them names and let them know I think they are stupid.

_____ 4. When people behave badly, I insult them in order to get them to behave better.

_____ 5. When people will not budge on an important issue, I get angry and say really nasty things to them.

_____ 6. When people criticize my faults, I do not let it bother me and do not try to get back at them.

_____ 7. When people insult me, I like to really tell them off.

_____ 8. I like making fun of people who do things which are very stupid in order to make them smarter.

Scoring Instructions for the Adolescent Verbal Aggressiveness Scale

1. Reverse the scoring for items 2 and 6. Use the following conversions: (5 = 1) (4 =2) (3 = 3) (2 = 4) (1 = 5). That is, for Items 2 and 6, if you scored a "5" change the score to a "1"; if you scored a "4" change the score to a "2" and so on.

2. Sum the scores on the eight items after this reverse scoring.

Both scales from "The Assessment of Argumentativeness and Verbal Aggressiveness in Adolescent Populations," by A. J. Roberto and M. Finucane, 1997, *Communication Quarterly*, 45, pp. 21–36. Copyright 1997 by Eastern Communication Association, Taylor & Francis.

Appendix C: Short-Form Versions of the Argumentativeness and Verbal Aggressiveness Scales

Short-Form Version of the Argumentativeness Scale

Instructions: This questionnaire contains statements about arguing controversial issues. Indicate how often each statement is true for you personally by placing the appropriate number in the blank to the left of the statement. Use the following scale:

1 = almost never true

2 = rarely true

3 = occasionally true

4 = often true

5 = almost always true

_____ 1. While in an argument, I worry that the person I am arguing with will form a negative impression of me.

_____ 2. I am energetic and enthusiastic when I argue.

_____ 3. I enjoy a good argument over a controversial issue.

_____ 4. I prefer being with people who rarely disagree with me.

_____ 5. I enjoy defending my point of view on an issue.

_____ 6. When I finish arguing with someone I feel nervous and upset.

_____ 7. I consider an argument an exciting intellectual challenge.

_____ 8. I find myself unable to think of effective points during an argument.
_____ 9. I have the ability to do well in an argument.
_____ 10. I try to avoid getting into arguments.

From "Subordinates' Satisfaction and Perceptions of Superiors' Compliance-Gaining Tactics, Argumentativeness, Verbal Aggressiveness, and Style," by D. A. Infante, C. M. Anderson, M. M. Martin, A. D. Herington, and J. Kim, 1993, *Management Communication Quarterly, 6,* pp. 307–326. Copyright 1993 by Sage Publications.

Short-Form Version of the Verbal Aggressiveness Scale

Instructions: This survey is concerned with how we try to get people to comply with our wishes. Indicate how often each statement is true for you personally when you try to influence other persons. Use the following scale:

1 = almost never true

2 = rarely true

3 = occasionally true

4 = often true

5 = almost always true

_____ 1. I am extremely careful to avoid attacking individuals' intelligence when I attack their ideas.

_____ 2. When individuals are very stubborn, I use insults to soften their stubbornness.

_____ 3. I try very hard to avoid having other people feel bad about themselves when I try to influence them.

_____ 4. If individuals I am trying to influence really deserve it, I attack their character.

_____ 5. I try to make people feel good about themselves even when their ideas are stupid.

_____ 6. When people simply will not budge on a matter of importance, I lose my temper and say rather strong things to them.

_____ 7. When individuals insult me, I get a lot of pleasure out of really telling them off.

_____ 8. When I attack a person's ideas, I try not to damage their self-concepts.

_____ 9. When I try to influence people, I make a great effort not to offend them.

_____ 10. When nothing seems to work in trying to influence others, I yell and scream in order to get some movement from them.

From "Subordinates' Satisfaction and Perceptions of Superiors' Compliance-Gaining Tactics, Argumentativeness, Verbal Aggressiveness, and Style," by D. A. Infante, C. M. Anderson, M. M. Martin, A. D. Herington, and J. Kim, 1993, *Management Communication Quarterly*, 6, pp. 307–326. Copyright 1993 by Sage Publications.

Appendix D: The Affective-Behavioral-Cognitive Scale (ABCAS)

Directions: This instrument contains statements concerning how you feel about and how you tend to behave when communicating with other people. For most of the items on this questionnaire you can choose one of seven possible responses. Many statements are similar to other statements. Do not be concerned about this. Please indicate in the space provided the degree to which each statement applies to you by marking whether you:

1 = Strongly Disagree

2 = Disagree

3 = Somewhat Disagree

4 = Not Sure

5 = Somewhat Agree

6 = Agree

7 = Strongly Agree

_____ 1. I tend to avoid opportunities to discuss my views on controversial issues.

_____ 2. Discussing controversial issues with another person sharpens my mind.

_____ 3. I participate frequently in controversial discussions.

_____ 4. When I overhear a controversial discussion, I try to join in.

_____ 5. I initiate discussions on controversial issues.

_____ 6. Controversial discussions are refreshing and satisfying.

_____ 7. Participating in discussions over controversial issues at social events makes these events more fun for me than they would be otherwise.

_____ 8. My friends and I engage in controversial issues.

_____ 9. Controversial discussions keep my personal relationships interesting.

_____ 10. When I think about having to discuss controversial issues with others, it bothers me.

Scoring Instructions for the Affective-Behavioral-Cognitive Scale (ABCAS)

1. Reverse the scoring for items 1 and 10. Use the following conversions: (5 = 1) (4 = 2) (3 = 3) (2 = 4) (1 = 5). That is, for Items 1 and 10, if you scored a "5" change the score to a "1"; if you scored a "4" change the score to a "2" and so on.

2. Sum the scores on the ten items after this reverse scoring.

Interpretation of ABCAS Scores

Mean = 45.09

Standard deviation = 9.86

Low Argumentativeness = Scores between 0–31

Moderate Argumentativeness = Scores between 32–55

High Argumentativeness = Scores between 56–70

From "Affective, Behavioral, and Cognitive Dimensions of Argumentativeness: A New Measure," by L. L. Hinkle, April 2003. Paper presented at the annual meeting of the Eastern Communication Association, Williamsburg, VA. Copyright by Dr. Lois L. Hinkle.

Appendix E:
The Indirect Interpersonal
Aggressiveness Scale

Instructions: This survey is concerned with how we try to get people to comply with our wishes. Indicate how often each statement is true for you personally when you try to influence other persons. Use the following scale:

1 = almost never true

2 = rarely true

3 = occasionally true

4 = often true

5 = almost always true

_____ 1. If someone intentionally treats me unfairly, I would spread rumors about him or her.

_____ 2. I would provide inaccurate information to a person who has been hostile or unfair to me.

_____ 3. I might "forget" to relay information to a person who has been hostile or unfair to me.

_____ 4. I would work "behind the scenes" to keep an enemy from getting what he or she wants.

_____ 5. If someone is a real jerk, I would harm his or her chances for success if given the chance.

_____ 6. I would facilitate the failure of people who have mistreated me.

_____ 7. Given the chance, I would keep a person who has mistreated me from getting a job or promotion that he or she really wants.

_____ 8. I would not warn a person who has mistreated me about a problem situation even though my information would allow him or her to avoid trouble.

_____ 9. I have destroyed one or more of another's belongings because he or she mistreated me.

_____ 10. I would try to keep important information from people who have been hostile toward me.

From "A 'Dark Side' of Communication Avoidance: Indirect Interpersonal Aggressiveness," by M. J. Beatty, K. M. Valencic, J. E. Rudd, and J. A. Dobos, 1999, *Communication Research Reports, 16*, pp. 103–109. Copyright by Eastern Communication Association, Taylor & Francis.

Appendix F: The Beliefs About Arguing Measure

Instructions: This questionnaire contains statements regarding your beliefs about arguing. Indicate your agreement or disagreement with each statement by using the following scale:

1 = strongly disagree

2 = disagree

3 = neither agree or disagree

4 = agree

5 = strongly agree

_____ 1. I enjoy a good verbal fight.

_____ 2. Arguing gives me insight into how others see the world.

_____ 3. Arguing increases my communication ability.

_____ 4. Arguing is a waste of time.

_____ 5. Arguing is a type of education.

_____ 6. When I do well in an argument, I experience a sense of power.

_____ 7. When I argue with someone, issues usually are not discussed fully enough.

_____ 8. Arguing creates tension between people.

_____ 9. Arguing is fun.

_____ 10. People will dislike me if I argue with them.

_____ 11. I find it difficult to state my case well when I argue.

_____ 12. Matters usually become worse between people when they argue with each other.

_____ 13. Arguing is an effective means of resolving differences between people.

_____ 14. Arguing usually leads to anger and unreasonable behavior.

_____ 15. Arguing is a type of inexpensive, enjoyable entertainment.

_____ 16. Unless an argument actually resolves an issue, it is not enjoyable.

_____ 17. Arguing provides an opportunity to persuade someone over to my side of an issue.

_____ 18. Arguing reduces aggression.

_____ 19. I rarely try to change others' opinions.

_____ 20. Arguments can be vicious.

_____ 21. It feels good, during an argument, to let out my feelings and support and defend my ideas.

_____ 22. When I argue, I don't feel good about myself.

_____ 23. Arguing helps resolve conflict.

_____ 24. Arguing is a hostile means of resolving differences between people.

From "Beliefs about Arguing as Predictors of Trait Argumentativeness: Implications for Training in Argument and Conflict Management," by A. S. Rancer, R. L. Kosberg, and R. A. Baukus, 1992, *Communication Education, 41,* pp. 375–387. Copyright 1992 by National Communication Association, Taylor & Francis.

Appendix G: Additional Resources on Argumentative and Aggressive Communication

Anderson, C. M., Raptis, P. R., Lin, Y., & Clark, F. R. (2000). Motives as predictors of argumentativeness and verbal aggressiveness of black and white adolescents. *Communication Research Reports, 17,* 115–126.

Aune, M., Hunter, J. E., Kim, H. J., & Kim, J. S. (2001). The effect of culture and self-construals on predispositions toward verbal communication. *Human Communication Research, 27,* 382–408.

Beatty, M. J., & McCroskey, J. C. (1998). Interpersonal communication as temperamental expression: A communibiological paradigm. In J. C. McCroskey, J. A. Daly, M. M. Martin, & M. J. Beatty (Eds.), *Communication and personality: Trait perspectives* (pp. 41–67). Cresskill, NJ: Hampton Press.

Bekiari, A., Kokarides, D., & Sakelariou, K. (2005). Verbal aggressiveness of physical education teachers and students' self-reports of behavior. *Psychological Reports, 96,* 493–498.

Bell, R. A., & Daly, J. A. (1984). The affinity-seeking function of communication. *Communication Monographs, 51,* 91–115.

Benoit, W. L. (2004). Election outcome and topic of political campaign attacks. *Southern Communication Journal, 69,* 348–355.

Bresnahan, M. J., & Cai, D. H. (1986). Gender and aggression in the recognition of interruption. *Discourse Processes, 21,* 171–189.

Cameron, K. A., Campo, S., & Brossard, D. (2003). Advocating for controversial issues: The effect of activism on compliance-gaining strategy likelihood of use. *Communication Studies, 54,* 265–282.

Cayanus, J. L., Martin, M. M., & Weber, K. D. (2005). The relationships between driver anger and aggressive communication traits. *Communication Research Reports, 22,* 189–197.

Chory-Assad, R. M., & Cicchirillo, V. (2005). *More evidence on the bi-dimensionality of the verbal aggressiveness scale: Relationships with hostility and self-monitoring.*

Paper presented at the annual meeting of the Eastern Communication Association, Pittsburgh, PA.

Darus, H. J. (1994). Argumentativeness in the workplace: A trait by situation study. *Communication Research Reports, 11,* 99–106.

DeWine, S., & Nicotera, A. M. (1989, October). *Understanding argumentativeness at work and at home.* Paper presented at the annual meeting of the International Communication Association, San Francisco, CA.

Downs, V. C., Kaid, L. L., & Ragan, S. (1990). The impact of argumentativeness and verbal aggression on communicator image: The exchange between George Bush and Dan Rather. *Western Journal of Communication, 54,* 99–112.

Feezel, J. D., Gordon, W. I., & Infante, D. A. (1991). Gender and the connotations of selected communication terms. *Ohio Speech Journal, 29,* 21–32.

Frankovsky, M. (1995). Multidimensional scale in argumentativeness. *Studies in Psychology, 37,* 157–158.

Frantz, C. M., & Seburn, M. (2003). Are argumentative people better or worse at seeing both sides? *Journal of Social and Personal Relationships, 20,* 565–573.

Gorden, W. I., & Infante, D. A. (1991). Test of a communication model of organizational commitment. *Communication Quarterly, 39,* 144–155.

Gordon, W. I. (1986, April). *Superior-subordinate argumentativeness and verbal aggressiveness.* Paper presented at the annual meeting of the Eastern Communication Association, Atlantic City, NJ.

Hample, D., Benoit, P. J., Houston, J., Purifoy, G., VanHyfte, V., & Warwell, C. (1999). Naïve theories of argument: Avoiding interpersonal arguments or cutting them short. *Argumentation and Advocacy, 35,* 130–139.

Harrell, W. A. (1981). Verbal aggressiveness in spectators at professional hockey games: The effects of tolerance of violence and amount of exposure to hockey. *Human Relations, 34,* 643–655.

Hartley, A. (2005, April). *The long term effects of viewing television violence on adult aggressive behavior.* Paper presented at the annual meeting of the Southern States Communication Association, Baton Rouge, LA.

Hatcher, A. (2005, April). *The long term effects of viewer characteristics on aggression.* Paper presented at the annual meeting of the Southern States Communication Association, Baton Rouge, LA.

Hinkle, L. L. (2003, November). *Family conflict communication model: Constructive and destructive conflict in communication.* Paper presented at the annual meeting of the National Communication Association, Miami Beach, FL.

Huessmann, L. R., Moise-Titus, J., Podolski, C. L., & Eron, L. D. (2003). Longitudinal relations between children's exposure to TV violence and their aggressive and violent behavior in young adulthood: 1977–1982. *Developmental Psychology, 39,* 201–221.

Infante, D. A. (1985). Inducing women to be more argumentative: Source credibility effects. *Journal of Applied Communication Research, 13,* 33–44.

Infante, D. A. (1989). Response to high argumentatives: Messages and sex differences. *Southern Communication Journal, 54,* 159–170.

Infante, D. A., Rancer, A. S., & Jordan, F. F. (1996). Affirming and nonaffirming style: Dyad sex, and the perception of argumentation and verbal aggression in an interpersonal dispute. *Human Communication Research, 22,* 315–334.

Infante, D. A., Wall, C. H., Leap, C. J., & Danielson, K. (1984). Verbal aggression as a function of the receiver's argumentativeness. *Communication Research Reports, 1,* 33–37.

Kassing, J. W., & Infante, D. A. (1999). Aggressive communication in the coach-athlete relationship. *Communication Research Reports, 16,* 110–120.

Kinney, T. A., Smith, B. A., & Donzella, B. (2001). The influence of sex, gender, self-discrepancies, and self-awareness on anger and verbal aggressiveness among U.S. college students. *Journal of Social Psychology, 141,* 245–275.

Kosberg, R. L., & Rancer, A. S. (1998). Enhancing argumentativeness and argumentative behavior: The influence of gender and training. In L. Longmire & L. Merrill (Eds.), *Untying the tongue: Gender, power, and the word* (pp. 251–265). Westport, CT: Greenwood Press.

LaMude, K. G., Scudder, J., & Simmons, D. (2003). The influence of applicant characteristics on use of verbal impression management tactics in the employment selection interview. *Communication Research Reports, 20,* 299–307.

Limon, M. S., & LaFrance, B. H. (2005). Communication traits and leadership emergence: Examining the impact of argumentativeness, communication apprehension, and verbal aggressiveness in work groups. *Southern Communication Journal, 70,* 123-133.

Lippert, L. R., Titsworth, B. S., & Hunt, S. K. (2005). The ecology of academic risk: Relationships between communication apprehension, verbal aggressiveness, supportive communication, and students' academic risk status. *Communication Studies, 56,* 1–22.

Logue, B. J. (1987, May). *Argumentativeness in the organization: Employees assess ts acceptability.* Paper presented at the annual meeting of the Eastern Communication Association, Syracuse, NY.

Martin, M. M., & Anderson, C. M. (1996). Communication traits: A cross-generalization investigation. *Communication Research Reports, 13,* 13–20.

Martin, M. M., Anderson, C. M., Weber, K., & Burant, P. A. (1996, November). *Verbal aggression, sarcasm, and criticism in stepparent relationships.* Paper presented at the annual meeting of the Speech Communication Association, San Diego, CA.

Martin, M. M., Rocca, K. A., Cayanus, J. L., & Weber, K. (2005, April). *The coach-player relationship: The impact of coaches' use of BAT's and verbal aggressiveness on player motivation and affect toward the coach.* Paper presented at the annual meeting of the Central States Communication Association, Kansas City, MO.

Martin, M. M., Weber, K., Mottet, T., & Koehn, S. C. (1998). The relationship of trait verbal aggressiveness and frequency of viewing and enjoyment of television sitcoms. *Communication Research Reports, 15,* 406–412.

Meyer, J. R. (2004). Effect of verbal aggressiveness on the perceived importance of secondary goals in messages. *Communication Studies, 55,* 168–184.

Murad, A. M. (2005, April). *Do family communication patterns affect an individual's verbal aggressiveness and state trait cheerfulness index?* Paper presented at the annual meeting of the Eastern Communication Association, Pittsburgh, PA.

Nicotera, A. M., Smilowitz, M., & Pearson, J. C. (1990). Ambiguity tolerance, conflict management style and argumentativeness as predictors of innovativeness. *Communication Research Reports, 7,* 125–131.

Nina, R. (1996, August). *Verbal aggressiveness, power and culture.* Paper presented at the 26th International Congress of Psychology, Montreal, Canada.

Olson, L. N. (2002). Exploring "common couple violence" in heterosexual romantic relationships. *Western Journal of Communication, 66,* 104–128.

Parke, A., & Griffiths, M. (2004). Aggressive behaviour in slot machine gamblers: A preliminary observational study. *Psychological Reports, 95,* 109–114.

Rancer, A. S. (1993). Communication styles and predispositions. In R. Ray (Ed.), *Bridging both worlds: The communication consultant in corporate America* (pp. 151–173). Lanham, MD: University Press of America.

Rancer, A. S. (1994). Teaching constructive means of handling conflict. *The Speech Communication Teacher, 8,* 1–2.

Rancer, A. S., Avtgis, T. A., & Kosberg, R. L. (1999, November). *Assessing aggressive communication in adolescents: Problems and alternatives.* Paper presented at the annual meeting of the National Communication Association, Chicago.

Rancer, A. S., & Dierks-Stewart, K. J. (1987). Biological and psychological gender differences in trait argumentativeness. In L. Stewart, P. Ting-Toomey, & S. Ting-Toomey (Eds.), *Communication, gender, and sex roles in diverse interaction contexts* (pp. 18–30). Norwood, NJ: Ablex.

Rancer, A. S., Jordan-Jackson, F., & Infante, D. A. (2003). Observers' perceptions of an interpersonal dispute as a function of mode of presentation. *Communication Reports, 16,* 35–46.

Riddle, B. L. (1997, November). *Aggressive communication in organizations.* Paper presented at the annual meeting of the National Communication Association, Chicago.

Rittenour, C., & Myers, S. A. (2005, April). *Adolescents' perceptions of interpersonal conflict and the impact on their aggressive communication traits.* Paper presented at the annual meeting of the Eastern Communication Association, Pittsburgh, PA.

Roberto, A. J., Meyer, G., & Boster, F. J. (2001). Predicting adolescents' decisions about fighting: A test of the theory of planned behavior. *Communication Research Reports, 18,* 315–323.

Rocca, K. A., & Vogl-Bauer, S. (1999). Trait verbal aggression, sports fan identification, and perceptions of appropriate sports fan communication. *Communication Research Reports, 16,* 239–248.

Rogan, R. G., & LaFrance, B. H. (2003). An examination of the relationship between verbal aggressiveness, conflict management strategies, and conflict interaction goals. *Communication Quarterly, 51,* 458–469.

Rudd, J. E. (1996). Communication effects on divorce mediation: How participants' argumentativeness, verbal aggression, and compliance gaining strategy choice mediate outcome satisfaction. *Mediation Quarterly, 14,* 65–78.

Sauders Wahba, J., & McCroskey, J. C. (2003, April). *Temperament and brain systems as predictors of assertive communication traits.* Paper presented at the annual meeting of the Eastern Communication Association, Washington, DC.

Schultz, B. (1982). Argumentativeness: Its effect in group decision-making and its role in leadership perception. *Communication Quarterly, 30,* 368–375.

Schommer, M. (1990). Effects of beliefs about the nature of knowledge on comprehension. *Journal of Educational Psychology, 82,* 498–504.

Simmons, D., Lamude, K. G., & Scudder, J. (2003). Correlates among applicants' communication apprehension, argumentativeness, and verbal aggressiveness in selection interviews. *Psychological Reports, 92,* 804–808.

Villagran, P., Johnson, A. J., Villagran, M. M., & Wittenberg, E. (2001, November). *Arguing in interpersonal relationships: The effects of argument type, resolution, and level of verbal aggressiveness.* Paper presented at the annual meeting of the National Communication Association, Atlanta.

Whaley, A. B. (1982). Televised violence and related variables as predictors of self-reported verbal aggression. *Communication Studies, 33,* 490–497.

Wigley, C. J. (1986, May). *Verbal aggression in interpersonal communication contexts.* Paper presented at the annual meeting of the Eastern Communication Association, Atlantic City, NJ.

Wigley, C. J. (1999). Verbal aggressiveness and communicator style characteristics of summoned jurors as predictors of actual jury selection. *Communication Monographs, 66,* 266–275.

Wrench, J. S. (2002). The impact of sexual orientation and temperament on physical and verbal aggression. *Journal of Intercultural Communication, 31,* 85–106.

Young, S. L., & Bippus, A. M. (2001). Does it make a difference if they hurt you in a funny way? Humorously and non-humorously phrased hurtful messages in personal relationships. *Communication Quarterly, 49,* 35–52.

References

AhYun, K. (1999). The effect of attitude similarity on interpersonal attraction: A test of the conversational expectation explanation. *Communication Research Reports, 16*, 249–255.

Ajzen, I., & Fishbein, M. (1980). *Understanding attitudes and predicting social behavior*. Englewood Cliffs, NJ: Prentice Hall.

Alberti, R. E., & Emmons, M. L. (1970). *Your perfect right: A guide to assertive behavior*. San Luis Obispo, CA: Impact Publications.

Allan, G. (1977). Sibling solidarity. *Journal of Marriage and the Family, 39*, 177–184.

Allen, J. J. (1986). A developmental approach to self-monitoring behavior. *Communication Monographs, 53*, 277–288.

Allen, M., & Preiss, R. W. (2002). Meta-analysis and interpersonal communication: Function and applicability. In M. Allen, R. W. Preiss, B. M. Gayle, & N. Burrell (Eds.), *Interpersonal communication research: Advances through meta-analysis* (pp. 3–12). Mahwah, NJ: Lawrence Erlbaum.

Allport, G. W., & Ross, J. M. (1967). Personal religious orientation and prejudice. *Journal of Personality and Social Psychology, 5*, 432–433.

American Psychiatric Association. (1987). *Diagnostic and statistical manual of mental disorders* (3rd ed., pp. 373–374). Washington, DC: Author.

Andersen, P. A. (1987). The trait debate: A critical examination of the individual differences paradigm in interpersonal communication. In B. Dervin & M. J. Voigt (Eds.), *Progress in communication sciences* (Vol. 7, pp. 47–52). Norwood, NJ: Ablex.

Andersen, P. A. (1999). *Nonverbal communication: Forms and functions*. Mountain View, CA: Mayfield.

Andersen, P. A., Lustig, M., & Andersen, J. F. (1987). Regional patterns of communication in the United States: A theoretical perspective. *Communication Monographs, 54*, 128–144.

Anderson, C. A., & Bushman, B. J. (2002). Human aggression. *Annual Review of Psychology, 53*, 27–51.

Anderson, C. M., & Martin, M. M. (1999). The relationship of argumentativeness and verbal aggressiveness to cohesion, consensus, and satisfaction in small groups. *Communication Reports, 12*, 21–31.

Anderson, C. M., Martin, M. M., Zhong, M., & West, D. (1997). Reliability, separation of factors, and sex differences on the assertiveness-responsiveness measure: A Chinese sample. *Communication Research Reports, 14,* 58–64.

Anderson, C. M., & Rancer, A. S. (2003, November). *Aggressive communication among incarcerated male youth: A two-part study.* Paper presented at the annual meeting of the National Communication Association, Miami Beach, FL.

Anderson, J., Schultz, B., & Courtney-Staley, C. (1987). Training in argumentativeness: New hope for nonassertive women. *Women's Studies in Communication, 10,* 58–66.

Andonian, K. K., & Droge, D. (1992, October). *Verbal aggressiveness and sexual violence in dating relationships: An exploratory study of antecedents of date rape.* Paper presented at the annual meeting of the Speech Communication Association, Chicago, IL.

Atkin, C. K., Smith, S. W., Roberto, A. J., Fediuk, T., & Wagner, T. (2002). Correlates of verbally aggressive communication in adolescents. *Journal of Applied Communication Research, 30,* 251–268.

Atkinson, J. W. (1957). Motivational determinants of risk-taking behavior. *Psychological Review, 64,* 359–372.

Atkinson, J. W. (1966). *An introduction to motivation.* New York: D. Van Nostrand.

Avtgis, T. A., Martin, M. M., & Rocca, K. A. (2000). Social support and perceived understanding in the brother relationship. *Communication Research Reports, 17,* 407–414.

Avtgis, T. A., & Rancer, A. S. (1997). Argumentativeness and verbal aggressiveness as a function of locus of control. *Communication Research Reports, 14,* 441–450.

Avtgis, T. A., & Rancer, A. S. (2002). Aggressive communication across cultures: A comparison of aggressive communication among United States, New Zealand, and Australia. *Journal of Intercultural Communication Research, 31,* 191–200.

Avtgis, T. A., & Rancer, A. S. (2005, April). *The efficacy of communication training programs: Are we selling our efforts short?* Paper presented at the annual meeting of the Eastern Communication Association, Pittsburgh, PA.

Avtgis, T. A., Rancer, A. S., & Amato, P. P. (1998). Self-handicapping orientation and tendencies toward verbal aggressiveness. *Communication Research Reports, 15,* 226–234.

Bacon, C. C., & Severson, M. L. (1986). Assertiveness, responsiveness, and versatility as predictors of leadership emergence. *Communication Research Reports, 3,* 53–59.

Bakker, C. B., Bakker-Rabdau, M. K., & Breit, S. (1978). The measurement of assertiveness and aggressiveness. *Journal of Personality Assessment, 42,* 277–284.

Bandura, A. (1977). *Social learning theory.* Englewood Cliffs, NJ: Prentice-Hall.

Bandura, A. (1978). Social learning theory of aggression. *Journal of Communication, 28,* 12–29.

Barge, J. K. (2001). Practical theory as mapping, engaged reflection and transformative practice. *Communication Theory, 11,* 5–13.

Baxter, L. A. (1992). Forms and functions of intimate play in personal relationships. *Human Communication Research, 18,* 336–363.

Bayer, C. L., & Cegala, D. J. (1992). Trait verbal aggressiveness and argumentativeness: Relations with parenting style. *Western Journal of Communication, 56,* 301–310.

Bayles, F. (2000, July 12). Hockey death no surprise to sports observers. *USA Today*, p. 3A.

Beatty, M. J. (1996). Thinking quantitatively. In M. B. Salwen & D. W. Stacks (Eds.), *An integrated approach to communication theory and research* (pp. 33–43). Mahwah, NJ: Lawrence Erlbaum.

Beatty, M. J. (1998). Future directions in communication trait theory and research. In J. C. McCroskey, J. A. Daly, M. M. Martin, & M. J. Beatty (Eds.), *Communication and personality: Trait perspectives* (pp. 309–319). Cresskill, NJ: Hampton Press.

Beatty, M. J., Burant, P. A., Dobos, J. A., & Rudd, J. E. (1996). Trait verbal aggressiveness and the appropriateness and effectiveness of fathers' interaction plans. *Communication Quarterly, 44*, 1–15.

Beatty, M. J., Dobos, J. A., Valencic, K. M., & Rudd, J. E. (1998, November). *A preliminary investigation into an unexplored "dark side" of communication avoidance: Indirect interpersonal aggressiveness.* Paper presented at the annual meeting of the National Communication Association, New York.

Beatty, M. J., & McCroskey, J. C. (1997). It's in our nature: Verbal aggressiveness as temperamental expression. *Communication Quarterly, 45*, 446–460.

Beatty, M. J., & McCroskey, J. C. (2001). *The biology of communication: A communibiological perspective.* Cresskill, NJ: Hampton Press.

Beatty, M. J., Plax, T. G., & Kearney, P. (1984). Communication apprehension and the Rathus Assertiveness Schedule. *Communication Research Reports, 1*, 130–133.

Beatty, M. J., Rudd, J. E., & Valencic, K. M. (1999). A re-examination of the verbal aggressiveness scale: One factor or two? *Communication Research Reports, 16*, 10–17.

Beatty, M. J., Valencic, K. M., Rudd, J. E., & Dobos, J. A. (1999). A "dark side" of communication avoidance: Indirect interpersonal aggressiveness. *Communication Research Reports, 16*, 103–109.

Beatty, M. J., Zelley, J. R., Dobos, J. A., & Rudd, J. E. (1994). Fathers' trait verbal aggressiveness and argumentativeness as predictors of adult sons' perceptions of fathers' sarcasm, criticism, and verbal aggressiveness. *Communication Quarterly, 42*, 407–415.

Bell, R. A., & Daly, J. A. (1984). The affinity-seeking function of communication. *Communication Monographs, 51*, 91–115.

Berkowitz, L. (1962). *Aggression: A social psychological analysis.* New York: McGraw-Hill.

Berkowitz, L. (1993). *Aggression: Its causes, consequences, and control.* New York: McGraw-Hill.

Berkowitz, L. (1998). Aggressive personalities. In D. Barone, F. M. Hersen & V. B. VanHasselt (Eds.), *Advanced personality* (pp. 263–285). New York: Plenum Press.

Berscheid, E., & Walster, E. H. (1978). *Interpersonal attraction.* Reading, MA: Addison-Wesley.

Bettinghaus, E. P., & Cody, M. J. (1994). *Persuasive communication* (6th ed.). Fort Worth, TX: Harcourt Brace.

Blickle, G. (1995). Conceptualization and measurement of argumentativeness: A decade later. *Psychological Reports, 77*, 99–110.

Blickle, G. (1997). Argumentativeness and the facets of the big five. *Psychological Reports, 81*, 1379–1385.

Blickle, G., Habash, A., & Senft, W. (1998). Verbal aggressiveness: Conceptualization and measurement a decade later. *Psychological Reports, 82*, 287–298.

Booth-Butterfield, M., & Brusberg, M. (1989, April). *Why don't I like my job? The interrelationships of perception of harassing communication, argumentativeness, and job satisfaction.* Paper presented at the annual meeting of the Eastern Communication Association, Ocean City, MD.

Booth-Butterfield, M., & Sidelinger, R. J. (1997). The relationship between parental traits and open family communication: Affective orientation and verbal aggression. *Communication Research Reports, 14*, 408–417.

Boster, F. J., & Levine, T. R. (1988). Individual differences and compliance-gaining message selection: The effects of verbal aggressiveness, argumentativeness, dogmatism, and negativism. *Communication Research Reports, 5*, 114–119.

Boster, F. J., Levine, T. R., & Kazoleas, D. (1993). The impact of argumentativeness and verbal aggressiveness on strategic diversity and persistence in compliance-gaining behavior. *Communication Quarterly, 41*, 405–414.

Boster, F. J., & Stiff, J. B. (1984). Compliance-gaining message selection behavior. *Human Communication Research, 10*, 539–556.

Bosworth, K., Espelage, D. L., & Simon, T. R. (1999). Factors associated with bullying behavior in middle school students. *Journal of Early Adolescence, 19*, 341–362.

Boyer, E. L. (1990, September 6). Ivory tower has grown too tall. *Los Angeles Times*, p. B11.

Breckler, S. J., Greenwald, A. G., & Wiggins, E. C. (1986, April). *Public, private, and collective self-evaluation: Measurement of individual differences.* Paper presented at the International Research and Exchange Board (IREX) Conference on Self and Social Involvement, Princeton, NJ.

Brenders, D. A. (1987). Perceived control: Foundations and directions for communication research. In M. McLaughlin (Ed.), *Communication yearbook* (Vol. 10, pp. 86–116). Beverly Hills, CA: Sage.

Bresnahan, M. J., Shearman, S. M., Lee, S. Y., Ohashi, R., & Mosher, D. (2002). Personal and cultural differences in responding to criticism in three countries. *Asian Journal of Social Psychology, 5*, 93–105.

Burgoon, J. K., & Hale, J. L. (1988). Nonverbal expectancy violations: Model elaboration and application to immediacy behaviors. *Communication Monographs, 55*, 58–79.

Buss, A. H., & Durkee, A. (1957). An inventory for assessing different kinds of hostility. *Journal of Consulting Psychology, 21*, 343–349.

Buss, A. H., & Perry, M. (1992). The aggression questionnaire. *Journal of Personality and Social Psychology, 63*, 452–459.

Byrne, D. (1971). *The attraction paradigm.* New York: Academic Press.

Cacioppo, J. T., Petty, R. E., & Kao, C. F. (1984). The efficient assessment of need for cognition. *Journal of Personality Assessment, 48*, 306–307.

Cacioppo, J. T., Petty, R. E., Kao, C. F., & Rodriguez, R. (1986). Central and peripheral routes to persuasion: An individual difference perspective. *Journal of Personality and Social Psychology, 51*, 1032–1043.

Cahn, D. D. (1984). Teacher-student relationships: Perceived understanding. *Communication Research Reports, 1*, 65–67.

Cahn, D. D. (1996). Family violence from a communication perspective. In D. D. Cahn & S. A. Lloyd (Eds.), *Family violence from a communication perspective* (pp. 1–19). Thousand Oaks, CA: Sage.

Cahn, D. D., & Shulman, G. M. (1984). The perceived understanding instrument. *Communication Research Reports, 1*, 122–125.

Cai, D. A., & Fink, E. L. (2002). Conflict style differences between individualists and collectivists. *Communication Monographs, 69*, 67–87.

Callan, V. J., & Gallois, C. (1983). Ethnic stereotypes: Australian and Southern-European youth. *Journal of Social Psychology, 119*, 287–288.

Canary, D. J. (1989). *Manual for coding conversational argument.* Unpublished manuscript, Pennsylvania State University.

Canary, D. J., Cody, M. J., & Marston, P. J. (1986). Goal types, compliance-gaining, and locus of control. *Journal of Language and Social Psychology, 5*, 249–269.

Canary, D. J., Cunningham, E. M., & Cody, M. J. (1988). Goal types, gender, and locus of control in managing interpersonal conflict. *Communication Research, 15*, 426–446.

Canary, D. J., Tanita-Ratledge, N., & Seibold, D. R. (1982, November). *Argument and group decision-making: Development of a coding scheme.* Paper presented at the annual meeting of the Speech Communication Association, Louisville, KY.

Caughlin, J., & Vangelisti, A. (2000). An individual difference explanation of why married couples engage in the demand/withdraw pattern of conflict. *Journal of Social and Personal Relationships, 17*, 523–551.

Centers for Disease Control. (2002, July). *Cohabitation, marriage, divorce, and remarriage in the United States* (Series 23, Number 22). Washington, DC: Author.

Centers for Disease Control. (n.d.). *Intimate partner violence: Fact sheet.* Retrieved July 5, 2004, from http://www.cdc.gov/ncipc/factsheets/ipvfacts.htm

Chan, K., & Elliott, R. G. (2004). Epistemological beliefs across cultures: Critique and analysis of belief structure studies. *Educational Psychology, 24*, 123–142.

Chen, G. M. (1994). Social desirability as a predictor of argumentativeness and communication apprehension. *Journal of Psychology, 128*, 433–438.

Chesebro, J. L., & Martin, M. M. (2003). The relationship between conversational sensitivity, cognitive flexibility, verbal aggressiveness and indirect interpersonal aggressiveness. *Communication Research Reports, 20*, 143–150.

Chesebro, J. L., & McCroskey, J. C. (2002). *Communication for teachers.* Boston: Allyn & Bacon.

Chory-Assad, R. M. (2002). The predictive validity of the verbal aggressiveness scale. *Communication Research Reports, 19*, 237–245.

Chory-Assad, R. M. (2004). Effects of television sitcom exposure on the accessibility of verbally aggressive thoughts. *Western Journal of Communication, 68*, 431–453.

Chory-Assad, R. M., & Cicchirillo, V. (2005, April). *More evidence on the bi-dimensionality of the Verbal Aggressiveness Scale: Relationships with hostility and self-monitoring.* Paper presented at the annual meeting of the Eastern Communication Association, Pittsburgh, PA.

Chory-Assad, R. M., & Tamborini, R. (2003, April). *Television sitcom exposure and aggressive communication.* Paper presented at the annual meeting of the Eastern Communication Association, Washington, DC.

Christie, R., & Geis, F. L. (Eds.) (1970). *Studies in Machiavellianism.* New York: Academic Press.

Christophel, D. M. (1990). The relationship among teacher immediacy behaviors, student motivation, and learning. *Communication Education, 37,* 233–240.

Cicchirillo, V., & Chory-Assad, R. M. (2005, April). *The relationship between video game play and trait verbal aggressiveness.* Paper presented at the annual meeting of the Eastern Communication Association, Pittsburgh, PA.

Cody, M. J., Canary, D. J., & Smith, S. W. (1994). Compliance-gaining goals: An inductive analysis of actors' goal types, strategies, and successes. In J. A. Daly & J. M. Wiemann (Eds.), *Strategic interpersonal communication* (pp. 33–90). Hillsdale, NJ: Lawrence Erlbaum.

Colbert, K. R. (1993). The effects of debate participation on argumentativeness and verbal aggression. *Communication Education, 42,* 206–214.

Cole, J. G., & McCroskey, J. C. (2003). The association of perceived communication apprehension, shyness, and verbal aggression with perceptions of source credibility and affect in organizational and interpersonal contexts. *Communication Quarterly, 51,* 101–110.

Comprehensive Health Education Foundation (1997). *Preventing violence: Changing norms in school communities.* Evanston, IL: Altschul Group.

Copstead, G. J., Lanzetta, C. N., & Avtgis, T. A. (2001). Adult children conflict control expectancies: Effects on aggressive communication toward parents. *Communication Research Reports, 18,* 75–83.

Costa, P. T., & McCrae, R. (1980). Still stable after all these years: Personality as a key to some issues in adulthood and old age. In P. B. Baltes & O. G. Brim (Eds.), *Lifespan development and behavior* (Vol. 3, pp. 65–102). New York: Academic Press.

Daly, J. A., & Bippus, A. M. (1998). Personality and interpersonal comunication: Issues and directions. In J. C. McCroskey, J. A. Daly, M. M. Martin & M. J. Beatty (Eds.), *Communication and personality: Trait perspectives* (pp. 1–40). Cresskill, NJ: Hampton Press.

Daly, J. A., Vangelisti, A., & Daughton, S. M. (1987). The nature and correlates of conversational sensitivity. *Human Communication Research, 14,* 167–202.

DeWine, S., Nicotera, A. M., & Parry, D. (1991). Argumentativeness and aggressiveness: The flip side of gentle persuasion. *Management Communication Quarterly, 4,* 386–411.

DiCioccio, R. L. (2000, April). *Aggression in friendship relationships: A communication model.* Paper presented at the annual meeting of the Eastern Communication Association, Pittsburgh, PA.

DiCioccio, R. L. (2001). *The development and validation of the Teasing Communication Scale.* Unpublished doctoral dissertation, Kent State University, Kent, OH.

Dowling, R. E., & Flint, L. J. (1990). The argumentativeness scale: Problems and promise. *Communication Studies, 41,* 183–198.

Eagly, A. H., & Chaiken, S. (1993). *The psychology of attitudes.* Orlando, FL: Harcourt Brace.

Edge, H. A., & Williams, M. L. (1994). Affirming communicator style of supervisor and subordinate use of upward influence tactics: An analysis of nonmanagerial and managerial employees. *Communication Research Reports, 11,* 201–208.

Elazar, D. (1972). *American federalism: A view from the states.* New York: Thomas Crowell.

Ennis, R. H. (1985). A logical basis for measuring critical thinking skills. *Educational Leadership, 43,* 44–48.

Epstein, S. (1979). The stability of behavior: 1. On predicting most of the people much of the time. *Journal of Personality and Social Psychology, 37,* 1097–1126.

Eysenck, H. J., & Eysenck, M., W. (1985). *Personality and individual differences: A natural science approach.* New York: Plenum.

Father accused of biting son's coach. (2001, March 8). *Akron Beacon Journal,* p. A17.

Fishbein, M., & Ajzen, I. (1975). *Belief, attitude, intention, and behavior: An introduction to theory and research.* Reading, MA: Addison-Wesley.

Fitzpatrick, M. A. (1977). A typological approach to communication in relationships. In B. D. Ruben (Ed.), *Communication yearbook* (Vol. 1, pp. 263–275). New Brunswick, NJ: Transaction Books-International Communication Association.

Fitzpatrick, M. A., & Badzinski, D. M. (1994). All in the family: Interpersonal communication in kin relationships. In M. L. Knapp & G. R. Miller (Eds.), *Handbook of interpersonal communication* (2nd ed., pp. 726–771). Thousand Oaks, CA: Sage.

French, J. R. P., Jr., & Raven, B. (1959). The bases for social power. In D. Cartwright (Ed.), *Studies in social power* (pp. 150–167). Ann Arbor: University of Michigan Press.

Galvin, K. (2003). The family of the future: What do we face? In A. Vangelisti (Ed.), *Handbook of family communication* (pp. 675–698). Thousand Oaks, CA: Sage.

Gass, R. H., & Seiter, J. S. (1999). *Persuasion, social influence, and compliance-gaining.* Boston: Allyn & Bacon.

Gass, R. H., & Seiter, J. S. (2003). *Persuasion, social influence, and compliance-gaining* (2nd ed.). Boston: Allyn & Bacon.

Geddes, D. S. (1990). Verbal aggression and argumentativeness: Regional differences. *Carolinas Speech Communication Annual, 6,* 44–56.

Geddes, D. S. (1992). Comparison of regional interpersonal communication predispositions. *Pennsylvania Speech Communication Annual, 48,* 67–93.

Gelles, R. J. (1997). *Intimate violence in families* (3rd ed). Thousand Oaks, CA: Sage.

Gerbner, G., Gross, L., Eleey, M. F., Jackson-Beeck, M., Jeffries-Fox, S., & Signorelli, N. (1977). TV violence profile No. 8: The highlights. *Journal of Communication, 27,* 171–180.

Gibb, J. R. (1961). Defensive communication. *Journal of Communication, 11,* 141–148.

Girion, L. (2000, December 10). Office pressure cookers stewing up "desk rage'; high-stress and high-tech leashes cause many workers to lose control. *Los Angeles Times,* p. W1.

Glascock, J. (2003). Gender, race, and aggression in newer TV networks' primetime programming. *Communication Quarterly, 51,* 90–100.

Glauser, M. J. (1984). Self-esteem and communication tendencies: An analysis of four self-esteem/verbal dominance personality types. *The Psychological Record, 34,* 115–131.

Gorden, W. I., & Infante, D. A. (1987). Employee rights: Context argumentativeness, verbal aggressiveness, and career satisfaction. In C. A. B. Osigweh (Ed.), *Communicating employee responsibilities and rights* (pp. 149–163). Westport, CT: Quorum.

Gorden, W. I., Infante, D. A., & Graham, E. E. (1988). Corporate conditions conducive to employee voice: A subordinate perspective. *Employee Responsibility and Rights Journal, 1,* 101–111.

Gorden, W. I., Infante, D. A., & Izzo, J. (1988). Variations in voice pertaining to dissatisfaction/satisfaction with subordinates. *Management Communication Quarterly, 2,* 6–22.

Guilford, J. P. (1959). *Personality.* New York: McGraw-Hill.

Hackman, M. Z., Johnson, C. E., & Barthel-Hackman, T. (1995). Correlates of talk-aholism in New Zealand: An intracultural analysis of the compulsive communication construct. *Communication Research Reports, 12,* 53–60.

Hall, E. T. (1976). *Beyond culture.* New York: Doubleday.

Hamilton, M. A., & Mineo, P. J. (2002). Argumentativeness and its effect on verbal aggressiveness: A meta-analytic review. In M. Allen, R. W. Preiss, B. M. Gayle, & N. Burrell (Eds.), *Interpersonal communication research: Advances through meta-analysis* (pp. 281–314). Mahwah, NJ: Lawrence Erlbaum.

Hample, D., & Dallinger, J. M. (1985a, November). *Cognitive editing of argument strategies.* Paper presented at the annual meeting of the Speech Communication Association, Denver, CO.

Hample, D., & Dallinger, J. M. (1985b). Unused compliance gaining strategies. In J. R. Cox, M. O. Sillars & G. B. Walker (Eds.), *Argument and social practice: Proceedings of the fourth SCA/AFA conference on argumentation* (pp. 675–691). Annandale, VA: Speech Communication Association.

Hample, D., & Dallinger, J. M. (1987). Individual differences in cognitive editing standards. *Human Communication Research, 14,* 123–144.

Harman, C. M., Klopf, D. W., & Ishii, S. (1990). Verbal aggression among Japanese and American students. *Perceptual and Motor Skills, 70,* 1130.

Harris, R. N., Snyder, C. R., Higgins, R. L., & Schrag, J. L. (1986). Enhancing the prediction of self-handicapping. *Journal of Personality and Social Psychology, 51,* 1191–1199.

Hays, E. R. (1970). Ego-threatening classroom communication: A factor analysis of student perceptions. *Speech Teacher, 19,* 43–48.

Heisel, A., D., LaFrance, B. H., & Beatty, M. J. (2003). Self-reported extraversion, neuroticism, and psychoticism as predictors of peer rated verbal aggressiveness and affinity-seeking competence. *Communication Monographs, 70,* 1–15.

Hinkle, L. L. (2003, April). *Affective, behavioral, and cognitive dimensions of argumentativeness: A new measure.* Paper presented at the annual meeting of the Eastern Communication Association, Washington, D.C.

Holden, R. R., & Fekken, G. C. (1989). Three common social desirability scales: Friends, acquaintances, or strangers? *Journal of Research in Personality, 127,* 553–554.

Hovland, C. I., & Janis, I. L. (Eds.). (1959). *Personality and persuasibility.* New Haven, CT: Yale University Press.

Hunter, J. E., & Boster, F. J. (1987). A model of compliance-gaining message selection. *Communication Monographs, 54,* 63–84.

Hurt, H. T., Scott, M. D., & McCroskey, J. C. (1978). *Communication in the classroom.* Reading, MA: Addison-Wesley.

Ifert, D. E., & Bearden, L. (1998). The influence of argumentativeness and verbal aggression on responses to refused requests. *Communication Reports, 11,* 145–154.

Ifert, D. E., Long, K. M., & Fortney, S. D. (1997, April). *Compulsive communicators are real people, too: Examining variation in communication apprehension, verbal aggressiveness, and argumentativeness.* Paper presented at the annual meeting of the Eastern Communication Association, Baltimore, MD.

Infante, D. A. (1981). Trait argumentativeness as a predictor of communicative behavior in situations requiring argument. *Central States Speech Journal, 32,* 265–272.

Infante, D. A. (1982). The argumentative student in the speech communication classroom: An investigation and implications. *Communication Education, 31,* 141–148.

Infante, D. A. (1987a). Aggressiveness. In J. C. McCroskey & J. A. Daly (Eds.), *Personality and interpersonal communication* (pp. 157–192). Newbury Park, CA: Sage.

Infante, D. A. (1987b, July). *Argumentativeness in superior-subordinate communication: An essential condition for organizational productivity.* Paper presented at the American Forensic Summer Conference of the Speech Communication Association, Alta, UT.

Infante, D. A. (1987c). Enhancing the prediction of response to a communication situation from communication traits. *Communication Quarterly, 35,* 308–316.

Infante, D. A. (1987d, May). *An independent-mindedness model of organizational productivity: The role of communication education.* Paper presented at the annual meeting of the Eastern Communication Association, Syracuse, NY.

Infante, D. A. (1988). *Arguing constructively.* Prospect Heights, IL: Waveland Press.

Infante, D. A. (1995a, November). *Spotlight on scholarship: Dominic Infante.* Paper presented at the annual meeting of the Speech Communication Association, San Antonio, TX.

Infante, D. A. (1995b). Teaching students to understand and control verbal aggression. *Communication Education, 44,* 51–63.

Infante, D. A. (2005). Corporal punishment of children: A communication theory perspective. In M. Donnelly & M. A. Straus (Eds.), *Corporal punishment of children in theoretical perspective*. New Haven, CT: Yale University Press.

Infante, D. A., Anderson, C. M., Martin, M. M., Herington, A. D., & Kim, J. (1993). Subordinates' satisfaction and perceptions of superiors' compliance-gaining tactics, argumentativeness, verbal aggressiveness, and style. *Management Communication Quarterly, 6*, 307–326.

Infante, D. A., Chandler, T. A., & Rudd, J. E. (1989). Test of an argumentative skill deficiency model of interspousal violence. *Communication Monographs, 56*, 163–177.

Infante, D. A., Chandler-Sabourin, T., Rudd, J. E., & Shannon, E. A. (1990). Verbal aggression in violent and nonviolent marital disputes. *Communication Quarterly, 38*, 361–371.

Infante, D. A., & Gorden, W. I. (1985a). Benefits versus bias: An investigation of argumentativeness, gender, and organizational communication outcomes. *Communication Research Reports, 2*, 196–201.

Infante, D. A., & Gorden, W. I. (1985b). Superiors' argumentativeness and verbal aggressiveness as predictors of subordinates' satisfaction. *Human Communication Research, 12*, 117–125.

Infante, D. A., & Gorden, W. I. (1987). Superior and subordinate communication profiles: Implications for independent-mindedness and upward effectiveness. *Central States Speech Journal, 38*, 73–80.

Infante, D. A., & Gorden, W. I. (1989). Argumentativeness and affirming communicator style as predictors of satisfaction/dissatisfaction with subordinates. *Communication Quarterly, 37*, 81–90.

Infante, D. A., & Gorden, W. I. (1991). How employees' see the boss: Test of an argumentative and affirming model of supervisors' communicative behavior. *Western Journal of Communication, 55*, 294–304.

Infante, D. A., Hartley, K. C., Martin, M. M., Higgins, M. A., Hur, G., & Bruning, S. D. (1992). Initiating and reciprocating verbal aggression: Effects of credibility and credited valid arguments. *Communication Studies, 43*, 183–190.

Infante, D. A., Myers, S. A., & Buerkel, R. A. (1994). Argument and verbal aggression in constructive and destructive family and organizational disagreements. *Western Journal of Communication, 58*, 1–7.

Infante, D. A., & Rancer, A. S. (1982). A conceptualization and measure of argumentativeness. *Journal of Personality Assessment, 46*, 72–80.

Infante, D. A., & Rancer, A. S. (1993). Relations between argumentative motivation, and advocacy and refutation on controversial issues. *Communication Quarterly, 41*, 415–426.

Infante, D. A., & Rancer, A. S. (1996). Argumentativeness and verbal aggressiveness: A review of recent theory and research. In B. Burleson (Ed.), *Communication yearbook* (Vol. 19, pp. 319–351). Thousand Oaks, CA: Sage.

Infante, D. A., Rancer, A. S., & Ambler, M. (1994). *A revised taxonomy of verbally aggressive messages*. Unpublished manuscript, Kent State University.

Infante, D. A., Rancer, A. S., & Womack, D. F. (2003). *Building communication theory* (4th ed.). Prospect Heights, IL: Waveland Press.

Infante, D. A., Riddle, B. L., Horvath, C. L., & Tumlin, S. A. (1992). Verbal aggressiveness: Messages and reasons. *Communication Quarterly, 40*, 116–126.

Infante, D. A., Step, M. M., & Horvath, C. L. (1997). Counterattitudinal advocacy: When high argumentatives are more persuasible. *Communication Research Reports, 14*, 79–87.

Infante, D. A., Trebing, J. D., Shepherd, P. E., & Seeds, D. E. (1984). The relationship of argumentativeness to verbal aggression. *Southern Speech Communication Journal, 50*, 67–77.

Infante, D. A., & Wigley, C. J. (1986). Verbal aggressiveness: An interpersonal model and measure. *Communication Monographs, 53*, 61–69.

Jacobson, N. S., & Gottman, J. M. (1998a, March/April). Anatomy of a violent relationship. *Psychology Today*, pp. 61–84.

Jacobson, N. S., & Gottman, J. M. (1998b). *When men batter women: New insights into ending abusive relationships.* New York: Simon & Schuster.

Janan Johnson, A. (2003, May). *Argumentativeness and verbal aggressiveness: Type of argument as a situational constraint.* Paper presented at the annual meeting of the International Communication Association, San Diego, CA.

Jay, T. (1992). *Cursing in America.* Philadelphia: John Benjamins.

Jenkins, G. D., Klopf, D. W., & Park, M. S. (1991, July). *Argumentativeness in Korean and American college students.* Paper presented at the annual meeting of the World Communication Association, Jyvaskyla, Finland.

Johnson, D. W., & Johnson, R. T. (1979). Conflict in the classroom: Controversy and learning. *Review of Educational Research, 49*, 51–70.

Johnson, J. G., Cohen, P., Smailes, E. M., Kasen, S., & Brook, J. S. (2002). Television viewing and aggressive behavior during adolescence and adulthood. *Science, 295*, 2468–2471.

Jones, E. E., & Rhodewalt, F. (1982). *Self-handicapping scale.* Unpublished manuscript, Princeton University and University of Utah.

Kassing, J. W. (1998). Development and validation of the organizational dissent scale. *Management Communication Quarterly, 12*, 183–229.

Kassing, J. W., & Avtgis, T. A. (1999). Examining the relationship between organizational dissent and aggressive communication. *Management Communication Quarterly, 13*, 100–115.

Kassing, J. W., Pearce, K. J., & Infante, D. A. (2000). Corporal punishment and communication in father-son dyads. *Communication Research Reports, 17*, 237–249.

Kassing, J. W., Pearce, K. J., Infante, D. A., & Pyles, S. M. (1999). Exploring the communicative nature of corporal punishment. *Communication Research Reports, 16*, 18–28.

Kaye, B. K., & Sapolsky, B. S. (2004). Talking a 'blue' streak: Context and offensive language in prime time network television programs. *Journalism and Mass Communication Quarterly, 81*, 911–927.

Kazoleas, D. (1993). The impact of argumentativeness on resistance to persuasion. *Human Communication Research, 20,* 118–137.

Kearney, P., Plax, T. G., & Allen, T. H. (2002). Understanding student reactions to teachers who misbehave. In J. L. Chesebro & J. C. McCroskey (Eds.), *Communication for teachers* (pp. 127–140). Boston: Allyn & Bacon.

Kearney, P., Plax, T. G., Hays, E. R., & Ivey, M. J. (1991). College teacher misbehaviors: What students don't like about what teachers say or do. *Communication Quarterly, 39,* 309–324.

Keen, J. (1996, October 9). Dole quips that he'll beat "Bozo." *USA Today,* p. A1.

Kennedy, G. A. (1991). *Aristotle on rhetoric.* New York: Oxford University Press.

Kim, M. S., Aune, K. S., Hunter, J. E., Kim, H. J., & Kim, J. S. (2001). The effect of culture and self-construals on predispositions toward verbal communication. *Human Communication Research, 27,* 382–408.

Kinney, T. A. (1994). An inductively derived typology of verbal aggression and its relationship to distress. *Human Communication Research, 21,* 183–222.

Kinney, T. A., & Segrin, C. (1998). Cognitive moderators of negative reactions to verbal aggression. *Communication Studies, 49,* 49–72.

Kippax, S., & Brigden, D. (1977). Australian stereotyping - A comparision. *Australian Journal of Psychology, 29,* 89–96.

Klopf, D. W., Thompson, C. A., & Sallinen-Kuparinen, S. (1991). Argumentativeness among selected Finnish and American college students. *Psychological Reports, 68,* 161–162.

Koper, R. J., & Boster, F. J. (1988). Factors affecting verbal aggressiveness and compliance gaining effectiveness: The relationship between communication rewards, communication approach/avoidance, and compliance gaining messages. In D. O'Hair & B. R. Patterson (Eds.), *Advances in interpersonal communication research* (pp. 129–146). Las Cruces, NM: CRC.

Kosberg, R. L., & Rancer, A. S. (1991). Training in argumentativeness. *Speech Communication Annual, 5,* 97–107.

Krcmar, M., & Sohn, S. (2004). The role of bleeps and warnings in viewers' perceptions of on-air cursing. *Journal of Broadcasting & Electronic Media, 48,* 570–583.

Lamude, K. G., Scudder, J., & Simmons, D. (2003). The influence of applicant characteristics on use of verbal impression management tactics in the employment selection interview. *Communication Research Reports, 20,* 299–307.

Lange, A. J., & Jakubowski, P. (1976). *Responsible assertive behavior.* Champaign, IL: Research Press.

Leary, M. R., Kowalski, R. M., Smith, L., & Phillips, S. (2003). Teasing, rejection, and violence: Case studies of the school shootings. *Aggressive Behavior, 29,* 202–214.

Lefcourt, H. M. (1982). *Locus of control: Current trends in theory and research* (2nd ed.). Hillsdale, NJ: Lawrence Erlbaum.

Leigh, G. K. (1982). Kinship interaction over the family life span. *Journal of Marriage and the Family, 44,* 197–208.

Lennox, R. D., & Wolfe, R. N. (1984). Revision of the self-monitoring scale. *Journal of Personality and Social Psychology, 46,* 1349–1364.

Levenson, H. (1973). Multidimensional locus of control in psychiatric patients. *Journal of Consulting and Clinical Psychology, 41*, 397–404.

Levine, T. R., & Badger, E. E. (1993). Argumentativeness and resistance to persuasion. *Communication Reports, 6*, 61–78.

Levine, T. R., Beatty, M. J., Limon, S., Hamilton, M. A., Buck, R., & Chory-Assad, R. M. (2004). The dimensionality of the verbal aggressiveness scale. *Communication Monographs, 71*, 245–269.

Levine, T. R., & Boster, F. J. (1996). The impact of self and others' argumentativeness on talk about controversial issues. *Communication Quarterly, 44*, 345–358.

Lim, T. S. (1990). The influence of receivers' resistance on persuaders' verbal aggressiveness. *Communication Quarterly, 38*, 170–188.

Lloyd, S. A., & Emery, B. C. (2000). *The dark side of courtship: Physical and sexual aggression.* Thousand Oaks, CA: Sage.

Loffredo, D. A., & Opt, S. K. (1998). Relating the MBTI to communication apprehension, receiver apprehension, and argumentativeness. *Journal of Psychological Type, 47*, 21–27.

Logue, B. J. (1987, May). *Argumentativeness in the organization: Employees assess its acceptability.* Paper presented at the annual meeting of the Eastern Communication Association, Syracuse, NY.

Lorr, M. (1991). An empirical evaluation of the MBTI typology. *Personality and Individual Differences, 12*, 1141–1145.

Lorr, M., & More, W. W. (1980). Four dimensions of assertiveness. *Multivariate Behavioral Research, 2*, 127–138.

Magnusson, D., & Endler, N. S. (1977). Interactional psychology: Present status and future prospects. In D. Magnusson & N. S. Endler (Eds.), *Personality at the crossroads: Current issues in interactional psychology* (pp. 3–35). Hillsdale, NJ: Lawrence Erlbaum.

Margoline, G. (1979). Conjoint marital therapy to enhance management and reduce spouse abuse. *Journal of Family Therapy, 7*, 13–23.

Markus, H. R., & Kitayama, S. (1991). Culture and the self-implications for cognition, emotion and motivation. *Psychological Review, 98*, 224–253.

Martin, M. M., & Anderson, C. M. (1995). Roommate similarities: Are roommates who are similar in their communication traits more satisfied. *Communication Research Reports, 12*, 46–52.

Martin, M. M., & Anderson, C. M. (1996). Argumentativeness and verbal aggressiveness. *Journal of Social Behavior and Personality, 11*, 547–554.

Martin, M. M., & Anderson, C. M. (1997a). Aggressive communication traits: How similar are young adults and their parents in argumentativeness, assertiveness, and verbal aggressiveness. *Western Journal of Communication, 61*, 299–314.

Martin, M. M., & Anderson, C. M. (1997b). Argumentativeness in roommates' relationships. *Psychological Reports, 80*, 142.

Martin, M. M., Anderson, C. M., Burant, P. A., & Weber, K. (1997). Verbal aggression in the sibling relationship. *Communication Quarterly, 45*, 304–317.

Martin, M. M., Anderson, C. M., & Cos, G. C. (1997). Verbal aggression: A study of the relationship between communication traits and feelings about a verbally aggressive television show. *Communication Research Reports, 14*, 195–202.

Martin, M. M., Anderson, C. M., & Horvath, C. L. (1996). Feelings about verbal aggression: Justifications for sending and hurt from receiving verbally aggressive messages. *Communication Research Reports, 13*, 19–26.

Martin, M. M., Anderson, C. M., & Sirimangkala, P. (1997, April). *The relationship between use of organizational conflict strategies with socio-communicative style and aggressive communication traits.* Paper presented at the annual meeting of the Eastern Communication Association, Baltimore, MD.

Martin, M. M., Anderson, C. M., & Thweatt, K. S. (1998). Aggressive communication traits and their relationship with the Cognitive Flexibility Scale and the Communication Flexibility Scale. *Journal of Social Behavior and Personality, 13*, 531–540.

Martin, M. M., Heisel, A. D., & Valencic, K. M. (2001). Verbal aggression in computer-mediated decision-making. *Psychological Reports, 89*, 24.

Martin, M. M., Koehn, S. C., Weber, K., & Mottet, T. P. (1997, May). *Verbal aggression in family sitcoms: Who said what to whom with what response.* Paper presented at the annual meeting of the International Communication Association, Montreal, Canada.

Martin, M. M., Mottet, T. P., Weber, K., Koehn, S. C., & Maffeo, V. P. (1998). The relationships of trait verbal aggressiveness and frequency of viewing and enjoyment of television sitcoms. *Communication Research Reports, 15*, 406–412.

Martin, M. M., & Rubin, R. B. (1995). A new measure of cognitive flexibility. *Psychological Reports, 76*, 623–626.

Martin, M. M., Weber, K., & Burant, P. A. (1997, April). *Students' perceptions of a teacher's use of slang and verbal aggressiveness in a lecture: An experiment.* Paper presented at the annual meeting of the Eastern Communication Association, Baltimore, MD.

Martin, M. M., Weber, K., & Mottet, T. P. (2003). Verbal aggression and viewing the world as a mean place. *Psychological Reports, 92*, 151–152.

Martin, M. M., Weber, K., Mottet, T. P., Koehn, S. C., & Maffeo, V. P. (1998). The relationship of trait verbal aggressiveness and frequency of viewing and enjoyment of television sitcoms. *Communication Research Reports, 15*, 406–412.

Marwell, G., & Schmitt, D. (1967). Dimensions of compliance-gaining behaviors: An empirical analysis. *Sociometry, 30*, 350–364.

McCrae, R. R., & Costa, P. T. (1987). Validation of the five-factor model of personality across instruments and observers. *Journal of Personality and Social Psychology, 52*, 81–90.

McCroskey, J. C. (1970). Measures of communication-bound anxiety. *Speech Monographs, 37*, 269–277.

McCroskey, J. C. (1978). Validity of the PRCA as an index of oral communication apprehension. *Communication Monographs, 45*, 192–203.

McCroskey, J. C. (1982). *An introduction to rhetorical communication* (4th ed.). Englewood Cliffs, NJ: Prentice Hall.

McCroskey, J. C. (1994). Assessment of affect toward communication and affect toward instruction in communication. In S. Morreale & M. Brooks (Eds.), *Assessing college student competency in speech communication* (pp. 56–71). Annandale, VA: SCA.

McCroskey, J. C. (1997). Self-report measurement. In J. A. Daly, J. C. McCroskey, J. Ayres, T. Hopf, & D. M. Ayres (Eds.), *Avoiding communication: Shyness, reticence, and communication apprehension* (pp. 191–216). Cresskill, NJ: Hampton Press.

McCroskey, J. C., Daly, J. A., Martin, M. M., & Beatty, M. J. (Eds.). (1998). *Communication and personality: Trait perspectives.* Cresskill, NJ: Hampton Press.

McCroskey, J. C., Heisel, A., D., & Richmond, V. P. (2001). Eysenck's Big Three and communication traits: Three correlational studies. *Communication Monographs, 68,* 360–366.

McCroskey, J. C., & McCain, T. A. (1974). The measurement of interpersonal attraction. *Speech Monographs, 41,* 261–266.

McCroskey, J. C., & McCroskey, L. L. (1988). Self-report as an approach to measuring communication competence. *Communication Research Reports, 5,* 103–108.

McCroskey, J. C., & Richmond, V. P. (1983). Power in the classroom I: Teacher and student perceptions. *Communication Education, 32,* 175–184.

McCroskey, J. C., & Richmond, V. P. (1993). Identifying compulsive communicators: The Talkaholic Scale. *Communication Research Reports, 10,* 107–114.

McCroskey, J. C., & Richmond, V. P. (1995). Correlates of compulsive communication: Quantitative and qualitative characteristics. *Communication Quarterly, 43,* 39–52.

McCroskey, J. C., Richmond, V. P., & Daly, J. A. (1975). The development of a measure of perceived homophily in interpersonal communication. *Human Communication Research, 1,* 323–332.

McCroskey, J. C., & Teven, J. J. (1999). Goodwill: A reexamination of the construct and its measurement. *Communication Monographs, 66,* 90–103.

McCroskey, J. C., & Young, T. J. (1981). Ethos and credibility: The construct and its' measurement after three decades. *Central States Speech Journal, 32,* 24–34.

Meyer, G., Roberto, A. J., Boster, F. J., & Roberto, H. (2004). Assessing the Get Real About Violence curriculum: Process and outcome evaluation results and implications. *Health Communication, 16,* 451–475.

Miller, G. R., Boster, F. J., Roloff, M. E., & Seibold, D. R. (1977). Compliance-gaining message strategies: A typology and some findings concerning effects of situational differences. *Communication Monographs, 44,* 37–51.

Miller, G. R., & Burgoon, M. (1978). Persuasion research: Review and commentary. In B. Rubin (Ed.), *Communication yearbook* (Vol. 2, pp. 29–47). New Brunswick, NJ: Transaction Books.

Miller, G. R., & Sunnafrank, M. J. (1984). Theoretical dimensions of applied communication research. *Quarterly Journal of Speech, 70,* 255–263.

Mischel, W. (1968). *Personality and assessment.* New York: Wiley.

Mongeau, P. A. (1989). Individual differences as moderators of persuasive message processing and attitude-behavior relations. *Communication Research Reports, 6,* 1–6.

Montgomery, B. M., & Norton, R. W. (1981). Sex differences and similarities in communicator style. *Communication Monographs, 48,* 121–132.

Mottet, T. P., & Richmond, V. P. (1998). Newer is not necessarily better: A reexamination of affective learning measurement. *Communication Research Reports, 15*, 370–378.

Myers, S. A. (1998). Instructor socio-communicative style, argumentativeness, and verbal aggressiveness in the college classroom. *Communication Research Reports, 15*, 141–150.

Myers, S. A. (2001). Perceived instructor credibility and verbal aggressiveness in the college classroom. *Communication Research Reports, 18*, 354–364.

Myers, S. A. (2002). Perceived aggressive instructor communication and student state motivation, learning, and satisfaction. *Communication Reports, 15*, 113–122.

Myers, S. A. (2003, April). *Argumentativeness and aggressiveness research in instructional communication contexts.* Paper presented at the annual meeting of the Eastern Communication Association, Washington, DC.

Myers, S. A., & Johnson, A. D. (2003). Verbal aggression and liking in interpersonal relationships. *Communication Research Reports, 20*, 90–96.

Myers, S. A., & Knox, R. L. (1999). Verbal aggression in the college classroom: Perceived instructor use and student affective learning. *Communication Quarterly, 47*, 33–45.

Myers, S. A., & Knox, R. L. (2000). Perceived instructor argumentativeness and verbal aggressiveness and student outcomes. *Communication Research Reports, 17*, 299–309.

Myers, S. A., & Members of COMM 2000. (2001). Relational maintenance behaviors and the sibling relationship. *Communication Quarterly, 49*, 19–34.

Myers, S. A., & Rocca, K. A. (2000a). The relationship between perceived instructor communicator style, argumentativeness, and verbal aggression. *Communication Research Reports, 17*, 1–12.

Myers, S. A., & Rocca, K. A. (2000b). Students' state motivation and instructors' use of verbally aggressive messages. *Psychological Reports, 87*, 291–294.

Myers, S. A., & Rocca, K. A. (2001). Perceived instructor argumentativeness and verbal aggressiveness in the college classroom: Effects of student perceptions of climate, apprehension, and state motivation. *Western Journal of Communication, 65*, 113–137.

Neer, M. (1987). The development of an instrument to measure classroom apprehension. *Communication Education, 36*, 154–166.

Neuliep, J. W. (1986). Self-report vs. actual use of persuasive messages by high and low dogmatics. *Journal of Social Behavior and Personality, 1*, 213–222.

Newman, J. (1991). College students' relationships with siblings. *Journal of Youth and Adolescence, 20*, 629–645.

Nicotera, A. M. (1993). Beyond two dimensions: A grounded theory model of conflict handling behavior. *Management Communication Quarterly, 6*, 282–306.

Nicotera, A. M. (1994). The use of multiple approaches to conflict: A study of sequences. *Human Communication Research, 20*, 592–621.

Nicotera, A. M. (1996). An assessment of the Argumentativeness Scale for social desirability bias. *Communication Reports, 9*, 23–35.

Nicotera, A. M., & DeWine, S. (1991). Understanding entry into controversy at work and at home. *Communication Research Reports, 8,* 89–99.

Nicotera, A. M., & Rancer, A. S. (1994). The influence of sex on self-perceptions and social stereotyping of aggressive communication. *Western Journal of Communication, 58,* 283–307.

Nicotera, A. M., Rancer, A. S., & Sullivan, R. G. (1991, November). *Race as a factor in argumentativeness, verbal aggressiveness, and beliefs about arguing.* Paper presented at the annual meeting of the Speech Communication Association, Atlanta, GA.

Noller, P., & Fitzpatrick, M. A. (1993). *Communication in family relationships.* Englewood Cliffs, NJ: Prentice Hall.

Norton, R. (1983). *Communicator style: Theory, applications, and mesaures.* Beverly Hills, CA: Sage.

Norton, R., & Warnick, B. (1976). Assertiveness as a communication construct. *Human Communication Research, 3,* 62–66.

Nussbaum, E. M., & Bendixen, L. D. (2003). Approaching and avoiding arguments: The role of epistemological beliefs, need for cognition, and extraverted personality traits. *Contemporary Educational Psychology, 28,* 573–595.

O'Brien, E. J., & Epstein, S. (1988). *MSEI: The multidimensional self-esteem inventory.* Odessa, FL: Psychological Assessment Resources.

Ohbuchi, K., & Fukushima, O. (1997). Personality and interpersonal conflict: Aggressiveness, self-monitoring, and situational variables. *International Journal of Conflict Management, 8,* 99–113.

O'Keefe, B. J., & Delia, J. G. (1979). Construct comprehensiveness and cognitive complexity as predictors of the number and strategic adaptation of arguments and appeals in a persuasive message. *Communication Monographs, 46,* 231–240.

Onyekwere, E. O., Rubin, R. B., & Infante, D. A. (1991). Interpersonal perception and communication satisfaction as a function of argumentativeness and ego-involvement. *Communication Quarterly, 39,* 35–47.

Pawlowski, D. R., Myers, S. A., & Rocca, K. A. (2000). Relational messages and sibling conflict. *Communication Research Reports, 17,* 271–277.

Payne, M. J., & Chandler-Sabourin, T. (1990). Argumentative skill deficiency and its relationship to quality of marriage. *Communication Research Reports, 7,* 121–124.

Pearce, K. J., & Berkos, K. M. (2003, October). *The effects of profanity use on teacher credibility and attractiveness.* Paper presented at the annual meeting of the Deutsche Gesellschaft fur Sprechwissenschaft und Sprecherziehung, Saarbrucken, Germany.

Perloff, R. M. (2003). *The dynamics of persuasion: Communication and attitudes in the 21st century* (2nd ed.). Mahwah, NJ: Lawrence Erlbaum.

Perse, E. M. (2001). *Media effects and society.* Mahwah, NJ: Lawrence Erlbaum.

Peterson, K. S. (2000, March 21). Say what: Pervasive profanity has turned self-expression to $#@*! *USA Today,* p. 9D.

Petty, R. E., & Cacioppo, J. T. (1986). *Communication and persuasion.* New York: Springer-Verlag.

Plax, T. G., Kearney, P., McCroskey, J. C., & Richmond, V. P. (1986). Power in the classroom VI: Verbal control strategies, nonverbal immediacy and affective learning. *Communication Education, 35*, 43–55.

Prunty, A. M., Klopf, D. W., & Ishii, S. (1990a). Argumentativeness: Japanese and American tendencies to approach and avoid conflict. *Communication Research Reports, 7*, 75–79.

Prunty, A. M., Klopf, D. W., & Ishii, S. (1990b). Japanese and American tendencies to argue. *Psychological Reports, 66*, 802.

Prusank, D. T., & Duran, R. L. (1996, November). *Parenting style, trait verbal aggressiveness, argumentativeness, and communication competence: The communicative patterns of parents and their children.* Paper presented at the annual meeting of the Speech Communication Association, San Diego, CA.

Rahoi, R., Svenkerud, P., & Love, D. (1994). *Searching for subtlety: Investigating argumentativeness across low-context cultural boundaries.* Unpublished manuscript, Ohio University, Athens, OH.

Rancer, A. S. (1995). Aggressive communication in organizational contexts: A synthesis and review. In A. M. Nicotera (Ed.), *Conflict and organizations: Communicative processes* (pp. 151–173). Albany: State University of New York Press.

Rancer, A. S. (1998). Argumentativeness. In J. C. McCroskey, J. A. Daly, M. M. Martin, & M. J. Beatty (Eds.), *Communication and personality: Trait perspectives* (pp. 149–170). Cresskill, NJ: Hampton Press.

Rancer, A. S. (2004). Argumentativeness, verbal aggressiveness and persuasion. In J. S. Seiter & R. H. Gass (Eds.), *Perspectives on persuasion, social influence, and compliance-gaining* (pp. 113–131). Boston: Allyn & Bacon.

Rancer, A. S., Avtgis, T. A., Kosberg, R. L., & Whitecap, V. G. (2000). A longitudinal assessment of trait argumentativeness and verbal aggressiveness between seventh and eighth grades. *Communication Education, 49*, 114–119.

Rancer, A. S., & Baukus, R. A. (1987). Discriminating males and females on belief structures about arguing. In L. B. Nadler, M. K. Nadler, & W. R. Todd-Mancillas (Eds.), *Advances in gender and communication research* (pp. 155–173). Lanham, MD: University Press of America.

Rancer, A. S., Baukus, R. A., & Amato, P. P. (1986). Argumentativeness, verbal aggressiveness, and marital satisfaction. *Communication Research Reports, 3*, 28–32.

Rancer, A. S., Baukus, R. A., & Infante, D. A. (1985). Relations between argumentativeness and belief structures about arguing. *Communication Education, 34*, 37–47.

Rancer, A. S., & Dierks-Stewart, K. J. (1985). The influence of sex and sex-role orientation on trait argumentativeness. *Journal of Personality Assessment, 49*, 69–70.

Rancer, A. S., & Infante, D. A. (1985). Relations between motivation to argue and the argumentativeness of adversaries. *Communication Quarterly, 33*, 209–218.

Rancer, A. S., Kosberg, R. L., & Baukus, R. A. (1992). Beliefs about arguing as predictors of trait argumentativeness: Implications for training in argument and conflict management. *Communication Education, 41*, 375–387.

Rancer, A. S., Kosberg, R. L., & Silvestri, V. N. (1992). The relationship between self-esteem and aggressive communication predispositions. *Communication Research Reports, 9*, 23–32.

Rancer, A. S., & Nicotera, A. M. (in press). Aggressive communication. In B. B. Whaley & W. Samter (Eds.), *Explaining communication: Contemporary theories and exemplars*. Mahwah, NJ: Lawrence Erlbaum.

Rancer, A. S., Whitecap, V. G., Kosberg, R. L., & Avtgis, T. A. (1997). Training in argumentativeness: Testing the efficacy of a communication training program to increase argumentativeness and argumentative behavior in adolescents. *Communication Education, 46,* 273–286.

Rathus, S. A. (1973). A 30-item schedule for assessing assertive behavior. *Behavior Therapy, 8,* 393–397.

Reardon, K. K. (1991). *Persuasion in practice*. Newbury Park, CA: Sage.

Reynolds, R. A. (1987, May). *Argumentativeness, need for cognition, and assertiveness as predictors of compliance gaining message strategy selections*. Paper presented at the annual meeting of the International Communication Association, Montreal, Canada.

Richmond, V. P. (2002a). Socio-communicative style and orientation in instruction. In J. L. Chesebro & J. C. McCroskey (Eds.), *Communication for teachers* (pp. 104–115). Boston: Allyn & Bacon.

Richmond, V. P. (2002b). Teacher nonverbal immediacy. In J. L. Chesebro & J. C. McCroskey (Eds.), *Communication for teachers* (pp. 65–82). Boston: Allyn & Bacon.

Richmond, V. P., & Gorham, J. S. (1996). *Communication, learning, and affect in instruction*. Edina, MN: Burgess International Group, Inc.

Richmond, V. P., Gorham, J. S., & McCroskey, J. C. (1987). The relationship between selected immediacy behaviors and cognitive learning. In M. McLaughlin (Ed.), *Communication yearbook* (Vol. 1, pp. 574–590). Beverly Hills, CA: Sage.

Richmond, V. P., & McCroskey, J. C. (1990). Reliability and separation of factors on the Assertiveness-Responsiveness measure. *Psychological Reports, 67,* 449–450.

Richmond, V. P., & McCroskey, J. C. (1992). *Power in the classroom: Communication, control, and concern*. Hillsdale, NJ: Lawrence Erlbaum.

Richmond, V. P., & McCroskey, J. C. (1995). *Communication: Apprehension, avoidance, and effectiveness* (4th ed.). Scottsdale, AZ: Gorsuch Scarisbrick.

Richmond, V. P., McCroskey, J. C., Kearney, P., & Plax, T. G. (1987). Power in the classroom VII: Linking behavior alteration techniques to cognitive learning. *Communication Education, 36,* 1–12.

Richmond, V. P., McCroskey, J. C., & McCroskey, L. L. (1989). An investigation of self-perceived communication competence and personality orientations. *Communication Research Reports, 6,* 28–36.

Richmond, V. P., McCroskey, J. C., & McCroskey, L. L. (2005). *Organizational communication* (3rd ed.). Boston: Allyn & Bacon.

Roach, K. D. (1992). Teacher demographic characteristics and level of teacher argumentativeness. *Communication Research Reports, 9,* 65–71.

Roach, K. D. (1994, April). *TA argumentativeness and power use in the classroom*. Paper presented at the annual meeting of the Central States Communication Association, Oklahoma City, OK.

Roach, K. D. (1995a). Teaching assistant argumentativeness: Effects on affective learning and students perceptions of power use. *Communication Education, 44*, 15–29.

Roach, K. D. (1995b). Teaching assistant argumentativeness and perceptions of power use in the classroom. *Communication Research Reports, 12*, 94–103.

Roberto, A. J. (1999). Applying the Argumentative Skill Deficiency Model of interpersonal violence to adolescent boys. *Communication Research Reports, 16*, 325–332.

Roberto, A. J., & Finucane, M. E. (1997). The assessment of argumentativeness and verbal aggressiveness in adolescent populations. *Communication Quarterly, 45*, 21–36.

Roberto, A. J., McClure, L., & McFarland, M. (2003, November). *The relationship between parent verbal aggression and child verbal aggression and self-esteem.* Paper presented at the annual meeting of the National Communication Association, Miami Beach, FL.

Rocca, K. A. (2004). College student attendance: Impact of instructor immediacy and verbal aggression. *Communication Education, 53*, 185–195.

Rocca, K. A., Martin, M. M., & Toale, M. C. (1998). Players' perceptions of their coaches' immediacy, assertiveness, and responsiveness. *Communication Research Reports, 15*, 445–450.

Rocca, K. A., & McCroskey, J. C. (1999). The interrelationship of student ratings of instructors' immediacy, verbal aggressiveness, homophily, and interpersonal attraction. *Communication Education, 48*, 308–316.

Rokeach, M. (1960). *The open and closed mind.* New York: Basic Books.

Roscoe, B., Goodwin, M. P., & Kennedy, D. (1987). Sibling violence agonistic interactions experienced by early adolescents. *Journal of Family Violence, 2*, 121–137.

Rosenberg, M. (1965). *Society and the adolescent self-image.* Princeton, NJ: Princeton University Press.

Rotter, J. B. (1954). *Social learning theory and clinical psychology.* Englewood Cliffs, NJ: Prentice Hall.

Ruben, D. H., & Ruben, M. J. (1989). Why assertiveness training programs fail. *Small Group Behavior, 20*, 367–380.

Rubin, A. M. (1993). The effect of locus of control on communication motivation, anxiety, and satisfaction. *Communication Quarterly, 41*, 161–171.

Rudd, J. E., Beatty, M. J., Vogl-Bauer, S., & Dobos, J. A. (1997). Trait verbal aggressiveness and the appropriateness and effectiveness of fathers' interaction plans II: Fathers' self-assessments. *Communication Quarterly, 45*, 379–392.

Rudd, J. E., Burant, P. A., & Beatty, M. J. (1994). Battered women's compliance gaining strategies as a function of argumentativeness and verbal aggression. *Communication Research Reports, 11*, 13–22.

Rudd, J. E., Vogl-Bauer, S., Dobos, J. A., Beatty, M. J., & Valencic, K. M. (1998). Interactive effects of parents' trait verbal aggressiveness and situational frustration on parents' self-reported anger. *Communication Quarterly, 46*, 1–11.

Sabourin, T. C., Infante, D. A., & Rudd, J. E. (1993). Verbal aggression in marriages: A comparison of violent, distressed but nonviolent, and nondistressed couples. *Human Communication Research, 20,* 245–267.

Sanders, J. A., Gass, R. H., Wiseman, R. L., & Bruschke, J. (1992). Ethnic comparison and measurement of argumentativeness, verbal aggressiveness, and need for cognition. *Communication Reports, 5,* 50–56.

Sanders, J. A., Wiseman, R. L., & Gass, R. H. (1994). Does teaching argumentation facilitate critical thinking? *Communication Reports, 7,* 27–35.

Schaefer, E. S. (1959). A circumplex model for maternal behavior. *Journal of Abnormal and Social Psychology, 59,* 226–235.

Schill, T. (1990). A measure of self-defeating personality. *Psychological Reports, 66,* 1343–1346.

Schill, T. (1995). Social skills of persons with self-defeating personality. *Psychological Reports, 77,* 632–634.

Schill, T. (1996). Self-defeating personality, argumentativeness, and assertive self-statements. *Psychological Reports, 79,* 1127–1130.

Schill, T., Morales, J., Beyler, J., Tatter, T., & Swigert, L. (1991). Correlations between self-handicapping and self-defeating personality. *Psychological Reports, 69,* 655–657.

Schraw, G., Bendixen, L. D., & Dunkle, M. E. (2002). Development and validation of the Epistemic Belief Inventory (EBI). In B. K. Hofer & P. R. Pintrich (Eds.), *Personal epistemology: The psychology of beliefs about knowledge and knowing* (pp. 261–275). Mahwah, NJ: Lawrence Erlbaum.

Schrodt, P. (2003a). Student perceptions of instructor verbal aggressiveness: The influence of student verbal aggressiveness and self-esteem. *Communication Research Reports, 20,* 240–250.

Schrodt, P. (2003b). Students' appraisals of instructors as a function of students' perceptions of instructors' aggressive communication. *Communication Education, 52,* 106–121.

Schrodt, P., & Wheeless, L. (2001). Aggressive communication and informational reception apprehension: The influence of listening anxiety and intellectual inflexibility on trait argumentativeness and verbal aggressiveness. *Communication Quarterly, 49,* 53–69.

Schullery, N. M. (1998). The optimum level of argumentativeness for employed women. *Journal of Business Communication, 35,* 346–367.

Schullery, N. M. (1999). Argumentative men: Expectations of success. *Journal of Business Communication, 36,* 362–381.

Schullery, N. M., & Schullery, S. E. (2003). Relationship of argumentativeness to age and higher education. *Western Journal of Communication, 67,* 207–224.

Schultz, B., & Anderson, J. (1984). Training in the management of conflict: A communication theory perspective. *Small Group Behavior, 15,* 333–348.

Segrin, C., & Fitzpatrick, M. A. (1992). Depression and verbal aggressiveness in different marital couple types. *Communication Studies, 43,* 79–91.

Seibold, D. R., Kudsi, S., & Rude, M. (1993). Does communication training make a difference?: Evidence for the effectiveness of a presentational skills program. *Journal of Applied Communication Research, 21,* 111–131.

Semic, B. A., & Canary, D. J. (1997). Trait argumentativeness, verbal aggressiveness, and minimally rational argument: An observational analysis of friendship discussions. *Communication Quarterly, 45,* 355–378.

Siegel, J. M. (1986). The multidimensional anger inventory. *Journal of Personality and Social Psychology, 51,* 191–200.

Sillars, A. L., Pike, G. R., Jones, T. R., & Redmon, K. (1983). Communication and conflict in marriage. *Communication yearbook* (Vol. 6, pp. 414–429). Beverly Hills, CA: Sage.

Simonelli, C. J., Mullis, T., Elliot, A. N., & Pierce, T. W. (2002). Abuse by siblings and subsequent experiences of violence within the dating relationship. *Journal of Interpersonal Violence, 17,* 103–121.

Singelis, T. M. (1994). The measurement of independent and interdependent self-construals. *Personality and Social Psychological Bulletin, 20,* 580–591.

Slater, M. D., Henry, K. L., Swaim, R. C., & Anderson, L. L. (2003). Violent media content and aggressiveness in adolescents: A downward spiral model. *Communication Research, 30,* 713–736.

Snyder, M. (1974). The self-monitoring of expressive behavior. *Journal of Personality and Social Psychology, 30,* 526–537.

Snyder, M. (1979). Self-monitoring processes. In L. Berkowitz (Ed.), *Advances in experimental social psychology* (Vol. 12, pp. 85–128). New York: Academic Press.

Sohlberg, S. C. (1976). Social desirability responses in Jewish and Arab children in Israel. *Journal of Cross-Cultural Psychology, 7,* 301–314.

Stewart, R. A., & Roach, K. D. (1993). Argumentativeness, religious orientation, and reactions to argument situations involving religious versus nonreligious issues. *Communication Quarterly, 41,* 26–39.

Stewart, R. A., & Roach, K. D. (1998). Argumentativeness and the theory of reasoned action. *Communication Quarterly, 46,* 177–193.

Strahan, R., & Gerbasi, K. C. (1972). Short, homogeneous versions of the Marlowe-Crowne social desirability scale. *Journal of Clinical Psychology, 38,* 191–193.

Sutter, D. L., & Martin, M. M. (1998). Verbal aggression during disengagement of dating relationships. *Communication Research Reports, 15,* 318–327.

Suzuki, S. (1998, May). *Argumentativeness and verbal aggressiveness: Effects of gender and low- and high-context communication.* Paper presented at the annual meeting of the International Communication Association, Jerusalem, Israel.

Suzuki, S., & Rancer, A. S. (1994). Argumentativeness and verbal aggressiveness: Testing for conceptual and measurement equivalence across cultures. *Communication Monographs, 61,* 256–279.

Swap, W. C., & Rubin, J. Z. (1983). Measurement of interpersonal orientation. *Journal of Personality and Social Psychology, 44,* 208–219.

Tamborini, R., Chory-Assad, R. M., Lachlan, K., Westerman, D., & Skalski, P. (2005, May). *Talking smack: Verbal aggression in professional wrestling.* Paper presented at the annual meeting of the International Communication Association, New York.

Tamborini, R., Skalski, P., Lachlan, K., Westerman, D., Davis, J., & Smith, S. L. (2005). *The raw nature of televised professional wrestling: Is the violence a cause for concern?* Unpublished manuscript, Michigan State University.

Tan, A. S. (1986). Social learning of aggression from television. In J. Bryant & D. Zillman (Eds.), *Perspectives on media effects* (pp. 41–55). Hillsdale, NJ: Lawrence Erlbaum.

Teven, J. J. (2001). The relationship among teacher characteristics and perceived caring. *Communication Education, 50,* 159–169.

Teven, J. J., Martin, M. M., & Neupauer, N. C. (1998). Sibling relationships: Verbally aggressive messages and their effect on relational satisfaction. *Communication Reports, 11,* 179–186.

Valencic, K. M., Beatty, M. J., Rudd, J. E., Dobos, J. A., & Heisel, A. D. (1998). An empirical test of a communibiological model. *Communication Quarterly, 46,* 327–341.

Vangelisti, A. L. (1994). Messages that hurt. In W. R. Cupach & B. R. Spitzberg (Eds.), *The dark side of interpersonal communication* (pp. 53–82). Hillsdale, NJ: Lawrence Erlbaum.

Vangelisti, A. L., Daly, J. A., & Friedrich, G. W. (1999). *Teaching communication: Theory, research, and methods* (2nd ed.). Mahwah, NJ: Lawrence Erlbaum.

Venable, K. V., & Martin, M. M. (1997). Argumentativeness and verbal aggressiveness in dating relationships. *Journal of Social Behavior and Personality, 12,* 955–964.

Waggenspack, B. M., & Hensley, W. E. (1989). Perception of the agumentativeness trait in interpersonal relationship situations. *Social Behavior and Personality, 17,* 111–120.

Wagner, J. (1980). Strategies of dismissal: Ways and means of avoiding personal abuse. *Human Relations, 33,* 603–622.

Wanzer, M. (2002). Use of humor in the classroom. In J. L. Chesebro & J. C. McCroskey (Eds.), *Communication for teachers* (pp. 116–126). Boston: Allyn & Bacon.

Weber, K., & Patterson, B. R. (1997). The effects of maternal verbal aggression on the adult child's future romantic relationships. *Communication Research Reports, 14,* 221–230.

Whaley, A. B. (1982). Televised violence and related variables as predictors of self-reported verbal aggression. *Central States Speech Journal, 33,* 490–497.

Wheeless, L. (1975). An investigation of receiver apprehension and social context dimensions of communication apprehension. *Speech Teacher, 24,* 261–268.

Wheeless, L., Preiss, R. W., & Gayle, B. M. (1997). Receiver apprehension, informational receptivity, and cognitive processing. In J. A. Daly, J. C. McCroskey, J. Ayres, T. Hopf, & D. M. Ayres (Eds.), *Avoiding communication: Shyness, reticence, and communication apprehension* (2nd ed.) (pp. 151–187). Cresskill, NJ: Hampton Press.

Wheeless, V. E., & Dierks-Stewart, K. J. (1981). The psychometric properties of the Bem Sex-role Inventory: Questions concerning reliability and validity. *Communication Quarterly, 29*, 173–186.

Wigley, C. J. (1987). Student receiver apprehension as a correlate of trait argumentativeness. *Communication Research Reports, 4*, 51–53.

Wigley, C. J. (1998). Verbal aggressiveness. In J. C. McCroskey, J. A. Daly, M. M. Martin, & M. J. Beatty (Eds.), *Communication and personality: Trait perspectives* (pp. 191–214). Cresskill, NJ: Hampton Press.

Wigley, C. J. (2003, April). *Temporal stability of the Verbal Aggressiveness Scale: State and trait influences.* Paper presented at the annual meeting of the Eastern Communication Association, Washington, D.C.

Wigley, C. J., & Graham, E. E. (1986, November). *Laudativeness: An interpersonal model and measure.* Paper presented at the annual meeting of the Speech Communication Association, Chicago, IL.

Wigley, C. J., Pohl, G. H., & Watt, M. G. S. (1989). Conversational sensitivity as a correlate of trait verbal aggressiveness and the predisposition to verbally praise. *Communication Reports, 2*, 92–95.

Will, G. (2003, August 5). Incivility poisoning the entire political landscape. *Akron Beacon Journal*, p. B3.

Wilson, B. J., Kunkle, D., Linz, D., Potter, W. J., Donnerstein, E., Smith, S. L., et al. (1997). *Violence in television programming overall: University of California, Santa Barbara Study, National Television Violence Study* (Vol. 1, pp. 3–268). Newbury Park, CA: Sage.

Wilson, J. F., & Arnold, C. C. (1983). *Public speaking as a liberal art* (5th ed.). Needham Heights, MA: Allyn & Bacon.

Wilson, S. R. (1998). Introduction to the special issue on seeking and resisting compliance: The vitality of compliance-gaining research. *Communication Studies, 49*, 273–275.

Yelsma, P. (1993). Correlations between self-defeating personality and self-esteem. *Psychological Reports, 72*, 1084–1086.

Zakahi, W. R. (1985). The relationship of assertiveness to communicative competence and communication satisfaction: A dyadic assessment. *Communication Research Reports, 2*, 36–40.

Zelli, A., & Huesmann, L. R. (1995). *Accuracy of social information processed by those who are aggressive: The role of beliefs about a hostile world.* Unpublished manuscript, University of Illinois at Chicago.

Index

About the Authors

Andrew S. Rancer (Ph.D., Kent State University) is Professor of Communication at The University of Akron in Akron, Ohio. He teaches communication theory, communication research, nonverbal communication, training methods in communication, and personality and communication to both undergraduate and graduate students. His research focuses on the role of argumentative and verbally aggressive communication and other personality traits across a wide variety of contexts. He has published in *Communication Monographs, Human Communication Research, Communication Education, Communication Quarterly*, the *Journal of Intercultural Communication Research*, and the *Journal of Personality Assessment*, among other publications. He has also published several book chapters and is one of the coauthors of the widely used textbook *Building Communication Theory*.

Theodore A. Avtgis (Ph.D., Kent State University) is Associate Professor of Communication at West Virginia University. He teaches research methods, communication theory, organizational communication, interpersonal communication, training and development, communication personality, and small group communication. His research focuses on the impact of personality on relationships and relational outcomes and, more specifically, the influence of argumentative and aggressive communication in the workplace and within the family. He has published in *Communication Education, Management Communication Quarterly*, and *Communication Research Reports*, among other publications.